Critique of Modernity

*For Adriana: a book
inspired by her life*

Critique of Modernity

Alain Touraine

Translated by David Macey

BLACKWELL
Oxford UK & Cambridge USA

Copyright © Alain Touraine 1995
English translation © Basil Blackwell Limited 1995

First published in French by Fayard as *Une Critique de la Modernité* in 1992

First published in English 1995

Blackwell Publishers, the publishing imprint of
Basil Blackwell Inc.
238 Main Street
Cambridge, Massachusetts 02142
USA

Basil Blackwell Ltd.
108 Cowley Road
Oxford OX4 1JF
UK

Library of Congress Cataloging-in-Publication Data

Touraine, Alain.
[Critique de la modernité.   English]
Critique of modernity / Alain Touraine : translated by David Macey.
    p.   cm.
Includes bibliographical references and index.
ISBN 1–55786–530–2 (alk. paper). – ISBN
1–55786–531–0 (pbk. : alk. paper)
1. History, Modern – Philosophy.   2. Civilization, Modern–
Philosophy.   I. Title.
D210.T68   1995
901 – dc20
                                                        94–21504
                                                        CIP

British Library Cataloguing in Publication Data

A CIP catalogue record for this book is available from the British Library.

Typeset in 10.5 on 12 pt Garamond
by CentraCet Limited, Cambridge
Printed in Great Britain by T.J. Press Ltd, Padstow, Cornwall

This book is printed on acid-free paper

Contents

Note to the Reader

My view that modernity is a tense relationship between Reason and the Subject is expounded in part III. Readers who wish to take Part III as their starting point may do so. Readers who are interested in the 'classical' conception which identified modernity with rationalization will find the history of its triumph and fall in Parts I and II.

Acknowledgements

This book took shape in the course of my seminar at the Ecole des Hautes Etudes en Sciences Sociales between 1988 and 1992. Its central ideas were presented on a number of occasions to a staff seminar at the Centre d'Analyse et d'Intervention Sociologiques (CADIS). My thanks are due to all those who assisted me with their comments and questions during those working sessions.

The first draft of this text was revised during the month I spent at the European University Institute of Florence at the invitation of Alessandro Pizzorno.

Simonetta Tabboni, Michel Wieviorka and François Dubet were kind enough to read the second draft. I am extremely grateful to them for their comments and criticisms.

Jacqueline Blayac and Jacqueline Longérinas produced both draft texts with their usual competence and energy. My warmest thanks are due to them for the care they devoted to my text.

A.T.

Introduction

What is the modernity whose presence has been so central to our ideas and practices for more than three hundred years, and which is now being challenged, rejected or redefined?

In its most ambitious form, the idea of modernity was the assertion that men and women are what they do, and that there must therefore be an increasingly close connection between production, which is made more efficient by science, technology or administration, the organization of a society governed by law, and a personal life motivated by both self-interest and the will to be free of all constraints. What could provide a basis for this correspondence between a scientific culture, an ordered society and free individuals, if not the triumph of *reason*? Reason alone could establish a correspondence between human action and the order of the world. Religious thought had indeed tried to do so, but was paralysed by the finalism characteristic of monotheistic religions based upon a revelation. Reason inspires science and its applications; it also requires the adaptation of social life to individual or collective needs. Reason replaces the reign of arbitrary power and violence with the legal State and the market. By acting in accordance with the laws of reason, humanity was advancing towards affluence, freedom and happiness.

It is this central assertion that is being challenged and rejected by critiques of modernity.

In what sense are freedom, personal happiness or the satisfaction of needs rational? We can accept that the arbitrary rule of the Prince and respect for local and guild customs were obstacles to the rationalization of production, which required the removal of barriers, the cessation of violence and the establishment of a legal State. Yet this has nothing to do with freedom, democracy and individual happiness, as the French are especially well aware, given that their legal State was constituted in the form of an absolute monarchy. The fact that the combination of rational legal authority and a market economy produced modern society is not enough to prove that the power of reason provides a link between growth and democracy. Far from it: there is a negative link between the two in that they both involve a struggle against tradition and arbitrary power, but there is no positive link. The same criticism applies, *a fortiori*, to the link that was presumed to exist between rationalization and happiness. Freedom from restrictions and traditional forms of authority permits but does not ensure happiness; it calls for freedom but at the same time subordinates freedom to the centralized organization of production and consumption. The assertion that progress leads to affluence, freedom and happiness, and that there is a close connection between these three objectives, is no more than an ideology to which history has constantly given the lie.

What is more, add the most radical critics, the so-called rule of reason increases the system's dominance over actors. It is a process of normalization and standardization which, having destroyed the autonomy of the workers, is now being extended to the world of consumption and communications. This domination may take either a liberal or an authoritarian form, but the goal of modernity is always, and especially when it calls for the freedom of the subject, the subordination of individual interests to the interests of a whole, be it the firm, the nation, society, or reason itself. Is it not in the name of reason that the domination of adult and educated Western men was extended throughout the world, and that they came to dominate women, children and workers as well as colonized peoples?

How could such criticisms fail to convince at the end of a century dominated by a communist movement which forced totalitarian regimes based upon reason, science and technology on one third of the world?

The West replies that that it has been suspicious of this voluntaristic rationalism and enlightened despotism ever since the French Revolution turned in to The Terror. It has gradually replaced a rationalist vision of the world and of human action with a more modest and purely instrumental conception of rationality. With the approach of a mass consumer society, rationality is, moreover, made to serve demands and needs which increasingly escape the restrictive rules of a rationalism corresponding to a productive society based upon accumulation rather than upon consumption on the part of the majority. A society dominated by consumption and, more recently, mass communications is in fact as far removed from the puritanical capitalism described by Weber as it is from Soviet-style appeals to the laws of history.

Other criticisms can, however, be made of this soft conception of modernity. It is fading in to insignificance. It grants the greatest importance to the most immediate, and therefore the least important, demands of the market. It is blindly reducing society to a market and ignores both the inequalities it exacerbates and the accelerating destruction of its natural and social environment.

In an attempt to escape both these criticisms, many people content themselves with an even more modest conception of modernity. In their view, the appeal to reason cannot found any type of society; it is a critical force which dissolves monopolies, guilds, classes, and ideologies alike. Great Britain, the Netherlands, the United States and France made their entry in to modernity through revolution and the rejection of absolutism. Now that the connotations of the word 'revolution' are negative rather than positive, we tend rather to speak of the 'liberation' of oppressed classes, colonized nations, downtrodden women and persecuted minorities. What is the result of liberation? Equality of opportunity according to some, and a well-tempered multiculturalism according to others. Yet is not political freedom merely a negative freedom which, according to Isaiah Berlin's definition, merely prevents anyone from coming to power or maintaining power against the will of the majority (Berlin 1969)? Is not happiness merely the freedom to obey one's own will or desires? In short, modern society tends to abolish all organizational forms and principles and to become no more than a multiple flow of changes governed by law and contracts, and therefore of personal, organizational or political strategies. Such consistent liberalism no longer defines any principles of government, management or education. It no longer guarantees the correspondence between system and actor which was the supreme goal of the rationalists of the Enlightenment. It means no more than a tolerance which is respected only in the absence of any serious social crisis and which works mainly to the advantage of those who have at their disposal the most abundant and varied resources.

Is not this soft conception of modernity self-destructive? This is the starting point for post-modern critics. Baudelaire (1863) saw in modern life, its fashions and its art, the presence of the eternal in the instant. Yet was this anything more than a transition from 'world-views' based upon stable religious or political principles, to a post-historical society in which the familiar and the unfamiliar, the ancient and the modern, coexist without claiming to be hegemonic? And is not this post-modern culture incapable of creating anything; is it not reduced to reflecting the creations of other cultures which do believe themselves to be in possession of a truth?

In both its hard and soft or modest forms, the idea of modernity, as defined by the triumph of either objective or instrumental reason, has lost its liberating and creative power. It is as powerless against the enemy, meaning the rise of separatism and racism, as high-minded appeals to human rights.

Do we therefore have to go over to the other side and join in the great return of nationalisms, particularisms, fundamentalisms – religious and otherwise – which seem to be gaining ground everywhere, in both the most highly modernized countries and in countries that have been brutally disrupted by forced modernization? Understanding the formation of these movements clearly requires a critical investigation of the idea of modernity, as developed in the West, but it in no sense implies that we must abandon the efficacy of instrumental reason, or the liberating power of critical thought and individualism.

This brings us to the starting point of this book. If we reject the return to tradition and community, we must look for a new definition of modernity and a new interpretation of our 'modern' history, which is so often reduced to meaning the necessary and liberating rise of reason and secularization. If modernity cannot be defined solely in terms of rationalization and if, conversely, visions of modernity as an incessant flow of changes fail to make due allowance for the logic of power and the resistance of cultural identities, is it not becoming clear that modernity can be defined precisely by the increasing divorce between the *objective* world created by reason in accordance with the laws of nature, and the world of *subjectivity*, which is primarily the world of individualism or, to be more accurate, of the call for personal freedom? Modernity destroys the sacred world, which was at once natural and divine, transparent to reason and created. It did not replace it with the world of reason and secularization or relegate final ends to a world that human beings could no longer attain; it introduced a divorce between a *Subject* which came down from heaven to earth and was humanized, and a world of objects manipulated by *techniques*. It replaced the unity of a world created by the divine will, Reason or History, with the duality of *rationalization* and *subjectivation*.

This book will trace these developments. It will begin by recalling the triumph of rationalist conceptions of modernity, despite the resistance of the Christian dualism that inspired the thought of Descartes, theories of natural law and the Declarations of the Rights of Man. It will then trace the destruction, in both thought and social practices, of that idea of modernity, and describe how the image of society as a flow of uncontrollable changes in which actors elaborate strategies for survival or conquest became completely divorced from the post-modern cultural imaginary. Finally, it will attempt to redefine modernity as a tense relationship between Reason and Subject, rationalization and subjectivation, the spirit of the Renaissance and that of the Reformation, between science and freedom. My position is as far removed from today's declining modernism as it is from the ubiquitous phantom of post-modernism.

Where is the main battle to be fought? Against the pride of modernist ideology, or against the destruction of the very idea of modernity? Intellectuals usually give the first answer. Whilst our century seems to technologists and economists to be the century of modernity triumphant, in intellectual terms it has been dominated by an antimodernist discourse. And yet, it seems to me that the real threat lies elsewhere. The real danger is that of a complete dissociation between system and actors, between the technical or economic world and the world of subjectivity. As our society comes increasingly to resemble a firm fighting for its survival in an international market, there is a widespread obsession with an identity which can no longer be defined in social terms. In poor countries it takes the form of a new communitarianism; in rich countries, that of narcissistic individualism. A complete divorce between public and private life would lead to the triumph of powers defined purely in terms of management and strategy. The majority would react by retreating in to a private space, and that would leave a bottomless void where there was once the public, social and political space that gave birth to modern democracies. This situation has to be seen as a regression towards the societies in which the powerful and the people lived in different worlds: a world of conquering warriors on the one hand, and on the other a world of ordinary people confined to a local society. It is above all obvious that the world is more divided than ever between the North, where instrumentalism and power reign supreme, and the South, which is paralysed with anxiety about its lost identity.

This representation does not, however, correspond to the whole of reality. We do not live entirely in a post-modern situation, and the dissociation between system and actor is not complete. We also live in a post-industrial society, though I prefer to speak of a 'programmed' society defined by the central importance of cultural industries – medical care, education, information – in which the central conflict is one between the apparatuses of cultural production and the defence of the personal subject. This post-industrial society constitutes a field of cultural and social action that is even more strongly constituted than industrial society, which is now in decline. The subject cannot be dissolved in to post-modernity because the subject asserts itself in a struggle against the powers that impose their domination in the name of reason. The unlimited extension of the interventions of powers frees the subject from any identification with its works and from over-optimistic philosophies of history.

How are we to recreate mediations between economics and culture? How are we to reinvent social life, and especially political life, when its almost universal state of decay is a product of the dissociation of instruments and meaning, means and ends? That will be the topic of a political sequel to these reflections, which represent an attempt to save the idea of modernity from both the conquering and brutal form it has been given by the West, and the crisis that has been affecting it for more than a century. The critique of modernity presented here is intended to extricate modernity from a historical tradition which has reduced it to rationalization, and to introduce the theme of the personal subject and subjectivation. Modernity is not based upon one single principle, and still less is it based simply upon the destruction of everything that stands in the way of the rule of reason. It is the result of a dialogue between Reason and Subject. Without Reason, the Subject is trapped in to an obsession with identity; without the Subject, Reason becomes an instrument of might. In this century, we have seen both the dictatorship of Reason and totalitarian perversions of the Subject. Is it at last possible for both figures of modernity, which have either fought or ignored one another, to begin to speak to one another and to learn to live together?

Part I

Modernity Triumphant

1

The Light of Reason

The Western Ideology

How can we speak of modern society unless we can at least agree upon a general principle that defines modernity? It is impossible to describe as 'modern' a society which tries primarily to organize and to act in accordance with a divine revelation or a national essence. But nor is modernity pure change or a mere sequence of events; it means the diffusion of the products of *rational* activity: scientific, technological and administrative activity. This is why it implies the increasing differentiation of the various sectors of social life – politics, the economy, family life, religion and, in particular, art. Instrumental rationality operates within specific types of activity and prevents any sector from being externally organized on the basis of its integration in to a general vision, or its contribution to the realization of what Louis Dumont calls a holistic societal project. Modernity precludes all finality. The secularization and disenchantment described by Weber (1904–5), who defines modernity in terms of intellectualization, marks the necessary break with the finalism of the religious spirit, which always invokes the end of history, meaning the final fulfilment of the divine project or the destruction of a perverted humanity which has betrayed its mission. The idea of modernity does not preclude the idea of the end of history, as we can see from Comte, Hegel and Marx, who are the great thinkers of historicism. But for them the end of history means, rather, the end of a prehistory and the beginning of a developmental process resulting from technological progress, liberated needs and the triumph of Spirit.

The idea of modernity makes science, rather than God, central to society and at best relegates religious beliefs to the inner realm of private life. The mere presence of technological applications of science does not allow us to speak of a modern society. Intellectual activity must also be protected from political propaganda or religious beliefs; the impersonality of the law must offer protection against nepotism, political patronage and corruption; public and private administration must not be the instruments of personal power; public and private life must be kept separate, as must private wealth, and State and company budgets.

The idea of modernity is therefore closely associated with that of rationalization. Abandoning one means rejecting the other. But is modernity reducible to rationalization? Is it the history of the progress of reason, and is that history also the history of freedom and happiness, of the destruction of 'traditional' beliefs, loyalties and cultures? The distinctive feature of Western thought, at the point when it identified most strongly with modernity, was the attempt to move from a recognition of the essential role of rationalization to the broader idea of a *rational society* in which reason would take control of not only scientific and technical activity, but also of the government of human beings as well as the government of things. Does this conception have a general value or is it no more than a particular historical experience, albeit one of immense importance? We must begin by describing the conception that views modernity and modernization as the creation of a rational society.

At times, society was imagined to be an order or an architecture based upon computation; at other times, reason became an instrument of individual interests and pleasure. This conception also used reason as a weapon to criticize all powers so as to liberate a 'human nature' that had been crushed by religious authority.

In all cases, rationalization was seen as the sole principle behind the organization of personal and collective life, and it was associated with the theme of secularization, or in other words with a refusal to define 'ultimate ends'.

Tabula Rasa

The most powerful Western conception of modernity, and the one which has had the most profound effects, asserted above all that rationalization required the destruction of so-called traditional social bonds, feelings, customs and beliefs, and that the agent of modernization was neither a particular category or social class, but reason itself and the historical necessity that was paving the way for its triumph. Rationalization, which was an indispensable component of modernity, thus also became a spontaneous and necessary modernizing mechanism. The Western idea of modernity merges with a purely *endogenous* conception of modernization. Modernization is not the achievement of an enlightened despot, a popular revolution or the will of a ruling group; it is the achievement of reason itself, and it is therefore primarily the achievement of science, technology and education. The sole goal of social policies for modernization must be to clear a path for reason by doing away with corporatist rules, defences or customs barriers, by creating the security and predictability required by business, and by training competent and conscientious managers and operatives. The idea may seem banal, but it is not, as the vast majority of countries in the world took very different roads to modernization. In most countries, the desire for national liberation, religious or social struggles, the convictions of new ruling elites or in other words social, political and cultural actors, played a much more important role than rationalization, which was paralysed by the resistance of tradition or private interests. The Western idea of modern society does not even correspond to the real historical experience of the countries of Europe, where religious movements, the glory of the king, the defence of the family and the spirit of conquest, financial speculation and social critiques played as important a role as technical progress and the diffusion of knowledge. It does, on the other hand, provide a model for modernization, for an ideology whose theoretical and practical effects have been considerable.

The West therefore lived and conceived modernity as a *revolution*. Reason takes nothing for granted; it sweeps away social and political beliefs and forms of organization which are not based upon scientific proofs. As Allan Bloom remarks (1987: 164):

> What distinguished Enlightenment from earlier philosophy was its intention to extend to all men what had been the preserve of only a few: the life lived according to reason. It was not 'idealism' or 'optimism' that motivated these philosophers but a new science, a 'method', and allied with them, a new political science.

For centuries, the moderns looked for a 'natural' model for the scientific understanding of society, be it a mechanical model, an organicist or a cybernetic model, or one based upon a general theory of systems. And their attempts to find a model were always based on the conviction that if the past were swept away, it would be possible to free human beings from inherited inequalities, irrational fears and ignorance.

The Western ideology of modernity, which we can describe as modernism, replaced the idea of the Subject and the related idea of God, just as meditations on the soul were replaced by the dissection of corpses or the study of the synapses of the brain. According to the modernists, neither society, history nor individual lives were determined by the will of a supreme being to whom one had to submit, or who could be influenced through magic. The individual was subject only to natural laws. Jean-Jacques Rousseau is part of this philosophy of Enlightenment because, remarks Jean Starobinski (1957), the whole of his work is dominated by a search for transparence and by a struggle against the obstacles that obscure knowledge and communication. The same spirit inspires his work as a naturalist, his musicological innovations, his critique of society and his educational programme. The spirit of the Enlightenment wanted to destroy not only despotism but also intermediary bodies, and the French Revolution did so. Society had to be as self-transparent as scientific thought. That idea is still very present in the French idea of the Republic, and in the conviction that the Republic is primarily the repository of the universal ideals of liberty, equality and fraternity. This paves the way for both liberalism and a potentially absolute form of power which is rational and communitarian. *The Social Contract* (Rousseau 1762a) heralded that power, and the Jacobins tried to construct it. It is the goal of all revolutionaries who seek to construct a power which is absolute because it is scientific, and which is intended to protect the transparency of society against arbitrary power, dependency and the spirit of reaction.

What applies to society also applies to the individual. The education of the individual must be a discipline which frees him from the narrow and irrational vision forced upon him by his family and his own passions. It must expose him to rational knowledge and prepare him to be part of a society which organizes the action of reason. The school must be a place which allows him to reject his background and which exposes him to progress, in the form of both knowledge and membership of a society based upon rational principles. The teacher is not an educator who intervenes in the private lives of children, and children are not mere pupils; the teacher is a mediator between them and the universal values of truth, good and beauty. The school must also replace privileged individuals, who are heirs to a discarded past, with an elite recruited through the impersonal ordeal of competitive examinations.

Nature, Pleasure and Taste

This revolutionary and liberating image of modernity is, however, not enough, and it must be completed by the positive image of a world governed by reason. Should we be speaking of a scientific or a rational society? This project was to lead revolutionaries to create a new society and a new man, and to impose, in the name of reason, much greater constraints than those imposed by absolute monarchies. Communist regimes were to construct a scientific socialism which had more in common with the iron cage described by Weber (1904–5: 181) than with freedom from need. The Enlightenment philosophers of the eighteenth century gave a very different answer: the arbitrariness of religious ethics must be replaced by an understanding of the laws of nature. Yet, if man is not to renounce his humanity as he lives in harmony with nature, an appeal to reason is not enough, firstly because it is not easy to reconcile arguments which result in a diversity of opinions and laws, and secondly because it is impossible to enforce the rule of reason in the same way that belief in a revealed truth can be enforced. It therefore has to be demonstrated that submission to the natural order of things is a source of pleasure, and that it corresponds to the rules of taste. This had to be proved in both the aesthetic realm and the ethical domain. This is what Jean Ehrard (1970: 205) calls 'the great dream of the century: humanity at peace with itself and with the world, and living in spontaneous harmony with the universal order'. Pleasure corresponds to the order of the world. As the same author remarks (1970: 187):

> Just as the reason of the mathematician is in harmony with the general laws of physical nature, so the man of taste spontaneously perceives the truth of absolute Beauty. A providential harmony ensures that the definition of the ideal Good coincides with the hedonistic laws of taste. An absolute is thus revealed within the relativity of pleasure.

It is Locke who formulates this conception of human beings (Locke 1690). He rejects Cartesian dualism, and therefore the idea of substance and the Cartesian conception of innate ideas; more specifically, he rejects the central role Cartesianism gave to the idea of God. Self-consciousness is no different to consciousness of things, and man's experience of his identity implies the unity of body and soul. The understanding does not give things a form; it is a reflection based upon sensations, and Locke stresses its passivity. Locke thus defines thought as having no transcendental guarantee, and as being detached from God: reason is purely instrumental. Nature imprints itself on man through his desires and the happiness that comes from acceptance of the law of nature or the misfortunes that befall those who disobey it.

Naturalism and recourse to instrumental reason are complementary, so much so that the combination will endure throughout the entire modern era until Freud, who, to borrow Charles Taylor's image, describes the Ego as a navigator who is trying to find his way between the pressures of the Self, the Super-Ego and social organization.

Similarly, the ethical thought of the Enlightenment is dominated
by the idea of man's natural goodness. Virtue moves him, and makes
him shed tears of joy and tears of pity. It is a source of rapture. And
if man fails to follow the path of virtue, it is because he, like Des
Grieux in *Manon Lescaut* (Prevost 1731), is a victim of fate or a
corrupt society. The language of the heart must make itself heard
despite the lies of words, and Marivaux's plays dramatize love's
triumph over the prejudices of education. Yet the triumph of good
would not be possible if virtue were not a source of pleasure. 'So as
to make the creature's happiness complete,' said Diderot, 'the favourable opinion of the mind is accompanied by the delicious and almost
divine stirrings of the heart.'

Without being as pessimistic about human nature as Pascal or La
Rochefoucauld, one wonders if it is in fact the case that only the good
can be a source of pleasure. Sade is more convincing when he describes
the pleasure of coercing, subjugating and humiliating the object of
one's desire, and causing him or her to suffer. This conception of
reason as a rational organization of pleasures will become more and
more difficult to accept. Why should we now describe as 'rational'
forms of mass consumption which have more to do with a search for
social status, a desire to seduce, or aesthetic pleasure? The spirit of
the Enlightenment was that of an educated elite of nobles, bourgeois
and intellectuals *avant la lettre*, and they enjoyed their pleasures
because these pleasures were liberating and, especially in Catholic
countries, gave them the satisfaction of scandalizing the Church. Yet,
as Edmund Leites has recently demonstrated (Leites 1986), even in
puritanism, the idea of constancy made it possible, especially in the
United States, to reconcile self-control with a rational search for
sexual pleasure. The link between reason and pleasure was supplied
by discourse and, if we understand the word in its secondary sense,
rationalization. The primary goal of this ethics and this aesthetic is
not, however, to construct an image of man; it is to eliminate all
images of man and to eradicate all references to Christianity's
teachings about the divine law and the existence of the soul, or in
other words the presence of God within every individual. The main
thing is to break free of all dualist thought and to establish a naturalist
vision of man. This is to be understood in more than a purely
materialist sense because in the Enlightenment era, the idea of *nature*
had a much wider meaning than it does today. As Cassirer explains
(1932: 242) so well:

> For the term 'nature' does not predicate merely the sphere of physical
> being from which the mind and soul is to be distinguished; it does not

oppose the 'material' to the 'spiritual'. 'Nature' at that time does not refer to the existence of things but to the origin and foundation of truths. To nature belong, irrespective of their content, all truths which are capable of a purely immanent justification, and which require no transcendent revelation but are certain and evident in themselves. Such truths are now sought not only in the physical but also in the intellectual and moral world; for it takes these two worlds together to constitute a real world, a cosmos complete in itself.

The main function of this concept of nature and of reason is to *unite man and the world*. This had already been done by the idea of creation, which was more often associated with than contrasted with the idea of nature, but the new concept made it possible for human thought and action to act upon nature by understanding and respecting its laws and without relying upon a revelation or the teachings of Churches.

Social Utility

The function of this appeal to nature is primarily critical or antireligious in that it is an attempt to give good and evil foundations which are neither religious nor psychological, but purely social. The idea that society is a source of values, that the good is what is *useful* to society and that anything which interferes with its integration and efficacy is evil is an essential element in the classical ideology of modernity. If men are no longer to submit to the law of the father, it must be replaced by the interests of brothers, and the individual must be subordinated to the interests of the collectivity. The Protestant and Catholic reformations produced the most religious version of this theme: the identification of the spiritual with the temporal took the form of an attempt to create a community of saints. When the Swabian peasants published their Twelve Articles in 1525 – a date which marks the beginning of the Peasants' War in Germany – they defined themselves as a community or Church. As a result they refused to allow priests to own land in their own right; they should be paid by the community. This text, which has been well analysed by Emmanuel Mendes Sargo (1985), is close to the later spirit of Calvinist Geneva, but it is also similar to the policy of the Jesuits who tried to convince Princes that they should rule *ad majorem Dei gloriam*. Before long, however, this vision became secularized, and the interest of the collectivity replaced the appeal to communal faith. Machiavelli's admiration for the struggle of the citizens of Florence against the Pope led him to formulate a new concept of politics: their love of their native city outweighed their fears for the salvation of their souls. This is why the Renaissance and subsequent centuries so readily turned to examples borrowed from Ancient Greece and Rome. Antiquity made a virtue of civic morality and recognized citizenship within a free *polis* as the supreme good.

The formation of a new way of thinking about politics and society is an essential corollary to the classical idea of modernity, which is associated with the idea of secularization. *Society* replaces God as the principle behind moral judgement and becomes, rather than an object of study, a principle that can explain and evaluate behaviour. Social science was born as a political science. It originally developed in the course of struggles against the Popes and Emperors whose interests were defended by Occam and Marsilius of Padua, but the major factor was Machiavelli's insistence on judging political institutions and actions without falling back upon moral, or in other words, religious criteria. Then came the idea, which was common to Hobbes (1651) and Rousseau (1762a) – and very different to Locke's analysis (Locke 1689) – that the social order is created by a decision on the part of individuals who submit to the power of Leviathan or to the general will, as expressed in the social contract. Hobbes's analysis predates the others, and represents the first great study of society to have been made since Machiavelli. According to Hobbes (1651: 91), the original condition of man is one of 'war of every one against every one', as 'every man has a right to every thing' (*jus in omnia*). The fear of death that results from this universal hostility leads to the establishment of peace, as all men surrender their individual rights to an absolute power. This does not abolish the individual's right to rebel against the sovereign, should the latter fail to guarantee the social peace. It would be more accurate to speak in this context of political philosophy rather than sociology as, unlike Locke, Hobbes and Rousseau do not take economic activity as the starting point for their analyses. Nor, unlike Tocqueville's (1835–40), do their analyses begin with cultural or social characteristics. They deal directly with power and its foundations. The idea of a social actor does not play any great role in this political philosophy – and still less does that of social relations. The only thing that matters is that the political order can be founded without recourse to religious principles. This is particularly important for Hobbes, who is criticizing the attempts made by various religious groups in England to justify their attempts to take power with arguments drawn from scripture and from their religious faith. From Loiseau and the jurists to Richelieu and Louis XIV, the formation of the absolutist State in France was similarly based upon the transition from *universitas* to *societas*. Bossuet's thought was discredited as the political and not the divine came to be seen as the social expression of the sacred. The French revolution took this development to extremes by identifying the nation with reason, and public-spiritedness with virtue. All subsequent revolutions imposed increasingly onerous duties on citizens, and the outcome was 'the cult of personality'. Writing at the height of the Enlightenment movement, Diderot contrasts individual passions with the rationality of the general will. Analysing the idea of natural right in the *Encyclopédie*, he writes:

> The man who obeys only his individual will is an enemy of the human race . . . the general will therefore exists within every individual. It is a pure act of the understanding which decides in the silence of the passions what a man may demand of his fellow and what his fellow is entitled to demand of him.

In very different terms, Rousseau attempts to defend a principle of citizenship which breaks with the inequality that dominates what the Scottish thinkers of his age were beginning to call civil society. For Hobbes, writing in the seventeenth century, and for Rousseau, writing in the eighteenth, the social order is neither bourgeois nor sacred, and must be based upon a free decision. That free decision itself is, however, an expression of the general will.

For Rousseau, the widely-used expression 'the general will' has a rationalist meaning. He firmly rejects the view that the general will defends the interests of the majority or the Third Estate; it applies only to the general problems of society, and therefore to its very existence, and what can that universalism be based upon, if not reason? There exists a natural order in to which man must be able to insert himself. When, acting under the influence of his desires and ambitions, he leaves that order, he abandons that natural existence and moves in to the domain of evil where individuals are divided and in conflict. The social contract brings about the appearance of the sovereign. The sovereign is both society itself, which, provided that it is on a small scale, constitutes a social body, and reason. Like all the philosophers of the Enlightenment, Rousseau refuses to see divine revelation as the organizing principle behind society and replaces it with reason. Rousseau's Sovereign anticipates Durkheim's collective consciousness, just as his thought, like that of Hobbes before him, lies at the origin of all sociologies that define the principal functions of a society and evaluate modes of behaviour in terms of the positive or negative contribution they make to integration and the ability of institutions to control personal passions and interests. Durkheim is in that sense an heir to the political philosophy of the seventeenth and eighteenth centuries, which was for a long time eclipsed by the triumph of historicism and the representation of society as a field for social conflicts between future and past, interest and tradition, and public life and private life. One of the great representational models of social life is beginning to take shape, and it centres on a correspondence between system and actors, institutions and socialization. Human beings are no longer created in God's image; they are social actors defined by roles, or in other words by modes of behaviour related to their status, and their behaviour must contribute to the smooth workings of the social system. Because human beings are what they do, they must no longer look beyond society, or to God, their own individuality or origins, for definitions of good and evil: their criteria must be what is useful or harmful to the survival and workings of the social body.

In this classical social thought, the notion of society – which we will go on using in this book to refer to a concrete aggregate defined by frontiers, recognized sources of authority, organs for the application of laws and a sense of belonging – takes on a different meaning. It is explanatory and not descriptive, as society and positions occupied within society are elements which explain modes of behaviour and their evaluation. This sociologism is a central element in the modernist vision.

This vision is reinforced by the optimism of an essay by Shaftesbury which was translated by Diderot's. Man, it is argued, is upright or virtuous when, without any ignoble or servile motives, he forces all his passions to conspire for the general good of his species; this requires a heroic effort and yet it never goes against his individual interests. It has to be admitted that this idea is as weak as theories about man's natural goodness or the correspondence between virtue and pleasure. And Mandeville's critique of the social order (Mandeville 1714) is as devastating as Sade's critique of the moral order. How can anyone deny the strength of his eulogy of private vices or of his peremptory statement that we must choose between virtue and wealth, salvation and happiness?

The weakness of this ethics, this aesthetic and this politics stems from the fact that the modernist ideology is not very convincing when it attempts to give modernity a positive content, even though it is powerful when it remains critical. The social contract can create a community which is as oppressive as the Leviathan who puts an end to the 'war of every one against every one' by making all submit to an absolute central power, but it was taken to be a call to overthrow powers which were based on nothing but tradition and a divine decision. The conception of modernity elaborated by the philosophers of the Enlightenment is revolutionary, but it is no more than that. It defines neither a culture nor a society; it inspires struggles against traditional society rather than shedding any light on the workings of a new society. We find the same lack of balance in sociology; ever since the end of the nineteenth century, the language of sociology has centred upon the contrast between traditional and modern, community and society (Tönnies), mechanical and organic solidarity (Durkheim) and ascription and achievement (Linton), the contrasting terms of the axes that define Parsons' 'pattern-variables' or, more recently, Louis Dumont's 'holism' and 'individualism'. In every case, the term defining modern society remains vague, rather as though only traditional society were organized around a positively defined principle and were therefore capable of managing institutional systems, and as though modern society were defined negatively in terms of its ability to dissolve the old order and not its ability to construct a new order.

The explanation for the weakness of modernist thought's propositions and the strength of its criticisms is that the call for modernity is defined not so much by its opposition to traditional society as by its struggle against the absolute monarchy. This was especially true of France, where Rousseau was as active as Diderot and Voltaire in the struggle against the monarchy, its religious legitimation and the privileges it guaranteed. In France, the idea of modernity remained a revolutionary idea for a long time because there was no possibility, as there had been in England after 1688 and the abolition of the absolute monarchy, of constructing a new social and political order. That was the task that occupied Locke on the ship which brought William of Orange to England. That is why the idea of modernity appealed to nature against society, and to a new absolute power against inequality and privilege. The modernist ideology was not bound up with the democratic idea; it was truly revolutionary, and criticized, first in theory and then in practice, the power of the king and the Catholic church in the name of universal principles and reason itself.

The identification of modernity with reason is French rather than English; the English Revolution and the Bill of Rights of 1689 called for the restoration of the traditional rights of Parliament, whereas the French Revolution, as it became more radical, called in the name of reason for the unity of the nation and for the punishment of the agents of the king and foreign powers.

Rousseau: A Modernist Critique of Modernity

The name of Jean-Jacques Rousseau has now been mentioned several times, and it has been associated with that of Hobbes. Yet although

Rousseau was a disciple of the *philosophes* and of Diderot in particular – it was while he was on his way to visit Diderot in prison in 1749 that, on the road to Vincennes, he had the flash of inspiration that produced the first *Discourse* he submitted to the Académie de Dijon in 1750 – his thought is in fact the first great internal critique of modernity, and contrasts the harmony of nature with the social confusion and inequalities of society. It is, however, not the first *Discourse* (Rousseau 1750) but the second (Rousseau 1754) that gives Rousseau's work its exceptional importance because it paves the way for *The Social Contract* (Rousseau 1762a). The idea that progress in the sciences and the arts leads to a fall in moral standards – an idea which was popular in Antiquity and which Hesiod, in particular, held dear – produces a brilliant dissertation but does not transform social thought. On the other hand, Rousseau does break with the optimistic rationalism of the Enlightenment when he denounces inequality in his second *Discourse*. At this point, he is very far removed from Hobbes. It is no longer the fear of war and death that leads human beings to create a social order and to transfer their rights to an absolute sovereign. It is the development of inequality within modern society that leads to the foundation of a political order, as opposed to civil society. For Rousseau, the appeal to the general will becomes a weapon in the struggle against inequality. In practice, the State, which is a community of citizens, is an essential counterweight to the social differentiation that results from modernization itself. Rousseau's anti-modernism is both revolutionary and communitarian. Communities, which are of necessity small, as was Athens and as are Geneva, Corsica and perhaps Poland, are contrasted with large societies whose unity is threatened by the division of labour and the search for profit. This return to the political is still – or was until recently – one of the central principles of the French Left, which readily identifies civil society with capitalism and the triumph of private interests with egotism, and sees itself as the champion of the republican State and national integration. It is suspicious of the notion of society, and prefers the idea of popular sovereignty, as embodied in the Nation-State. This mystique of the political will reach its apotheosis with Hegel's analysis of the State as society (*Staatsgesellschaft*). According to the Rousseau of *The Social Contract*, it is only by being citizens that we begin to become human. That idea was to inspire the most ambitious attempts to create a new society, or in other words a new political power which could give birth to a new man. Modernism makes a virtue of the collective will to struggle against inequality and the negative effects of the increase in wealth. The struggle is waged in the name of nature, which is transformed in to popular sovereignty in order to establish an alliance between man and nature. Rousseau is, however, aware that the general will cannot go on existing in this pure form, and cannot override the interests of individuals and social categories in any absolute sense. He has no illusions about what an *embourgeoisé* Geneva would be like. Whereas Montesquieu and Voltaire attempt to make the contradiction between economic modernity and citizenship acceptable by placing restrictions on political power, Rousseau experiences it as something insurmountable and tragic because, as he writes at the very beginning of Book I of *Emile* (Rousseau 1762b), it is based upon the contradiction between the natural order and the social order. Jean Starobinski (1957) stresses the importance of the dichotomy between being and seeming, which is found in its most elaborate form in the 'Profession of Faith of A Savoyard Vicar' (*Emile* Book IV). Here, natural religion is contrasted with dogmas, which vary from one society to another and which can therefore be denounced as relative and artificial. How is this contradiction to be overcome? Not by going back to primitive society, which was amoral rather than moral in any positive sense, but by overcoming social contradictions and constructing a communicative society based upon an intuitive knowlege of the truth.

Rousseau criticizes society, its artifices and its inequalities, but he does so in the name of Enlightenment, even though he does increasingly turn against the *philosophes* who were once his friends. He appeals to nature because it is the realm of order and harmony, and therefore reason. He wants to replace man within that order, and to allow him to escape the confusion and chaos created by social organization. That is the goal of education, as expounded in *Emile*: the production of a natural, good and reasonable being who is capable of sociability.

This naturalism is a critique of modernity, but it is a modernist critique which goes beyond the philosophy of the Enlightenment, and it is an enlightened critique. From Rousseau, who in this sense is a forerunner of Kant, to the mid twentieth century, intellectuals will combine their critiques of social injustice with the dream of a self-transparent *polis*, of a philosophical return to being and reason. That dream will often take the political form of a new society constructed under their leadership once they – the servants of reason – have been brought to power by the people's rebellion against a society of appearances and privileges. Jean-Jacques Rousseau inaugurates the internal critique of modernism. Rather than opposing power in the name of personal freedom or collective traditions, it opposes disorder in the name of order, private interests in the name of nature and community.

Yet is not Rousseau also the author of the *Confessions* (1778), the *Rêveries* (1782) and the *Dialogues* (1772–6), and the archetype for individual resistance to society? Rousseau does not in fact oppose social power in the name of a moral subject; he feels that he has been rejected by society and is therefore obliged to bear witness to the truth and even to denounce his own weaknesses as the products of a depraved society. If defined in positive terms, his individualism is primarily a naturalism and his psychology and conception of the understanding are similar to Locke's, especially in that he gives primacy to sense perception.

The idea that modernity will in itself lead to a rational social order is acceptable to Voltaire – an admirer of the success of the English bourgeoisie and a past master at reconciling his conscience and his own interests – but not to Rousseau. Society is not rational and modernity is divisive rather than unifying. The mechanisms of self-interest must be opposed by the general will, and especially by the return to nature, or in other words to reason. The alliance between man and the universe must be re-established. Rousseau is the source of both the idea of popular sovereignty, which will inspire democratic and authoritarian regimes alike, and the idea that the individual represents nature against the State. For Rousseau, the radical critique of society leads to the idea of a political sovereignty which serves the cause of reason. Bernard Groethuysen (1949) analyses the transition from *The Social Contract*'s call for republican despotism to the character depicted in the *Confessions*:

> Rousseau might be compared to a modern revolutionary who, being aware that society is not what it should be, contemplates both the socialist and the anarchist solution. He finds that the two forms of political regime are incompatible but, being above all a revolutionary, he espouses both ideals because both are opposed to existing society.

It would be a mistake to transform Rousseau in to a romantic, as in the interval separating *The Social Contract* and *Emile* he introduces the theme of the construction of a social 'We' that transcends the individual and raises him to a higher level. We must, on the other hand, agree with Groethuysen that the break with society is all-important and is the key to understanding both the creation of a political utopia and the loneliness of an individual who, in the name of truth, challenges a society obsessed with pride and appearances.

Kant too will say that the sovereign Good is defined in terms of the unity of virtue and happiness, and therefore of law and individual, system and actor. And how can that unity be attained, if not by raising man above his inclinations, and above any object or form of behaviour that can be identified with the good, by elevating him towards the universal that exists within him, namely reason, which allows man to commune with the universe? This is the underlying principle of Kant's eminently modern ethics, which replaces external ideals and commandments with a reform of the will. The union of the will and reason renders the latter practical. The Good is an action which conforms to reason, and it is therefore subject to the ethical law of finding universals in particulars, both by opting for potentially universal modes of behaviour and by taking man as an end and not a means. Man is a moral subject, not when he seeks his happiness or what he has been taught to see as virtuous, but when he submits to duty, or in other words to the ascendancy of universals. And his duty is to know. As Kant puts it: 'Dare to know! Have the courage to use your own understanding' (cited, Cassirer 1932: 163). The categories of the understanding and the categories of the will can be unified only as the result of the striving that leads man to posit the immortality of the soul and the existence of God, which provide the basis for the never-ending attempt to attain a potentially universal mode of action. The transcendence of all hypothetical imperatives leads to the categorical imperative to submit to the law which proclaims that the will must conform to the universal law of nature.

There is a striking parallel between Kant's ethics and Rousseau's politics. Rousseau argues the case for the absolute submission of the individual to the general will. He constructs a society which is both a product of the will and natural, or in other words which ensures that individual and collectivity can commune with one another, and which founds the social bond as both necessity and freedom. Neither Rousseau nor Kant chooses happiness against reason, or reason against nature; they reject both the stoic reduction of happiness to virtue and the epicurean illusion that virtue lies in the quest for happiness. Writing at the height of the Enlightenment (*Aufklärung*), their main purpose is to unify reason and the will, to defend a freedom which is not so much a revolt against the social order as a submission to the natural order.

This is the central principle behind the 'illuminist' conception of what had yet to be called modernity, but which must be retrospectively known by that name. It is not a philosophy of progress, but almost its antithesis, namely a philosophy of order which combines classical and Christian thought. It can be seen as a break with tradition or as a secular mode of thought which destroys the sacred world, but at a deeper level, it must be seen as a new and powerful attempt to preserve, within a culture that has indeed been secularized, *the unity of man and the universe*. The philosophy of the Enlightenment will be followed by a final attempt at unification with the historicism of idealist philosophies of progress, but after Rousseau and Kant, man will never again be at one with the universe. The universe will become history in action, and man will no longer submit completely to the universalist call of reason. Man will no longer see reason as a principle of order, but as the ability to transform and control, and lived experience, both individual and collective, will rebel against it.

The modernist ideology is the final form of the belief that man and nature form a unity. Modernity, identified with the triumph of reason, is the final form taken by the traditional search for the One, for Being. After the Enlightenment, this metaphysical will becomes either nostalgia or revolt, and the inner man will become increasingly divorced from an external nature.

Capitalism

The modernist ideology, which corresponds to the historically specific form of Western modernization, triumphed with the philosophy of the Enlightenment, but its triumph was not restricted to the domain of ideas. The same ideology was also dominant in the economic domain, where it took the form of capitalism, which is not reducible to either the market economy or rationalization. The market economy corresponds to a negative definition of modernity; it signals the disappearance of all holistic controls over economic activity, and the independence of economic activity from both the characteristic goals of political or religious power, and the effects of traditions and privileges. Rationalization, for its part, is, as we said at the beginning of this chapter, an indispensable element in modernity. The capitalist model of modernization, on the other hand, is defined by a type of leading actor: the capitalist. Whereas Werner Sombart thought that economic modernization had resulted in the breakdown of social and political controls, in the opening up of markets and continued rationalization, and therefore in the triumph of profit and the market, Weber argues against this purely economic definition and defines the capitalist as a specific social and cultural type in both his *The Protestant Ethic and the Spirit of Capitalism* (Weber 1904–5) and his *Economy and Society* (Weber 1922). Weber's general intention is to demonstrate how the great religions either facilitated or hindered modern secularization and rationalization. In the case of Christianity, he concentrates mainly on the Reformation and the Calvinist idea of predestination, which replaces 'otherworldly' asceticism with 'worldly' asceticism. The capitalist sacrifices everything, not to money, but to his calling – *Beruf* – and to work. Work does not guarantee his salvation, as the Catholic Church believed, but it may reveal signs that he is one of the elect – *certitudo salutis* – or at least bring about the detachment from the world demanded by his faith. Reformation man turns his back on the world. Milton's *Paradise Lost* ends, Weber reminds us (1904–5: 87–8), with a call for action in the world that goes against the spirit of the *Divine Comedy*.

This celebrated thesis is open to question for two reasons. The first is historical. Everyone knows that capitalism initially developed in Catholic countries like Italy and Flanders. We might add that the most strictly Calvinist countries did not experience any noticeable economic development, that Calvinist Scotland for a long time lagged behind Anglican England, that northern countries remained under-developed for a very long time, and that Amsterdam was brought to the forefront of the capitalist world by the Arminians or Remon-strants, who were much less strict than the Calvinists of Geneva, a city which experienced neither any conspicuous economic activity nor any noteworthy academic activity in the sixteenth century (it was only with the arrival of the French Cartesians a hundred years later that the University of Geneva became a centre for intellectual production). On the other hand, in seventeenth-century England and in the emergent United States, where Franklin was the emblematic figure, the presence of Calvinism had been attenuated and austerity had given way to a highly secularized utilitarianism. It is therefore difficult to explain the development of capitalism in terms of the influence of the most puritanical forms of Calvinism. What Weber is trying to understand is, rather, a particular or extreme type of economic activity: not the modern trader or industrialist, but the capitalist in the strict sense of the term. The capitalist is fully immersed in economic activity and his ability to invest depends upon his personal savings. He is interested in neither speculation nor luxury, and regards the things of this world with the indifference recommended by St Paul.

The second reason is closer to Weber's own central line of inquiry. Does a given faith encourage the appearance of a particular form of economic activity? How can we accept such a paradox, given that the religious spirit, as transformed and revived by the Reformation, is indeed a worldly asceticism resulting in a detachment from worldy goods and that it is difficult to reconcile this with a life devoted to work, trade and profit? We thus arrive at a more limited interpretation of the realities analysed by Weber. The essential factor is not, it would appear, faith, and therefore a religious culture, but the breakdown of the social bonds imposed by the fear of being judged by a hidden God. It is the breakdown of the family, of relations based upon friendship, and a rejection of religious institutions which, following the example of the Popes and Cardinals of the Renaissance, made no distinction between the sacred and the profane, faith and wealth, or religion and politics. This brings us back to Weber's theme of disenchantment, of the break with all forms of interpenetration of the sacred and the profane, or of being and phenomena, to borrow Kant's terminology. It is in chapter 4 that Weber goes furthest in this direction. If we interpret his thought in this restricted way, it is quite consonant with the whole of the classical Western idea of modernity, which Weber sees as intellectualization, as a break with the 'meaning of the world' and action in the world, with the elimination of the finalism of religions, revelation and the idea of a Subject. The importance of protestantism does not stem from the content of its faith, but from its rejection of the enchantment of the Christian world, which was previously defined by both the role of the sacraments and the temporal power of Popes.

Weber's thought therefore does not coincide with a general definition of modernity, but with *capitalism*, with the economic form of the Western ideology of modernity, seen as a break and a *tabula rasa*. The Reformation itself and the subsequent transformation of catholic piety, thanks to François de Sales in particular, gave rise to a different ethics inspired by a faith which was quite different to the fear and trembling of those who awaited a decision from a God they could not influence. Whilst capitalism did therefore help to create an *ethos* favourable to capitalism, it also made a major contribution to the development of an ethics of conscience, piety and intimacy which led in a different direction, towards, that is, a *bourgeois* individualism which can be contrasted with the spirit of capitalism, just as Pascal contrasted the order of charity with that of reason. Capitalism, which Weber analyses in such depth, is therefore not the economic form of modernity in general, but the form of a particular conception of modernity based upon a break between reason and belief. Reason breaks with all social and cultural loyalties. Phenomena amenable to analysis and computation become divorced from both Being and History. Hence the violence – inspired by the principle of a *tabula rasa* – that accompanied capitalist modernization. Violence ensured the dominance of capitalism, but it also resulted in tragic divisions that cannot possibly be seen as a necessary precondition for modernization.

Weber's definition of capitalism – a particular social form of economic rationalization – is also central to the thought of Karl Polanyi (1944) and Joseph Schumpeter (1912). Polanyi gives central importance to the divorce between market and society, which is

symbolized by the repeal of the Poor Laws in 1834 and by the break
with social and political interventions such as the sixteenth-century
Poor Laws, the Statute of Artificers, and the later Speenhamland
System. The same divorce between economy and society led Schumpeter to predict the collapse of a capitalism which no longer enjoyed
the support of public opinion in the capitalist countries.

Is this divorce a permanent and necessary element in modernization? Certainly not. Very few countries, even in the modern world,
have experienced a purely capitalist form of development. France did
not, as industrialization there was the result of State *dirigisme*. Nor
did Germany, where Bismarck eliminated the bourgeoisie of Frankfurt, or Japan, where the State has played a central role in economic
development ever since the Meiji revolution, to say nothing of
countries where the capitalist bourgeoisie was either much weaker or
non-existent. The distinguishing feature of the English, Dutch and
especially the American capitalist model is the creation of a space for
autonomous action on the part of private agents of economic development. It should also be added that industrial capitalism was largely
based upon the exploitation of a workforce, whereas Weber's analysis
tends to apply to a pre-industrial or 'household' economy in which
the success of productive or commercial undertakings depends primarily on the capitalist's ability to limit his consumption in order to
invest. The interest of Weber's analysis of capitalism is therefore that
it concentrates upon on a historical case in which religious beliefs
made a direct contribution to the divorce between an economic logic
and the rest of social and political life. What Weber is describing is
not modernity as such, but a *particular* mode of modernity characterized by both a high concentration of resources for economic rationalization and the harsh repression brought to bear on traditional
cultural and social loyalties, on the personal need to consume and on
all social forces – women and children as well as workers and
colonized peoples – identified by capitalists as belonging to the realm
of immediate needs, indolence and irrationality.

Because Western modernization occurred much earlier than any
other form of modernization and because it had a dominant role in
the European States and then in the United States for three hundred
years, thinkers in those countries often identify their modernization
with modernity in general, rather as though the break with the past
and the formation of a truly capitalist elite were necessary and central
preconditions for the formation of a modern society. The dominant
model of Western modernization minimizes the action of a will
influenced by cultural values or political objectives, and therefore
does away with the idea of *development*, which is based, in contrast,

on the interdependency of economic enterprises, social movements and state political intervention and which has, increasingly, become more important than the purely capitalist model. This brings out the complexity of Weber's analysis, which is based upon the general idea that social behaviour is culturally determined, but also attempts to show the shaping of an action which is divorced from all world-views, governed by instrumental rationality alone, and acknowledges only the law of the market. As a result, Weber himself had a tragic awareness of the impasse facing a modern society trapped in to instrumental rationality, devoid of meaning and constantly set in motion by charismatic action and therefore by an ethics of conviction (*Gesinnung*) that modernity seeks to eliminate in favour of rational, legal authority and an ethics of responsibility (*Verantwortung*).

Capitalism, the appeal to a natural ethics and the idea of the *tabula rasa* combine to define particular aspects of the modernist ideology of the West. It should not be identified with modernity in general and it would be dangerous to recommend it to the entire world or to enforce it as the 'one best way', to borrow an expression from F. W. Taylor.

The Modernist Ideology

This classical conception, which is at once philosophical and economic, defines modernity in terms of the triumph of reason, liberation and revolution, and modernization as modernity in action, as a purely endogenous process. History books rightly describe the modern period as lasting from the Renaissance to the French Revolution and the beginnings of large-scale industrialization in Great Britain. The societies in which the spirit and practices of modernity developed were attempting to put things in order rather than to set them in motion. Trade and exchange became organized. A public administration and a legal State were created. Books were circulated, along with critiques of traditions, taboos and privileges. At this time, the principal role was played by reason rather than by capital and labour. These centuries were dominated by jurists, philosophers and writers – all men of the book – and the sciences observed, classified and categorized phenomena in order to discover the order of things. Throughout this period, the idea of modernity – which was present, even if the word was not – gave social conflicts the form of a struggle between reason and nature, and the established powers. This was not simply a conflict between the Ancients and the Moderns; nature or even the word of God were being set free from forms of domination which were based upon tradition rather than history and which spread the darkness that would be dispelled by the Enlightenment.

The classical conception of modernity is therefore primarily the construction of a rationalist image of the world which integrates man in to nature, the microcosm in to the macrocosm, and which rejects all forms of dualism of soul and body, the human world and transcendence.

Anthony Giddens (1990) provides a highly integrated image of modernity as a world-wide project of production and control with four main dimensions: industrialism, capitalism, the industrialization of war and the surveillance of every aspect of social life. He adds that the central tendency within the modern world is towards an increasing globalization which takes the form of the international division of labour and the formation of world-economies. It also results, however, in an international military order and the strengthening of Nation-States with centralized systems of control. This vision combines elements of faith in and doubts about accelerated modernization, and gives particular emphasis to the idea of system by extending Durkheim's notion of organic solidarity. According to Giddens, modern society is usually thought of as a system which is capable of 'reflexivity', or in other words capable of acting upon itself. This means that it is the antithesis of the natural societies in which individuals can commune directly with the sacred by means of traditions, or even in the absence of traditions. Modern societies, in contrast, reject both the individual and the sacred in favour of a self-generating, self-controlled and self-regulating social system. There thus emerges a conception of modernity which actively eliminates the idea of a Subject.

This classical conception of modernity, which dominated Europe and then the whole of the Westernized world before retreating in the face of critiques and transformations of social practices, has as its central theme the identification of social actors with what they can produce thanks to either the triumph of scientific and technical reason or society's rational responses to the needs and desires of individuals. This is why the modernist ideology is primarily an assertion of the death of the Subject. The dominant current in Western thought from the sixteenth century to the present day is *materialist*. Reliance upon God and references to the soul are constantly regarded as the heritage of a traditional thought that has to be destroyed. The struggle against religion, which was so intense in France, Italy and Spain and which was so central to the thought of Machiavelli, Hobbes and the French *Encyclopédistes*, was not simply a rejection of the divine-right monarchy, of an absolutism that had been strengthened by the Counter-Reformation or of the subordination of civil society to the alliance of throne and altar. It was also a rejection of transcendence and, in more concrete terms, of the divorce between body and soul. It was a call for the unification of the world and for thought to be dominated by reason or the quest for interest and pleasure.

We therefore have to recognize the vigour, even the violence, of the classical conception of modernity. It was revolutionary, like any call for liberation, like any refusal to compromise with traditional forms of social organization and cultural belief. A new man and a new world had to be constructed by turning away from the past and the Middle Ages, by rediscovering the Ancient World's faith in reason, and by according a central importance to labour, the organization of production, freedom of trade and the impersonality of laws. Disenchantment, secularization, rationalization, rational legal authority, and an ethics of responsibility: the now classic concepts developed by Max Weber provide a perfect definition of this modernity, but it has to be added that it was also bent on conquest, that it established the dominance of rationalizing and modernizing elites over the rest of the world by organizing trade and factories, and through colonization. The triumph of modernity meant the suppression of eternal principles, the elimination of all essences and of artificial entities such as the Ego and cultures in favour of a scientific understanding of bio-psychological mechanisms and of the unwritten and impersonal rules that govern the exchange of commodities, words and women. Structuralist thought was to radicalize this functionalism, and to take to extremes the elimination of the subject. Modernism is an antihumanism, because it is well aware that the idea of man is bound up with the idea of the soul, which necessarily implies the idea of God. The rejection of all revelation and of all moral principles creates a vacuum which is filled by the idea of society, or in other words of social utility. Human beings are no more than citizens. Charity becomes solidarity, and conscience comes to mean respect for the law. Jurists and administrators replace prophets.

The world of reason, pleasure and taste that the philosophers of the Enlightenment opened up for the moderns is either oblivious to internal social conflicts, or interprets them as the irrational's resistance to the progress of reason. The modernists have a clear conscience: they are bringing light in to the darkness, and place their trust in the natural goodness of human beings, in their ability to create rational institutions and above all in their self-interest, which prevents them from destroying themselves and leads them to tolerate and respect the freedom of others. This world advances under its own impetus, and thanks to the conquests of reason. Society is no more than the sum of the effects of the progress of knowledge. Affluence, freedom and happiness progress as one, as they are all products of the application of reason to every aspect of human existence. History is no more than the rise of the sun of reason in the firmament. There cannot be any divorce between man and society. Ideally, man is a citizen, and private virtues contribute to the good of all. The world of the enlightenment is transparent but, like a crystal, it is also self-contained. The modernists live in a self-contained world, protected from everything that disturbs reason and the natural order of things.

The attempt to construct a rationalized society ended in failure, primarily because the idea that a rational administration of things can replace the government of men is tragically mistaken and because social life, far from being transparent and governed by rational choices, proved to be full of powers and conflicts, whilst modernization itself proved less and less endogenous and increasingly stimulated by a national will or social revolutions. Civil society was divorced from the State, but whilst the birth of industrial society signalled the triumph of civil society, it was the State that championed national modernization in the nineteenth century. The increasing divorce between modernity and modernization, and between capitalism and nationalism, destroyed the dream of a modern society defined by the triumph of reason. It paved the way for the invasion of the classical order of modernity by the violence of power and the diversity of needs.

What remains of the modernist ideology? Criticism, destruction and disenchantment. Not so much the construction of a new world as the will to destroy and the joyful destruction of everything that stands in the way of reason. The idea of modernity does not derive its strength from its positive utopia – the construction of a rational world – but from its critical function. And it retains its strength only so long as the past continues to resist.

That resistance was so strong and lasted so long, especially in France where the absolute monarchy claimed to be founded upon divine right, that the main concern of the philosophy of the Enlightenment was, from Bayle onwards, the struggle waged against religion, or rather against the Churches, in the name of natural religion, or sometimes scepticism or even militant atheism. Cassirer (1932) rightly points out that this was primarily a French position and that both the German *Aufklärung* and the English Enlightenment were on better terms with religion. Yet throughout Europe, the new philosophy rejected the authority of tradition and placed its trust in reason alone. This critical thought and trust in science were to remain the principal strength of a conception of modernity which associated the idea of progress with that of tolerance, particularly in the thought of Condorcet (1795). Its destructive work was, however, more convincing than its constructive work, and its social practices did not correspond to the ideas of the philosophers, whose critique of superstition was more formidable than their analysis of social transformations.

Before we turn away from modernism, it should not be forgotten that it was associated with the jubilatory liberation of individuals who were no longer content to escape political and cultural controls by taking refuge in private life, and who proclaimed their right to satisfy their needs, to criticize princes and priests and to defend their own ideas and preferences. Whilst the exclusive trust they placed in instrumental reason and social integration was fraught with danger, the joyous destruction of the sacred and its taboos and rites was an indispensable part of the entry in to modernism. Rabelais is the exemplary representative of this lust for life, food and learning, this desire for pleasure and this wish to construct a new world shaped by the imagination, desires and reason rather than sacred texts, customs or established hierarchies. Today's advanced industrial societies are far removed from this initial liberation, and feel trapped by their products rather than by traditional privations, but they are also in danger of being drawn to the dream of a closed communitarian society which is protected from change. The best defence against this return to a closed community is a combination of Rabelais's appetite and Montaigne's doubts. If we are to defend ourselves against all the forms of repression that are brought to bear in the name of the State, money or reason itself, we must constantly go back to the flamboyance of the Renaissance and to the beginnings of modernity, to the solitary triumphal march of Guidoriccio da Fogliano, as depicted by the Siennese painter Simone Martini, and to the laughter of Molière's servants. A critique of the modernist ideology must not lead to the return of what it destroyed.

2

The Soul and Natural Law

The Augustinian Resistance

Modernist thought asserts that human beings belong to a world governed by natural laws. Reason can discover those laws, and is itself subject to them. Modernist thought also identifies the people, the nation and human beings in general with a social body. It too functions in accordance with natural laws, and must rid itself of irrational forms of organization and domination that fraudulently attempt to gain legitimacy by appealing to a revelation or a supra-human decision. For modernist thought, human beings exist in the world and are therefore social beings. The degree of violence with which it challenges religious thought varies as the links between political power and religious authority change.

It is not surprising that this thought should have encountered great resistance. It was resisted in the name of respect for the customs, and therefore the particular history and culture, of particular social groups. Yet the resistance offered by local and national life or established beliefs never succeeded in blocking the use of new techniques or emigration from the countryside to the cities for any great length of time. In more general terms, the only critiques that had any weight were those which accepted the central role of reason in defining human beings and evaluating behaviour. Just as it would be an error to waste time on criticizing scientific medicine in the name of therapeutic methods whose results have not been scientifically evaluated, a critique of modernity must not stray in to irrationalism and traditionalism.

The naturalist and materialist image of modernity was, on the other hand, constantly and vigorously challenged by the religious thought which, in the West, also made an active contribution to the development of rationalist thought. Let us go back to Weber's famous analysis. Modernity does not mean the elimination of the sacred. It means that otherworldly asceticism is replaced by a worldy asceticism which would be meaningless if it appealed to one or another form of the divine or the sacred. At the same time, the world of phenomena becomes divorced from the world of revelation or being-in-itself. Secularization is only one half of the disenchanted world, the other being an appeal to a Subject which is now out of reach, but which is still one of its constant references. Weber did not accept the simplistic answers of positivism and scientism. On the contrary, he argued strongly against the positivism and scientism of German historians and jurists during the famous conflict over method (*Methodenstreit*). He bequeaths to us a contradictory image of society. Society is characterized by the contradiction between rationalization and the war between the gods, and that between rational legal authority and charisma. And, we might add, between capitalism and the nation. It seems to me impossible to go beyond this fragmentation and this dualist thought. They may well take on different forms or a different content, but they still provide the basis for our critique of modernist rationalism.

Modern history is not the linear development of a supposedly autopoietic rationalization. This chapter is a reminder that a dualism originating in Christianity played an important role in the formation of modernity. It was so thoroughly destroyed by the modernist ideology that the eighteenth century marked the beginning of a long rationalist period which many have identified with modernity itself. Yet, as we shall see in part II below, when that ideology began to be affected by an intellectual, social and political crisis in the second half of the nineteenth century, new questions came to be asked about modernity. The outcome was the revival of a dualism which had, it was believed, been destroyed for ever by the power of industry and war. This chapter is therefore devoted both to a cultural tradition which seemed to have been defeated by the philosophy of the Enlightenment, and to the origins of the more personal considerations to which part III will be devoted.

The philosophers of the Enlightenment saw Christianity as a system which tended to sanctify the established order, and the historical realities of the Europe of the Counter-Reformation more than justified their revolt against the alliance of throne and altar. Yet it is precisely the reality of divine-right monarchy that raises doubts about the accuracy of the criticisms directed against Christianity. Marcel Gauchet is right to contrast Christianity with religion (Gauchet 1983), if we understand that term in the specific sense of the organization of the social around the sacred, or in other words the enchantment of the world, in Weber's sense. All revealed religions, and especially Judaism, which is the earliest of them, in fact introduce the principle of the *subjectivation of the divine*, and this is the *beginning of the disenchantment of the world*. Christianity takes that tendency still further by breaking the link between religion and a people and by giving 'the people of God' a non-social meaning. It divorces temporal and spiritual power rather than merging the two. Modern thought was the creation of those who supported the Emperor in his struggle against the Pope, and one of its branches was to lead to Luther. Christianity breaks with classical Greek thought, whereas the modernist ideology remains faithful to it by identifying the good with social utility and, therefore, the man with the citizen. Greek culture is both an enchanted thought – as is Christian thought – and a religion without transcendence, a cosmology in which the idea of Creation plays only a limited role. What is more important, neither the idea of personality nor that of personal relations between a human individual and a god figures in it. Jean-Pierre Vernant (1989) analyses the absence of subjectivity in Greek culture in these terms:

> The *psyche* is an impersonal or supra-personal entity that exists in each of us. It is a soul within me, rather than *my* soul. Firstly, because this soul is defined by its radical opposition to the body and to everything relating to the body, and therefore has nothing to do with our individual characteristics ... and secondly because this *psyche* is an internal *daimon*, a divine being or a supernatural power whose place and function within the universe transcend our individuality.

Michel Foucault (1984a, 1984b) describes how this conception collapsed in the third and fourth centuries, when an image of the Ego began to take shape.

This reference to Christianity is, however, still too general. Christianity as such is too disparate a historical set, and we have to isolate an intellectual tradition which gives particular importance to personal relations between human beings and God, namely Augustinianism. Its modern expressions are to be found in the thought of Descartes, in theories of natural law and even in the thought of Kant, which already anticipates the sociology of Max Weber.

A famous text provides an immediate introduction to this intellectual tradition. It is taken from the opening pages of Book X – the most important book – of St Augustine's *Confessions* (Augustine 400: 212):

> I asked the sea and the chasms of the deep and the living things that creep in them, but they answered, 'We are not your God. Seek what is above us.' I spoke to the winds that blow, and the whole air and all

that lives in it. It replied, 'Anaximenes is wrong. I am not God.' I asked the sky, the sun, the moon and the stars, but they told me, 'Neither are we the God whom you seek.' I spoke to all the things that are about me, all that can be admitted by the door of the senses, and I said, 'Since you are not my God, tell me about him. Tell me something of my God.' Clear and loud they answered, 'God is he who made us.' I asked these questions simply by gazing at these things, and their beauty was all the answer they gave. Then I turned to myself and asked, 'Who are you?' 'A man,' I replied. But it is clear that I have both body and soul, the one the outer, the other the inner part of me. Which of those two ought I to have asked to help me find my God? With my bodily powers I had already tried to find him in earth and sky, as far as the sight of my eyes could reach, like an envoy sent on a search. But my inner self is the better of the two, for it was to the inner part of me that my bodily senses brought their messages. They delivered to their arbiter and judge the replies which they carried back from the sky and the earth and all that they contain, those replies which stated, 'We are not God' and 'God is he who made us.'

It is because he turns towards 'the inner part' that Augustine departs from the Platonic thought to which he remains so close in other respects. Whilst he thinks that everything that exists is beautiful because everything belongs within the rational order of Creation, he does not discover God through the beauty of his works, but by turning towards the inner man. The light he discovers there is the light of reason, but in more general terms it is the light of the soul, which God created in his own image. This brings us very close to the Cartesian *cogito*. Augustine wrote his *Confessions* because recollection is an intellectual activity. It is therefore a rational activity, and it allows him to make a transition from the outer part to the inner part.

This dualism is constantly present in Luther, who divorces philosophy from religion, and the realm of reason from that of faith. The break with the vision that integrated man in to nature is in itself an appeal to experience and affectivity, and a challenge to reason. It thus makes it possible to think about existence in non-rationalist terms and fosters a conception of man which, whilst it is theocentric and not anthropocentric, still plays an essential role in the history of Western humanism. Both the Reformation and Jansenism, which did not break with the Catholic faith or the Catholic church, enriched freedom of conscience, in spite of the fact that the very expression is incompatible with the Lutheran idea of a *servo arbitrio* (Luther 1525).

Luther's work is usually defined in terms of his struggle against the Church, and rightly so, as that is what makes it part of the general trend towards secularization. He fought the Church and the increasingly dense network of mediations and magical practices it had created between men and God. Luther wanted above all to break with all intermediaries and even with the sacraments in order to make men submit once more to the word of God. He denounced piety, good works and all the means Christians used to try to ensure their salvation. Even Christians wallowed in sin and concupiscence, which they could never succeed in conquering, and Luther abandoned them to the will of God, whose justice – and it is love and not repression – is the only path to salvation. The true Christian is not the pious man, but the man who is transported by his faith in God, even though he cannot live his life in the certainty of being saved. This direct conflict between the human world and the divine world results in a denial of free will, and the aging Luther broke with Erasmus and his *De Libero Arbitrio* (1523) by writing a *De Servo Arbitrio* (Luther 1525). Luther's austerity does not lead to pietism, which was a later development, but it does make it impossible to give a liberal interpretation of his thought. Luther's thought, and especially the great writings of 1520, is diametrically opposed to the idea that the merits of a pious and virtuous life might reinforce the effects of divine grace, which is central to Catholic ethics, though it also reappears in many different guises in protestant ethics from Melanchthon onwards. The central principle behind Luther's thought is the subordination of the human person to a principle of action: God. To cite only one of so many famous texts, the following quotation is from the 'Disputation Concerning Man' (Luther 1536: 139):

> Those who say that natural things have remained untainted after the fall philosophize impiously in opposition to theology. The same is true of those that say that a man 'in doing what is in him' is also able to merit the grace of God and Life. Also, those who say that the light of God's countenance is in man, as an imprint on us, that is, free will which forms the precept right and the will good . . . In like manner, that it rests with man to choose good and evil, or life and death.

In the 'Heidelberg Disputation' (1518: 41), Luther writes more succinctly: 'The love of God does not find, but creates, that which is pleasing to it. The love of man comes in to being through that which is pleasing to it.' Luther's thought inaugurates an intellectual tradition which challenges both Enlightenment rationalism and Christian-inspired humanism. It subordinates man to a meaning, to a Being who dominates him, and love and faith are his only means of surrender.

All this seems to trap Luther in to an otherworldly asceticism, but his ethical anti-individualism also leads to a secularized and communitarian image of the people of God. It took both the form of the

revolutionary messianism of the Swabian peasants and that of nationalism: Luther was and is a central reference for the German nationalism which found its initial expression in what Lucien Febvre (1928)
calls 'spiritual territorialism'. It is as though the dangerous aspects of
opposition to critical rationalism were already apparent at the very
beginning of modern times. Yet, at the same time, how can we fail to
recognize that this theology of faith, and the Jansenism that followed
it, is one of the main sources of ethical individualism? It appeals to
the responsibilities of human beings who have been freed from
mediations between heaven and earth, and whose solitude and very
impotence allows them to see the self as a personal Subject.

In terms of the history of ideas, the most important lesson to be
learned from Luther's thought is that it condemned to failure the
attempts of the small group of humanists and followers of Erasmus
who tried to reconcile the spirit of the Renaissance with that of the
Reformation, and faith with knowledge. The history of modernism is
marked from the outset by a split, not between progressives and
traditionalists, but between those who created the twin components
that will henceforth constitute modernity. On the one hand, we have
those who defend reason, and often reduce it to being an instrument
promoting a happiness which will once more make human beings a
part of nature; on the other, we have those who embark upon the
difficult adventure of transforming the divine subject in to a human
subject. They can only do so by taking the most indirect and most
paradoxical path: they must use faith or even predestination to
destroy social man.

The divorce between the two faces of modernity is irrevocable. On
the one hand, we find a regression to millenarianism; on the other,
modernity is reduced to meaning the quest for a utility defined by
merchants. Ignoring both these extremes, the history of modernity
will be a constant dialogue between rationalization and subjectivation.
No compromise is possible. The moving grandeur of the sixteenth
century is that it did not surrender to any great unitary myth. It
surrendered to neither absolute monarchy, Enlightenment nor Progress. In the midst of the ruins of the enchanted world, it rejected the
illusions of the humanists and lived the necessary and creative
lacerations of an emergent modernity. As we reach the end of the
millennium, are we not closer to the tragic beginnings of modernity
than to the apparent triumph of the centuries of Enlightenment and
revolutions?

Many thought that the break with the sacred and magical world
would make way for a world governed by reason and self-interest.
Above all, it would be one world in which there could be no darkness

and no mysteries: a world of science and instrumental action. The modernism whose effigy presides over the beginning of this book seemed to triumph for a long time, and it was only in the second half of the nineteenth century, with Freud and Nietzsche, that it came under criticism and began to disintegrate. Yet from the outset, and particularly during the Reformation and the seventeenth century, it was complemented or challenged by a force which was just as powerful as rationalization: *subjectivation*. The disintegration of the sacred world, and the accelerating divorce between the world created by man and the world of the divine creation triggered two contradictory but related tendencies, and both were far removed from modernist naturalism. On the one hand, the extra-human or divine Subject was replaced by man-as-subject. As a result, the view that the human person was a network of social roles and individual particularities gave way to an uneasy self-consciousness and a will to freedom and responsibility. On the other hand, we also see a return to a God who is no longer identified with a world which is sanctified or made divine through redemption, but who is defined in terms of his distance, his absence and the arbitrary nature of his grace. The teachings of the Reformers, Bérulle, and the French school of spirituality centre on the personality of Christ. This is Augustine's twofold heritage. Modernity did not replace a world which was divided between the human and the divine with a rationalized world. It did quite the reverse. It destroyed the enchanted world of magic and sacraments, and replaced it with two forces: reason and the Subject, rationalization and subjectivation. The tragic history of modernity is the story of the stormy relationship between the two. The religious Reformations went far beyond the rationalism of the Renaissance: humanists appealed to conscience and piety, whilst their opponents stressed the arbitrary nature of the will of God.

Even within the Catholic world, religious thought was torn between contradictory tendencies and riven by violent polemics, notably between what Henri Bremond calls devout humanism, and the Jansenists and other extreme Augustinians, who were close to the Reformers and convinced of the need for absolute submission to efficacious grace. One tendency within the latter school believed that reason was deceptive because it was dominated by natural instincts. This was the view taken by La Rochefoucauld and Pascal. Pascal attempts to humble the pride of the intellect and to focus on the direct conflict between the order of the body and the order of charity, yet he still has to rely upon reason to discover the human condition. The central figure in Catholic thought is Francis of Sales. Whilst the author of the *Introduction to the Devout Life* (1608; the definitive version dates from 1619) was a devout humanist, he was also the bishop of a diocese near Geneva and was influenced by protestantism. His *Traité de l'amour de dieu* (1616) is influenced both by Augustinianism and by the mystical experience of Jeanne de Chantal. This quasi-pietism, which prefigures Fénelon, does not, however, preclude a certain trust in human nature, and above all a desire to define a piety designed not for members of religious orders but for lay people. This was a piety for everyday life and for family life. For Francis de Sales, the entry in to modernity did not eradicate the reference to a distant and omnipotent God, but this did not signal a return to the religious order of things. It implied that the church must be neither worldly nor, above all, monarchical. Francis de Sales thus appeals to both the consciousness and the freedom of the human subject.

To conclude, let us go back to Augustine. Can we say that Augustine, or the Lutherans, Calvinists and Jansenists who are his distant descendants, resisted modernity and promoted a mysticism rather than an ethics, whereas his contemporary Pelagius or the Jesuits of the seventeenth century were more worldly and therefore more 'humanist'? The moralizing appeal to man is, however, always transformed in to respect for rules that conform to the interests of society. At best, as in Pelagius's case, it is ennobled by a reference to the virtues of the citizens of Antiquity. And the ethics that makes such a powerful appeal to conscience soon socializes man to such an extent that he is totally integrated in to the social world and begins to serve the collective consciousness, the common good or established powers, whatever name they go by. Conversely, the appeal to God, which appears to deny man's humanity, can have the opposite effect. It subordinates man to God, but it also implies that the meaning of living in God is to be found within the soul itself, as we can see from Augustine's account of his own conversion (*Confessions* VIII). This dualism is self-destructive when it becomes manichaean, or when the principle of good becomes completely divorced from that of evil, but it is also the starting point for any construction of a Subject which does not coincide with the social roles of the Ego. This Subject does not identify the man with the citizen and therefore recognizes the role of subjectivity, which is so alien to the Graeco-Roman tradition. The Augustinians, like their master, are painfully aware of the presence within them of what they call original sin, or, more accurately, concupiscence. The Ego's moral control over the individual is disrupted by sexuality, by the desire for women that enflamed Augustine, and which can be dominated only by a force 'deeper than my inmost understanding and higher than the topmost height that I could reach' ('*interior intimo meo, superior sumo meo*'; Augustine 400:

62). The unity between the rule of the good and respect for the good is replaced by the battle between God and Evil. The twofold and contradictory nature of man is revealed: God's creature bears the mark of original sin, which explains both why redemption is for all and why many are called but few are chosen. The Ego is fragmented, but there is still the possibility that an 'I' can be partially reconstructed as a result of the struggle between the Id and something higher than the Ego. What appears, at every moment in history, to be an antihumanism is, on the contrary, the starting point for the discovery of the Subject in Western culture.

This brief return to the religious origins of individualism takes us in a very different direction to that taken by Louis Dumont. Dumont (1983) contrasts individualism or the ideology of modern society, with the holism that characterizes other societies, and which is as typical of the Greek city-states as it is of the Indian caste system. Yet in his studies on Christianity, Louis Dumont himself speaks of the transition from 'an otherworldly individual' to the 'individual in the world'. By using these expressions, he reveals that in traditional societies the ascetic who lives in God coexists alongside the individual who is identified with a social role legitimized by a natural or divine order. Similarly, in the modern world, individual freedom coexists alongside an individuality defined in terms of identification with social roles. In Calvin's Geneva, the social order was originally contained within the Church and was imposed upon all with a rigidity consistent with the idea of predestination. That conception later became secularized and the individual became a citizen or a worker, but he was still subordinated to the social system and the holistic demands of a collective consciousness. The modern world which freed the individual therefore also made the individual submit to new laws, whereas the religious world – Buddhist or Christian – asserted both the freedom of the individual in God and the subordination of the individual to tradition. Individualism is not specifically associated with the modern world. Forms which subordinate the individual to the collectivity are to be found in all societies, ancient and modern. And the individual is never defenceless against the collectivity. This is why the contemporary return of religions or a religious-inspired ethics should be seen both as the community's revenge on modern individualism, and as the individual's revenge on the social and political mobilizations associated with modernization, which take on an extreme form in totalitarian regimes.

Our society is not individualistic because it is rationalist, secularized and production-oriented; it is individualistic despite the constraints and the normalization forced upon individuals by centralized production and management. To a large extent, it is the influence of ethical and social conceptions which are religious in origin that makes it individualistic. When he recalls the religious origins of individualism Louis Dumont himself argues along similar lines, especially when he writes (Dumont 1983: 64): 'There is within the very internal constitution of what we call the modern "individual in the world", an unnoticed but essential element of otherworldliness.' It is not, however, enough, to argue that the otherworldly individual marks an intermediary stage between the holism of old and modern individualism, as the modern world poses as great a threat to individualism as the ancient world. We thus find the constant and parallel presence of the moulding of the individual by society and the liberation of the individual. Without that liberation, it would be impossible for individuals to transform society.

These assertions may occasion some surprise. Should we not be contrasting Augustine's pessimism and the idea that human nature is corrupt and incapable of rising unaided to the level of the divine, with the optimism of the humanists, beginning with the Christian humanism which, from Marsilio Ficino to Erasmus, was open to the sciences and trusted in reason? And do we not have to agree with Cassirer (1932: 137–8) that there is a great continuity between this humanism, which seemed at first to have been marginalized by the Reformation, the natural religion of the eighteenth century, and the thought of Rousseau and Kant? This is a paradox only if we reduce ancient culture to the idea of human impotence, and modern culture to the opposite view. In traditional culture, there is in fact a conflict between the cosmological world-view in which everything is a manifestation of the omnipotence and goodness of God, and a meditation on evil, the fall and original sin that results in submission to divine grace. The same dualism can be seen in modern thought. Whereas the philosophers of the Enlightenment reconstruct a rationalist view of the world and man, Augustine's descendants discover a human subject who is dominated, exploited or alienated by society, but who has become able to give his freedom a positive content through labour and protest. It was in the seventeenth century that Augustinianism was 'modernized', mainly by Descartes and Pascal. Their similarities are greater than their differences, and Pascal had to resort to reason in order to condemn reason.

Descartes: A Modernist in Two Senses

The Subject and reason must coexist within the human being. The thinking that dominates modernity in its nascent phase does not reduce human experience to instrumental thought and action. And nor does it appeal to tolerance or even to Montaigne's scepticism in an attempt to reconcile reason and religion. Nascent modernity is dominated by the thought of Descartes, not because he is the herald of rationalism, but because he puts modernity on a sound footing and because his dualistic thought, which would soon be attacked by the empiricists but extended by Kant, beckons to us across two centuries of Enlightenment philosophy and progressive ideology and teaches us to redefine modernity.

Descartes frees himself from the world of sensations and opinions. That world is so deceptive that it does not allow him to work backwards from facts to ideas and to the discovery of the world order created by God, as Aquinas did. His distrust of all experiential data not only allows him to discover the rules of the Method that can protect him from illusions; it also allows him to discover the *cogito* in a surprising way. Whilst engaged on scientific work and in formulating the principles of the scientific thought that will supposedly make men the masters and possessors of nature, he suddenly digresses in to the *cogito* and writes in part IV of the *Discourse* (Descartes 1637: 127)

> From this I knew I was a substance whose whole essence or nature is simply to think, and which does not require any place, or depend on any material thing, in order to exist. Accordingly this 'I' – that is, the soul by which I am what I am – is entirely distinct from the body, and indeed it is easier to know than the body, and would not fail to be whatever it is, even if the body did not exist.

Let us ignore the objections raised against this argument by Hobbes and by Arnaud, who is the author of the third and fourth 'Objections' to the *Meditations*, and trace the implications of this radical dualism. The existence of God cannot be demonstrated on the basis of observations of the world. Such observations confuse two substances: the realm of souls and the realm of bodies. On the other hand, my idea of God is inexplicable if God does not exist. It is the idea of God that demonstrates the existence of God. According to part IV of *The Discourse* (Descartes 1637: 128):

> I decided to inquire in to the source of my ability to think of something more perfect than I was; and I recognized very clearly that this had to come from some nature that was in fact more perfect . . . the idea had been put in to me by a nature truly more perfect than I was and even possessing in itself all the perfections of which I could not have any idea, that is – to explain myself in one word – by God.

This argument is much closer to our concerns than St Anselm's proof, which Kant will describe as the ontological argument, and which Descartes expounds in the fifth *Meditation*. The detachment from immediate experience and opinion permitted by reason therefore both leads the human mind to discover the divinely created laws of nature, and allows man to define his own existence as that of a creature made in God's image. Man is a creature whose thought is the mark left by the divine workman when his work was done. As Descartes concentrates increasingly on the problems of ethics, especially in his correspondence with Princess Elisabeth, the greater his insistence on the divorce between, on the one hand, the world of reason and wisdom and, on the other, the world of the will and free will. With Descartes, whose name is so often associated with reason, what Horkheimer will call objective reason begins to break down and to be replaced by subjective reason – Charles Taylor (1989: 156) calls them substantive and procedural reason – whilst the freedom of the human Subject is asserted and experienced in the consciousness of thought. The Subject is defined in terms of reason's control over the passions, but is primarily a creative will, an inner principle of conduct, and not in terms of harmony with the world. Hence the image of the hero created by Corneille, who is seen by Cassirer (1932) as a good disciple of Descartes, though Charles Taylor (1989: 154) is more alert to the differences between aristocratic honour and the Cartesian appeal to self-consciousness. The Corneillean hero is motivated by a love which transcends the self, by a demand and not by shared sentiments. As Descartes himself puts it in the fourth *Meditation* (Descartes 1641: 40):

> It is only the will, or freedom of choice, which I experience within me to be so great that the idea of any greater faculty is beyond my grasp; so much so that it is in virtue of the will that I understand myself to bear in some way the image and likeness of God.

He therefore gives paramount importance to generosity. Article 153 of *The Passions of the Soul* (Descartes 1649: 384) provides the explanation:

> Thus I believe that true generosity, which causes a person's self-esteem to be as great as it may legitimately be, has only two components. The first consists in his knowing that nothing truly belongs to him but this freedom to dispose his volitions, and that he ought to be praised or blamed for no other reason than his using this freedom well or badly. The second consists in his feeling within himself a firm and constant resolution to use it well – that is, never to lack the will to undertake

and carry out whatever he judges to be best. To do that is to pursue virtue in a perfect manner.

Jean-Paul Sartre saw this ethics of freedom as prefiguring his own ideas. As a result of the importance he accords to free will, Descartes emphasizes the role of friendship, or the recognition of the other as Subject. He is therefore in the tradition of Montaigne and breaks with the social ethics that evaluates virtue in terms of the individual's devotion to the collective good.

There is no conflict between the two faces of man – rational knowlege of divinely-created laws – and will and freedom. They complement one another to the extent that will and generosity are supported by reason and, in more concrete terms, because, if man is a thing that thinks, this implies, according to the third *Meditation*, that he is also 'a thing that doubts, affirms, denies . . . which imagines and has sensory perceptions'. Descartes adds that he is also 'a thing that understands a few things, is ignorant of many things, loves, hates, is willing, is unwilling' (Descartes 1641: 24). He does not say 'It thinks within me' (*cogitatio sum*); he says 'I am thinking.' His philosophy is not a philosophy of Mind or of Being; it is a philosophy of the Subject and of Existence. The result is a trust in man which cannot be reduced to the power of scientific thought. Ferdinand Alquié comments (1950: 198): 'Whilst God created truth and nature, it is man who, in the technical era, will, thanks to his understanding of truths, rule over a nature which has no end or form of its own, and which will therefore yield to man's ends, receive his form and take on his face.' Man is not nature, but nor can he identify with God or Spirit. He exists between two orders; he dominates nature by deciphering it, and his soul bears the mark of God and recognizes that God, who is present in his thoughts, is greater than him. This is consistent with the general trend towards secularization and the rejection of all immanence. The world of nature and the world of God are separate, and communicate only through man. Man's action subordinates the world of things to his needs; his will does not merge with God, but discovers within itself an I which is distinct from his opinions, sensations or needs. This I is therefore the Subject. It is this aspect of Descartes that meant so much to Paul Valéry (1925: 839). He saw the philosopher's use of the 'I' as his most obvious break with 'the architecture of scholasticism'.

Descartes frees himself from the idea of the Cosmos. The world no longer has any unity; it is no more than a set of objects available for scientific research. The principle of unity now applies to a creator who can be perceived only through the thought of God, and therefore through the Cogito. This approach is the complete antithesis of an idealism. Consciousness is grasped in its finitude, its temporality. Just as man cannot identify completely with God, God must not be transformed in to a temporal and historical being made in man's image. Man is midway between God and nature.

The idea that man, being both body and soul, has a twofold nature is also central to the thought of Pascal: 'Man is to himself the greatest prodigy in nature, for he cannot conceive what body is, and still less what mind is, and least of all how a body can be joined to a mind. This is his supreme difficulty, and yet it is his very being' (Pascal 1669: 94). The text is followed by a quotation from St Augustine, as handed down by Montaigne. The famous fragments about the thinking reed (Pascal 1669: 95) take up the same idea:

> Man is only a reed, the weakest in nature, but he is a thinking reed. There is no need for the whole universe to take up arms to crush him: a vapour, a drop of water is enough to kill him. But even if the universe were to crush him, man would still be nobler than his slayer, because he knows that he is dying and the advantage the universe has over him. The universe knows none of this. Thus all our dignity consists in thought.

For both Pascal and Descartes, thought and personal experience are unitary and not contradictory, and together they are a source of religious inspiration. We therefore have to question the identification of rationalism with an antireligious mode of thought which all too easily moves from being a social critique of the Church and religious practices to being a materialism which fails to see that the religious Subject has been transformed in to a human Subject.

Man is part of Creation and he must at the same time surrender to the truth. His twofold nature means that he cannot, as Pascal tries to do, completely contrast the divine world with the human world, the order of charity with the order of reason. Man must take responsibility for his passions, which are – as a result of the hypophysis – signs of the concrete unity of body and soul. In 1640, Descartes told Newcastle that 'I attribute all the sweetness and happiness in this life to the use of the passions.' He said the same thing to Princess Elisabeth in 1645 when he replied to the objections of Regius, who wanted completely to divorce body and soul. Descartes's dualism is complemented by the primacy he accords to existence. His world is neither that of nature nor that of the universal Spirit. It is the world of a man who doubts and who is therefore divorced from God. Yet that man finds a solid support only within himself thanks to an inversion which allows the Subject or the I to appear within the Ego.

The rationalism of the Enlightenment believed that human freedom lay in the triumph of reason and the destruction of beliefs. It therefore imprisoned man within nature and necessarily destroyed any principle of the unity of man. And it not unreasonably reduced the Ego to being no more than an illusion or a false consciousness. Descartes takes a very different line, as his trust in reason leads him to reflect on the human subject, which is not merely God's creature, but a creature made in the image of its Creator. If our image of modernity is purely negative or critical, we inevitably see Descartes as one of the initiators of modern rationalism, and the defenders of the 'Cartesian' spirit are often reduced to that status. On the contrary, it is legitimate to see him as the principal agent of the transformation of Christian dualism in to a modern idea of the Subject.

Locke's Individualism

Whilst faith in reason has always been the starting point for the idea of modernity, there is, in law, political thought and philosophy, a divide between naturalism, and the related idea that society is a social body, and an individualism that is central to the formation of the notion of the Subject. Descartes's grandeur stems from the fact the rationalist author of the *Discourse on the Method* also defends an extreme dualism which transforms the Christian idea of a creature made in the image of its Creator, in to a philosophy of the personal Subject. Political and social thought is also marked by the divergence between two currents deriving from the same source. Once the Good ceases to be defined in terms of a divine imperative or the Ten Commandments handed down by Moses, one current of thought asserts that ethics and politics must be governed by the idea of the common good or of the interest of society. The prime exponent of this conception is the Cicero of *De re publica*. For this current, the central ideas are those of contract and obligation, and right is defined in terms of obedience to the law, which can take either an authoritarian or a democratic form. The modern expression of this conception is the view that the law must conform to a common utility which is defined in terms of peace and the preservation of individual and collective life. This appeal to natural law and reason does not, however, always lead to the idea that society is based upon a contract, as it does for Hobbes and Rousseau. That idea was inspired by the revolutionary spirit of the eighteenth century. What is known as the common good can easily be transformed in to State power, which views its positive right as being based solely upon its own interests. Descartes's contemporary Hugo Grotius in 1625 argued against the

modern theory of the absolute State associated with Machiavelli or
Jean Bodin by advancing the idea of *natural law*, which he defines in
Platonist terms as a body of juridical ideas or principles existing prior
to any particular situation or even the existence of God. Even if there
were no such thing as a circle, argues Grotius, the radii of a circle
would still be equal. Right is a creation of the mind, and it is as
rigorous as mathematics. Pufendorf will make the same comparison
in even more forceful terms in 1672.

This defence of right, which is distinct from and independent of
politics and based purely upon reason, represents, together with
Cartesian thought, the principal moment in the transformation of the
old Christian dualism in to a philosophy of the Subject and of
freedom. Grotius was not satisfied with the relative autonomy the
theologians granted *lex naturalis*, as opposed to *lex divina*. Above all,
he did not accept the extremist position of Calvin, who completely
denied the autonomy of human law in the name of the omnipotence
of elective grace, and his trust in reason led him to support the
Arminians or Remonstrants and, after their defeat, to lose the
positions he held in Amsterdam.

This view that natural law is an object of scientific study can also
be found in Montesquieu (1750), who studies social experiences in an
attempt to identify the spirit of the laws, or in other words the
'necessary relations deriving from the nature of things' that govern
the coherence and spirit of legislation. There is an enormous difference between this and the hesitant positions of Voltaire, and especially
Diderot's surrender to pragmatism. When Diderot speaks of efficacy
and when D'Alembert speaks of our duties towards our fellows, the
law reverts to being social, whereas Grotius and Montesquieu are
primarily concerned with restricting power and divorcing the theory
of law from theology.

It may seem surprising to relate the rationalism of the theorists of
natural law to the position of Locke, whose theory of human
understanding plays such a central role in the philosophy of the
Enlightenment. One is tempted, rather, to contrast Rousseau's social
revolt and Locke's 'bourgeois' theory. Yet it is the Rousseau of the
Second Discourse (1750), the *Emile* (1762b) and the *Social Contract*
(1762a) who is central to the philosophy of the Enlightenment, whilst
Locke supplies new foundations for the divorce between individual
and society. As we shall see, the difference between their theories can
be clearly seen in the French and Virginian Declarations of Rights.

Locke's starting point is that because God has granted him an
understanding which guides his actions, man enjoys free will and is
free to act. The primary meaning of action is labour. The law of

nature is the law of the common ownership of the land and all its products. Yet whilst certain men live, like the American Indians, in accordance with the law of nature, others transform and increase natural resources through their labour, and that gives them a right of ownership. Paragraph 27 of the second *Treatise* (Locke 1690b: 287–8) provides the starting point for the argument that will justify the existence of property, money and inequality:

> Though the earth and all inferior creatures be common to all men, yet every man has a property in his own person; this nobody has any right to but himself. The labour of his body and the work of his hands we may say are properly his. Whatsover, then, he removes out of the state that nature hath provided and left it in, he hath mixed his labour with and joined to it something that is his own, and thereby makes it his property. It being by him removed from the common state nature placed it in, it hath by this labour something annexed to it that excludes the common right of other men. For this labour being the unquestionable property of the labourer, no man but he can have a right to what that is once joined to, at least where there is enough and as good left in common for others.

The transition from common ownership to individual property therefore transforms the role of the law: far from being based on the common good, it must protect the freedom to act, to trade and to own property. Locke departs from Hobbes in that he does not confine himself to the purely political argument that the social contract which founds political society is based upon fear of violence and war. He gives natural law a political expression which brings it in to conflict with the hereditary monarchy defended by Sir Robert Filmer, who is the target of the first *Treatise* (Locke 1690a). He thus establishes a complete discontinuity between the state of nature and social organization. He underlines this by recalling that the political system was established not as a response to the state of nature, but to the state of war which destroyed it. Louis Dumont rightly sees Locke as inaugurating the transition from holism to individualism. The analysis of a community and the needs of its members is replaced by an analysis of labour and property, which must be protected by laws. That Locke is still concerned with community can, however, be seen from the way in which he justifies rebellion against oppression (Locke 1690b: 398–405). He does not defend rebellion, but he does condemn magistrates who are guilty of 'breach of trust' for having broken the covenant that made them agents of the common good. They are unworthy governors who destroy public order. Both political theory and economic theory argue that there cannot be a complete divorce between the rights of the individual and the preconditions for peace and social life.

This conception gives Locke a central position in the history of ideas, as he combines the individualist idea that property and wealth are based upon labour, with a reference to a human order whose nature is parenthetically defined by Louis Dumont: '(or what remains of the cosmic order)'. As Raymond Polin argues (Polin 1953), interest and morality thus converge thanks to the existence of God. Locke defends both the individualism that is present in all dualist thought, and the naturalistic deism of the philosophy of the Enlightenment. That unity will be gradually replaced by the growing opposition between the empiricism that leads to positivism, or even a Rousseauist sociologism, and the idea of natural law, which will inspire all the social movements that resist the established order.

Hobbes, Locke and Rousseau are equally revolutionary or, if we prefer to put it that way, are the first to define the democratic thought that rejects the legitimation of political power in terms of inheritance of the will of God, but they found political society on quite different bases. The goal of all these thinkers and all theorists of natural law is of course to found political society on a free decision taken by individuals, on a covenant or an act of trust. The words they use can, however, mask very different conceptions, as Pufendorf is aware when he advances the idea of a double covenant: first, a covenant of association and then a covenant of submission. This creates contradictions but does not resolve them. Locke emphasizes consent under constraint, the rule of the majority, and not the general will; in his view, the law means the protection of individual rights and not, as Hobbes thought, the constitution of a pacified social order. Locke also elaborates a theory of citizenship, yet he still sees civil society as a means of providing the natural rights of man with real guarantees. His thought, like the Bill of Rights of 1689, which is quite in keeping with the political positions of this Orangeman – even though the *Treatise* was conceived before the revolution of 1688-- stresses the independence of citizens rather than the construction of a community which benefits from the transfer of individual rights to a sovereign authority. He is reluctant to talk about the Sovereign; on the other hand, he stresses the importance of trust and the participation of all – the word 'people' had negative connotations in Locke's day – in the workings of institutions. Being a Whig, he believed in citizenship, but put more emphasis on the rights of citizens than on national unity.

Pufendorf, who was Locke's exact contemporary, also departs from Grotius and Cumberland. His dualism is similar to that of Descartes, and completely divorces physical beings (*entia physica*) from ethical beings (*entia moralia*). The latter do not originate in nature. Nature gives rise to judgements of utility or pleasure, but moral judgement implies 'a directive norm that we term a law', he writes in his *Elementa Jurisprudentiae Universalis* (1658). Being the law of reason, Pufendorf's law may, it is true, relate to the criterion of social utility and to that extent there is no disagreement between Grotius and Pufendorf, though the latter does place more emphasis on the distinction between 'what must be' and 'what is'. Rather than judging acts in terms of their consequences, he judges them in terms of intentions and their relationship with a divine law. He thus departs from the so-called modern conception of law, and his theories pertain to the world of religious thought – Buddhist as well as Christian – which seeks to provide an ethics of intention and which is more concerned with purity than law.

Locke's arguments seem far removed from any ethical absolutism, and even from any religious content, and his main purpose is to combat absolute monarchy. And yet, he ensures the transition from a religious definition to a secularized definition of a human actor who never completely identifies with the political society to which he belongs. The right to own property, the right to freedom and the right to resist oppression are the principles that found civil society. And civil society cannot become either a monarchic or a democratic Prince. Spanish theologians like Suarez and Las Casas protested against the massacres perpetrated by the conquistadores and pointed out that the Indians were as much the creatures of God as the Spaniards. Political power and its armed might must respect the equality of God's creatures, and should not treat some of them as though they were animals or objects to be sold on the market. The fact that the argument is couched in terms of the law of nature or reason, rather than of the mark left by the creator on his creatures, does not indicate a break in ethical thinking, but when these arguments give way to arguments that give a central role to social utility – defined in either Christian or secularized terms – the conception of ethical or political life does change considerably. We should not leap to the conclusion that modernity is to be equated with utilitarianism or that modern thought is concerned only with contracts, the law and the equilbrium or integration of society. The principle of normativity and the 'consequentialism' introduced by religion is replaced by the appearance of a human actor defined in terms of action, will and freedom, and, in more concrete terms, labour. The idea of the social contract, which inspired both absolutism and revolution – which is why they are so similar – dissolves the Subject in to the political community, the sovereign people or the nation, as the French

Revolution put it. In contrast, the idea of natural law, as conceived by Locke and Pufendorf, founds the duality of civil society and State, the rights of man and political power, and those rights give rise to both bourgeois thought and the workers' movement, or in other words to modes of thought and action which are assumed to represent social actors.

We have, then, two conflicting currents of thought, but they can converge. For one, which stems from Machiavelli, the important thing is to free the State from the dominance of the Church, and to breathe new life in to the model of Republican Rome bequeathed by Livy. This triumph of Reason of State has both positive and negative effects. It leads, on the one hand, from the theocracy of Geneva to the idea of popular sovereignty, to the modern conviction, which has very deep roots in France, where anticlericalism has played a major role, that the rationalism of the State is the precondition for the freedom of citizens, and that individuals will flourish only if they take part in public life. On the other hand, it can – and always does – lead to the absolute authority of a State, be it authoritarian or popular, based upon a contract, a general will or the revolutionary uprising of a people.

The political philosophy of the public contract can be contrasted with that of the private contract or trust, to use the term Locke borrows from private law. Whereas the first current of thought, which derives from nominalism, believes only in positive law, the second gives natural law the meaning conferred upon it by the Declarations of Rights, a meaning which was already present in the writings of the English Levellers of the seventeenth century. The first current is remembered mainly for the revolutions it inspired, whilst the second might be termed 'bourgeois', but it has to be said that whereas the former has given rise to terror and totalitarian regimes, every social movement has been inspired by the second. This duality means that it is impossible to establish too close a connection between the foundation of the State and modern individualism. Whilst that association does correspond to the thinking of those Régis Debray calls 'republicans' (Debray 1989), it is rejected by democrats, whom Debray himself defines in terms that signal his own fidelity to the republican idea. It should be obvious that the author is a 'democrat'.

The Declaration of the Rights of Man and of the Citizen

Despite the increasing strength of naturalism and empiricism, which prefigure the scientism and positivism of the nineteenth century, the seventeenth and eighteenth centuries are still strongly influenced, at the intellectual level, by the secularization of Christian thought and by the transformation of the divine Subject in to a human subject. As a result of Cartesian dualism, the idea of natural law, and then the thought of Kant, the human subject becomes less and less absorbed in the contemplation of an increasingly hidden being, and becomes an actor, a worker and a moral conscience.

The period ends with a great text: the Declaration of the Rights of Man and the Citizen, which was adopted by the Assemblée Nationale on 26 August 1789. Its influence was much greater than that of the American declarations, and its meaning is very different to the English Bill of Rights of 1689. This is a great text, not simply because it proclaims principles which contradict those of the absolute monarchy and which are, in that sense, revolutionary, but because it marks the culmination of two hundred years of debate and because it gives expression to the idea of the rights of man, which contradicts the revolutionary idea. The French Declaration of Rights was promulgated just as a period dominated by English thought was giving way to a period of revolutions which was to be dominated by the French political model and by German thought. It is the last text publicly to proclaim the twofold nature of modernity and to define it as a combination of rationalization and subjectivation. The long century that followed was dominated by the triumph of historicism and its monism.

The text has been so closely identified with the principles of democracy and the overthrow of the Ancien Régime in France and many other countries, that we assume, when we read it with the respect it deserves, that it has a unity which makes it difficult to understand. Similarly, Clemenceau's insistence in 1889 on defending the heritage of the Revolution as a whole made it difficult, if not impossible, to analyse the ten-year period that began with the proclamation of national sovereignty and ended with a military *coup d'état*. It is, on the other hand, clear that two conflicting themes run through the Declaration: individual rights and the general will, which are usually associated with Locke and Rousseau respectively. The two are so intertwined that the central issue is that of the unity and coherence of the Declaration. This historic text is evoked here because it has more to do with individualistic than holistic thought, to adopt Louis Dumont's dichotomy, and because it is marked by the influence of the English and the Americans rather than that of French patriots. The balance of power and influence was soon to be inverted and to lead to the triumph of a revolution that was increasingly alien and hostile to the individualism of the rights of man. It is in that sense that this Declaration marks the end of the pre-revolutionary period, whereas the Declaration of 1793 is fully implicated in a revolutionary logic. That the theme of individual rights is preeminent is clearly demonstrated by the preamble, which elevates 'the inalienable and sacred rights of man' above a political system whose 'acts' can at any moment be compared with the goals of all political institutions, and which can therefore be evaluated with reference to social integration, the common good or what we would now call the national interest. Article II lists the principal rights: freedom, property, safety and resistance to oppression. The right to own property is specified by article XVII, with which the Assemblée Nationale ended its work. Article IV is part of the same individualistic logic. Man, however, is contrasted with the figure of the citizen constructed by the very first article, which asserts that 'Social distinctions can only be based upon social utility', and especially by articles II and VI, which expound the ideas of the nation and the general will. As Hegel observes in his *Philosophy of Right* (Hegel 1821: 156), these conceptions are contradictory:

> If the state is confused with civil society, and if its specific end is laid down as the security and protection or property and personal freedom, then the interest of the individuals as such becomes the ultimate end of their association, and it follows that membership of the state is something optional. But the state's relation to the individual is quite different from this. Since the state is mind objectified, it is only as one of its members that the individual himself has objectivity, genuine individuality, and an ethical life. Unification pure and simple is the true content and aim of the individual, and the individual's destiny is the living of a universal life.

The opposition between the two conceptions is not one between traditional holism and modern individualism; it is one between the two faces of modernity. On the one hand, the absolutism of the divine law is replaced by the principle of social utility: man must be regarded as a citizen, and he is all the more virtuous if he sacrifices his selfish interests to the salvation and victory of the nation. On the other hand, individuals and social categories defend their interests and values against a government whose call for unity hinders their individual initiatives, and therefore limits its own representativity.

This contradiction cannot be overcome by a better understanding of the nation – which means not the State, but the people and therefore the general will – as that reference is part of one of the two conceptions the Declaration is trying to reconcile, and the experience of history makes it quite impossible to identify the common good and the rights of man with the unanimism of a crowd. The Declaration of 1789 provides a different and more elaborate answer. It is the law that reconciles individual interest with the common good. The formula was almost a truism at the end of a century in which social thought merged with or was dominated by the philosophy of right. The law is seen as the expression of the general will and the instrument of equality, but it also has the task of indirectly defending individual freedoms by defining 'limits' which make the freedom of all compatible with respect for the rights of others. This is an outline theory of democracy (the word itself is never used). This regime combines the plurality of interests with the unity of society, freedom and citizenship, by appealing to a law whose only principles are those of mediation and reconciliation. The law is, in general terms, limited and fragile, but it is still indispensable. This conception of law is less ambitious and above all less authoritarian than that of the legists who constructed the legal State, usually within the framework of an absolute monarchy, and who turned the law in to an instrument which subordinated the individual to a common good redefined in terms of collective utility. Here, in contrast, the law is elevated above the natural rights of man; it is therefore responsible for reconciling the interests of the individual with those of society. This is no Rousseauist utopia, as the individual may be egotistical or dishonest, and as the word 'society' may mask the individual interest of governments, technocracy or bureaucrats.

Most of the Declaration's articles, from articles V and VI onwards, specify the conditions for the application of the law, and in particular the workings of justice. The primacy of the rights of man is therefore restated, particularly in article XI, which introduces the principle of *habeas corpus*, and in article X, with its strange formulation 'No one shall be persecuted because of his opinions, even his religious opinions', which gives secularism a form which is far removed from the antireligious spirit of the rationalists of the nineteenth century. Here, secularism takes the form of respect for basic freedoms, and therefore for the cultural and political diversity in which the rights of man are embodied. The Declaration in fact concludes, not with article XVII, which deals with property and which has already been cited, but with article XVI. It is dedicated to Montesquieu and the very terms in which it is formulated – 'Any society in which rights are not guaranteed and in which the separation of powers is not determined, has no constitution' – makes it absolutely clear that individual rights and freedom take precedence over political integration and order.

The revolutions that did away with the absolute monarchy in England, in the former English colonies that became the United States of America, and in France were therefore defined by an overlap between Enlightenment thought and Cartesian and Christian dualism.

Bourgeois individualism, which long outlived this period, combined the consciousness of the personal Subject with the triumph of instrumental reason, ethical thinking with scientific empiricism, and the creation of economic science, notably by Adam Smith.

The history of the next two centuries was to be that of the increasing divorce between two principles that are very closely associated in Locke's thought: the defence of the rights of man and instrumental rationality. As the latter constructs a world of techniques and powers, the appeal to human rights will become increasingly dissociated, firstly in the workers' movement and then in other social movements, from trust in instrumental reason. Swept along by progress, humanity begins to wonder if it might not be losing its soul, or might not have sold it to the devil in exchange for its domination over nature. This was not yet the case in the eighteenth century because the struggle against the traditions and privileges of the Ancien Régime was still the dominant concern until the upheavals of the French Revolution, the Napoleonic Empire and the industrial revolution that began in Great Britain resulted in the romantic crisis which made it impossible to assert that inner experience and instrumental reason were one and the same. That is why the Declaration of Rights is both bourgeois and influenced by the theory of natural law; its individualism is both an assertion of a triumphal capitalism and of an ethical consciousness's resistance to the power of the Prince. The Declaration of Rights is the supreme creation of modern political philosophy and it already displays the contradictions that will tear apart industrial society.

The End of Pre-revolutionary Modernity

The triumph of freedom in France and, a few years earlier, in the United States of America when they freed themselves from colonial dependence, put an end to the three-hundred-year period that historians call the 'modern period'. I have attempted to remind the reader that this is not simply a period of secularization, rationalization and capitalism. In contrasting this critical and rationalist conception of modernity, which is identified with the disenchantment of a world that had for so long been populated by gods and numina, with the complementary but contrasting image of the birth of the Subject, of the progress of Subjectivation, I am attempting to get away from an evolutionism which is popular precisely because it is so simplistic. I am attempting to show that modernity is not simply a transition from the sacred to the profane or from religion to science, and above all to replace the modernist ideology which completely identifies modernity with rationalization with a vision which has a very different meaning and very different implications. Modernity, that is, is the ever-increasing divorce between the world of nature, which is governed by the laws discovered and used by rational thought, and the world of the Subject. In the latter, there are no transcendental principles to define the good, which is replaced by the right of every human being to freedom and responsibility. The principles bequeathed to the world by the French Revolution – liberty, equality and fraternity – stem neither from the idea of secularization nor from an empiricism which is naturally more sensitive to inequalities of all kinds, but from the founding theme of natural law.

I am attempting to replace the image of the Enlightenment dispelling the fog of the past, first in the heights of society and then over a broader area, with that of two conflicting trends in thought and social organization. We can call one *capitalism*, and the other the *bourgeois* spirit. On the one hand, man is freed from all social bonds and, because he may be one of the elect, adopts a strict self-discipline, but also imposes a repressive order on those who do not live in justice or beneath the gaze of God. He therefore constructs a society which is fair, elitist, strict and efficient, and which transforms faith in to practical activities. On the other, we have the discovery of self-consciousness which is concerned with what Montaigne called 'that mistress form', or in other words the individual personality, and therefore a love which escapes the domain of the philosophy of law.

It is quite possible to combine the two images. There is so little distance between them that they often merge, especially in the seventeenth century, but also on the eve of industrialization. And yet they look in opposite directions. One constructs a society based upon production, labour, savings and sacrifices; the other seeks happiness and stresses the importance of private life. Public and private life begin to be divorced, and will move further and further away from one another. The same duality can, as I have shown, be seen in Jean-Jacques Rousseau, who founds a society in which the general will is almost necessarily transformed in to an integrative and intolerant collective consciousness, but who also displays a sensitivity which is closer to that of Montaigne than that of the Genevans of Calvin's day.

The above comments also apply to Catholic countries. On the one hand, they resist secularization by giving very enormous power to a Church armed with the sacraments and by recognizing the divine right of absolute monarchs. On the other, they preserve the separation of the spiritual and the temporal in the form of ultramontanism and the new piety born of the catholic Reformation. Rather than contrasting Catholics who are attached to the past with Protestants who look to the future, it would therefore be more accurate to contrast the creation of a personal Subject with the use of religious values to reinforce social order, as both tendencies are visible within both camps within a divided Christianity. Right down to the present day, the reference to religion has been used to reinforce the established order just as often as it has been used to encourage rebellions against that order.

The history of religious life, especially in what we call the Judaeo-Christian world, is primarily the history of the increasing divorce between a rationalism which stems from Plato and Aristotle, and which is then transformed by the theologians, and the mysticism of the Subject, of a personal Self which finds itself by becoming lost in the love of God. The divorce is now complete. Hence the conflict between societies – from the United States to some Islamic societies – which claim to be based on religious principles, and social movements which appeal to personal and collective freedom, or which are struggling against power in the name of faith. We now feel that we have very little in common with the thought of the seventeenth and eighteenth centuries, which was still attempting to reconcile the law of reason and divine revelation. As we have seen, the two were reconciled thanks to the idea of society, which was understood to mean a trade in commodities and ideas and therefore an organic division of labour. Hence the central role played in classical intellectual life by social thought and, more specifically, political philosophy. Its centrality implies that the increasing divorce between these two currents of thought, between the religious life and social organization, means that we will have to relinquish all images of the ideal society.

In his great book *Sources of the Self* Charles Taylor (1989) broadly identifies modernity with the formation of the Self, with the affirmation of the inner man, and his vision almost marginalizes what he calls (Taylor 1989: 321–54) the 'radical enlightenment', meaning primarily the work of those the French describe as the *philosophes* of the eighteenth century: Diderot, Helvétius, d'Holbach and even Condorcet. In Taylor's view, extreme materialism had less influence than the transformation of moral feelings and the image of man. I agree with him as to the central importance of the theme of the Subject, but it declines in the eighteenth century to the extent that it is still bound up with a Christian vision that loses ground whilst secularization spreads, whilst bourgeois individualism is and will be increasingly subordinate to capitalist rigour. This paves the way for the triumph of historicism and even scientism, which will lead in the nineteenth century to the almost complete eclipse of the idea of the Subject. As confidence in a conquering and liberating reason fades, the idea of the Subject then undergoes a renaissance.

This renaissance was obvious in the strange way the French celebrated the bicentenary of the Revolution. The longstanding and prevailing idea that the Revolution represented the victory of science, reason and of individuals who understood the laws of History was rejected. And as the idea of a united Europe precluded too boisterous a celebration of a nation struggling against princes and an antirevolutionary coalition of European armies, the French remembered only the Declaration of the Rights of Man, and thus celebrated the least revolutionary act. They celebrated the one act that has least to do with historicist thought, and which most closely relates the transformation of French society to that of English society and to the birth of American society. This choice is symbolized by François Furet's victory (Furet 1978) over the descendants of Albert Mathiez (1925–7).

We are, then, witnessing a resurrection of the pre-revolutionary period and pre-revolutionary thought at the very time when the word *democracy* tends to replace the word 'revolutionary' in our discourse because we now have mixed feelings about all philosophies of progress. We rarely reject them, but we often find the Enlightenment as dazzling as it is illuminating. Above all, we are afraid of becoming purely social human beings who are completely dependent on a political power, as we know that power never coincides with the general will, which is more mythical than real. The return of the religious is, of course, often an antimodernist development; it is a reaction against secularization and an attempt to reconstruct a community by combining spiritual and temporal power, but it is also an attempt to reintroduce a non-social force in to social life, to reintroduce an ethics of conviction in to a world dominated by the ethics of responsibility, to adopt Weber's terminology. As at the beginning of the modern era, we are now witnessing a convergence between three great forces: rationalization, an appeal to human rights, and religious communitarianism. And who would be as bold as to claim to be certain that only the first defends modernity, that the second means no more than respect for the consumer and that the third is completely reactionary?

The inescapable conclusion is that the two poles of modernity – rationalization and subjectivation – are becoming divorced, whereas our former world, which was dominated by a combination of philosophy and Christian theology, habitually thought in terms that were at once magical and rationalist, Christian and Aristotelian. This divorce will eventually affect every domain. The idea that human behaviour can and must be completely confined by rationality and its universalism is being challenged both by those who explore the personality, by nationalisms and, more recently, by analysts of mass consumption and mass communications.

The greatest thinkers of the seventeenth century tried to prevent this fragmentation by transforming religiously-inspired thought and the idea of the soul in to the idea of a free subject, but this does not mean that they were content with an individualist empiricism, or with a utilitarianism which would make social organization intelligible. Descartes, Grotius and Locke tried to overcome the great break between Luther and Erasmus, between the Reformation and the Renaissance, that occurred at the beginning of the sixteenth century.

The seventeenth and eighteenth centuries did not, however, have to choose between two orientations that were in open conflict, because their common hostility to both the trends they had inherited outweighed the battle they were fighting within modernity itself.

This is why the long modern period ends with the French Revolution and with the industrialization of Great Britain. The new industrial societies acquired such a capacity for transforming themselves that they whole-heartedly adopted the haughtiest and most masterful conception of their modernity. There was no longer such a thing as human nature, and man no longer had natural rights: he was no more than what he did, and his rights were social rights. Reason was no longer thought or the discovery of an order; it became a force that could transform history, and the idea of society, which had been mechanical, now became organic. As a result, the divorce between subject and society disappeared. Man became a truly social and historical being. The triumph of the modernist ideology was so complete and so violent that it was a century before it was challenged and before the gap between rationalization and the personal Subject could reappear.

3

The Meaning of History

Historicism

The primary effect of accelerated economic modernization was to transform the principles of rational thought in to general social and political objectives. In the seventeenth and eighteenth centuries, both political leaders and social thinkers discussed order, peace and freedom in social terms; throughout the long nineteenth century, which lasted well in to the twentieth, they transformed a natural law in to a collective will. The idea of *progress* is the clearest expression of this politicization of the philosophy of the Enlightenment. The advance of reason no longer merely requires the removal of the obstacles in its path; modernity is something to be loved and willed. The goal is to organize a self-motivating society which can create modernity. The social thought of the period is, however, still dominated by the identification of social actors with natural forces. This is true of both capitalist thought, which adopts as its hero the entrepreneur who is motivated by the quest for profit, and socialist thought, for which the workers' movement is an expression of productive forces that are trying to escape the contradictions in which they are imprisoned by capitalist relations of production. Social and political liberation represents a return to nature or to Being, and scientific reason will reunite man with the universe. Condorcet (1795) was confident that the progress of the human spirit would ensure universal happiness; in the nineteenth century, it was believed that political and social mobilization, and the will to happiness were the motors behind industrial progress. Labour, organization and investment would create a technologically-based society that would generate affluence and freedom. Modernity had been an idea; it was now primarily a will, but that did not destroy the link between human action and the laws of nature and history. There is, then, a basic continuity between the century of the Enlightenment and the era of progress.

For less subtle thinkers, this meant quite simply the victory of positive thought, and therefore the dissolution of subjectivity in to the rationality of scientific objectivity. Until the beginning of the twentieth century, scientism enjoyed great success in intellectual life. The break with the scientistic belief that once the facts had been clearly established, the laws of historical evolution would be revealed, came with the development of the social sciences and especially the work of Weber in Germany and Durkheim in France. These famous debates, which were continued by Simiand and then by Marc Bloch and Lucien Febvre, had more far-reaching effects in Germany than in France.

Historicist thought is of much greater interest. Whether or not it takes an idealist form, it identifies modernization with the development of the human spirit, and the triumph of reason with that of freedom, the formation of the nation or the final triumph of social justice. For some, the correspondence between economic activity and social organization provides an infrastructure which determines every manifestation of political and cultural life. Whilst this idea does introduce an economic determinism, greater importance should be accorded to the assertion that all forms of collective life are manifestations of a society's ability and will to produce and transform itself.

Social thought has distanced itself from historicism with such violence, especially in recent decades, that we have almost forgotten what it once represented, but it would be foolish to consign it to the 'dustbin of history' without further ado. Earlier modes of thought had investigated the nature of politics, religion, the family and especially law, and therefore the causal relations that existed between these different orders of reality. Did ideas determine politics, or was politics determined by the economy? What are the causes that bring about the victory of a nation, or the decline and fall of the Roman Empire? Historicism replaced these questions with an analysis that defined phenomena in terms of their position on a tradition–modernity axis. Marxist thought itself is not so much an economic determinism as an expression of the view that society is a product of the practice of labour and of the contradictions between the rational development of the productive forces and profit, and between the direction or meaning [*sens*] of historical evolution and the irrationality of private interests. And the image of communism it proposes is not that of a rationalized society, but that of a society in which each will receive in accordance with their needs. Historicist thought in all its forms is dominated by the concept of *totality*. It replaces the concept of institution, which had been so central for the previous period. This is why the idea of progress insistently identifies economic growth with national development. As we can see from both the predominantly German concept of a national economy and the French idea of the nation, which is associated in republican and secular thinking with reason's triumph over tradition, progress implies that social and economic modernity takes the concrete form of the formation of the *nation*. This same theme was taken up by the educational ideology of the Third Republic, and it was only in the second half of the twentieth century that it began to fade. Modernity is therefore not divorced from modernization, as was the case with the earlier philosophy of the Enlightenment, but it does take on greater importance in a century when progress no longer means intellectual progress alone. It now means the development of forms of production and labour at a time when industrialization, urbanization and the extension of public administration are having a drastic effect on the lives of most people. Historicism asserts that the internal workings of a society can be explained in terms of the developments that are taking it in the direction of modernity. In the last analysis, any social problem is a struggle between the past and the future. The sense [*sens*] of history refers to both the direction in which it is moving and its signification. History will lead to the triumph of modernity, and modernity means complexity, efficacy, differentiation and therefore rationalization. History is also the emergence of a consciousness that is synonymous with reason and will, and that consciousness will replace submission to the established order and to the heritage of the past.

The historicist vision has often been criticized for being inhuman. It has been accused of justifying the increasingly absolute power of the leaders of economy and society over individuals, particular groups and minorities. It would, however, be a mistake to reduce it to the subordination of individual life and thought to impersonal economic forces. Historicism, and all that it implied for better and for worse, was a voluntarism rather than a naturalism. In that sense, the idea of a *subject*, which is identified with the idea that history has a meaning and direction, is ubiquitous in the nineteenth century – the century of great epic and lyrical narratives. It had been marginalized by the philosophies of the eighteenth century, which were suspicious of its religious origins. The nineteenth century in fact sees the convergence of two intellectual currents – idealism and materialism – and the disappearance of the old dichotomies between reason and religion, the ethics of responsibility and the ethics of conviction, and the world of phenomena and the world of noumena. The most important thing of all is that society's practices of production and culture are unified within a nature which is fully committed to its own modernization. The idea of modernity is triumphant and will not tolerate the existence of anything else. The moment when we began to think of ourselves in purely historical terms is a central moment in our history.

How did this fusion come about? How did the heritage of Locke come to be combined with that of Rousseau, the liberalism of the defender of the rights of man with the idea of the general will? How was the eighteenth- and nineteenth-century divorce between these currents replaced by a single intellectual system, by a belief in progress that had both the mobilizing power of a religion and the obviousness of a scientific truth? The primary reason for the transformation was the French Revolution, and not the industrial revolution. Whilst the latter did reinforce evolutionary and even positivist thought, it was the French Revolution that introduced the idea of a historical actor in to both thought and history. It was the Revolution that introduced the idea that individuals or social categories had a rendezvous with destiny or a historical necessity. And it did so outside the religious context of the Judaic idea of a chosen people. The Revolution that turned France upside down was not simply French, whereas the Glorious Revolution of 1688 was and remains a specifically English phenomenon. Those who took part in the French Revolution, those who had heads cut off and those whose heads were cut off, those who experienced the revolutionary *journées* as the soldiers of Year II, not to mention the Bonaparte who was transformed in to Napoléon, were all epic figures whose historic significance goes far beyond their individual personalities. In a very short and compressed space of time, they all lived through the clash between a millenary past and a future which could be measured in centuries. In such a situation, how could the divorce between natural objectivity and human subjectivity be sustained?

The idea of *progress* has a central or intermediary place between the idea of rationalization and that of development. The latter accords primacy to politics, the former to knowledge. The idea of progress asserts that development policies and the triumph of reason are one and the same. It foreshadows the application of science to politics, and therefore identifies a political will with a historic necessity. To believe in progress means loving the future, which is both unavoidable and radiant. The Second International, whose ideas spread to most countries in Western Europe, expressed the same view when it asserted that socialism would emerge from capitalism once capitalism had exhausted its ability to create new productive forces and when it called for collective action on the part of the workers and intervention on the part of their elected representatives. To borrow one of

Nietzsche's most famous expressions, we might even speak of an *amor fati* or love of destiny.

According to this view, social conflicts are primarily conflicts between the future and the past, but the victory of the future is ensured not only by the progress of reason, but also, and especially, by economic success and successful collective action. This idea lies at the heart of all versions of the belief in modernization. The influential sociologist Seymour Martin Lipset has attempted to demonstrate that economic growth, political freedom and personal happiness increase at the same rate, and that this synchrony has to be termed progress. How is progress to be brought about? Initially through the rationalization of labour, which was to be the great slogan of industry from Taylor and Ford to their enthusiastic disciple Lenin. Secondly, and most importantly, through the action of a political power which can mobilize energy – a term borrowed from physics – so as to accelerate modernization. Which means that local traditions and loyalties have to be subordinated to a high degree of national integration. The correspondence between reason and will, the subordination of the individual to society, and the subordination of society to the modernization of production and the might of the State, make possible a collective mobilization. And the call for rationalization, which is always elitist, is powerless to resist it.

Revolution

This is why historicist thought is closely associated with the *revolutionary* idea. The idea is present from the very beginnings of modernist thought, but after the French Revolution it acquires a central role which it will lose only with the departure of many Central and Eastern European countries from the Communist system in 1989. The revolutionary idea combines three elements: the will to liberate the forces of modernity, the struggle against an *ancien régime* that is an obstacle to modernization and the triumph of reason, and the assertion of a national will identified with modernization. All revolutions are modernizing, liberating national. Historicist thought is weaker when, as in the very centre of the capitalist system, the economy seems to govern history and when it is possible to dream of the withering away of the State. Conversely, it grows stronger when a nation identifies its renaissance or independence with modernization, as was the case in Germany and Italy, and then in a great number of countries in Europe and other continents. The universalism of the Enlightenment concerned only an elite, and sometimes only the immediate entourage of enlightened despots; the idea of revolution rouses nations, or at least a vast middle class. France became a beacon for these international revolutionary movements, even though it was Germany which saw the broadest development of a revolutionary political movement, and even though the revolution which was to exert the greatest influence on the twentieth century occurred in Russia. The explanation is that in France the 'Great Revolution' led to an exceptionally close association between the destruction of the Ancien Régime and the victorious nation's triumph over a coalition of Princes and internal enemies. This political vision was so powerful that its effects are still felt today, even though the political, social and intellectual situation has changed completely. Intellectuals and politicians continue to celebrate a revolutionary nationalism. Without it, the strange alliance between communists and socialists which lasted, with one interruption, from 1972 to 1984 would have been inconceivable.

All these ideas, which are in fact sentiments rather than ideas, come together with a passion in the work of Michelet. From the *Introduction à l'histoire universelle* (Michelet 1831) to *Le Peuple* (Michelet 1846) and the *Histoire de la Révolution française* (Michelet 1852–3), no theme is more central to Michelet than the history of France, viewed as that of a person and nation willingly sacrificed for the cause of justice. His passion for the Revolution stems from the fact that it was the creation of a people who saved freedom at Valmy and Jemmapes and, more generally, from the fact that it created a unity between reason and faith and thus ensured the victory of freedom over fatality, and the victory of justice over grace, as Michelet himself puts it. From 1843 onwards, Michelet became not simply anticlerical – this was the moment when he published his attack on the Jesuits (Michelet 1843) – but antireligious. He abandoned his work on the Middle Ages, developed a passion for the Renaissance, and then flung himself in to the study of the Revolution. Yet when he speaks of the modern world, he constantly speaks of faith and love, and of the rediscovery of a unity that lies beyond the the class struggle. This unity is the unity of France, of the *patrie*, and in Michelet's view it is best symbolized by the Fête de la Fédération of 14 July 1790. As he adds that the people could create justice and freedom only by making sacrifices and shedding its own blood, all the major themes of historicist thought are present in his work, which is as much a philosophy of history as an exercise in historiography: belief in an evolution towards freedom, the identification of justice with a nation, namely France, a quest for the unity of *la patrie* which transcends social divisions, and the dream of a new religion which will at last be able to unite society. Modernity is the reign of love and justice, the reconciliation of the elements of a Whole which is not merely the sum of its parts, but the goal towards which each individual element is striving.

Even when it takes an attenuated form, the revolutionary idea is a much more powerful mobilizing force than that of natural selection, which reduces history to a struggle won by the fittest, or in other words the strongest. How could the majority be inspired by an ideology which celebrates the victory of minorities? Historicism and its practical expression, namely revolutionary action, mobilize the masses in the name of the nation and history, and against the minorities who are blocking modernization in order to protect their interests and privileges. François Furet has demontrated (Furet 1988) that the idea of the French Revolution and especially the thought of Robespierre, who was its greatest actor, centred upon the assertion that the revolutionary process was natural but must also be a matter of will, that the Revolution was as much the creation of virtue as of necessity. That is why the body politic had to be as pure as a crystal and cleansed of all dross, of all the traitors who were plotting on behalf of tyrants. The Revolution is defined by the dominance of political categories over all other categories and therefore by the closure of the political universe as it strives for purity, mobilizes its forces and unleashes its armies against internal enemies, and especially against revolutionaries who have betrayed the spirit of the Revolution. Hence the importance of the public meetings of the Clubs and of the speeches of the Jacobin leaders. Their speeches do not supply a programme, but rather a defence of revolutionary purity, of the internal dynamic of the Revolution, and a tireless denunciation of the luke-warm, who inevitably become traitors. Furet (1988: 397) sums up the idea of Revolution thus: 'The French idea of revolution is characterized by an extraordinary emphasis on the political and on the new State's ability to change society.' A few pages earlier, he spells out what this implies: 'The Republic presupposes that people and State are by their very nature inseparable.'

It was therefore extremely difficult to separate out social problems from political problems. In that sense, the best and most critical observer is Marx, who denounces the 'political illusion' that was so powerful in France, especially during the Paris Commune. The majority aped the Commune of 1793, got drunk on revolutionary rhetoric and dared to expel from their ranks a minority which included representatives of the International. In France, the dominance of political forces over social forces did not disappear after 1848 and 1871; it could be found intact in the Common Programme of the Left in 1972. The nineteenth century was an epic century, even though we have long been taught to see it mainly as the century which saw the birth of large-scale industrialization. Those who spoke of an age of revolutions were right to see this political definition as carrying more weight than the idea of industrial society. That idea often introduces an economic determinism which obscures the mechanisms that shape such a society, whereas the theme of revolution, even when applied to countries which did not experience the destruction of their political institutions, does underline the great strength of a mobilization which serves the cause of progress, accumulation and might.

The long nineteenth century was therefore no longer dominated by the divorce between the world of techniques and the world of consciousness, of objectivity and subjectivity; on the contrary, it strove, with an effort without historical precedent, to make the individual a public being, not in the Athenian or Roman sense of the word or by subordinating the individual to the *polis*, but by overcoming the dichotomy between the spiritual and the temporal in the name of the meaning of history, and therefore in the name of the historic mission of every social actor.

This is a military rather than an industrial vision, and it mobilizes rather than organizes. Thanks to an apparent paradox, we have to look to economic life to see the presence of subjectivation. It was dominated rather than being truly suppressed. As we have already seen, subjectivation was of such importance in the pre-revolutionary period that the rationalism of the Enlightenment never succeeded in masking it. For it is not so much self-interest that resists the general mobilization of society, as *labour*. According to Weber's analysis, labour was a calling. Many entrepreneurs acted in its name, and it also became the central justification for the workers' movement. In industrial society, such an appeal to the Subject is inseparable from conflicts over labour. In his own view, the entrepreneur represents labour and reason, as opposed to the routine and traditionalism of wage-earners, whereas militant workers denounce the irrationality of profit and the crises that destroy human labour, which is the productive and progressive force *par excellence*.

The Subject could be shaped by the long-standing Christian tradition only because the Ego was torn between sin and the grace of God; in industrial society it was strengthened by being transformed in to a social movement. At the same time, it risked destruction when that movement became a new emblem of the State, progress and historical necessity, just as the individual risked absorption by divine grace. Once again, the Subject could assert its presence only by taking the risk that it might vanish by becoming either an almost natural force or a power whose legitimacy is based upon natural laws.

Whilst social actors and their conflicts do resist the evolution of the historical totality, it is immediately obvious that there is no solid basis for the identification of economic growth, or in other words industrialization, with national, social and collective action, or of history with the Subject. Historicist thought triumphed in the margins of modernity. It had more difficulty in gaining acceptance in the heartlands of a triumphant industrial capitalism or in countries where the national question was more important than the economic and social question, or even came in to conflict with it. That is why historicism was primarily a German mode of thought which subsequently spread throughout continental Europe during the turmoil brought about by the beginnings of capitalism and the formation of revolutionary movements. It had immense influence across a huge area thanks to Herder, Marx and then Lenin. Yet it had no effect on either Great Britain or the United States, and permeated French political culture to only a limited degree. In nations that were part of the Austro-Hungarian, Turkish or Russian Empires, the struggle for independence often took precedence over the desire for modernity. When, on the eve of the First World War, the Czech workers were forced to decide if they were primarily workers or primarily Czechs, they decided they were first of all Czechs, and national movements were often dominated by the old ruling classes or by intermediary categories whose relationship with modernity was ambiguous. At the opposite extreme, in 'central' countries, the appeal to the market, the concentration of capital and the rationalization of production methods suppressed the idea of modern, or even industrial, society and led to a brutal divorce between public and private life, between modernization and consciousness. Men's dominance over women therefore took an extreme form. Men were identified with public life, whereas women were confined to private life but made up for their lack of rights and power by exercising great authority over their families and the education of their children. Squeezed between a 'savage' capitalism and outbreaks of nationalism, historicist thought and historicist movements always remained fragile. This was especially true in France, which was subject to the rule of both the financial bourgeoisie and the control of a nationalist State. Society enjoyed only a limited autonomy, and social thought was more often a history of the nation than a sociology of modernity, at least until the success of the Durkheimian school, which coincided with the limited emergence of a solidarist politics.

The historicist integration of public and private life thus had an effect on cultural production too. It meant that this was the period of the *novel* – a genre defined by the correspondence between a biography and a historical situation. Novels lose their power if the central character is no more than a symbol of a collective history or if, conversely, that character lives in a purely private space.

Modernity without Revolution: Tocqueville

To conclude this general description of the idea of progress, we must at least sketch a portrait of someone who rebelled against this progressive philosophy of history. I cannot think of a more interesting example than Tocqueville. He seems at first to share the idea that history has a meaning or direction, that an unavoidable natural necessity governs the transition from aristocracy to democracy, from inequality and barriers between castes and classes to an equality of condition which means not so much the absence of differences as the removal of obstacles to mobility. Tocqueville does not believe that America is different to Europe; he does believe that America provides a clear picture of the future towards which France and Europe are heading in an indirect and very contradictory way. Yet no sooner has he expressed this idea than, in the second volume of *Democracy in America* (Tocqueville 1835–40), he gives this evolution a different meaning. Increasing equality leads to the concentration of power. Tocqueville's subsequent argument appealed mainly to aristocrats and all those who remained attached to social and cultural traditions, but it was relevant to all: given that it had rooted out all particularisms, traditions and customs, was not modern society becoming an atomized crowd that gave free reign to absolute power and its excesses? Tocqueville asks himself why America did not succumb to the tyranny of the majority or of a dictator. His initial answer was that it has a federal government, that its provinces and districts are autonomous, and that the judiciary is independent, but these explanations were not enough: these were manifestations of democracy rather than its cause. Tocqueville then comes to the main issue: religion. In chapter IX of the second part of volume one, he asserts that religion introduces the principle of equality between men and then, adopting a more complex argument, claims that by leaving Heaven to deal with the problem of ultimate ends, it limits conflict and, so to speak, secularizes politics. Tocqueville is not indulging in tautology when he states that manners and ideas determine equality, which then defines democracy. Not only is democracy a social phenomenon before it becomes a political phenomenon; it is cultural rather than social. Convictions and manners thus become divorced from social and political organization; they act upon them and can also come in to conflict with certain tendencies within modernity.

Although it was very influential in Great Britain and the United States, Tocqueville's work was for a long time marginal to social thought in France, presumably because it contradicted the integrated and monolithic vision of modernity, and the martial image of wealth, freedom and happiness advancing side by side which had been disseminated and popularized by the ideologies and politics of modernity. Tocqueville completely rejected the revolutionary idea which dominated French thought and asserted that a unitary and voluntarist movement was leading modern society towards freedom and equality. He fully supported the overthrow of the Ancien Régime, but he rejected the Revolution, and to that extent he had a great deal in common with many other thinkers of his day and, as we shall see, with Auguste Comte. He accepted the decline of the *notables* and the intermediary bodies, and the gradual victory of equality, or in other words the lowering of social and cultural barriers. He supported the separation of Church and State, because he had seen its beneficial effects in the United States, but his thought is steeped in the tradition of natural law and Christian spiritualism. Tocqueville dreams retrospectively of an English-style historical continuity which both modernizes and restricts the central power. He adopts Montesquieu's theories and transports them to a new world. He reduces the United States to a seventeenth- and eighteenth-century society which was far removed from what it had become since Jackson, and even further removed from what it was at a time when the industrial North was poised to destroy the plantation economy of the South. Current French interest in Tocqueville is part of a broader trend. The political philosophy of the eighteenth century has great attractions for all those who want to escape from the ruins of historicism. Whilst Tocqueville is a post-revolutionary and a convinced believer in the triumph of equality, he is still looking for a force that can resist mass society and its most dangerous product: the concentration of power. He finds that force in 'manners', and therefore in the influence that an ethical and religious conception can have on economic and social organization, as we can see from the titles of the four parts of volume 2, which deal respectively with the influence of democracy, or in other words the spirit of equality, on science and the arts, on opinions and sentiments, on manners and on political society in the United States. The intellectual quality of Tocqueville's analyses does not mean that they are not part of the political culture of the seventeenth and eighteenth centuries, to which Americans remain more attached than the French. The Subject in whose name Tocqueville challenges economic and political modernization is still the Christian subject whose origins lie, according to Tocqueville, in the irrepressible human need for hope.

What possible influence could such ideas have at a time when philanthropists and socialists were drawing attention to the increase in poverty, when the European and American world was being swept along by an industrial revolution which may not, according to historians, have deserved its name, but which certainly brought about such an upheaval in material and mental life that it was no longer possible to speak of man in general or to investigate the moral or religious foundations of the social order? Our encounter with Tocqueville is therefore a final farewell to the theory of natural law and Christian and Cartesian dualism. The combined effects of the French Revolution and the transformations of the economy that began in Great Britain were sweeping the European world and, before long, the greater part of the planet in to a modernity that was not confined to the world of ideas. It created a society and social actors who are defined by their actions rather than by their nature. Political philosophy was giving way to political economy.

Nostalgia for Being

The entry in to historicism and the technological world signalled by the unpheavals of the French Revolution and industrialization in England provoked more extreme resistance than that put up by Tocqueville, who rejected the Revolution and looked for modernity in the realization of the ideas of the seventeenth and eighteenth centuries. The entry in to History, the transition from ideas to practices and the untranscendable divide that had been created between phenomena and Being, generated a nostalgia for Being, for the principle behind the unity of the natural world and the human world and therefore behind a rationalist vision. That nostalgia would grow so powerful as to become the principal force behind the intellectual reaction against modernity. In his triumph, Prometheus mourned the lost beauty of Olympus. The disenchantment of the world described by Weber inevitably led to attempts to lend it a new enchantment. Attempts to recreate the pre-revolutionary world of particularisms and privileges were of no great importance. Tocqueville was as well aware as Guizot or Thiers of the futility of these reactionary longings in both the intellectual and the political realm. Attempts to lend the world a new enchantment that took a pre-romantic or *romantic* aesthetic form were much more important. A nostalgia for Being challenged the triumph of modernizing rationality in a very different way to the Cartesian I or the individual rights of theorists of natural law. Germany had not been affected by the political modernization that had transformed Great Britain and then

France, but with Schiller, Hölderlin and then Schelling it saw the rise of a nostalgia for Being that would never disappear from German thought and which was often to take the form of an antimodernist critique, particularly with the Frankfurt School of philosophers in the mid twentieth century.

The Reconstruction of Order

The most elementary form of historicism is obsessed with the idea of destroying the old order and with the search for a new order. This mode of thought is the complete antithesis of that of great liberals like Tocqueville. It does not invent any new relationship between progress and social integration; on the contrary, it distrusts triumphal individualism and, in an attempt to ward off its dangers, invents a new order, a new principle of social integration. Auguste Comte is the best representative of this tendency. A reference to modernity is, however, both central and constant throughout his work, even though it is usually remembered by posterity for the law of the 'three states', which holds that the decline of the theological state and the upheavals of the metaphysical state will be followed by the advent of the positive state. Yet it would be dangerous to see Auguste Comte as the prophet of the victory of the scientific spirit. He is not even convinced that the natural sciences contain any specific truth; it is possible, he says, that there are several specific theories which explain various orders of phenomena without merging in to a general theory of nature. Above all, and like his master Saint-Simon, he is not so much convinced that progress will lead from one state to the next, as aware of the transition from an organic era to a critical era, from community to market individualism. Sociology, which owes its name to Auguste Comte, was to a large extent born of the anxieties of the intellectuals of the post-revolutionary period. Their main concern was to reconstruct order, and this could not mean the order of the Ancien Régime. This preoccupation is constant throughout the whole century. It emerged in Germany when it too was thrown in to turmoil by modernity – Tönnies contrasts community with the emerging society in the hope of finding a way back to commununity (*Vergemeinschaftung*) – and we can now find it in the work of Louis Dumont, whose holism–individualism dichotomy expresses a fear that individualism will triumph. According to Comte, the jurists of the Revolution replaced the concrete with the abstract and freed the individual, but at the same time condemned the individual to dreams, madness and solitude.

This vision of modernity could not be further removed from the idea of a personal Subject. Comte wanted to dispel the illusions of individualism and to make the transition from I to We. That is why, the views of Littré and John Stuart Mill notwithstanding, we have to agree with Henri Gouhier (1988) and conclude that there is no real break between the two major stages in Comte's intellectual life. There is no real break between the *Cours de philosophie positive* and the appeal to the religion of humanity which dominates the *Système de politique positive* (Comte 1851–4). The two stages are of course divided by the decisive encounter with Clotilde de Vaux in 1845, but that lasted for only a few months, as she died in 1846. The positivists abandoned the attempt to create a new religion and rejected the claim that 'the living are always, and increasingly, governed by the dead', but Gouhier is quite right to stress that Comte's central idea and the goal of his action is the discovery that the inevitable – but possibly temporary – triumph of individualism would give way to a new principle of social integration. Positivism and the search for social integration converge. Categories which relate to things more directly – the proletariat, women (and especially 'uneducated' women) – have the greatest awareness of the unity of humanity, whereas intellectuals tend to take a metaphysical view of things. More generally, society must be a community or an order, and the supreme virtue of the scientific spirit is that it provides a defence against subjectivity and personal interest. Comte's thought is hostile to social and political struggles because it accords absolute primacy to the creation of an order which allows the human race to become part of the universal tendency to 'preserve and perfect the Great Being'. The positive spirit is therefore, according to Auguste Comte (1844: 56), diametrically opposed to the concern for man displayed by the philosophers of natural law:

> Because of its characteristic reality, the positive spirit, in contrast, is directly and effortlessly social, insofar as that is possible. In its view, man does not exist in any real sense; Humanity is the only thing that can exist because we owe our whole development to society, no matter how we look at it. If the idea of society still seems to be an intellectual abstraction, that is mainly because of the philosophical *ancien régime*. Truth to tell, it is the idea of the individual that is abstract, at least insofar as it applies to our species. The whole of the new philosophy will constantly strive to reveal, in both the active and the speculative life, the connection that binds us all together in so many different ways, and to make us unthinkingly familiar with the innner feeling of social solidarity, suitably extended to all times and all places.

What can this Humanity that exists outside individuals be, if not society itself? What can the solidarity that must become the main source of personal happiness be, if not an equivalent to 'species' amongst other animals? Historicist thought paves the way for this identification of personal freedom with participation in a collectivity, for the anti-Christian and anti-liberal position which subordinates individuals to representatives of society or, to put it in more concrete terms, to those who hold power. In Comte, it also has authoritarian connotations which can be explained in terms of the experience of revolution and the subsequent fear that the breakdown of society would lead to the reign of interest and violence. His attacks on intellectuals, 'men of letters', parliamentary debates and social struggles were to have a long and active posterity, largely because of the idea that true freedom is the product of social integration and that solidarity allows everyone to take part in the life of the whole social body. Whilst it is true that historicism centres on a call for political, social and national mobilization in the service of modernization, the positivists reduce that call to a minimum. Their trust in modernizing leaders is conditional upon their ability to encourage the religion of humanity, which can be regarded as a preliminary – and still utopian – definition of socialism to the extent that it implies a purely social or functional conception of man. This positivism is closer to the sociologism of the political philosophy of Hobbes and Rousseau than to the analysis of the social conflicts of industrial society made by Proudhon and especially Marx. The difference is that political philosophies of modernity legitimized absolute power in order to free society from religious power. After the French Revolution, the goal was to recreate a communitarian power and a religion of progress and society. Like the Saint-Simonianism which provided it with its starting point and which had a more direct influence on the new leaders of industry, positivism soon disintegrated in to an appeal to science and growth on the one hand, and the dream of establishing a new Church on the other. The desire to reconcile reason and faith, which is so similar to that of Michelet, persisted throughout the century, and influences Durkheim's attempts to recreate order within movement, and to ensure organic solidarity within a utilitarian society subject to permanent change.

The 'Beautiful Totality'

The weakness of positivism stems from the fact that it is alien to the cultural traditions it attempts to challenge. It devotes all its energies to the resolution of the contemporary problem of recreating order within movement. And the solution it offers applies only to a society which can be seen as an organism requiring both a diversity of organs and a unitary life and energy. But what answer does it have to the most important debate in seventeenth- and eighteenth-century thought: the difficult reconciliation of natural law and individual interest, universals and particulars, reason and sensation? The religion of humanity exists between these two worlds, yet it is difficult to see how it can become established in either of them. Positivist politics therefore had no impact on social practices.

In his formative years, Hegel, in contrast, identified himself with the French Revolution, and personal freedom with the transformation of society. He adopted the revolutionary cry of 'Freedom or death'. And his philosophy is an attempt to synthesize subjectivity and totality by making a twofold critique of an abstract ethics and of a civil society based upon individual interests. The young Hegel initially defines his position by criticizing Kant and abstract morality (*Moralität*). He constructs an ethics or an ethical domain (*Sittlichkeit*), which cannot be separated from institutions, or from active participation in freedom. Citizenship is the highest form of freedom. Hegel is therefore critical of natural law. His central theme is close to Rousseau: the universal can be realized only in the particular, which thus becomes singularity. The history of the world is not a linear evolution, but a sequence of emblematic figures and cultures, each representing the action of the universal within history. Christ is a prime representative of the subjectivity that is inscribed in history, and the French Revolution will be another. Christ destroys Jewish legalism and the correspondence between the spiritual and the temporal that was common to both the Jews and the Greeks. Yet the individuality of Christ also lies in the fulfilment of his messianic destiny, and his sacrifice is an *amor fati*.

History is thus the product of two complementary processes: estrangement and integration. Hegel comes close to the Christian tradition when he writes in the *Phenomenology* (Hegel 1807: 758):

> Spirit is knowledge of self in a state of alienation of self: spirit is the being which is the process of retaining identity with itself in its otherness. This, however, is Substance, so far as in its accidents substance at the same time is turned back in to itself; and is so, not as being indifferent towards something unessential and, consequently, as finding itself in some alien element, but as being there within itself, i.e. so far as it is subject or self.

The same point is made in still more general terms in the 'Preface' (Hegel 1807: 80): everything depends upon 'grasping and expressing the ultimate truth not as Substance but as Subject as well'.

This alienation and the birth of subjectivation that results from it also leads, however, to mediations and thus to the integration of will and necessity. Their complete reconciliation comes about when freedom exists both as reality, as necessity and as subjective will. What being can achieve this concrete freedom? The citizen, as created by the French Revolution. This citizen is, however, also a citizen of a concrete historical nation or *Volk*. In this sense, Hegel is a successor to both Herder and Luther and the ancestor of the culturalists who reject the abstract universalism of reason. They do not resist it in the name of an unrestricted theory of difference which quickly becomes both absurd and destructive, but in the name of the idea, which is of central importance to Herder, that every nation and every culture with any historical reality can participate in the progress or reason, and has the right to do so.

It is at this point that Hegel departs furthest from eighteenth-century French thought and its individualism, and is most consciously true to the German notion of Development. The Subject is not an abstract being. It is present in collective achievements and collective life, and especially in the great religions which have marked the development of humanity. Humanity moves from one historical figure to the next, and not from one level of rationalization to the next. Hegel thus rejects the dualism that dominated philosophical thought from Descartes to Kant and, therefore, moralistic judgements on history. He comes close to the preoccupations of his own day when he sees in civil society the subordination of man to the laws of production and labour, and looks to citizenship, and therefore to a relationship with the State, to remedy that dependency. That idea still prevails today as sections of both the Left and the Right identify the State with history and reduce social life to the defence of immediate interests, and thus reintroduce a new dualism which is as dangerous as Christian dualism was liberating. The individual is no longer an embodiment of universal values; the State realizes them in history. Civil society must be transcended or, to put it in concrete terms, controlled by the State. This vision has a tragic grandeur; it is the story of a hero for whom death is the realization of a destiny, just as it was for Christ. Christ is the exemplary representative of the unhappy consciousness: he internalizes the fall of the world, but fulfils the will of his Father in doing so. Hegel does not go back beyond Christianity to the Greek *polis*, or to the identification of man with citizen. He concentrates on Christianity, on the moment of the divorce between the temporal and the spiritual, of the substitution of morality for faith. The creation of a private religion is seen as the birth of the subjectivity without which Spirit cannot exist for itself.

Spirit can only encounter itself by becoming divided, by breaking with nature and by becoming freedom.

And yet, asks Marx, does not Hegel reconcile totality and alienation only in the form of ideas? Does not the theme of estrangement and subjectivity lead to that of struggles between masters and slaves? At the same time, the reference to totality is transformed in to either the creation of an absolute power (a successor to Rousseau's general will), or the absorption of all historical actors in to Absolute Spirit. Hegel's own work thus ceases to be a philosophy of history and becomes a philosophy of Mind which elevates art, religion and philosophy above social life.

Hegel's philosophy may not have to choose between a rightist interpretation that sees the State as the realization of Spirit, and a leftist interpretation that transforms the estrangement of Spirit in to real contradictions between nature and society, reason and profit, and challenges the cultural and religious ideologies that conceal this truly social struggle. It is, however, difficult to apply such philosophical ideas to historical practices without introducing a contradiction between the assertion of subjectivity and the movement towards totality, and thus destroying historicism's dream of uniting Subject and history. The same agonizing struggle can be found in Marxism, which is both an economic determinism and a call for liberating action on the part of the proletariat.

No one pursued the intellectual ambitions of historicism further than Hegel, and no one did more to integrate the two intellectual traditions of the pre-revolutionary period, namely a vision of the Subject and a belief in progress and reason. His philosophy of history has a tragic power and it is closer to the Christian history of the redemption than to the intellectual optimism of a Condorcet. After Hegel, it is no longer possible, as it was in the eighteenth century, to speak of social actors in ahistorical terms. Both reason and the Subject have become history.

Praxis

The most dangerous aspect of historicist thought is the subordination of social actors to the State, which is seen as the agent of historical transformation. Subjectivity is seen merely as a necessary moment in the emergence of 'mind objective' and then Absolute Spirit. There is an underlying tendency in historicism to speak in the name of a Subject identified with history, and to eliminate subjects, or in other words the actors who are trying to transform their situation in order to gain greater freedom.

The historicist thought of Marx, Hegel and Comte introduces the idea that men make their own history only to destroy it, for history is the history of reason or, and this is merely a different version of the same general belief, of a progression towards the transparence of nature. The thought of the seventeenth and eighteenth century was dominated by the encounter between reason and the Subject, between utilitarianism and natural law; the historicism of the nineteenth century absorbs the Subject in to reason, freedom in to historical necessity, and society in to the State.

It is in the thought of Marx that the philosophy of history achieves its most tragic vision of the contradiction between its liberating force and the subordination of the subject to History. No other tendency within social thought asserts with such force that men make their own history. Marx's first impulse is to look for the practices that lie behind the abstract categories of religion, law and politics. This is why, as we have already seen, he denounces the priority given to political categories in France. He regards Robespierre's doctrinarianism and Napoleon's autocracy as masking the triumph of bourgeois idealism just as he sees the leftist rhetoric of the leaders of the Commune as masking the weakness of the French working class, and the juridical category of property as concealing labour and social relations of production. No matter whether he is speaking as an economist, a philosopher or a leader of the International, Marx constantly refers to the 'positive humanism' which will result in 'the destruction of the *estranged* character of the objective world', as he puts it in the third of the *1844 Manuscripts* (Marx 1844: 395).

Marx is the sociologist of industrialization. He is discussing a society which is dominated by the factory and not the market. He is not preaching the respect for the rule of law, and therefore of ethics, which would ensure the peace and justice that are essential to trade; he is observing an industrial world in which men are reduced to the status of commodities, in which wages tend to fall to a level which will merely ensure biological reproduction of the labour force, and in which man's 'species-being' is destroyed by the domination of money, objects and individualist ideologies. The highest expression of this vision is to be found in the 'Theses on Feuerbach', and especially in their opening sentence: 'The chief defect of all previous materialism – that of Feuerbach included – is that things [*Gegenstand*], reality, sensuousness are conceived only in the form of the *object*, or of *contemplation*, but not as *human sensuous activity*, *practice*, not subjectively' (Marx 1845: 421). 'Practice' means primarily the social relations of production. The social science of action was born of texts like this. Even though the collapse of historicism, especially in the last quarter of the twentieth century, makes Marx's thought seem remote indeed, we still have to recognize its greatness.

What is this Subject, this species-being or social being which is alienated or exploited? Being an economist and a political militant, Marx gives central importance to absolute proletarianization, and to the contradiction between the situation of the proletariat and human creativity. This is an objective contradiction rather than an actual conflict, as there was as yet little conflict in a society where the workers' movement was still far from being an important and autonomous actor. Marx's thought is not an analysis of social conflicts, but an analysis of the contradiction between the productive forces and the totality on the one hand, and between class domination and individualist ideology on the other. Marx looks to nature to defeat capitalism, and not to a social movement. The action of proletarians and their International cannot be a set of demands put forward by an interest group in the name of its rights: it is quite the opposite, namely the transformation of alienated workers in to a force that can shatter these contradictions, and the sole basis for its capacity for action is its support for productive forces which have been imprisoned by capitalism. There will be no movement unless it serves the cause of progress, and progress itself means progress towards totality, or in other words towards the liberation of nature, of the productive forces and, at a still deeper level, human needs.

At no point does Marx found a sociology of social movements, even though he makes such a sociology possible with his destructive critique of 'institutional' illusions and his constant reminders that practice is primary. Their complete alienation prevents the workers from becoming the actors of their own history. The destruction of capitalist domination will not bring about the triumph of a dominated actor who, according to the Proudhonist vision, takes control over production. It will bring about the abolition of classes and the triumph of nature. Marx's thought by no means anticipates the reformist or social-democratic vision of working-class, trade-union and political action as promoting the rights of the workers and strengthening their influence over economic and social decisions. Its radicalism is so extreme that it sees all institutions and all ideologies as concealing interest and domination. It believes that capitalist exploitation can be fought only by the irrepressible power of nature, progress and nature, and by the pressure of human needs.

Marx's thought eliminates the social actor. It contains no reference to either the eighteenth-century vision of man as ethical being, or a social movement guided by the values of freedom and justice. Some may find these words disturbing. Marx was, after all, the most active leader of the International Working Men's Association and the most constant adversary of the subordination of the labour movement to political action. These are valid objections, but they are no argument against the interpretation given here. Marx believes that nature, rather than social action, is the force that will overcome the contradictions of class society. He has much more in common with the great destroyers of the idea of modernity – Nietzsche and Freud, whom we will meet in part II – than with the revolutionary syndicalists.

That is the concrete meaning of the historical materialism expounded in *The German Ideology* (Marx and Engels 1845–6). Its classic expression can be found in the preface to the *Contribution to the Critique of Political Economy* (Marx 1859: 20–1):

> In the social production of their existence, men inevitably enter in to definite relations, which are independent of their will, namely relations of production appropriate to a given stage in the development of their material forces of production. The totality of these relations of production constitutes the economic structure of society, the real foundation, on which arises a legal and political superstructure and which correspond definite forms of social consciousness . . . It is not the consciousness of men that determines their existence, but their social existence that determines their consciousness. At a certain stage of development, the material productive forces of society come in to conflict with the existing relations of production or – this merely expresses the same thing in legal terms – with the property relations within the framework of which they have operated hitherto. From forms of development of the productive forces these relations turn in to their fetters. Then begins an era of social revolution.

These last words of the *Critique* state (1859: 21): 'Mankind thus inevitably sets itself only such tasks as it is able to solve' – a formula which will justify the economism of the Second International and of the many reformers who, whilst they are opposed to violent revolutionary action, share its view, which is common to every manifestation of historicist thought, that the meaning of action lies in historical evolution. That evolution will lead to the liberation of nature or a return to nature, and not to the construction of an institutional and ethical world based upon absolute principles.

Marx is eminently modern in that he defines society as a historical product of human activity, and not as a system organized around cultural values or even a social hierarchy. He does not, however, equate the modernist vision with individualism; on the contrary, the man he describes is primarily a social man who is defined by his position in a mode of production, in a technical world and in property relations. He is defined by social relations rather than by the rational pursuit of his interests. Social man cannot be described in terms of the holism–individualism dichotomy, Louis Dumont's efforts notwithstanding. Social man escapes both categories, as neither defines human beings in truly social terms.

Marx does not in fact defend the 'rights of man' or the ethical Subject. The alienating constructs of the social order are contrasted with human need, and it may already be possible to equate this need with what Nietzsche and then Freud will call the Id. Historicism eliminates Christianity's ethical God. It initially replaces God with a mere will to reconcile progress with order. At a less superficial level, Hegel then replaces God with the dialectic that will lead to the triumph of Absolute Spirit. By giving more importance to social and economic practices, Marx transforms the dialectic in to a rational and natural drive which will demolish the defences erected by the ruling class and its agents. An obsession with totality is central to all these intellectual endeavours, and totality is the meaningful principle that replaces both divine revelation and natural law. None of them makes allowance for the appearance within civil society of the social actor, initially in the form of the bourgeois and then in that of the workers' movement. Historicism does indeed subordinate History to a philosophy of History, and the social to the non-social, which it variously defines as reason, spirit or nature.

This vision of society is perfectly in keeping with the experience of the first industrial societies, which were dominated by an almost unfettered capitalism, but it also makes an essential contribution to the theory of the personal Subject. Even though working-class action cannot, according to Marx, be successful unless it moves in the same direction as History, it does make it impossible to represent society as either a machine or an organism. The elimination of God and the rejection of social utilitarianism opens up two avenues for the assertion of freedom: either a return to Being through art, sexuality or philosophy, or an assertion of the Subject and the freedom of the Subject – which may prove to be derisory if that freedom is not embodied in a struggle against the dominant forces. Marx, like Nietzsche, rejects any appeal to the Subject, but the workers' movement, from which his work is inseparable, was, once the bourgeois revolutions had run their course, the principal expression of the appeal to the Subject. As in so many other cases, practice was ahead, of theory.

Practice was, however, usually crushed by theory and the political action it inspired. Political leaders increasingly claimed to have a monopoly on transforming of the action of the proletariat and oppressed nations – which in itself, they claimed, could never be anything more than the negation of the negation – in to positive action which could reconcile man and nature, will and reason. Marxism rarely leads to a sociology of collective action. It is in fact precisely because Marxism has produced so few analyses of collective action and social movements that we have to recognize the lasting importance of Georg Lukács's *History and Class Consciousness* (Lukács 1923). Written shortly after the First World War, his book, which is at once central and marginal, marks the end of the history of Hegelian Marxism and foreshadows the triumph of totalitarianism. According to Lukács, the bourgeoisie is aware of its interests and does have a subjective class consciousness, but does not, and refuses to have, any consciousness of the *totality* of the historical process. It had such a consciousness when it was struggling against feudalism; it loses it when it is attacked by the proletariat, and therefore cannot analyse social relations because it divorces the objective from the subjective. The proletariat, in contrast, does achieve a class consciousness, but in Lukács's view this is by no means a class subjectivity. On the contrary, it means the identification of the interests of the proletariat with historical necessity. 'The proletariat is, then, at one and the same time the product of the permanent crisis in capitalism and the instrument of those tendencies which drive capitalism towards crisis' (Lukács 1923: 40). The same point is later made (1923: 177) with even greater clarity: 'This consciousness is nothing but the expression of historical necessity. The proletariat "has no ideals to realize".' Lukács then adds (1923: 178) that the proletariat 'can never "in practice" ignore the course of history, forcing upon it what are no more than its own desires or knowledge. For it is itself nothing but the contradictions of history that have become conscious.'

Praxis is neither the mere defence of interests nor the pursuit of an ideal. It identifies the interests of a class with its destiny or with a historical necessity. Being exploited, alienated and repressed, the workers can no more spontaneously arrive at this consciousness of the totality than can any other social category. It is the revolutionary party that embodies consciousness-in-itself. Only the Party can bring about the extraordinary inversion that transforms a totally alienated class in to a revolutionary actor capable of completely rejecting class society and liberating humanity. At the time when he wrote these pages, Lukács was a member of the Communist Party and had been a minister in Béla Kun's government, but he had also defended the workers' councils. His Leninism therefore must not be caricatured, but he does say that: 'The revolutionary victory of the proletariat does not imply, as with former classes, *the immediate realization of the socially given existence of the class*, but, as the young Marx clearly

saw and defined, its *self-annihilation*' (Lukács 1923: 71). According
to Lukács himself, it is not the masses, but a Party which understands
the meaning of history and which is guided by revolutionary intellectuals, that brings about the transition to the consciousness of totality
which turns the proletariat in to a Subject-object whose praxis
transforms reality. '*The proletariat only perfects itself by annihilating
and transcending itself, by creating the classless society through the
successful conclusion of its own class struggle.*' All these formulations,
which are central to not only Lukács's thought but to revolutionary
Marxist thought as such, despite the debates between competing
tendencies, justify the absolute power of the revolutionary Party. The
Party is the agent of a historic mutation, of the transition from a class
society to a classless society.

Some were still more radical, like Régis Debray in his *Revolution
in the Revolution?* (Debray 1967), and the theorists of the *foco
revolucionario*. In their view, the dependency of Latin America – and
other regions – on imperialism was so complete that not only mass
action but even the existence of a revolutionary party was impossible.
Only the armed action of a mobile guerrilla force could attack
imperialism's weakest link: the corrupt and repressive national State.
Its mobility meant that it had no roots in the population. The divorce
between the working class or the peasantry, and the revolutionary
has never been more complete. Guevara launched his anti-imperialist
struggle in Bolivia without reaching any agreement with either the
miners, who were the main trade-union power in the country, or the
Communist Party. He based his guerrillas in a rural area where
the farmers spoke Guarani rather than Spanish; they had also enjoyed
the benefits of agricultural reform. As a result, he was soon defeated
and killed. Intellectuals and other political militants joined guerrilla
campaigns in many countries where they had no social roots, and the
victory that was achieved in Cuba inevitably led to a dictatorship
without the proletariat. This is the example that proves the rule, but
it does bring out the logic of revolutionary Marxist action. It is true
that its triumph did bring about the transition from a class society to
a classless society, but the abolition of classes worked to the advantage
of absolute power and its apparatus. They exercised a permanent
terror which eventually became more technocratic and bureaucratic,
but Cuba remained a police-state opposed to the autonomy of social
actors and their freedom of expression.

Marxist thought cannot lead to the formation of a social movement.
Socialism, in the form given it by Marxism – and this is its most
influential form – was not the political wing of the workers' movement; that role was played by social democracy. The workers'

movement sought to give a social actor the ability to act autonomously, and that presupposed a reliance upon ethical principles of
equality and justice which could create a democratic politics. Marxist
socialism, in contrast, is hostile to class subjectivity and alien to
democracy, and is concerned less with justice than with the fulfilment
of a historic destiny. Even though Marx, like Hegel before him, was
aware that he was constructing a philosophy of the Subject, he
understood it to mean something very different to our modern
understanding of subjectivity or subjectivation, or even freedom and
responsibility. Luckás was quite right to say that 'it is not the primacy
of economic motives in historical explanation that constitutes the
decisive difference between Marxism and bourgeois thought, but the
point of view of totality' (Lukács 1923: 27). No individual actor can
adopt this point of view; it is inevitably that of a truly political agent
of historical necessity who seizes absolute power in order to realize
that necessity.

Whilst subjectivity appears to be bourgeois, visions which appeal
to a historical totality, be they revolutionary or petty-bourgeois, as
Mathiez liked to say of Michelet, identify a class or a nation with the
natural movement of history, and therefore with an idea, that real
social actors are no longer anything more than references. At the level
of practice, they are the 'masses', and they need a party of intellectuals
to speak in their name. The vision of a humanity which creates its
own history and overthrows the deceptive illusions of essences and
the principles of law and ethics in order to understand and transform
itself through its practices, leads to the subordination – violent or
moderate, totalitarian or bureaucratic – of social actors, and particularly classes, to the absolute power of a political elite which proclaims
its legitimacy in the name of its supposed understanding of the laws
of History.

Farewell to Revolution

We now know from experience that progress, the people and the
nation do not fuse in to a revolutionary enthusiasm or a historical
force against which the barriers erected by money, religion and law
are powerless. The historic synthesis dreamed of the age of revolutions was never spontaneously realized, Michelet's dreams notwithstanding. It simply gave birth to the absolute power of revolutionary
leaders who identified with the purity and unity of the Revolution.
The unity of the historical process was realized only through the
replacement of a plurality of social actors and the complexity of
their relations with the One of the nation, of the people or of a

besieged community under martial law, and where traitors had to be punished.

Revolutions have always turned their back on democracy and imposed unity – and it is inevitably the unity of a dictatorship – on the diversity of a class-divided society. Indeed, it was precisely because social actors failed to take an active role in public life – even in France where universal suffrage was introduced in 1848 – that the political elite was able to establish its domination over the people and over social classes. The process began with the Terror and was made permanent by the totalitarian regimes of the twentieth century.

If we accept for a moment the idea, which I defend throughout this book, that modernity is defined by an increasing divorce between rationalization and subjectivation, it is clear that the affirmation of the basic unity of the natural laws of history and collective action implies a rejection of modernity. If that affirmation is not confined to a small circle of ideologues, it inevitably leads to the construction of an absolute and repressive power. That power then imposes an artificial and authoritarian unity on both the world of the economy, which thus loses its internal rationality, and the world of social actors, who are denied their identity in the name of their universal mission. The era of Revolutions led by tortuous paths to the Terror, to the repression of the people in the name of the people, and to the execution of revolutionaries in the name of the revolution. Because it asserts the unity of modernity and social mobilization, it leads to economic failure and to the disappearance of society, which is devoured by a Saturn-like State.

The triumph of progress necessarily leads to this naturalization of society. Anyone who opposes modernity and its revolution is therefore regarded as an obstacle, as an anti-social element who must be eliminated by skilled gardeners with a talent for weeding. Modernity completely self-destructs at the very moment when ideology is loudly equating a will with a necessity, when it is turning history in to both a progression towards freedom and the liberation of nature, when it thinks it can bring about the triumph of the social by dissolving it in the cosmos. This extreme idea of modernity has never become completely dominant in the most active centres of Western modernization, where political power has not gained control over the economy and culture, but as modernization spreads to the regions where it encounters the greatest obstacles, it becomes increasingly voluntarist and is increasingly identified with the revolutionary idea.

The first duty of today's intellectuals is therefore to proclaim that the great historicist synthesis was a dangerous dream and that revolution has always been the antithesis of democracy. Modernity does not mean the triumph of the One. Modernity means that the One disappears and is replaced by the management of the difficult but necessary relationship between rationalization, and individual and collective freedom.

Christian thought and natural law were defeated by the philosophy of the Enlightenment. We therefore have to ask ourselves what form the return to subjectivity will take now that historicism has been defeated. The formula has at least two advantages. The first is that it distances us from both the eighteenth and the nineteenth centuries and therefore obliges us to accept both the appeal to reason and the liberation of the personal Subject. The second is that we have to situate our arguments in historical terms. This obviously does not mean situating them in terms of a sequence of forms of modernization or stages of economic growth. It means that we must look for forms of self-production of society which will provide a new definition of relations between efficacity and freedom. As we have seen, modernism initially prioritized the destruction of the past, liberation and openness. Philosophies of history and progress then gave modernity a positive content. They called it 'totality', and the word is close enough to 'totalitarianism' for its ambiguities and dangers to be obvious. Is it possible to conceive of a new historical situation, of a new type of society in which modernity is defined, not in terms of a single and totalizing principle, but in terms of new tensions between rationalization and subjectivation?

Part II

Modernity in Crisis

1

The Decay of Modernity

A Crisis in Three Stages

The liberating force of modernity is exhausted as modernity triumphs. The call for enlightenment is overwhelming when the world is plunged in to darkness and ignorance, in to isolation and slavery. Is it still liberating in a great city which is lit up night and day, where the flashing lights solicit consumers or indoctrinate them with State propaganda? Rationalization is a noble word when it introduces the scientific and critical spirit in to domains hitherto dominated by traditional authorities and the arbitrary decisions of the mighty; it becomes a fearful word when it designates Taylorism and other managerial methods which destroy the craft autonomy of workers and force them to submit to rates of production and orders that claim to be scientific. They are of course no more than ways of maximizing profits and they pay no heed to the physiological, psychological and social realities of human labour.

Once, we lived in silence; we now live with noise. Once, we were isolated, and now we are lost in the crowd. Once, we received too few messages, and we are now bombarded with them. Modernity has uprooted us from the narrow limits of the local cultures in which we once lived; it has cast us in to a mass society and a mass culture as well as giving us individual freedom. For a long time, we fought the old regimes and their heritage; in the twentieth century, the most dramatic calls for liberation are directed against the new regimes, the new society and the new man that so many authoritarian regimes have tried to create. Revolutions are directed against revolutions and the regimes that were born of them. Modernity's great strength was its ability to open up a world which was once closed and fragmented. It becomes exhausted as trade intensifies, as the population rises and as the density of capital, consumer goods, instruments of social control and arms increases.

We wanted to leave our communities and to begin to build a mobile society; we are now trying to escape the crowds, the pollution and the propaganda. Some flee from modernity. The majority do not, as the centres of modernity have accumulated the disposable resources on such a scale and dominate the whole world so completely that there are no more pre-modern places and no more noble savages, merely reserves of raw materials and labour power, army training areas and rubbish dumps littered with tin cans and television programmes. Most people are no longer satisfied with the oft-proclaimed opposition between a shadowy past and a brilliant future, or even a radiant future, to borrow the grating title of Zinoviev's attack on the hypocrisy of the Soviet bureaucracy. The point is not so much to reject modernity as to discuss it, to replace the image of a modernity that is implacably opposed to tradition with an analysis of both the positive and negative aspects of its cultural objectives and the relations of dominance or dependency, integration or exclusion that give the cultural theme of modernity a truly social content. Whereas odes to modernity have often called upon all moderns to form a united front, and in more concrete terms for the subordination of all to the elite who are in charge of modernization, the *critique of modernity* does not usually lead to its rejection. As the original meaning of the term suggests, it means separating out its elements. It means analysing and evaluating all of them, rather than becoming trapped in to an all or nothing attitude which makes us accept anything because we are afraid of losing everything.

That the idea of modernity should have become exhausted was inevitable; it was defined, not as a new order, but as a movement, as a creative destruction, to borrow Schumpeter's definition of capitalism (Schumpeter 1912). Mobility was attractive to people who had long been trapped in immobility; it becomes tiring and leads to vertigo when it is incessant and results only in its own acceleration. It is because modernity is a critical rather than a constructive notion that a critique of modernity must be hypermodern. Such a critique provides a defence against nostalgia, which, as we know, can easily take a dangerous turn.

The exhaustion of modernity is quickly transformed in to a disturbing feeling that action is meaningless when its only criteria are those of instrumental rationality. Horkheimer denounces the debasement of 'objective reason' in to 'subjective reason', of a rationalist worldview in to a purely technical activity which makes rationality serve needs, be they the needs of a dictator or the needs of consumers, which are no longer subject to reason and the principles it uses to regulate both the social and the natural order. This anxiety results in a reversal of perspective. Modernity was suddenly rebaptized 'the eclipse of reason' by Horkheimer (1947), Adorno and all those they influence far beyond the Frankfurt School itself. Their arguments are an extension of the doubts voiced by Weber, who is the greatest analyst of modernity. Secularization and the disenchantment of the world, the divorce between the world of phenomena, or the realm of technical activity, and the world of Being, which comes in to our lives only through moral duty and aesthetic experience, trap us in an iron cage, to use the famous phrase which ends Weber's essay on *The Protestant Ethic and the Spirit of Capitalism* (Weber 1904–5). The same theme later reappears in the early work of Jürgen Habermas. Weber defines modernity in terms of the rationality of means, as opposed to the rational goal of values. In more concrete terms, he contrasts the ethic of responsibility which characterizes modern man with the ethic of conviction which, like charismatic authority, can intervene in a rationalized world only in exceptional circumstances. According to Weber's image of the modern world, the rationalization of daily life coexists alongside an occasional war between the gods. There have been many moderate expressions of this Kantianism in European countries. It inspired, for instance, the founders of secular education in France at the end of the nineteenth century. A number of them were protestants, and their secularism was in no sense hostile towards religious convictions. They wanted to draw clear boundaries between private convictions and public life. The educational system was part of the latter, and it recognized only rational and critical thought. The separation of Church and State suited the purposes of a 'progressive' middle class. It allowed it to defend itself against both the Catholic bourgeoisie, and a revolutionary workers' movement which was challenging that moderate tolerance in the name of societal counter-project. According to Weber, modernity destroys the alliance between heaven and earth. It robs the world of its enchantment and does away with magic, but it also destroys rationalist cosmologies and effectively puts an end to the reign of instrumental rationality. The God suppressed by modernity was both the God who created an intelligible world and the God of priests and sacraments. Whether or not we accept Kant's dualism or Weber's reinterpretation thereof, it is no longer possible to believe in a world order or in the total unity of natural phenomena and to view human actions as no more than a particular instance of that unity.

The great rationalist intellectuals reject this image of a total disenchantment. They are still enchanted, not by the memory of Arthurian legends, but by the idea of the Logos bequeathed them by so many centuries of Graeco-Christian thought. Horkheimer provides the most powerful expression of this nostalgia for objective reason. Exile, Hitler's destruction of German culture, and the extermination of the Jews of Europe, most of whom identified – more so than any other social group – with the universality of reason, provide a ready explanation for his tragic feeling that the eclipse of objective reason would inevitably lead to a crisis in a disoriented bourgeois society, and thence to Nazi barbarism. Marxism often gave a new lease of life to a positivism which saw itself as the heir to the great thinkers of Antiquity and provided worried intellectuals with the reassuringly integrated and stable image of a rational world order. The Frankfurt School was the *locus classicus* for this combination of nostalgia for a world order and a social critique that combined political progressivism with cultural traditionalism.

These two stages in the crisis of modernity – the exhaustion of the initial liberation movement and the loss of meaning in a culture which felt itself to be trapped by technology and instrumental action – led to a third stage which was still more radical in that it challenged not modernity's deficiencies, but its positive objectives. It has been obvious since the first chapter of this book that the disappearance of the metasocial foundations of ethics resulted in the triumph of social ethics, utilitarianism and functionalism. Social utility is the criterion for the good. We have to be good citizens, good workers, good fathers or good daughters. The idea of right is now inseparable from that of duty, even though the Constituent Assembly resolved that the Declaration of the Rights of Man and the Citizen should make no mention of duties. Yet is the society everyone is being asked to serve simply the general will, as described by Rousseau, and to which magistrates, or in other words the State, must remain subordinate? How can we escape the conclusion that the Whole is something other than the sum of its parts and that it tends to dominate them? Does anyone still believe that the interests of the State and those of individuals are identical, or that the individual and the citizen are one and the same? The separation of Church and State is a mere preliminary to something more important and more radical: the separation of society and State. This means that we have to abandon the idea that *society* is a whole, a social system or a social body, and emphasize the contradiction between the idea of society and the reality of social life, which is open, changeable and pluralistic.

These three critiques of modernity take social thought further and further away from its starting point. The liberating impulse behind modernity has always consisted in resisting a will transmitted by rules and laws, and the impersonal obviousness of scientific truth, economic success and technical efficiency. Because it contradicted prophets and conquerors, the spirit of modernity appealed to those who distrusted systems and wanted not so much to build a new world as to discover unexplored horizons, to live in a world that was in search of something rather than a world of certainties. They wanted, that is, to live in a world of freedom and tolerance rather than one of order and principles. And yet modernity suddenly begins to look like an instrument for control, integration and repression; Foucault, like many others, denounces modern societies' tendency to extend the field of moralization. We are no longer simply required to obey the policeman's orders. We are now being asked to believe in them, to adapt our feelings and desires to the rules of social success and to a social hygienics which is often couched in the language of science. If society's increased reflexivity is an expression of modernity, surely modernity implies power rather than rationalization, constraints rather than liberation. Social thought now feels that it is trapped by a modernity it distrusts. Some intellectual currents are attempting to change the way modernity is defined, but others reject it entirely or are attempting to halt history or at least to prioritize equilibrium rather than progress. Still others fling themselves in to an extreme modernity because, in their view, it is accelerating so fast as to abolish itself. These responses remain, however, relatively marginal and the critique of modernity is more likely to lead to the fragmentation of the idea than to its being replaced by something else.

We now have to describe the decay of modernity because, if this hypothesis is correct, our field of social and cultural action has to be understood as encompassing all the shattered fragments of modernity. What might be termed *post-modern* culture, were it not that the term now applies to a more restricted domain of ideas, has no discernible central principle; it brings together conflicting tendencies and seems to be torn in different directions. What is the common factor in all the disparate aspects of the culture and society that developed from the mid nineteenth century onwards? Is there any common theme to the work and contributions of modernity's greatest adversaries whose writings have, together with those of Marx, dominated intellectual life for more than a hundred years, namely Nietzsche and Freud? And yet it is possible to find the unity of a process behind this cultural kaleidoscope: the decay of modernity. Let us begin, then, by describing its fragmentation.

Four Fragments

1. The most powerful reaction against modernity is a stubborn resistance against the voluntarism of modernizing powers. As we have seen, Christian

spiritualism, as transcribed by theories of natural law, was the main obstacle to political power during the first stages of modernity. But if God is absent, the only defence against an invasive social power is the devil. Man – a creature of God imprinted with the mark of his creator's freedom – is replaced by a being of desire. The Ego is no more than an envelope for the Id and for *sexuality*, which attempts to recover its vital energy by breaking through the barriers erected by social conventions and moralizing agencies. The new anthropology is modern because it is an extreme form of the struggle against religion and, more specifically, Christianity. This is the central theme of the work of Nietzsche and Freud, but it is also an antimodern theme in so far as it ignores man's historical being and concentrates upon his anthropological nature. There is, then, an eternal struggle between desire and the law.

Privacy came to be seen, especially in late eighteenth-century Britain and France, as something separate from religious life. As a result of the protestant and catholic Reformations and the importance accorded to piety and confession, it had already become an autonomous part of the religious life. It was rapidly secularized; the confession of sins was transformed in to psychological counselling or even psychoanalysis. It was the discovery of what Nietzsche called the Id that did most to destroy the rationalist idea of consciousness. The word itself was then bequeathed by Groddeck (1923) to Freud, who acknowledges his debt (Freud 1923: 362).

2. The economy of *consumption* cannot be reduced to an anthropology of desire, as it cannot be dissociated from industrial rationalization. Jean Fourastié (1950) and Colin Clark have become famous for their accounts of recent and accelerated productivity gains. Nineteenth-century economists did not give productivity gains the importance they merit. From the end of the nineteenth century onwards, our societies began to make the transition from an almost stable equilibrium or long cycles, to growth. The image of 'take off' accurately captures the mutation. Despite a hundred years of industrial revolution, industrializing societies experienced few far-reaching changes in consumption or ways of life, but despite crises and wars, consumption was revolutionized between the end of the nineteenth century and the end of the twentieth. At the same time, labour came to have a much less important role in life as the working year became shorter and as periods of study and retirement became longer. The proto-modern economy, which was a production economy, was dominated by the scientific and technical spirit; the economy defined by mass production and consumption is dominated by the market and marketing. This spectacular change was symbolized by the victory, after the First World War, of Alfred Sloane and General Motors, who paid attention to customer demand, over Ford, the hero of industrial revolution and the author of the famous 'Any colour you like, as long as it's black'. Rationality cannot but be instrumental now that it is required to meet demands which are as much expressive of a search for social status symbols, an attempt to seduce or a desire for exoticism as of a search for labour-saving devices, rapid mobility or foodstuffs of guaranteed quality that can be prepared rapidly.

3. Within the domain of production, the idea of *organization* becomes central. Whilst the great figures of nineteenth-century capitalism were bankers, and in France the brothers Pereire in particular, management specialists and captains of industry came to the fore at the turn of the century, especially in the United States. The 1920s were a period of rationalization, especially in Germany, and trade unions in the United States and France adapted, as did the German unions, to the new themes of productivity and Taylorism. The factory is both a decision-making centre and a system for mobilizing financial and human resources, and it now plays the role that once devolved upon capitalism. Increasingly, social struggles occur inside the factory, so much so that the factory occupation became the ultimate weapon in both the United States and France during the Popular Front period. As we reach the end of the twentieth century, it may seem that there has been a return to the reign of financial capitalism, but observers like Lester Thurow (1993) and Michel Albert (1991) rightly criticize those who overlook the central role of the production unit.

4. Social struggles often merge in to *national* struggles. Like the *Zollverein* which, by turning the German states in to a single market, paved the way for both economic development and the political unification of Germany in 1871, they too claim that their goal is modernization. Their effect is, rather, to introduce or revive the idea of cultural identity. The defence of national languages was an essential part of the rise of nationalities: one of its later triumphs was the revival of Hebrew in the new state of Israel. Every nationality tries to define and expand its territory, creates symbols of its collective identity, arms itself and acquires a collective memory. The trend became very general. Throughout this period, even Great Britain and France, which had so readily identified with the universal values of economic, institutional or political modernity, developed a heightened consciousness of their national identities.

The nation becomes divorced from reason and independence increasingly takes precedence over modernization. Whereas the two goals were closely related in Germany, Italy and Japan in the second half of the nineteenth century, the goal of national independence has become so important in most of the world in the twentieth century that it is more likely to be allied with a popular fundamentalism than with the liberalism of the new bourgeoisies, or even with the voluntarism of state apparatuses.

A Hidden Unity

This rapid survey of the main forces – *sexuality*, *commodity consumption*, *the company* and the *nation* – which have dominated the social and cultural scene for the last hundred years can provide no more than a preliminary overview by drawing our attention to the apparent heterogeneity of a scene that we can no longer call a society. We have the impression of living in a fragmented world, in a non-society,

	BEING	CHANGE
INDIVIDUAL	Sexuality	Consumption
COLLECTIVE	Nation	Company

Figure 1

because personality, culture, economics and politics all seem to be moving in different directions. Before we even begin to explore these four worlds, let us try, however, to put some order in to this apparent incoherence, not in order to promote an image of a new society but, on the contrary, to show that all these social or cultural forces result from the decay of classical modernity.

How can we situate in relation to one another sexuality, commodity consumption, the factory as organization and central site of social conflicts, and the nation or nationalism? The most obvious factor is the dissociation between the order of change and the order of being, which were once associated in the idea of modernity – which meant both rationality and individualism. The constant changes that take place in production and consumption are increasingly divorced from the recognition of an individual personality which is both a sexuality and a collective cultural identity. Rather than gradually disappearing before the transparence of rational thought, social and cultural reality is invading the space of modernity on two fronts. And there appears to be no principle to reunite the various forces that occupy the fragmented world of modernity. The long century that stretched from the mid 1800s to the mid 1900s, and even beyond, saw the fragmentation of the rationalist world, but not its replacement by another unifying principle or by a new and more complex model.

Secondly and more simply, the personal order has become divorced from the collective order. On the one hand, we have sexuality and consumption, and, on the other, the factory and the nation.

It is not difficult to reconcile these dichotomies. The hope that endogenous modernization and the triumph of the light of reason and the laws of nature would dispel the illusions of consciousness, the lies of ideologies and the irrationality of traditions and privileges, has given way to the brutal recognition of forces whose diversity disorganizes the social and cultural field. The idea of modernity has been replaced by that of modernizing action, which mobilizes non-modern forces and frees individuals and a society that had hitherto been prisoners of the divine law and then of impersonal laws of nature. The cultural and social field in which we have been living since the end of the nineteenth century has no unity: it constitutes, not a new stage of modernity, but its decay. Perhaps no other civilization has lacked a central principle to this extent. No great religion exercises a dominant influence in this secularized culture where the separation of Church and State is a fundamental principle. Yet, at the same time, nostalgia for the past and a lost order has never been weaker. Our rapid survey of the shattered fragments of modernity has shown that each of them bears the mark of a voluntarist modernity. This is obvious in the case of the elements that define the new producer–consumer society; it is also obvious in the case of nationalisms, which are never traditionalisms. Matters are more confused when we turn to the great thinkers of the Id. Nietzsche and Freud are resolute antimodernists, but they are also rationalists who believe that it is possible to free man from the fetters created by a moralizing culture. That is why I think this historical set can best be described as *postmodern*. This definition, which may seem paradoxical, should be an antidote to facile optimism and should remind us that this so-called century of progress has, at least in Europe, also been seen as a century of crisis, and often of decline and disaster. The great upsurge of Western industrialization was accompanied by a broad intellectual movement which was criticial of modernity, especially in Germany and turn of the century Vienna. More than fifty years later and after having been influenced by the radical criticisms of Jean-Paul Sartre, the period in French history that Jean Fourastié (1950) describes as 'the thirty years of glory' [*les trente glorieuses*] was dominated by the antimodernist and deeply pessimistic thought of the descendants of Nietzsche, and especially by Michel Foucault. It is impossible to think of one French intellectual of any importance who has celebrated modernity. Even Raymond Aron, who comes closest to playing that role, was a politician rather than an economist, and was too aware that the problems of war and peace were more important than those of production and consumption, not to be influenced by the dominant pessimism, which in his view was justified by the cold war and the expansion of totalitarian regimes (Aron 1969). The image of our century painted by statisticians is in open contradiction with that elaborated by our most important thinkers and writers, from Thomas Mann to Jean-Paul Sartre. The divorce between acts and meaning, between the economy and culture, provides the best definition of the crisis of modernity.

Throughout the long nineteenth century – the century of modernity triumphant – we lived and thought inside the model of the national class society, and we eventually made it the concrete expression of modernity. We asserted – in ways that varied from country to country

– that the economy, society and the existence of the nation were as closely related as the fingers of our hands. We claimed that collective experience had a basic unity, and were quite happy to call it 'society', whilst Talcott Parsons did more than anyone else to convince us that politics, economics, education and justice were the four main functions of that social body. Modernity was defined at once by an increase in trade, the development of production, wider participation in political life, and the formation of nations and Nation States. The French pragmatically recognized the correspondence between these factors, whilst the United States interpreted it in more voluntarist and therefore more juridical terms, and whilst the Germans gave it a more prophetic and cultural content.

A century later, most intellectuals on both the left and the right stress what Daniel Bell calls the cultural contradictions of capitalism (Bell 1976) and the increasingly divergent norms that govern production, consumption and politics. Does the France of the late twentieth century still have any faith in the image of a republican, universalist and modernizing nation that is still promoted by a few intellectuals and political leaders? Does anyone listen to them seriously? Isn't what is known as the crisis in education primarily a recognition of these cultural contradictions and of the breakdown of the system of norms and values that schools, the family and all the other agencies of socialization are supposed to hand on to new members of society? The national consciousness which was the other side of revolutionary liberation is now its antithesis. And the twentieth century has too many reasons to associate nationalism with anti-progressivism for us to be able to understand our last Jacobins. Mass consumption is certainly one of the motors behind economic growth, but who would now defy all the ecological warnings and claim that all its effects are positive? Who would dare to sing the praises of rationalization in the way that Taylor (1914) did almost a hundred years ago? Each of these shattered fragments of modernity is marked by both modernity and the crisis of modernity. Everything in our society and culture is marked by the same ambiguity. Everything is both modern and antimodern, so much so that it is scarcely an exaggeration to say that the surest sign of modernity is the antimodern message it sends out. Modernity is self-critical and self-destructive. It is *heautontimorou- menos*, to cite the poet who, along with Théophile Gautier, was the first to launch the theme of modernity (Baudelaire 1857). According to Baudelaire (1863), modernity means the presence of the eternal in the instant, in the ephemeral. It is the beauty of fashion, which changes every season. His definition implies the feeling that, just as love is dissolved in to desire, the eternal will eventually be dissolved in to the instant to such an extent that it can be grasped only by an awareness of its absence and by the fear of death.

The picture is still incomplete. As the full, global model of modernity, which was at once cultural, economic and political, breaks down in to sexuality, consumption, company and nation, rationality is reduced to being a residue. Instrumental rationality or *technique* comes to mean the search for the most efficient means to achieve goals which in themselves escape the criteria of rationality, and to satisfy choices which are sometimes made on the basis of criteria that make no reference to rationality. Technical reason is now the servant of repressive policing as well as of social solidarity. It is the servant of mass production, but also that of military aggression, propaganda and advertising, regardless of the content of the message it delivers. Technical reason is rarely discussed, because it is clear to most people that it leaves them no choice as to the ends of their actions.

And yet many intellectuals follow Weber's example and denounce the reign of instrumentalism and the cult of technology and efficiency. These criticisms are based upon an awareness of the decline of objective reason and of the rationalist worldview, which may or may not have been governed by a rational God who guaranteed our reason's ability to understand the laws of the world. Yet their claims to have a social and political content are groundless. Their denunciations of technocrats are equally weak. It is as though the hold of technical rationality were so powerful that it replaces all finalities. It is too easy to denounce the ubiquity of technicians and it is dangerous to believe that they are running a world governed by mere engineers of the human soul and of society. The world of technology, or the world of means, is all the more subordinated to the world of personal or collective ends now that the link between objective and subjective reason has been broken, and now that technology is no longer exclusively the servant of a rationalist worldview or the commandments of a philosopher-God or a mathematician-God.

The denunciation of technology is a particular form of nostalgia for Being; it sustains every ideology that seeks to make one of the fragments of our shattered modernity the central principle of the modern world. One ideology argues that nationality is all, and that we must recreate self-contained communities that can resist outside aggression; another argues that, on the contrary, national traditions and defences must be swept aside so as to facilitate the operations of the transnational companies whose technologies and products can be found everywhere; a third argues that the market is replacing every other principle of social organization. According to the fourth, we must surrender to pansexualism, as it is the one thing which can unite

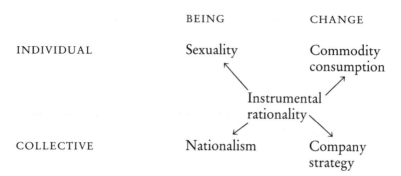

Figure 2

all human beings in the new Dionysian cult that is being spread by television and video cassettes.

Given this cultural chaos and the fragmentation of modernity, we may well ask ourselves if it is possible to reconstruct a coherent cultural world. I will try to do so, and the first two parts of this book do no more than supply the preparatory materials for that attempt. The alternative is to come to terms with chaos, to accept a basic pluralism of experiences and values, and simply to organize a society which is tolerant, pluralistic and in search of authenticity. Weak as it may be, the reference to instrumental rationality has a major role in that it prevents each of the fragments of our shattered modernity from severing its links of interdependency with the others. It prevents them from believing themselves to be completely different, sovereign and therefore obliged to wage a holy war on the others.

Technical rationality restricts each cultural tendency's claims to be dominant, and therefore prevents them from transforming themselves in to social forces in search of political hegemony. In the best-case scenario, we find at the centre of post-modern society – that of yesterday and that of today – a value vacuum which guarantees the autonomy of technical rationality and makes it possible to protect the power vacuum at the heart of society which Claude Lefort (1981, 1986) rightly regards as the first principle of democracy.

The shattering of modernity can be represented as in figure 2. It should be recalled that this table must be read in two complementary ways. It describes the fragmentation of modernity, and therefore lists forces which tend to become antimodern, as all critical schools of thought say so consistently and so firmly, whatever their respective orientations. Sexuality and consumption involve both consumption and destruction; in business policy, profit or power tends to outweigh the function of production, and nationalisms, like all differentialisms, bear within them the seeds of war. Yet, as I have said, each of these elements also expresses one of modernity's demands: national independence is a precondition for economic development; sexuality is a challenge to norms designed to ensure social integration and cultural reproduction; the output of great factories is consumer-led and designed to meet increasingly varied demands. This modernizing function always implies an alliance with instrumental rationality, whilst attacks on technology are associated with the antimodern and fundamentalist tendencies within each of these fragments of our shattered modernity.

The above assertion cannot replace the search for a central cultural principle that allows the reconstruction of an integrated cultural field, but it does define a limit which cannot be crossed in any circumstances. If rationalization is no longer the principle that integrates our culture, that culture cannot be reunified around opposition to rational thought and action. Irrationalism leads to extreme fragmentation, to a complete divorce between elements that were once integral parts of the model of objective rationality. That is why denunciations of technology are dangerous and have usually inspired totalitarian thinking, rather than liberal or anarchistic thinking. It is possible to denounce the reign of profit, the destruction of the environment or the commodification of sex. In all these cases, it is possible to have a debate and to exchange arguments. Denunciations of technology, on the other hand, are all the less justifiable in that they have never been able to demonstrate that, in a modern society, means become ends. Some technical experts have, especially in periods of crisis, defended the technocratic cause against both capitalism and social and cultural traditions which they regard as obstacles to growth. This school of thought, whose most eloquent spokesman is Thorstein Veblen in the United States, has never become dominant because no society is simply a machine, and no State is simply a bureaucracy. The weakness of our societies does not stem from the disappearance of ends which have been destroyed by the internal logic of technical means, but from the decay of the rationalist model, which has been destroyed by modernity itself, and therefore by the separate development of logics of action which no longer refer to rationality: the search for pleasure, for social status and for profit or power.

2

The Destruction of the Ego

Marx, Once More

The presence of Marx at the beginning of this cultural critique of modernity may seem surprising, as I have, in classical fashion, described him as one of the greatest thinkers of modernity. His desire to invert Hegel's thought is too great for him not to belong to the same cultural world as his master and adversary. The inversion does, however, constitute a break with the idealism of philosophies of history. Progress is no longer seen as the triumph of reason or the realization of Absolute Spirit. It is seen as the liberation of a natural energy and natural needs that come in to conflict with institutional and ideological constructs. The divorce between the spiritual and the temporal, which was overcome by idealism, returns in force. Indeed, it returns in such an extreme form that it extends beyond the domain of institutions and even the political scene itself. On the one hand, we have need; on the other, profit. Between the two, we have not merely a conflict that might result in a compromise, but a contradiction which will be overcome only when a liberating rebellion and the development of the productive forces finally converge with the socialization of production and socialism, to bring about the naturalization of society and the elimination of the obstacles created by consciousness. Marx's principal intellectual adversary is therefore the idea of the Subject. The conflict is one between need and profit; anything representing society or the personality, a model of society or a human model, or individual or collective subjectivity, is a ruse on the part of the bourgeoisie. Consciousness is always a false consciousness. This justifies the role of revolutionary intellectuals. They are by no means agents who raise consciousness; their role is to decipher the laws of history. To that extent, Marx remains a historicist. Social life is no more than a struggle between use-value and exchange-value, between the productive forces and social relations of production.

There is no room in Marx's work for a worker-Subject, perhaps because he was writing at a time of extreme proletarianization. Exploitation stems from the fact that the price capitalists pay for the labour that is produced is the minimum required to reproduce labour-power, or in other words the continued existence of the worker. Marx brushes aside the objection that unskilled labourers who are paid minimal wages coexist alongside skilled workers, some of whom enjoy a favourable position in the labour market and who will create the workers' movement. Marx eradicates the figure of the skilled worker, who must in my view be central to any study of the workers' movement, and peremptorily states that skilled and complex labour is no more than a compound form of simple and unskilled labour.

There is, then, a link between Marx's great themes: laws of historical development and technological and economic determinism; the contradiction between the natural history of humanity, and class domination; a critique of consciousness on the grounds that it is an effect of bourgeois domination; an absence of class actors. All these themes combine to define the motor-role of revolutionary intellectuals armed with a science of history.

Marx is the first great post-modern intellectual because he is an antihumanist and because he defines progress as the liberation of nature, and not as the realization of a conception of man. His conception of totality varies from text to text, and even from one stage in his life to the next, but his work does have its unity: materialism, and therefore the struggle against subjectivity. That is Marx's sociological heritage. The appeal to consciousness, to intentional action and, *a fortiori*, values, is 'petty-bourgeois', and its only function is to conceal exploitation and its purely economic logic. Even today, Marxists sense that they have much more in common with the liberals who defend an extreme methodological individualism than with social reformers, and they have yet to withdraw their denunciations of social democrats.

The important thing about Marxist thought and its struggle against utopian socialism or left-Hegelians is that it replaces a rebellion waged in the name of the human Subject with an analysis of the contradictions of capitalism. It contrasts capitalism, not with values, but with the natural energy of the productive forces – including human labour – and the pressure of needs which will eventually be freely expressed in communist society. Its polemical and political force is unrivalled, precisely because it makes a frontal assault on the moralism of philanthropists, reformers and utopians and, above all, because it gives a revolutionary counter-elite complete control over the meaning of political action. In the mid nineteenth century, the triumph of Victorian society was complete and the spirit of the institutions that served triumphant capitalism had been successfully transformed in to moral convictions and rules for the organization of collective life. Marx flung a stone in to a pond, and the ripples are still spreading.

We can conclude that the brutality of capitalist industrialization and the complete break between economy and society explain why Marxism prevailed over the study of social movements and over democratic reforms for so long in Europe, particularly in countries where absolute political power was most successful in blocking the autonomous organization of the workers' movement. Capitalism and the State combined to crush democracy's social actors with such violence that Western society saw only the struggle labour and production were waging against violence and profit, and relegated any reference to the goals of action to the realms of ethics and art.

Nietzsche

The industrial society that took shape in Europe and then in North America seemed to have been cut in two by the brutality of capitalism. On the one hand, there was the world of interest and individuality which, according to Schopenhauer (1818) was a tavern full of drunkards in aesthetic terms, a madhouse in intellectual terms and a den of thieves in moral terms. On the other, there was the impersonal world of desire, which did not communicate with the world of calculation. There was no longer any connection between the instrumental reason that served possessive egotism, and the forces of life, the body and desire, which could not be perceived through representation, but only through intuition. Kant's dualism became tragic. In Schopenhauer's view, man was wretched because he was torn between his desire to live on a cosmic scale and the tendency towards individuation. Schopenhauer's answer was that we must choose. We must free ourselves from individuation and a liberal conception of right which merely prevents the will of others from encroaching on our will, not in order to abandon ourselves to desire, but to de-individualize desire, to free ourselves from desire by reaching nirvana. Schopenhauer was interested in Buddhism, but he was also influenced by Madame Guyon's quietism. His ascetic nihilism liberates the will to life through art, philosophy and a meditation upon death.

At the very beginning of the nineteenth century, Schopenhauer distances himself from the world of reason, science and technology which, in his view, is a world of egotism and de-socialization. He does not do so in order to recreate an impossible order, but in order to turn to life and desire, or in other words to the impersonal element in lived experience, rather than the conscious or voluntarist element. We must destroy the Ego and the illusion of consciousness, just as we must distrust the illusion of the social order, which simply protects egotistical appetites. How can critical thought and action not reject the illusions of the Ego, individualism and the social order, and how can the most vigorous ethical and social thinkers from Schopenhauer to Bergson not defend life against technology, and continuity and the collective against discontinuity and the individual? It would be a grave mistake to try to find the birth of the Subject in this intellectual movement: on the contrary, it is hostile to the idea of the Subject. But we do find within it the destruction of the Ego and a critique of individuation, and whilst they are certainly far from being central to the construction of the Subject, it would be impossible without them.

Nietzsche rejects Schopenhauer's answer but adopts his critique of individualism. He sees himself as a modern, and claims to be an heir to the Enlightenment, and to Voltaire in particular, notably because he rejects Christianity. Men have become divorced from the gods, but that break is not the end of a world. It is both a liberation that opens up a new era and a murder which leaves man covered in guilt. 'God is dead', he writes in *The Gay Science* (Nietzsche 1882: 181). He then adds 'We have killed him' and goes on:

> God is dead. God remains dead. And we have killed him. How shall we comfort ourselves, the murderers of all murderers? What was holiest and mightiest of all that the world has yet owned has bled to death under our knives: who will wipe this blood off us? What water is there for us to clean ourselves? What festivals of atonement, what sacred games shall we have to invent? Is not the greatness of this deed too great for us? Must we ourselves not become gods simply to appear worthy of it? There has never been a greater deed; and whoever is born after us – for the sake of this deed he will belong to a higher history than all history hitherto.

The death of God also signals the death of metaphysics. Metaphysics is defined as a quest for the correspondence between Being and thought, or for their unity, and it has gone on from Parmenides to Plato, from Descartes to Spinoza. In the middle of the century of historicism, Nietzsche replaces Being with becoming, substance with action and what he might, like Marx, call praxis. The transvaluation of all values that he announces replaces adaptation to the rational order of the world with a celebration of will and passion. He writes (Nietzsche 1885: 41):

> We have abolished the real world: what world is left? the apparent
> world perhaps? . . . But no! *with the real world we have also abolished
> the apparent world*! (Mid-day; moment of the shortest shadow; end of
> the longest error; zenith of mankind; INCIPIT ZARATHUSTRA).

Nothing could be more modern than this attack on Kant. Nietzsche's
contempt for metaphysics is so great that it could be ascribed to
Auguste Comte. Yet this modernity is traversed by a number of
different paths. The most popular leads to utilitarianism, which
Nietzsche calls English thought and which he violently rejects. It is
impossible to live when we are enclosed in the apparent world.
French civilization is as loathsome as English thought. It is lifeless
and its cultural objects float in a void.

If we abandon the classical paths to modernity, we can avoid
utilitarianism by going back to the idea of natural law and to Christian
thought. We can centre our reflections on the idea of the subject and
that of democracy. Yet none of the thinkers who dominate the crisis
of modernity – Marx, Nietzsche and Freud – made that choice. And
it was Nietzsche who rejected it most violently.

His central argument is outlined in *The Genealogy of Morals*
(Nietzsche 1887). Some are weak and others are strong. Some rule
and others are ruled. Some are birds of prey and others are lambs.
Relations between the two are material relations and are devoid of
any ethical element. These are the relations of life, the relations that
exist between individuals and species. In order to escape power
relations which are not in their favour, the weak, however, intepret
their enemies' strength as wickedness. They therefore assume the
existence of a will or an essence which motivates action. This gives
birth to the notion of a subject. It is as irrational and artificial as the
notion of thunder, which the ignorant introduce to explain an
electrical discharge. That notion also becomes a Subject, and takes the
form of Jupiter. Anything that introduces a general intention and a
consciousness in order to explain behaviour is an instrument to
defend the weak. It therefore destroys the order of nature and creates
essences, or the principles that Auguste Comte saw as the foundations
of juridical and metaphysical thought. As Gilles Deleuze (1962: 44)
so accurately puts it: 'Consciousness is never self-consciousness, but
the consciousness of an Ego as opposed to the Self, which is not
conscious. It is not the consciousness of a master, but the consciousness of a slave, as opposed to a master who does not need to be
conscious.'

The important thing here is Nietzsche's violent rejection of the idea
of the Subject and of Christianity in particular. Christianity is a

religion of the weak. So too was the psychologism of Socrates and his pupil Euripides, which destroyed the spirit of Greek tragedy. According to *The Genealogy of Morals* (Nietzsche 1887: 180),

> This sort of person requires the belief in a 'free subject' able to choose indifferently, out of that instinct of self-preservation which notoriously justifies every kind of lie. It may well be that to this day the subject, or in popular language the soul, has been the most viable of all articles of faith simply because it makes it possible for the majority of mankind – i.e., the weak and oppressed of every sort – to practice the sublime sleight of hand which gives weakness the appearance of free choice and one's natural disposition the distinction of merit.

In *Beyond Good and Evil*, the critique concentrates on the philosophers of the Subject, with particular reference to Descartes's *cogito*. 'In the past . . . one said "I" is the condition, "think" is the predicate and conditioned . . . Then one tried . . . to fathom . . . whether the reverse was not perhaps true: "think" the condition, "I" conditioned; "I" thus being only a synthesis *produced* by thinking' (Nietzsche 1888: 81). Using terms very similar to those later used by Freud, Nietzsche describes consciousness as a social construct bound up with language and communication, and therefore with social roles. What is most personal is also what is most conventional and mediocre. Consciousness is, Nietzsche writes in *The Gay Science* (1882: 84), 'the last and latest development of the organic and hence also what is most unfinished and most unstrong. Consciousness gives rise to countless errors that lead an animal or man to perish sooner than necessary.' One is inevitably reminded of Marx's contrast between the productive forces, which are creative expressions of life and energy, and relations of production, which are constructs of consciousness – and for Marx this means the consciousness of the ruling class.

In Nietzsche's view, modernity has until now meant the triumph of consciousness, which turns against itself by identifying with a god, with a non-human force to which man has to submit. Modernity has led to nihilism, to the exhaustion of man. Christianity projected all man's power in to the divine universe, and left him with weakness as his only possession. Hence his decadence and inevitable disappearance. The inversion of values will lead him to reject this alienation and allow man to recover his natural being, his vital energy and his will to power.

Only the renuciation of the ideal and of God, and only the triumph of life over the will to death can bring about this liberation. There is, however, an incessant struggle between these conflicting forces, as any desire dreams of its fulfilment and thus gives birth to an ideal. At the end of the century, Weber will return to the theme of asceticism, which is so important to Nietzsche, but he stresses the transition from otherworldly to worldly asceticism in order to explain the rise of capitalism, and therefore a world of rich and poor and not a world of weak and strong. Nietzsche, in constrast, brutally contrasts the asceticism of priests and philosophers who extol silence, poverty and chastity, with the will to power. The explanation is that Weber is writing of the economic and social world, and Nietzsche of the world of thought, as he accuses the philosophers of having turned modes of behaviour appropriate to their own work in to universal virtues. This shift of perspective has decisive implications. Unlike Weberean man, Nietzschean man is not a social man. Nietzsche looks to the past for his models, to Ancient Rome and to the Italian Renaissance. The *virtù* of the Renaissance is the highest expression of a will to power that has acquired a taste for knowledge. We have killed God, and our guilt feeds on our desire for submission and redemption. We must therefore go beyond murder, beyond good and evil, and rediscover or create a natural existence which is free of all asceticism and all alienation. Doing so requires a combination of desire and reason, domination and self-control. This is not an internalization but a liberation of the self, a return to Dionysus. This was the primary theme of the young Nietzsche who wrote *The Birth of Tragedy* (Nietzsche 1872) and saw in Wagner a return to Dionysus, yet only a few years later Nietzsche denounced the composer of *Parsifal* for having reverted to a Christian morality. Gilles Deleuze is right to say that Dionysus is contrasted with Socrates and Jesus rather than with Appollo, who is his necessary complement. For Dionysus is life, and therefore a supra-individual principle.

Nietzsche escapes English utilitarianism only by outflanking the Christian idea of the Subject, by moving further and further away from empiricism and by rising above individuality. He is fascinated by the Eleusinian rites because we find 'a recognition that whatever exists is all of a piece, and that individuation is the root of all evil; a conception of art as the sanguine hope that the spell of individuation may yet be broken, as an augury of eventual reintegration' (Nietzsche 1872: 67). This is a nostalgia for Being, a desire to go beyond consciousness – or against consciousness – and to return, to the One, which is not the divine world but a world that predates the gods, a world of paganism in which man himself is a god, a demigod or a hero. Our civilization has no myths. It has lapsed in to decadence – and France is at once the most brilliant and the worst example of that decadence. It is attempting to recreate a foundation myth and is exhausting itself by trying to find that myth in past civilizations. *The Birth of Tragedy* (Nietzsche 1872: 103–4) teaches us that there is a more direct way to taste the delight of existence. We must

> look for this delight not in the phenomena but behind them . . . For a brief moment we become, ourselves, the primal Being, and we experience its insatiable hunger for existence . . . Pity and terror notwithstanding, we realize our great good fortune in having life – not as individuals, but as part of the life force with whose procreative lust we have become one.

According to Nietzsche, the Dionysiac myth which escapes the constraints of social life can appear only when the union between a people and a civilization disappears. In France, its disappearance has come about in an exemplary, if dangerous form. The Dionysiac myth can only be a German myth, precisely because it is asocial and does not correspond to any national consciousness. Ever since Luther's day, Germany has been the land of 'becoming', of a will-to-be that has never been exhausted in political and social forms. Only the German spirit can fight modern decadence and the degeneration of the European race. It is difficult to interpret this argument, which is far removed from the nationalism, bureaucracy and militarism of Bismarck's State. We also know that Nietzsche was, in his day, one of the few resolute opponents of anti-Semitism. It would therefore be a mistake to confuse him with the Nazism that claimed to be his heir. Nietzsche did not identify with the nation or the German *Volk*. The historical manifestation of the Being or the One to which he refers does, however, have as its vehicle the will of a people, and more specifically the will of the German people, who have 'risen up in profound disgust' against ' "modern ideas" ' (Nietzsche 1888: 185). Nietzsche constantly refers to 'slave peoples'. Because of his origins, he identifies to some extent with Russia and Poland, but his main identification is with the German people. He contrasts the German people with both French civilization and English thought, and the same contrast will be drawn in different terms by Tönnies, whose dichotomy between society and community (Tönnies 1957) is not without a certain nostalgia for community, or a certain nationalism.

For the philosophy of the Enlightenment, society and history were two aspects of a single reality. That idea is still very much present in French thought, which identifies France with the triumph of reason and freedom. This new alliance between the temporal and the spiritual leaves no space for the freedom of anyone who is not defined in terms of their participation in progress, as embodied in the nation. German thought, of which Nietzsche is a prime representative, dissociates nation and rationalization. He attacks abstract men who have no constructive myths, abstract education, abstract law and the abstract State in the name of the national myth, of something more profound than a collective will, namely the very life-force of a concrete historical Being. Nietzsche's thought is an appeal to both Being and the movement of the nation's self-assertion. The appeal to Being takes him beyond good and evil, and allows him to reconcile freedom and necessity. In *The Gay Science*, he writes (Nietzsche 1882: 223): 'I want to learn more and more to see as beautiful what is necessary in things; then I shall be one of those who make things beautiful. *Amor fati*: let that be my love henceforth.'

The superman is capable of an *amor fati* and knows that, as Zarathustra puts it, 'the wickedness in man is necessary for the best in him' (Nietzsche 1883–92: 235). Nietzsche is clearly not calling for the liberation of the instincts. He is calling for their spiritualization, for the transformation of nature in to a work of art and for an acceptance of the Eternal Return: 'Everything goes, everything returns; the wheel of existence rolls for ever. Everything dies, everything blossoms anew; the year of existence runs on for ever' (Nietzsche 1883–92): 234). This elevation to Being and art is consistent with the central current in German thought from Schiller to Hölderlin and the young Hegel, all of whom studied together in the Stift in Tübingen. It is associated with the national spirit, as all three reject a modernity which they identify with social integration, moralization and bourgeois civilization.

The association is fragile: the appeal to the people rapidly becomes nationalism and comes in to conflict with aestheticism. But it is no more fragile than the Christian consciousness or the social demands that provide the basis for modern democratic action. In the very moment of its triumph, utilitarianism finds itself faced with two adversaries. They sometimes seem to have a lot in common, but they are in fact diametrically opposed to one another: Nietzschean paganism and the democratic spirit, which is based upon the defence of the weak and the exploited as well as on the idea of human rights. Intellectuals of my generation often opted for Nietzsche's anthropological critique of bourgeois civilization rather than for the social critique of capitalist domination, even though the expansion of totalitarian regimes did produce some convergences and similarities that were more apparent than real, as the 'grand politics' Nietzsche dreamed of in his last years was anything but democratic. The inversion of values now comes to be typified by the transition from the Revolution to Napoleon. Nietzsche's politics was intended to be a struggle against decadence, or in other words against Christianity, socialism and the slave morality. But is it in fact a politics? The struggle against Christianity and against Kantian ethics is primarily intended to free man, an 'animal with the right to make promises' according to the opening words of the second essay on *The Genealogy of Morals* (Nietzsche 1887: 189), and one capable of turning life in to what *The Gay Science* calls 'a means to knowledge'. Nietzsche concludes thus: 'With this principle in one's heart one can live not only boldly but gaily, and laugh gaily too. And who knows how to laugh anyway and live well if he does not first know a good deal about war and victory' (Nietzsche 1882: 255).

All Nietzsche's themes are contained in the words 'rejection of Christian morality', 'gaiety' and 'war'. The common factor between them is above all the critique of a modernity identified with both utilitarianism and the subordination of individual Being and the life it contains, to the interests of social and economic organization. Nietzsche's critique is radical only because it is antisocial, as is the hostility of so many artists and intellectuals to a civil society and a democracy they identify with a philistine capitalism. His thought sheds light on a major aspect of the fragmented modernity we described in the previous chapter. Nostalgia for Being and an appeal to national energy are the two main forms of resistance to modernity, of the return to something that lies beyond the social, and which can replace the God who died. With Nietzsche, thought becomes antisocial and antimodern. Sometimes it will become antibourgeois, and sometimes it will become antidemocratic, but it will always be wary of any face-to-face encounter between the forces and social actors of modernity. Irrespective of whether it appeals to the unity of Being, the national spirit or the evolution of history, it always takes the path that leads to a return to the One, to a Whole. As a result, the twentieth century will be a century of confrontation in which societies will do their utmost to serve their gods, and will hurl themselves in to a struggle to the death over the empty tomb of the God of Christians. Nietzsche himself avoids this all too real war, partly because he refuses to make an absolute break with Christianity. *Beyond Good and Evil* and the final pages of *The Genealogy of Morals* re-establish a certain continuity with the religion that associates suffering with willing and the figure of Christ, and which taught that 'It is necessary that the emotions be cooled' (Nietzsche 1887: 291) and must be sublimated in to the passion of love. As historicism and trust in progress become exhausted, Nietzsche's thought takes on increasing importance and eventually becomes dominant. In France, for example, it inspired the reaction against the ideology of modernization that accompanied the period of rapid economic growth which

followed the Second World War. Gianni Vattimo (1985) rightly
describes Nietzsche as the source of post-modernism. Nietzsche was
the first to show the exhaustion of the modern spirit in 'epigonism'.
More generally, he is the best representative of the philosophical
obsession with a lost Being, of the nihilism that triumphed after the
death of God. Contemporary thought is characterized by an increasing divorce between those who, following Marx, make, not Being,
but the struggle waged against social domination in the name of the
human subject or nature, the principle of order and of the unity of
the world, and those who, inspired by Nietzsche, turn towards a
Being-in-the-world. This is a form of energy, but it is also the
bearer of a tradition, a culture, or a history. It is therefore defined
by its nationalism. Nietzsche was both the first to denounce the
modernist illusion, or the idea that there is a correspondence between
personal development and social integration, and the philosopher
who imbued sectors of European thought with a nostalgia for Being
that has often led to the celebration of particular natural and cultural
beings.

Post-Nietzschean modernist thought is critical, and it is challenged
by the rise of an antimodern school of thought which concentrates its
attacks on the idea of a Subject. This is an anthropological and
philosophical mode of thought and it comes in to conflict with the
social sciences, which have an almost natural affinity with modernity.
It is not nostalgic for the past, but refuses to identify actors with their
achievements. Nietzschean thought escaped modernism by reintroducing an ahistorical Being, but that Being can no longer mean the
world of Platonic ideas or the divine Logos. It is a relationship with
the Id, or consciousness of desire. Man does not transcend his history
because his soul is made in God's image, as Descartes would have it,
but because he is inhabited by Dionysus, by the impersonal power of
desire and sexuality, of a nature that exists within man. Whereas
Enlightenment thought believed reason to be a universal and looked
to a lucid will-power to control the passions, Nietzsche and then
Freud argue that the universal emerges in the unconscious and its
language, in the desire that breaks down the barriers of interiority.
This inversion can take the form of the most extreme antimodernism,
but it is also the precondition for the creation of a subject which is
synonymous with neither the individual Ego nor the Self constructed
by society. This Subject is defined by a relationship with the self and
not by institutionalized cultural norms, but it can only exist if we can
discover the path that leads from the Id to the I, and that path must
bypass an Ego that is identified with reason. Nietzsche did not
concern himself with the I; the love of destiny (*amor fati*) that he

proclaims is intended to free man from all the decadent tendencies – Christian, democratic and feminine – that result in subjectivation.

Nietzsche's thought easily becomes a nostalgia for Being and a fascination with the nation as living community. It led Heidegger, who was steeped in Nietzsche, to ally himself with Nazism, and it is not possible to isolate Nietzsche himself from the rise of nationalisms in Central Europe which signals the first great crisis in the modernist ideology. It would, however, be as great an exaggeration to identify Nietzsche with a nationalist drive (*Drang*) as it would be to regard his anthropology as a necessary response to utilitarianism and social conformism. A thinker can be seen as a particular element in a cultural configuration involving other elements, which are not ideas but collective social and political forces. We might also recall that Nietzsche himself reminds us that a thinker exists at the heart of a society divided by conflicting interests. Consciousness and interiority are instruments for the defence of the poor; life is a matter for the powerful. Nietzsche's dichotomy between active and reactive forms of behaviour is indeed a social dichotomy, and it is no accident that his attacks should be directed against the weak, democracy and women. His attitude is, I believe, of crucial importance, and I intend to defend the opposite point of view by demonstrating in this book that the theme of the Subject no longer means a search for metasocial foundations for the social order, and that the Subject is not a new name for the One God, reason or history. On the contrary, the Subject is a social movement, the act of defending the dominated against the dominant, who do identify with their achievements and desires. In modern society, naturalism and materialism are the philosophy of the dominant, whilst those who are caught up in networks of dependency must establish a relationship with themselves and assert themselves as free subjects because they cannot know themselves through their achievements and their social relations, as they are alienated and dominated. By attacking the idea of consciousness and the Subject, Nietzsche identifies with the masters and thus indicates *a contrario* the path that has to be taken by a philosophy of the Subject. A philosophy of the Subject is inevitably a sociology of the Subject, as the subject can be constituted only by breaking the bonds of dependency. And democracy, which is so often attacked by intellectuals in the name of both an elitist reason and the will to power, means creating guarantees that protect the weak and allow them to establish the relationship with the self that we call democracy. Democracy is the force that allows us to attempt to reconquer the social space our dominators control by describing it as natural, as alien to consciousness, or as conforming to the evolution of history or the nature of human beings. And how, finally, can we forget that the triumph of modernity also signalled the triumph of virility and of the divorce between men, who were identified with both reason and will, and women, who were reduced to being no more than tradition and passion?

The master–slave dichotomy dominates the entire century from Hegel to Marx and then Nietzsche. This means that we have to defend or reject the Subject within a class-divided society where the elite identifies with progress, and where all dominated categories fall back not only on an identity, which is always defined by a tradition, but an interiority or consciousness which, even when they use traditional language, is the only free space for the organization of their counter-offensive.

Let us accept that idea that the utilitarianism and the religion of society that imprison modern man in an iron cage can be attacked from two different directions. Nietzsche attacks it from the side of the Id, of the life that rebels against the norms of order and against moralization. It can also be attacked from the side of the I and its freedom, of social movements that fight against a social order which the masters try to pass off as natural. It is important to recognize the difference between these two currents of thought, as they are more decisive than their common will to attack social utilitarianism and sociological functionalism. Critiques of the bourgeois order that are made in the name of life and desire can drift in to either leftism or fascism, but they are always hostile to democracy and especially to what is dismissively termed 'social democracy'.

As my analysis begins to trace the decline of the historicism whose triumph over Christian dualism has already been described, it is impossible for me to distance myself from Nietzsche without at the same time recognizing that it is essential to support his attacks on positivism and on an increasingly suffocating historicism. The Subject or the consciousness he rejects is closer to what sociology calls socialization, meaning the internalization of social norms or moralization, than to what I mean by the idea of the Subject: the consciousness of the Zek who resists the concentration camp or the idea of human rights which resists the arbitrariness of absolute power.

Nietzsche is not the only great intellectual figure to have fought the modernist ideology. Broadly speaking, philosophers of history and society identify with one or another aspect of the crisis of modernity. They often ally themselves with the national theme, as we have already seen with Michelet in France, and as we shall see with the vast majority of German intellectuals and *a fortiori* those of the Danube countries. More often still, they are obsessed with the search for Being, which they will find in nature, in beauty and especially in life, or more specifically in sexuality. *Philosophies of life* are both an intellectual expression of modernity and a reaction against the intellectualism of a culture reduced to instrumental rationality. It was only with the work of Bergson that they reached France. It is easy to contrast them with a sociology of the Subject, but it is more useful to recognize that they provide the starting point that allows thought to break free of a rationalism which is increasingly being swallowed up by conformism and social utilitarianism. They are the starting point for a critical tendency without which the constitution of the Subject would be inconceivable, even if there is considerable tension between all philosophies of Being and all notions of the Subject.

I took Nietzsche as a starting point because, whilst he is obviously completely opposed to the redefinition of modernity I am proposing, the idea of the Subject cannot be introduced prior to the destruction of Enlightenment rationalism, which reduced modernity to rationalization and secularization. Thanks to Nietzsche, social life becomes enchanted once more, and I see the idea of the Subject as a central element in that process.

Freud

Freud takes the destruction of the Ego, which may be defined in terms of the internalization of social norms, to its most extreme conclusions. His work is the most systematic attack ever to have been made on the ideology of modernity. The unity between actor and system, between the rationality of the technical world and personal ethics, gives way to a divorce between the individual and the social, between pleasure and the law. These worlds are so completely different that it is impossible to interpret them as one. Freud's central assertion has therefore been interpreted in contrasting ways. For some, Freud is a pessimist who regards the subordination of individual instincts to the rules and constraints of social life as essential. For others, Freud is the man who revealed, and therefore liberated, sexuality. It is impossible to accept this duality, which corresponds to the starting point for Freud's reflections and not their point of arrival. On the other hand, we do have to recognize that it never disappears and that Freud's thought is incompatible with any attempt at moralization and socialization. It is so radical that it has an explosive power. Freud declares war on consciousness and the Ego: 'Psychoanalysis cannot situate the essence of the psychical in consciousness, but is obliged to regard consciousness as a quality of the psychical, which may be present in addition to other qualities or may be absent'

(Freud 1923: 351). The inversion is analogous to that brought about by Nietzsche. The starting point is not consciousness but the unconscious, and that term is not to be understood in the secondary sense of a repressed psychical content, but in the primary sense of a deep psychical activity. Consciousness is no more than an envelope which comes in to contact with the reality it perceives. This psychical activity calls for a biological and even a physical analysis. Human beings are inhabited by instincts which create needs, or in other words tensions, and the organism attempts to satisfy them in order to return to a state of equilibrium. Taken to extremes, this view means that the organism strives to reduce the tension and therefore to return to inertia. The clearest expression of this thesis is to be found in *Beyond the Pleasure Principle* (Freud 1920: 308–9):

> *It seems, then, that an instinct is an urge inherent in organic life to restore an earlier state of things*, which the living entity has been obliged to abandon under the pressure of external disturbing forces; that is, it is a kind of organic elasticity, or, to put it in another way, the expression of the inertia inherent in organic life.

Freud almost immediately adds (Freud 1920: 310–11) the even more radical comment:

> If we are to take it as a truth that knows no exception that everything living dies for *internal* reasons – becomes inorganic once again – then we shall be compelled to say that *'the aim of all life is death'* and, looking backwards, that *'inanimate things existed before living ones'*.

He has already (1920: 310) spelled out the main implications of his claims:

> Let us suppose, then, that all the organic instincts are conservative, are acquired historically and tend towards the restoration of an earlier state of things. It follows that the phenomena of organic development must be attributed to external disturbances and diverting influences.

These texts could not be further removed from representations which, like those of Fromm, regard sexuality as the natural setting for sociability and a desire for the other, and therefore for the pansexualism which has spread throughout contemporary culture (Fromm 1942). Freud's thinking becomes increasingly radical, especially after the tragic experience of the First World War and its devastation. He now begins to attach great importance to aggressivity and the death instinct. At this point, his thought is similar to that of Hobbes. The natural state is a state of universal war and, far from being based upon human beings' natural tendencies, the organization of social life must break with them. The realm of the law is contrasted with that of the drives, the reality principle with the pleasure principle. In her recent *L'Ombre de l'objet*, Marie Moscovici (1990) emphasizes this strand in Freud's thought by stressing the role of hatred and aggressivity in both his work and that of Winnicott. In *Totem and Taboo* (Freud 1913) Freud explains the formation of social rules in terms of the murder of the father and the murderous brothers' establishment of the law that puts an end to violence. The important role played by hypnosis in the development of his thought is one illustration of how Freud's analyses of the instincts and the search for pleasure completely eradicate subjectivity and intentionality.

Pleasure is contrasted with the law, and both are external to consciousness. The Ego is almost powerless against both the law, which is primarily repressive, and the Id. Adaptation to the social world requires repression. It is fear of castration that makes the child turn away from its mother and orients it towards reality. The law inculcates the idea that members of society must be subordinate to society's interests. Socialization and the internalization of norms, which functionalist sociologists describe as acquired characteristics, are seen as a process of repression which is never stabilized.

Whilst this initial image of Freud's thought is open to criticism, it does have one virtue in that it reveals that the nature of capitalist society is being interpreted in terms of psychical life. Capitalist society is not simply an acquisitive society, but above all the site of the break, which is so well described by Polanyi (1944), between the economy and cultural beliefs or forms of social organization.

This image of capitalist society is consonant with the way in which that society experiences itself. It is expressed in its social norms and its so-called values, and it is based upon a complete divorce between, on the one hand, individual interests and the market, defined as being non-social, as a battlefield and as the site of a struggle to the death, and on the other, the law or, more specifically, the discipline which imposes upon beings of desire the constraints that turn them in to social beings. The capitalist world sacrifices neither the violence of money nor the rigour of the social order; it knows that both are essential to its workings, and this implies both the liberation of acquisitive instincts and the imposition of strict rules in both productive labour and education. The pleasure–law dichotomy explains why capitalist society is based upon the twin dichotomies between, on the one hand, a bourgeoisie motivated by acquisitive desires and workers subject to discipline, and, on the other, economic activity, which is public and therefore dominated by competition or money, and private life, which is where we learn to obey laws, rules and conventions. This gives capitalist society its highly distinctive characteristics; the instincts are set free in public life, and it is in private life that the weight of the law makes itself felt. As a result, superficial thinkers believe that in such a society, individuals are completely socialized and controlled. In capitalist society, the liberation of instincts that other societies accept in private life, occurs in public life, in economic life and in the market, which is a place of violence, aggressivity and death. This is of course the main theme of many nineteenth-century novels, and especially of the novels of Balzac.

Freud's analysis can be the source of a possible inversion, or even of the transcendence of the divorce between pleasure and reality. Those who define communism as 'to each according to their needs' dream of a naturalized society. In more realistic terms, the action of the workers' movement and social reforms have done a great deal to attenuate the divorce between economy and society that defined capitalist society in its pure state. Freud himself, however, did not think along these lines. He had no notion of revolutionary consciousness and action precisely because his approach made it impossible to define human behaviour in terms of action and intentionality. It is time to point out that, whilst this simplistic image of the complete break between pleasure and reality, between individual instincts and social order, does have a permanent critical value, it overlooks the greater part of Freud's analysis. More specifically, it overlooks the theme of the libido on the one hand, and those of guilt and sublimation on the other.

The *libido* differs from the other instincts in that it is a desire for an object rather than for satisfaction. The lines cited earlier introduce a dichotomy between the life instincts and the death instinct, between object relations and the destruction of the object, between an attachment to the object – which is what we usually mean by 'love' – and the repetition of a desire which is attached only to itself. At the same time, the law is not something that remains external to the individual. It enters in to the individual, governs him to some extent and instils the guilt born of desire's resistance to the law.

Finally, we have to ask if the super-ego is inevitably repressive, and this raises the most difficult problems of all. The super-ego is capable of both meeting the demands of the Id and giving them a sublimated meaning. As a result, it becomes the creator, not of the Ego, but of the Subject. To sum up, the divorce between the agencies of psychical life – unconscious, preconscious and conscious, to use the terminology of Freud's first topography – has to give way to a more dynamic relationship between the agencies which are redefined as the Id, the Super-Ego and the Ego. The history of the individual is not simply, or even primarily, that of the growing conflict between pleasure and the law, or of the final submission of the former to the latter. It is also the history of the transcendence of the primal fusion with the mother and the concomitant rejection of the father, and of the transition from Oedipal conflict to identification with the father. The father is not only a repressive figure who threatens to castrate the child who desires its mother. *The Ego and the Id* is quite explicit on this point (Freud 1923: 376):

> The ego ideal is therefore the heir of the Oedipus complex, and thus it is also the expression of the most powerful impulses and the most important libidinal vicissitudes of the id. By setting up this ego ideal, the ego has mastered the Oedipus complex and at the same time placed itself in subjection to the id. Whereas the ego is essentially the representative of the external world, of reality, the super-ego stands in contrast to it as the representative of the internal world, of the id.

We have moved from a confrontation between the Id and the Super-Ego, to use Freud's new terminology, to an alliance between the Super-Ego and the Id against the Ego, which is still regarded as a set of social identifications. This alliance is known as sublimation: 'What has belonged to the lowest part of the mental life of each of us is changed, through the formation of the ideal, in to what is highest in the human mind by our scale of values' (Freud 1923: 376). Religion, morality and what Freud himself calls 'a social sense' (1923: 377) are all products of sublimation.

Is it an overstatement to say that Freud's thought is initially motivated by the will to destroy the dominant image of the Ego and consciousness but that, whilst he never abandons that critical project, he ultimately replaces the Ego with the I? Can we not understand the famous formula 'Where id was, there ego shall be' (Freud 1933: 112) as indicating that the two operations complement one another? The Ego is made subordinate to the Id, but part of the Id is subsequently transformed in to a Super-Ego which is no longer a law external to the individual, but a Subject. The Subject is no longer the internalized representative of the law, but an instrument for liberation from social constraints. Whereas there was initially a caesura between the agency of repression and the repressed, part of the great reservoir of libido – the Id – now becomes the Super-Ego. The Id is differentiated and transformed in to the Super-Ego and Ego, which is now defined in a new sense as an I. To be more specific and to adopt the suggestions made in 'On Narcissism: An Introduction' (which was published in 1914, or in other words before *Beyond the Pleasure Principle* and *The Ego and the Id*), the libido, which was originally directed towards the Ego (primary narcissism), is later projected on to external objects.

The cathexis of the Ego still persists, however, and is related to object-cathexes 'much as the body of an amoeba is related to the pseudopodia which it puts out' (Freud 1914: 68). Primary narcissism then gives way to a seondary narcissism which is directed not towards the Ego, but towards the Super-Ego: 'It would not surprise us if we were to find a special psychical agency which performs the task of seeing that narcissistic satisfaction from the ego ideal is ensured and which, with this end in view, constantly watches the actual ego and measures it by that ideal' (Freud 1914: 89). Sublimation and secondary narcissism explain the shaping of the moral conscience, and there is no longer any divorce between ego-instincts and object-libido. The instincts of self-preservation are also libidinal in nature, according to the 'Autobiographical Study' of 1925 (Freud 1925: 240). Whereas identifications subordinate the individual to society, narcissism is a libidinal return to the self. It has no pathological meaning, but it does allow a non-sexual focus on the self. Laplanche and Pontalis (1967: 433) summarize Freud's analysis clearly: 'The transformation of a sexual activity in to a sublimated one . . . is now said to require an intermediate period during which the libido is withdrawn on to the ego so that desexualization may become possible.'

This return to the self is of particular importance in a mass society in which every member of a crowd strives to identify with leaders who exercise a hypnotic influence. Thanks to sublimation and the libido it supplies, the Super-Ego gives the individual the ability to resist this seduction and manipulation. It would be a mistake to privilege these aspects of Freud's thought, though they are a characteristic expression of the group of texts which gives the clearest account of his metapsychology (Freud 1915). But it would also be a mistake to say that the absolute contradiction between pleasure and the social law results in an unrelieved pessimism on Freud's part. The repressed also plays a positive role to the extent that it is sublimated, though this does mean that instinctual representations become separated from their 'quota of affect', which then seeks new representatives in order to enter the conscious system. The moral conscience can only be shaped in relation to repression and anxiety, but it is not reducible to either. Freud is as far removed from the hedonistic ethics of the twentieth century as he is from the old ethics of guilt. In the later part of his life, he does attach great importance to the death instinct, or Thanatos, but he does so in order to contrast the ego-instincts with the quest for pleasure – which, as Marcuse (1955) says, inevitably leads to nirvana and to death. The creative role of Eros is a unifying factor to the extent that its primary function is sexual reproduction, and it is sublimated in to what Freud himself calls love.

Eros can, however, also lead to the loss of the Ego if it is dissolved in to its identifications. Only the return to the self, and in particular secondary narcissism, makes it possible to avoid the twin dangers of solipsism and the loss of the self in the object. It thus makes possible the construction of a personality which is no longer a thin envelope for the Id which comes in to contact with the outside world, as it is in Freud's initial description of the Ego.

The absolute divorce between pleasure and the law can lead to an authoritarian and very masculinist conception of the formation of the personality. It is tempting to say that girls do not completely break off their relationship with the mother in order to identify with a model of their own sex, and therefore remain within the order of the imaginary, to use Lacan's terminology, and have greater difficulty in entering the order of the symbolic, or in other words culture. If, on the other hand, we stress the continuity between the Id and the Super-Ego and the invasion of the ego-ideal by the libido, there is no longer the same absolute divorce between the imaginary and the symbolic, and the theory of the personality can be feminized to a certain extent. The personality is shaped by what pragmatists call an internal conversation – a conversation between the I and the Ego, according to Mead (1934) – and therefore, in Lacan's view, by a divorce between the 'I' of the enunciation and the 'I' of the utterance. The communication that exists between these two Subjects must be given the same importance as their divorce. This thesis, which can be found mainly in the second part of Freud's *oeuvre* but which is not marked by the extreme pessimism of his final writings, is quite opposed to the vision imposed by a certain rationalism. Rationalism identifies the Subject with reason and its triumph over the passions. This conception had already been abandoned by Descartes, as we are reminded by Lacan, in whose view the 'I' of the philospher's 'I am' does not coincide with the I of the *cogito*'s 'I am thinking'. The formation of the subject is not merely a departure from the individual and an identification with the group and the categories of rational action; it is bound up with a desire for the self and at the same time with a desire for the other.

Freud teaches us to mistrust the 'inner life' because it is full of alienating identifications and inculcated social models. We will not find the I within the Ego, but in the refusal to divorce the I from the Ego. We must therefore look for the I outside the Ego, reject the correspondence between the individual and society, and connect the defence of the individual with a revolt against the established order.

There are similarities between the thought of Freud and that of Nietzsche, but the differences between them are greater. Freud himself emphasizes that they have something in common on a number of occasions, as in his 'Autobiographical Study'. Both are in conflict with the dominant themes of socialization and moralization. Both refuse to give consciousness a central role, and replace it with an analysis that begins with the Id and life, or in other words desire and sexuality. But they then go their separate ways. In *Beyond the Pleasure Principle*, Freud openly admits that he does not believe that there is any widespread 'untiring impulsion towards further perfection' (Freud 1920: 315). He is therefore much more pessimistic than Nietzsche about the possibility of inverting values, as human culture is primarily a matter of the repression of the instincts. In *Group Psychology and the Analysis of the Ego*, however, he states (Freud 1921: 156) that Nietzsche's superman was a leader with 'few libidinal ties; he loved no one but himself, or other people only in so far as they served his needs'. Whereas Nietzsche attempts to escape the pressures of society by going back to Being because he does not accept that the Great Pan is dead, Freud attempts to construct the personality on the basis of relations with others and the relationship between the desire for the object and the relationship with the self. This allows him to explore the transformation of the Id, an impersonal force external to consciousness, in to a force that can construct the personal Subject on the basis of relations with human beings.

Critiques of modernity that are influenced by Nietzsche lead to a rejection of modernity; those influenced by Freud lead to a quest for individual freedom. The difference between them should not, however, be allowed to mask their common pessimism and their rejection of modernist illusions, and especially the dangerous tendency to identify personal freedom with social integration. Nietzsche revives the world that existed before Christianity; Freud gives birth to the personal subject in a secularized world where it is in danger of being crushed by guilt or by alienating social and political identifications. Yet it has to be admitted that their influences often converge and lead many intellectuals to reject society completely in the name of desire – a word which, for historical reasons, they use in preference to 'will to power', on the grounds that it has been reduced to a network of rules and constraints. This radical antimodernism finds the notion that everything is political or the idea of social choice quite alien, and can therefore result in all sorts of choices. It becomes a new twentieth-century form of 'artistic' hostility to the bourgeois world. Freud's thought can, however, lead in a different direction. His antimodernism leads him to seek resistance to social controls in the language of the unconscious. He is as close to religion in general as he is far removed from Christianity. Freud has a particular influence on surrealist thought. Its radical critique of bourgeois society will also be associated with the liberation of the unconscious by means of the derangement of the senses and by techniques such as automatic writing.

The differences between sexuality and object-libido, and the Ego-instincts must not, on the other hand, be forgotten. Sexuality is relational. It is primarily an instinct to reproduce, and it is therefore a search for an encounter between two individuals of different sexes. Above all it must be recalled that the libido penetrates the Super-Ego, which is therefore not simply repressive, and which is indeed an ego-ideal. We thus have an outline conception which sees social action as a precondition for a self-consciousness which is neither neurotic nor narcissistic. Why do we have to choose between these lines of thinking, both of which stem from Freud's thought? It seems preferable to stress that they complement one another, which does not mean that there is no tension between them. The critical side to Freud's thought is the destruction of the Ego and the awareness of the repressive, inevitable and unacceptable nature of the social order. Its educational side stresses that the Subject can recathect the interpersonal or social situations in which it finds itself. The contradiction between the two is much closer to reality than the sharp contrast some have tried to establish between a pure analysis of the symbolism of the unconscious, and a 'revisionist' school which is primarily therapeutic and designed to adapt the individual to society – an idea which certainly cannot be ascribed to either Freud, Erich Fromm, author of *Fear of Freedom* (Fromm 1942) and analyst of fascism, or Karen Horney.

Freud has had a much wider influence than Nietzsche. The only escape from modernity offered by Nietzsche is art and nostalgia for the Whole, for the vanished world where 'all is order and beauty, luxury, calm and voluptuousness', to cite Baudelaire's 'Invitation au voyage'. Freud's thought takes the destruction of the Ego to extremes, but at the same time it also explores the paths that must be taken by any theory of the Subject.

Herbert Marcuse (1955) follows those paths systematically, and realizes that only a truly social critique can reintroduce the idea of a Subject. That notion is the product of an intellectual current born of the encounter between Freudian thought and the revolutionary movement in the 1920s and 1930s. At first sight, Marcuse seems to be even more pessimistic than Freud himself, as he contrasts the constraints of social life with the free flowering of pregenital sexuality. Yet that theme is quickly transformed, as sexuality cannot flower without some support in social experience. That is the core of

Marcuse's thought. What Freud saw as social reality is, for Marcuse, divided in to two contrasting realities: on the one hand, activity or labour, and, on the other, the truly social domination that is exercised in labour, and particularly in Taylorized industries. Labour is not solely a matter of suffering and constraint, as it can also be a relationship. What is more important, it can have a libidinal or relational content which becomes more and more real as we leave proto-industrial society and enter the tertiary sector where communication takes the place of manufacture. The contradiction between these two aspects of social activity is exacerbated to the point where, according to Marcuse, the negative aspects of labour in an advanced industrial society have more to do with social domination than with constraints at work. The 'leftist' condemnation of a class domination which destroys the desire for affective relations is therefore complemented by the great faith in modernity displayed by the 'Flower Generation' and the young people who gathered at Woodstock. At this point, Marcuse takes up a theme which is, as we have seen, of great importance in Freud's thought: the Id penetrates the Super-Ego. More specifically, he shares Roheim's view that 'in sublimation we have no ground wrested from the id by the super-ego, but quite to the contrary, what we have is super-ego territory inundated by the id' (cited, Marcuse 1955: 177). Sexualized libido is sublimated in to civilization because it is primarily a social bond.

For the purposes of our analysis, it is, however, more pertinent to note that Marcuse, like Roheim, realizes that the libido can be sublimated only if it becomes a social phenomenon, as this takes us away from the crude dichotomy between pleasure and reality. Only the relationship with the other can prevent the self-destruction that threatens the libido, and that threat is very much present in the consumer society. Marcuse retreats from the absolute condemnation of technology which so marked the Frankfurt School, and adopts a Marxist perspective by associating the productive forces with the libido and contrasting them with capitalist relations of production. Total rejection of a modern society reduced to the triumph of instrumental rationality implies a nostalgia for Being and a pre-industrial model of society which is often identified with the Greek *polis*. Marxism, in contrast, has every faith in modernity, and concentrates criticisms on its mode of social management and not its instrumentalism.

The rejection of the discourse of order and of the mechanisms of identification with leaders led to a *rapprochement* between Marx and Freud, and after the First World War this gave rise to important intellectual trends which took their inspiration from the work of both. At that level, both Freud and Marx remain faithful to the central inspiration behind the social sciences: a distrust of the categories of practice and empiricism. The most mundane categories, or those which are most strongly influenced by norms, are not the most objective. On the contrary, they are the most direct expression of relations of domination. The starting point for social science will always be a distrust of 'the social', and it must distance itself from anything that reduces the workings of society to a technico-adminis- trative operation. Industrial society is no more governed by instru- mental reason alone than any other society. Marx reminds us of the role of profit, and Freud of the accumulation of power on the part of leaders who encourage members of the crowd to identify with them. Being a historicist, Marx contrasts the ruses of social domination with the natural logic of the productive forces. Being both more of a traditionalist and more modern, Freud contrasts them with the power of reason. Yet he also contrasts them with the principles of a universal ethics similar to that of Jesus: love one another. He thus introduces the idea of the Subject. At the end of 'Group Psychology and the Analysis of the Ego' (Freud 1921), Freud contrasts the army with the church. In the army, soldiers identify with their leaders and, through them, the organization and the society it defines. According to Freud, the Christian, in contrast, does not identify with Christ in order to be absorbed in to him. He seeks to imitate him, or in other words to submit, like Christ, to the universal ethics of charity. Identification with the group is contrasted with the imitation of a charismatic figure who is no more than the embodiment of a value. Like Marx and like Nietzsche, Freud thus appeals to a form of desocialization and breaks with the tradition that came in to being with Rousseau and the Revolution and which was spread by the nationalisms that became so widespread in the nineteenth, and especially the twentieth, centuries. This desocialization, which can lead us back through art to Being, is the basis for all critical thought. It can take us back to the rationalist tradition of the Enlightenment, but it can also take us back to Christian and Cartesian dualism. It can also make the individual the main source of resistance against social domination, and its individualism can enable it to defend either specific needs and an individual's freedom of initiative, or the right of every individual to construct him or herself by resisting the logics of domination as a personal Subject.

For more than a hundred years, debates within social thought have claimed that these various answers are mutually exclusive, yet they all refuse to identify the actor with the system. But only one of the thinkers who dominate our age – Freud, at least in part – puts us on the track of the Subject, whereas Marx wanted to see the triumph of nature, and Nietzsche, the triumph of Dionysus.

Fin de Siècle Sociology

Whereas Nietzsche and Freud make devastating attacks on the rationalist image of man, sociology seems to defend modernity and rationalization. Yet is not this image false? Sociology is in reality part of a *fin de siècle* school of thought which distrusts the spirit of the Enlightenment and rediscovers, thanks to Nietzsche and Freud, the power of the will and of unrestricted desires, as opposed to instrumental reason. It is no paradox to say that the philosopher to whom the emergent discipline of sociology refers most directly is Schopenhauer. This is especially true of Durkheim, who was actually nicknamed 'Schopen' by his students. His struggle against the utilitarian conception of the contract is based on the idea of the duality of human nature – *homo duplex* – or, more specifically, on the idea that the world of representations – the world of society – comes in to conflict with the world of will and desire. The opposition he establishes between the world of representation and the world of will derives directly from Schopenhauer. And his conception of *anomie* refers to a conflict between the limitations imposed by social rules, and the unbounded desire that is to be found in human beings. Durkheim is close to Freud, especially in his *Moral Education* (Durkheim 1925). Like Freud, be believes that, being creatures of desire, human beings find it increasingly difficult to overcome the constraints imposed by modern society. Yet, again like Freud, he also maintains that society imposes the moral rules that will allow reason to triumph over desire. To that extent, he disagrees with Tönnies, who comes close to arguing that the artificiality of society must not destroy the natural strength of community. Durkheim's rationalism is not an elementary sociologism. Like Schopenhauer, and like Hobbes before him, Durkheim believes that the individual is an egotistical and violent creature, and that a contract and the idea of justice are the only things that can erect adequate barriers against the forces of destruction. That is why, unlike the utilitarians, he argues for a strong State that is capable of establishing a necessary compromise between the interest of society and individual desires and of ensuring that it is respected.

The emergent discipline of sociology breaks with the spirit of the Enlightenment. Even Weber stresses the non-rational character of Calvinist values and regards the prophet as the central figure in social and political life. In an essay on Schopenhauer and Nietzsche written in 1907, Simmel, for his part, gives an even more central role to the will to life, which he sees as the source of both morality and immorality.

This is why sociology is no stranger to the *fin de siècle* awareness of the decline of the West, or in other words of the crisis in Enlightenment rationalism which first began in Germany.

The triumph of capitalism made it so obvious to sociologists and economic historians alike that the will to profit and power, the war in the market and the constraints imposed on workers by the factory, could not be reduced to a more moderate image of rationalization, that it forced them to abandon the rationalist image of man.

Sociology is too stong and too diverse an intellectual movement for it to be reducible to this image. It understands both the power of the desire for wealth and the extent of the destruction that has been inflicted upon society. It sometimes calls upon the workers to resist, but it usually calls for State intervention. In both cases, it argues against utilitarianism, just as Durkheim argues against Spencer, and it is therefore inscribed within the general trend towards the destruction of the rationalist conception of man that was launched by Nietzsche and Freud. To that extent it is far removed from the functionalist vulgate that will triumph in the mid twentieth century. That vulgate lacks the tragic power of the works of Weber or Durkheim, which are dominated by the image of a break or conflict between opposing forces: on the one hand, social rationality, and, on the other, conviction or personal desire. It is true that, like Freud himself, sociologists remain convinced that the social order is based upon the triumph of reason and the subordination of desire to rules, and that they are therefore the heirs of the political thinkers of the seventeenth and eighteenth centuries. What is still more important is that they reject ideologies of progress. Sociology was born pessimistic, and Freud's sociological works, which were written in the second half of his life, are part of the same current. Both Freud and sociology are aware that desire and reason are incompatible and that reason implies social rules. If human nature is dual, we have to abandon the idea that there can be some correspondence between institutions and motivations. It is largely irrelevant that this struggle between the individual and civilization is often described in terms that evoke the first wave of Western industrialization and massive proletarianization, rather than the consumer society that will emerge only after the First World War in the United States and only after the Second in Europe. Greater prosperity and the diversification of consumption will simply cure modern society of its initial optimism. As Durkheim reminds us, the advance of modernity leads to diminished happiness and increased dissatisfaction and frustration.

Two Critiques of Modernity

Both liberal and Marxist versions of modernist thought are based upon the assertion that there is a correspondence between the liberation of the individual and historical progress, and both therefore dream of creating a new man in a new society. Nietzsche and Freud, in contrast, destroy the idea of modernity. Is it an overstatement to claim that their destruction of modernism is final, that it is as complete today as it was at the end of the nineteenth century and that the great period of growth that followed the Second World War did not lead to a revival of philosophies of progress? The influence of the Communist Party, especially in France, explains the survival of a highly ideological 'progressivism', but that influence was not great enough to give rise to new expressions of faith in the future. On the contrary, it had the opposite effect and led to a denunciation of the general crisis of capitalism and of relative, or even absolute, pauperization, and this destroyed the socialist belief that faith in the revolutionary working class is inseparable from the economy's natural tendency to evolve towards a greater 'socialization' of production.

Nietzsche and Freud make it impossible to go on seeing the individual as a worker, a consumer or even a citizen. The individual has ceased to be a purely social being and has become a being of desire inhabited by impersonal forces and languages, as well as an individual or private being. This means that the Subject has to be redefined. The Subject was once the link between the individual and a universal such as God, Reason or History; now that God is dead, reason becomes instrumental and history is dominated by absolute States.

Given this situation, how can the individual escape the laws of his interests, which are also the laws of social utility? Most thinkers fall back on the idea that human beings must rediscover, usually through art, their true nature, which has been repressed or perverted by the strengthening of social controls. Life must be turned in to a work of art, and we must rediscover the beauty of the correspondences that unite human beings with the world. Freud was more drawn to the foundation myths of ancient societies, but their discovery is also an aesthetic experience, as the religious objects of those ancient cultures have been bequeathed to us in the form of works of art. Most philosophical critics of modernity are drawn to the return to Being, to the Whole, and that increasingly distances them from the social critique of modernity, which must be based upon a new conception of the Subject, defined as a desire for freedom and a will to be an autonomous social actor.

Whilst their respective critiques of modernity contradict one another, in destroying the myth of modernity, Nietzsche and Freud do revive a dualism that had long been destroyed by the spirit of the Enlightenment and philosophies of progress. Even though their main enemy is Christianity and its definition of the Subject as a human soul created by God in his own image, they contrast Being with action. They are looking for something basic, natural and biological, as opposed to the social, which they see as the ultimate expression of what Nietzsche calls nihilism. Nihilism deprives human beings of all their creativity and projects it in to society, which is modernity's god. There is therefore a conflict between a utilitarian society and individuals driven by the life-force of Eros. Nietzsche and Freud make similar criticisms of modern society, but whereas Nietzsche rejects completely the idea of a Subject and the trend towards subjectivation introduced by Christianity, Freud does not divorce the destruction of the Ego and consciousness from the quest for an I which can reconcile the libido and the law by rejecting both self-destructive desire and the authority of leaders. Which is why this book will constantly move away from Nietzsche, but stay within Freud's shadow.

In a modern society where mobility and indeterminacy have replaced order and 'states', the destruction of the Ego does more than any other transformation to signal the end of classical modernity. For a long time, modern society appeared to be the antithesis of traditional society because it claimed that, rather than having to occupy one particular position, the individual had to identify with a universal reason, and that education would teach children the higher and impersonal values of knowledge and art. Nietzsche and Freud can be regarded as the founders of post-modernism, and thanks to them classical modernity now seems to have more in common with traditional religious society than with the twentieth century's experience of modernity. The reign of reason is still universal, but Tocqueville was quite justified in saying that, in modern society, everything boils down to private life. The triumph of individualism, which is the counterpart to the destruction of the Ego, defines a new modernity, and obliges us to revise the analyses bequeathed us by philosophies of Enlightenment and Progress. To speak of an 'analysis' is in fact inadequate because, as the nineteenth century came to a close, a number of important cultural attitudes became divorced from one another and because the difference between them opened up a boundless field for a cultural critique (*Kulturkritik*).

The most violent reaction, which is dominant in Viennese culture, is the crisis of individual identity. Jacques Le Rider (1990), like Karl Schorske (1980) and a number of others before him, reminds us of the dominant features of this crisis, which basically affected masculine identity and Jewish identity. The destruction of identity created a non-integrated and unstable world of identifications. According to writers like Robert Musil, who was writing slightly later, this indeterminacy of the Ego had both positive and distressing aspects (Musil 1930–3). All were agreed, however, that man was losing his 'qualities', as Musil puts it. He had made a close study of the psychology of Mach, who describes the Ego as being 'beyond redemption' [*Unrettbarisch*]. In sociology, Georg Simmel gave a central role to the replacement of the rational law by the individual.

This extreme individualism is, however, intolerable, as it means that there can be no answer to questions about identity, and no acceptance of personal and social determination. 'Am I a man or a woman' was the question that drove Schreber mad. 'Am I Jewish or German?' was a question that brought more than one Jewish intellectual close to anti-Semitism. The destruction of the Ego means that we can have no intellectual peace of mind, but it leads in two different directions.

The first, and the most important in cultural terms, was the return to the *totality* inaugurated by Schopenauer and then Nietzsche. Robert Musil speaks of a man without qualities in Mach's sense of the term. Master Eckhart used the word in a similar sense when he defined God as 'the being without qualities' and called on man to return to the path that would bring him closer to God and take him beyond all personal and social determinations. Like Nietzsche, Musil attemps to find reconciliation within the totality. The late nineteenth century was dominated by mysticism and by every possible variation on the philosophy of life.

This return to art and to the One appealed only to those who wanted to save their individuality in this way and who saw themselves as geniuses. The exhaustion of both traditionalist society and classical rationalist thought also provoked a broader movement which sought to defend collective identities. It went hand in hand with the rise of nationalisms and resulted in the blinding clarity of Nazism. Women were so defined as to be subordinate to men, Jews so as to be exterminated, and the nation so as to proclaim the superiority of the German race and nation. The intellectual heirs of the Enlightenment fought nationalism, which began in both Vienna and in Paris at the time of the Dreyfus Affair. Yet both liberal intellectuals and nationalists were incapable of overcoming the crisis in modernity. They tried to rediscover the unity of a worldview, be it rationalist or populist. The result was an increasingly pathetic discourse on the one hand, and an increasingly savage baying on the other.

These desperate attempts did nothing to prevent the decay of the rationalist conception of modernity reaching its logical conclusion. We will now examine the exhaustion of the modernist ideology before attempting in part III to find a way out of a crisis affecting both Enlightenment, reason and historical progress.

3

Nation, Company, Consumer

The Actors of Modernization

The intellectual critique of historicist optimism has always been complemented by a historical and practical critique of positivist illusions. According to this critique, modern or industrial society is not reducible to the triumph of computation and rational legal authority; it is the product of companies, is supported by a national consciousness and is increasingly led by consumer demand. None of the three actors of modernization can be reduced to an instrumental action.

Nations are defined in terms of their culture rather than economic action. Companies are as interested in profit and power as in the rational organization of production. Consumer choice is increasingly influenced by various personal factors as a rising standard of living allows us to satisfy needs which are less basic and therefore less influenced by traditional rules and status. The fragmentation of the classical idea of modernity or of the ideology of Enlightenment and progress is as much a product of the rediscovery of these actors as a product of the thought of Nietzsche and Freud. I will attempt to demonstrate in this chapter that each actor – nation, company and consumer – corresponds to one of the cardinal points of this shattered rationalist modernity, just as the anthropologies of the Id elaborated by Nietzsche and Freud occupy the fourth. Theories and practices alike must be regarded as complementary manifestations of the same general cultural crisis: the crisis of modernity. Sexuality, nationalism, profit and needs are indeed forces, and the relations, complementarities and, above all, the oppositions that exist between them are the flesh and blood of industrial society. Those who view modernity simply as the triumph of instrumental rationality are fighting such an impoverished image that they cannot win any real victory and are using theoretical formulations against the action of the real forces that are at work in industrial society: sexuality, nationalism, profit and needs. We must look at every dimension of society and consider its economic practices as well as its philosophical ideas.

Nation

Are the actors of social life the bearers of modernity, or do they obey a different logic of action? It is the first answer that gives classical theories of modernity their force. The nation is modernity's political form because it replaces traditions, customs and privileges with an integrated national space reconstructed by a law inspired by the principles of reason. Similarly, the company is a rational actor, and turns science in to a production technique whose rationalization-effect is judged by the market. As for consumption, it is less and less determined by the state of manners and by the symbolic value that every culture ascribes to certain commodities; it is governed by rational choices between forms of satisfaction which have been reduced to a common denominator, namely the price of commodities and services.

The modernist thesis was expressed most forcefully in connection with the nation, but it is also here that it meets the greatest resistance. The thesis has been widely accepted in France, where Louis Dumont can write (1983: 21): 'The nation is a total society made up of people who consider themselves to be individuals.' But it is a British author who gives it its most elaborate expression. Ernest Gellner (1983) defines a nation as a combination of a political unit and a culture, and demonstrates how modern or industrial societies need a national culture, or in other words a culture which is constructed by and for the nation. It swamps traditional and local cultures which resist change. Yet it is by no means the existence of a national culture that founds the nation and nationalism. The opposite is true: it is the Nation-State which produces a national culture, notably through education. This is a Durkheimean vision in which the national culture has the role of creating a collective consciousness. The State diffuses, spreads and imposes a culture which has already been elaborated and above all, a language which becomes a national language thanks to the educational system, the public administration and the army. This is an eminently rationalist and modernist conception, and its main goal is to combat nationalisms and populisms which claim to make politics serve the nation or people – *Narod* or *Volk* – as though they existed prior to the State. In that respect, Gellner comes close to the French tradition which regards the State – from the kings of France to the

French Revolution and the successive Republics – as having constituted the nation and even France itself. He tends, however, to apply
his thesis mainly to recently-formed nations and criticizes their
favourite theme of the national renaissance. They mistake a birth
[*naissance*] for a renaissance. This general thesis has, however, met
with serious objections, as commercial and industrial modernity
results in the universalist ideas of production, rationalization and the
market rather than the idea of the nation. Many ruling elites have
tried at all cost to insert their countries in to international trade
networks and have had to combat certain forms of economic, social
and cultural life in the attempt. In many cases, those who produce
and disseminate knowledge also rebel against nationalism.

As we move further away from the centres of economic development, we begin to find a divorce between modernity and modernization, and between society and State, as the State is the creator of
modernity and not its manager. It is in the name of national
independence that the State fights foreign enemies and modernizes
the economy and society, as Napoleon did in his struggle against
England and as Emperor Meiji when he began to industrialize Japan
in order to save it from American or Russian domination. Like Japan
and like many countries after them, Germany and Italy associated
modernization with the defence or restoration of a national culture.
When faced with a modernity identified with English trade or the
French language, a nation State's only means of defending its independence was to mobilize its non-modern resources, be they cultural,
social or economic. Just as landowners like the Prussian Junkers and
especially the Japanese Daimyos have often been the driving force
behind capitalist development, it was an appeal to traditional social
loyalties that allowed countries which were later-comers to modernity
to mobilize their resources. This trend has become more and more
pronounced and it culminates in Islamism, which is far removed from
traditionalism or even Muslim pietism. It usually mobilizes modernizing elites, and especially science students and medical students. In
this case, the theme of a national cultural renaissance comes in to
conflict with that of liberal modernity.

Elsewhere, and especially in Latin America, the combination of
nationalism and modernism takes more variable forms. The association between the two gave birth to the continent's only true fascist
movement – *integralismo* – in pre-war Brazil. Elsewhere, the dominant form is the national-populist regime which attempts to involve
broad sectors of the new urban population in political life. Modernizing themes are as important as the appeal to nationalism. Gellner is
therefore right when he states that nationalism comes from above or

from the State, but wrong in that he fails to see that the State has to rely upon history and inherited particularisms in order to mobilize forces capable of resisting the hegemony of the great central powers. Nationalism means the mobilization of the past and tradition in the service of the future and modernity. It opens up a territory's culture or cultures to modernity and rationalization, but it also constructs a national being which is modernizing rather than modern. The further the country is away from the centres of modernity and the more it feels threatened by a foreign imperialism, the more nationalism becomes attached to its origins and traditions. The nation is not the political figure of *modernity*; it is the main actor of *modernization*. This means that it is a non-modern actor and the creator of a modernity which it will both try to control and relinquish to some extent in exchange for the internationalization of its production and consumption.

Having examined the centre's view of the periphery, we must also look at the periphery's view of the centre. Africans and Latin Americans quite rightly suspect that not everything that comes to them from Great Britain, France or America is an expression of modernity. Those countries also export colonial domination and often impose cultural models which are quite simply alien. When the French taught Algerians about 'Our ancestors the Gauls', or when the United States supplied Latin American universities with textbooks that discussed the agriculture of Kansas and not that of the Altiplano, how could anyone mistake colonialism for modernization? This was simply a matter of conquest. It was only because they were so arrogant that the dominant countries could identify their nationalism with the universalism of reason.

These modernizing nationalisms are now largely a thing of the past, as the economy and culture are increasingly transnational, not that that prevents certain countries – the United States today and, perhaps, Japan tomorrow – from having cultural control over most of the news that is broadcast across the planet. There has therefore been a violent break between modernization and nationalism for a long time. Nations, which are non-modern agents of modernization, are increasingly becoming forces which resist modernization and disseminate openly anti-universalist ideas, culminating in the assertion of the absolute superiority of particular cultures or even races. This inversion of the alliance between the nation and modernity took extreme forms as industrialization progressed in nineteenth- and twentieth-century Europe. The large-scale industrialization of Germany in the late nineteenth century resulted in the rise of a nationalism which had a profound influence in intellectual circles, especially after Bismarck.

Weber was both a liberal – he was opposed to anti-Semitism – and a nationalist. Anti-Semitism replaced anti-Judaism when the rejection of a Jewish culture confined to the *shtetls* of Eastern Europe gave way to fear of the emancipated Jew who was identified with the universalism of science, trade and art. German and French nationalism became anti-Semitic in order to defend traditional national cultures which were steeped in history against a rationalism which was supposedly rootless and pernicious. The outcome was the Nazi policy of extermination and the Vichy government's discriminatory and repressive measures.

It was therefore only in highly specific situations – that of the entry in to modernity of pioneering nations like Great Britain, France and, a little later, the United States – that the nation was identified with a new openness and the abolition of cultural barriers and traditions. The alliance between nation and modernity rapidly became more complex wherever modernization ceased to be liberal and became voluntaristic, and wherever it mobilized the past in order to construct the future rather than simply opening up the nation to the winds of change. The nationalist consciousness has finally turned against modernity: it has become fundamentalist and rejects as foreign agents or satanic forces all those who do not identify completely with a cultural heritage which is often interpreted in biological terms.

How can anyone fail to see that the modern industrial world is not a vast machine, but a constellation of dominant and dominated nations which are either confident or doubtful about their ability simultaneously to retain their identities and to participate more fully in international trade. Auguste Comte thought that the growth of industry would make war ridiculous: improving industrial productivity would produce more wealth than conquest. History proved him wrong, just as it proved wrong all those who believed that the universal values of reason would increasingly replace social, cultural and national particularisms. The actors of history are more than agents of modernity. The great idea of the modernists – that there would be a correspondence between system and actor in modern society as the actors internalized society's norms – has been inverted and overtaken by historical reality. The old is used to create the new, and particularisms are used both to promote and resist universalism, despite the widespread intellectual conviction that modernization meant a transition from particularism to universalism, from belief to reason. A social actor can never be reduced to a function of a system, just as a society is never merely a link in a history whose meaning must be deciphered by philosophers or economists. The divorce between modernity and the actors of a modernizing society may be either partial or complete, but it lies at the origin of the crisis of the classical ideology of modernism, which was based upon the assertion that there was an absolute correspondence between the two.

The divorce between a universalist modernity and modernization, which takes particular national or local roads and mobilizes particularist resources, takes a more radical form in the late twentieth century than it did in the last century, when it was still possible for the Austro-Marxists, in particular, to attempt to reconcile the social question and the national question. There are fewer and fewer national roads to modernization, as modernity increasingly divorces flows of wealth and information on the world market, from identification with a cultural and social ensemble. Public space and even social and political life are in danger of being destroyed by the gulf that is opening up between economic and cultural modes of behaviour, between the objectivity of the market and the subjective consciousness of belonging. Unlike the Germans and the Japanese of the last century, the Québécois do not dream of creating a national economy. On the contrary, and like Europe's Flemings and Catalans, they want to combine direct participation in the North American economy with a defence of their cultural identity. In similar fashion, although the Slovenes and Croats have demanded independence, their intention is to become part of the single European market before the Macedonians and Montenegrins do so.

Nationalism is especially dangerous when it becomes an instrument in the hands of a modernizing, authoritarian and nationalist State which appeals to the artificially reconstructed idea of the *Volk* to produce, at best, a National State or, at worst, a totalitarian power in the name of *Ein Volk, Ein Reich, Ein Führer* (one People, one State, one Leader). The assertion that there is some correspondence between modernity and nation, in both its colonial and its nationalist form, has had a destructive effect, whereas the divorce between economic modernity and national consciousness, which can certainly divide society in to two superimposed and quasi-autarkic zones has not had such tragic effects. This dissociation seems to me to be an important aspect of the shattering of the classical idea of modernity and of conceptions of modernization which regarded industrialization, democratization and the formation of nation States as three interdependent aspects of a single general process. Both liberals like Seymour Martin Lipset and Marxists like Eric Hobsbawm (1990) still cling to this idea, but it must be firmly rejected. On the contrary, the idea that there is an increasing divorce between the supposed attributes of a rationalization which can be identified with modernity, is much more in keeping with the modern world.

Company

It seems more difficult not to regard the company as the agent of modernity, defined as rationalization. The management of a company implies efficient production, an ability to respond to demands expressed through the market, a search for the highest possible profit and the diversification of investments, and all these acts appear to be so many applications of economic rationality. Yet doubts begin to arise when one thinks of the minor role given to the company in analyses of economic activity. Discussion initially focused on capital, economic cycles and, to a lesser extent, the effects of technological innovation on economic activity. The second period in the analysis of production was dominated by the idea of rationalization. Yet from Taylor and Ford to the golden age of American business schools in the 1950s and 1960s, the factory was seen purely as the concrete context for modernization. Experts advised management to apply the principles of Enlightenment rationalism, to define functions and hierarchical levels, to plan the flow of information, ideas, commodities and men, or in a word to introduce order and clarity in to companies which were becoming ever more complex. Management science, which spread from the United States to Europe after the Second World War, therefore applied general values to particular situations, and even made great use of case-studies. But was the idea of the company central during this period, which marked the apotheosis of American industry? Not at all. Taylor and Ford regarded the shop floor and work stations as the main focus for their interventions, and management theory talked, not about companies, but about *organizations*, and thus replaced a real economic actor with general principles. In a rather different mode, there was much talk, in both the public and the private sector, of the role of the technocrats whose technical, administrative or financial knowledge made them professional experts on production. The rationalizers and organizers were the real agents of economic activity, and the idea of the company was marginalized.

At the same time, a very different image of the company was also beginning to emerge. It denied that the factory had any importance in itself, and viewed it as the site of a class struggle and of the workers' movement. There was a struggle between labour and capitalist profit, between craft autonomy and working-class culture, and an economic power. That power was expressed through class barriers, authoritarian forms of command, and a divorce between conception and execution which was not simply the product of scientific management, but rather the expression of class rule. The workers' movement and the factory were always seen as conflicting or mutually hostile realities. The workers' movement existed both at the level of the workplace, the work station and the shop floor, and at the level of society as a whole. It set class against class, not in the way that one culture or social group is set against another, but in the way that one social mode of utilizing industry, machines and labour organization comes in to conflict with another. That is why, when it was strong, the workers' movement encouraged both direct confrontation – direct-action syndicalism, which is often described as revolutionary syndicalism – and a political struggle between socialism and capitalism. The factory was non-existent at either level of collective action. It played a secondary role in the eyes of both technical and financial managers and wage earners, who saw it merely as a manifestation of a class society. It is because this vision, which elevated trade-unionism in to a social movement, does not correspond to contemporary realities that the company can now be seen as an autonomous economic actor.

The company is no longer regarded as a concrete expression of capitalism; increasingly, it is seen as a strategic unit in a competitive international market and as an agent for using new technologies. It is best defined in terms of the management of markets and technologies rather than in terms of rationalization or class rule. The transition from an analysis based on social classes or rationalization to one defined in strategic terms completely changes the way we look at the company. If we speak of rationalization and class conflict, we retain the classical image of modernity and its social applications; when, in contrast, the company is defined in military–'strategic' terms rather than industrial terms, the actor is much more than an agent of modernization.

Joseph Schumpeter attached great importance to the role of the entrepreneur (Schumpeter 1912). His argument borders on the paradoxical when he describes capitalism as becoming a slave to routine because competition is lowering the rate of profit. Capitalism is condemned to death and must eventually be replaced by a planned economy. In Schumpeter's view it survives only because of the intervention of entrepreneurs who reintroduce the warrior values of the aristocracy in to a humdrum world. They are primarily agents of innovation. As a result of the clash between the industrial armies of America and Japan, and the victory of the latter, our vision of the factory is changing rapidly. Whilst American enterprise was channelled in to both rationalization and the market or flexibility, Japanese enterprise sees itself quite literally as *enterprise*. It prioritizes the definition of its goals and then mobilizes its technical and human resources in order to achieve them. The attempt to integrate the company leads to a reduced social differentiation at work, but that does not rule out authoritarian labour relations. Once we begin to speak of a business strategy rather than of general rules of rationalization, the company becomes a crucial actor in social life, and our analysis can no longer simply view it as the basic unit of the capitalist system. Hence the growing divorce between a highly formalized macro-economics, which is useful for decision-making at government level, and a micro-economics which has more in common with management studies and the sociological approach. The central theme of this chapter is the divorce between the study of the system and the study of actors. The distinction applies at the level of company, nation and consumption, and it is designed to destroy our image of modernity, or the idea that actors are defined in terms of their conformity or non-conformity to the meaning or direction of History, which will bring about the gradual triumph of rationality.

Consumption

It is in this domain that it is most difficult to conceptualize the break between system and actors. Our thinking about consumption has long been dominated by two types of explanation. According to one, consumption can be represented as a sliding scale with essential commodities such as food at one extreme and with commodities involving the greatest freedom of choice, such as leisure, at the other extreme. Clothing and housing come somewhere in between. According to the other, consumption is the language of social levels. We all believe that our tastes are determined by our position in society and our tendency to either upward or downward mobility; consumption appears to be strictly determined by social status. This representation, like the representation that reduced the nation or the company to forms of modernity, was quite in keeping with a definition of modernity appropriate to a productivist society. Those who insist that there is a close and direct connection between modernity and rationalization have always denounced the consumer society in an attempt to defend the idea of a productivist society based upon labour, the rational organization of production, savings and national integration. Hence the success of Weber's essay on the relationship between protestantism and capitalism (Weber 1904–5). The reassuring thing about Weber's image of capitalism was its asceticism: consumption was sacrificed to science and the cult of objective reason. For a long time, our image of modernity was associated with the Christian idea of renunciation and the simple life, and with a distrust of pleasure. Both State schools and Church schools taught us to control our desires in order to become good workers, good citizens, good fathers and, *a fortiori*, good mothers. The similarities between the language they used were greater than the differences between them. It is also true that for a long time – most of the nineteenth century – industrialization had no great impact on modes of consumption, and that Fourastié (1950) could describe the post-war period as *les trente glorieuses* because it was characterized by a very high level of saving and investment. It is also true that, throughout this period, the needs met by production related primarily to material domestic amenities, and were therefore inscribed mainly within the context of an industrial society. It was only after 1968 – the date has been chosen for its symbolic value – that the countries of Western Europe began to enter the consumer society the United States had entered much earlier, or in other words after the great depression and the war.

This transformation is so recent and so far-reaching that we have yet to assimilate it. The word 'consumption' still has negative connotations, whereas 'production' has positive connotations, and rationalist theories of consumption – both positive and criticial – are stepping up their efforts to make consumption an attribute of either a standard of living or of the mode of the system's dominance and control over actors.

Such rearguard actions are futile. It is impossible to reduce consumption to self-interest or social status. It is also influenced by seduction, and by a retreat in to tribalism and narcissism, and none of these aspects can be reduced to the image of a social pyramid based upon production.

What might be called traditional consumption, which was subordinate to productive activities, had three main goals: reproducing labour-power, symbolizing status, and relating to the non-utilitarian world of ideas. Although it is obviously not unrelated to income, so-called mass consumption also has three aspects: physical and cultural reproduction gives way to the formation of new communities or tribes. The social hierarchy of patterns of consumption is disrupted by the birth of Toffler's 'prosumer', or in other words a consumer who is also the productive company's finality; school or university students, hospital patients and television audiences are all 'prosumers'. The appeal to high culture is, finally, transformed in to a defence and affirmation of the individual personality. Both the old and the new modes of consumption can be either defensive, imitative or liberating. For the purposes of our analysis, however, the important point is that, as the world of consumption changes, the consumer becomes divorced from his or her position in the social order and the actor becomes divorced from the system. More so than any other social change, our entry in to the consumer society means that we are leaving modern society, as the best way to define modern society is to say that modes of behaviour are defined by the actor's position – before, after, above, below – within the process of modernization. The social and economic armature of behaviour suddenly cracks and actors are situated in relation to themselves and to messages sent out by an enormous audience, or by their membership of restricted primary groups. When he speaks of a society of the simulacrum or of signifiers without signifieds, Baudrillard exaggerates the extent to which we have broken with modernity, but his formulations do have the virtue of stressing a loss of social references which other interpretations try to deny or conceal. The actor is no longer, as Weber thought, reason or tradition. The actor is in search of himself. He is a seducer, a *groupie*, a spectator, an inhabitant of the ecosystem or a member of a gang.

This world of consumption is as alien to the world of the company as it is to the world of the nation. It has much more in common with the world of the libido, even though it is much further removed from it than those who speak of the eroticization of consumption think. Eros, the nation, the company and consumption are the shattered fragments of a modernity which once meant rationalization and the identification of human beings with their social roles. The logic of production and that of consumption are now quite foreign to one another. It is only – at least in their official ideologies – in the caricatural communist societies that are collapsing before our very eyes that there is any correspondence between the two. We are as afraid of the idea of a *society* in which every element corresponds to every other element as we are of an educational system which merely trains us for social roles.

The idea of modernity replaced God with society. Durkheim is quite explicit about this – more so than anyone else. The crisis of modernity is now leading to the disappearance of the idea of *society*. That idea was once a unifying principle, and even the principle of good, whereas evil was defined as anything that hindered social integration. We had to play our parts, fulfil our functions, and we also had to know how to welcome newcomers and re-educate deviants. The idea of modernity has always been associated with the construction of society: a mechanical society was transformed in to an organism, in to a social body whose every organ contributed to its smooth workings. Society was both a sacred body and an eternal soul which could transform savages in to civilized human beings, warriors in to citizens, and violence in to law. This representation has not vanished, and it still colours official discourses, but it has lost its power. For the most part, we believe in the need for public order and for social rules. We are as afraid of violence as we are of loneliness, but we have also learned to defend individuals against citizens and society, and to refer to what we once called integration as control or manipulation.

The shattering of modernity in to four fragments scattered to the four cardinal points of social life is also a fourfold liberation movement. Nietzsche and Freud asserted the rights of Eros in the face of social laws and moralization; national gods rise up and resist the universalism of the market; industrial and banking empires – the lords of industrial society – become concentrated and assert their desire for conquest and power in the face of the frigid advice of textbooks on management; desires escape social controls because they are no longer associated with a social position. Such is the social scene that was born of the decay of the model which identified modernity with the triumph of reason.

Technology

Is this fragmentation complete? If it were, modernity would be a thing of the past. It is not complete and the situation I am describing must be defined simply as a century-long crisis within modernity. Although I have on a number of occasions spoken of post-modern thought, usually with reference to Nietzsche and Freud, that was no more than a way of stressing the importance of the divorce they inaugurated. It would be paradoxical to describe as 'post-modern' a period which everyone regards as the period of the triumph of modernity. The truth lies midway between that over-superficial image and the idea that the critique of modernity had already triumphed by the end of the nineteenth century. This crisis situation must be precisely defined. The fragmentation and decline of objective reason leads to a gradual divorce between four cultural worlds: Eros, consumption, the company and the nation, but the four are connected by instrumental reason, though it would be more accurate to speak of technology. This is in line with the visions of Weber and Horkheimer. Reason is now purely instrumental: the rationality of means has replaced the end-oriented rationality characteristic of an industrial society which gave central importance to the production and large-scale distribution of capital equipment and consumer goods. What functionalist sociologists call 'the social system' is no more than a technical apparatus, and social actors are only partially integrated in to it. Weber stressed this point when, like Kant before him, he spoke of the divorce between moral values and instrumental reason, and when he evoked the 'war between the gods', which is also a war between firms and nations that continues as technology develops. That is technology's positive role: it protects everyone against cultural totalitarianisms.

This technical world does not exist in isolation; it ensures communications between the various cultural worlds. Without it, they would all become introverted, and in the final chapter of part II, we will describe post-modernity as a complete dissociation between technology and these cultural worlds, which now cease to be bound up with an instrumental action. Nations can assert their independence and difference; they must also run an administration, organize production and consumption and equip armies. All that implies a reliance upon technology, even in the case of theocratic or fundamentalist regimes. Companies are primarily agents of economic change rather than organizations, but they are also sets of production and communication techniques, even though our modern golden boys reduce the business world to financial deals and are oblivous to the requirements of production. Rational calculation is still present in the domain of consumption, as are choices expressing our personalities or cultural preferences. Nietzsche and Freud, finally, are far from being anti-rationalists. Nietzsche in particular has an aesthetic conception of the will to power and sees in the uncontrolled expression of feeling the triumph of moralization, and therefore the destruction of the ethics of the strong. For his part, Freud contrasts the pleasure principle and the reality principle, but not in order to free the latter from the former. On the contrary, he contrasts them in order to preserve the tense relationship between the two, and his way of treating neuroses is rationalist and diametrically opposed to more recent methods designed to promote the free expression of deep drives. Such methods belong to a post-modern culture in which the instrumental and the expressive are dissociated or even quite alien to one another.

In schematic terms, modernity can be defined as follows. Instrumentality is the linchpin, but it is not modernity's integrating principle. Followers – and opponents – of the Frankfurt School who claim that technology is industrial society's only legitimizing principle and that it is therefore technocratic, are therefore mistaken. This is indeed a strange idea when we apply it to a century which has seen Hitler and Stalin, Mao and Fidel Castro, and Roosevelt and de Gaulle, to mention only a few major political leaders who were quite clear about the source of their legitimacy. Can any concrete society or country be said to be governed by a technocracy? A Soviet-style *nomenklatura* is the antithesis of a technocracy; economic choices and careers are sub-ordinated to the power of the political apparatus. Similarly, under capitalism, the search for profit does not always lead to the develop-ment of the productive forces. On this point, the Marxists are right and all those who, like James Burnham, denounce the managerial revolution in superficial terms, are wrong. The theme of 'technology triumphant' is no more than an error of judgement on the part of those who, be they leftists or hyper-liberals, see in modernity only the replacement of objective reason by subjective reason. Modern society may well be in crisis but it is also alive with warring gods and warring techniques. And the violent upheavals of the twentieth century should make us wary of the image that puts scientists – or, in more general terms, professionals – at the top of the social pyramid, when they are in fact technicians and play a much more modest role. The dangerous thing about this ideology is that it suggests that modern society is no more than a field of forces from which actors have been eliminated, whereas modernity, crisis or no crisis, abounds in actors who proclaim their convictions, fight their enemies and call for the renaissance of the past and the creation of the future.

In a more limited form, this ideology has helped to sustain the technological determinism which often finds its way in to the expression 'industrial society'. It suggests that technology determines the professional and, above all, the social division of labour, rather as though society were a vast company. As a young reseacher, I argued against this theme and demonstrated that the scientific management labour and rationalization, which is a central element in industrial production, meant that the system of production, in all its economic and social aspects, dominated labour and destroyed its autonomy, and that this invasion of the world of the skilled worker explained the rise of the workers' movement (Touraine 1955).

Georges Friedmann (1963) criticized my position, which was based on shop-floor observations, mainly at the Renault factory, for its failure to see that, in industrial society, what he termed the techno-logical environment and, more generally, technological civilization, enjoyed an increasing autonomy from social relations of production. We live in a world of production techniques and, increasingly, communication techniques which distract us from our true concerns and condemn us to 'diversion'. I use Pascal's phrase because this is indeed a religious critique which contrasts the spiritual and contem-plative needs of the soul with the instrumentalism and utilitarianism of technical civilization. Witness the recurrent calls for the supplement of the soul that is supposedly needed by a society which is so powerful in material terms and so poor in spiritual terms.

Georges Friedmann's work has played such an important role in thinking about industrial society that he deserves a careful answer, especially now that his main themes have been adopted and reinterpreted by ecologist ideologies. I fear that it surrenders too easily to the post-modernist temptation, which is so conspicuous in the work of the Frankfurt School, to reduce modernity to technology, rather as though social actors, their power relations and their cultural preferences, could be dissolved in a sea of technology. This argument is a good answer to the schematic Marxism which sees industrial society simply as a mask for capitalist profit and reduces social conflicts to a war between contradictory interests. We do live in an industrial society *too*, and not simply in a capitalist society or a national society, but the distinguishing feature of the industrial society that replaced the pre-industrial rationalism of a market and statist society, is that, as Marx was the first to realize, it gives class relations and social relations the form of a technical organization of labour. If we do have to adopt Georges Friedmann's analysis of technological civilization, it is not because it allows us to avoid analysing social relations, but for the opposite reason. He helps to introduce the idea that the central conflict is no longer one between reason and belief, but one between the personal Subject and the apparatuses of production, management and communication. That vision is rejected or despised by all those who want to eradicate the social actor and the Subject and try to persuade us that we live in a crystalized society with an intangible structure and hierarchy, and which, like the societies of ants or bees, devotes all its energies to controlling its members. Georges Friedmann is right to say that labour does not simply mean that proletarians are exploited by capitalists or bureaucrats; at a deeper level, it also means that the personal Subject is alienated and loses its ability to construct and defend its identity because of rules which are often, and on inadequate grounds, described as scientific, and because of the apparatuses of power. It is because our society is technology-based that power is not instrumental, that it is exercised through violence, the search for profits and power, and the spirit of conquest. We have not moved from a traditional society based upon privilege, to a modern society based, for better or worse, on technology. We live in a society in which means were completely divorced from ends. Far from determining or absorbing ends, the same means could therefore be used for both good and evil ends, for both reducing inequality and exterminating minorities. The increasingly dense networks of techniques and signs in which we now live, and which orient and govern the ways in which we behave, by no means imprison us in a technological world and by no means destroy social actors. They impose neither a logic of efficacy and production nor a logic of control and reproduction. The image of technocracy triumphant is pathetically inadequate if we contrast it with the increase in consumption, the rise of nationalisms and the might of transnational companies.

4

Intellectuals Against Modernity

Intellectuals inspired the trend towards rationalization by associating the progress of science with a critique of past institutions and beliefs. From the Medici era onwards, intellectuals were quite prepared to serve enlightened princes, regardless of their authoritarianism. After centuries of modernism, however, relations between intellectuals and history underwent an inversion in the twentieth century. There are two reasons for this, and they are contradictory rather than complementary. The first is that modernity became mass production and mass consumption, and that the pure world of reason was invaded by crowds who made the instruments of modernity serve the most mediocre, even the most irrational, demands. The second is that, in the twentieth century, the world of modern reason became subordinate to modernization policies and nationalist dictatorships. Many intellectuals, especially in France but also in the United States, tried to preserve their traditional alliance with 'progressive forces' as long as possible. The colonial wars waged by their countries, especially in Indochina and Algeria, led them to defend national liberation movements. They did so with courage and conviction, and opposed the governments of their own countries. Yet at the same time they clung in varying degrees to the idea that regimes born of an anticapitalist or anti-imperialist struggle were 'progressive'. They therefore displayed a strange indulgence or even a blind sympathy to the most repressive Communist regimes, and some made extremely serious errors of judgement about Mao's cultural revolution or terrorist activity in Western Europe. Yet it soon became clear, even to the most backward of them, that they had to stop supporting these bad causes. Many intellectuals then discovered, especially after 1968, a new philosophy of history in antimodernism. They burned their old idols and denounced the modern world because it had destroyed reason. This satisfied both their anti-mass elitism and their hostility towards modernizing dictatorships. In the 1970s in particular, antimodernism became dominant and almost hegemonic.

Whereas the intellectuals of the mid nineteenth century were inspired by a dream of the future, those of the mid twentieth century are overwhelmed by a sense of impending disaster and by the conviction that everything is meaningless and that there are no more social actors. They once believed that ideas ruled the world; they are now reduced to denouncing the irresistible rise of barbarism, absolute power or State monopoly capitalism.

Intellectual life thus became divorced from social life and intellectuals became trapped in to an overall critique of modernity which both led them to an extreme radicalism and marginalized them to an increasing extent. For the first time in a long time the social, cultural and political transformations that are occurring in the world seem to defy analysis: whilst the information supplied by the experts is indispensable, it does not in itself produce the interpretations that intellectuals seem incapable of supplying. Before we go on to explore the extreme forms of the decay of the modernist ideology, we must describe how intellectuals drifted in to antimodernism.

Horkheimer and the Frankfurt School

The most important intellectual group was undoubtedly the Institute for Social Research (*Institut für Sozialforschung*), even though it no longer existed when its influence, which was for a long time limited by exile, finally began to spread. The Institute was founded in Frankfurt in 1923 and Max Horkheimer was its director from 1931 until his return to Germany after the war. The history of the Institute and its main researchers has been written by Martin Jay (1973) and others.

The Frankfurt School takes as its starting point what it sees as the obvious divorce between praxis and thought, between political action and philosophy. Horkheimer and his friends therefore reject both Weimar's social-democratic reformism and Bolshevik power in the Soviet Union. They do not recognize the existence of any historical actors – not even the proletariat or Lukács's vision of the Party – and therefore inaugurate a total critique of modern society and especially of its culture. They distance themselves from political and social reality to such a degree that these Jewish intellectuals who had been forced in to exile wrote little about the Jewish problem. Their most important studies of anti-Semitism appeared as part of their famous study of the authoritarian personality (Adorno et al. 1950), which owes at least as much to the American human sciences as it does to their own insights. It was not begun until 1944, and was not published until 1950.

The Frankfurt School philosophers take the view that the world in which they live has seen the collapse of objective reason, or in other words of the rationalist worldview. It might be said that they regret the capitalism of old, which could sustain the great trend towards rationalization, whereas the world of economic crisis, which is also the world of large-scale industry and Taylorism as well as Nazism and Stalinism, is simply a world of power and money. It is dedicated to the pursuit of material interests which are destroying the life of the mind, and acknowledges no higher principle of rationality. Individualism is the enemy of reason, which is the fundamental form of Being. Ever since Locke and all the utilitarians, subjective reason had been replacing ideas with ideologies which serve the interests of profit, and the universalism of the Enlightenment with the triumph of particularisms, and especially nationalisms. The correspondence between individual and society, which was once guaranteed by reason, has disappeared. The break is of course an old one, and dates back to the time of Socrates. It became more pronounced in the early modern period, notably with the figure of Hamlet, but in the twentieth century it affects everything. Modern man no longer acts in accordance with the universal rules of reason. In his *Critique of Instrumental Reason*, Horkheimer writes (1974: vii): 'Reason for a long period meant the activity of understanding and assimilating the eternal ideas which were to function as goals for men. Today, on the contrary, it is not only the business but the essential role of reason to find means for the goals one adopts at any given time.' He then accuses Weber of having celebrated the triumph of functional rationality over substantive rationality, which is tantamount to accepting the decline of objective rationality and the triumph of instrumental rationality. To adopt the dichotomy introduced by Walter Benjamin, who was close to the Institute, creative experience (*Erfahrung*) has been replaced by lived experience (*Erlebnis*). Having been divorced from reason, the individual Subject is becoming dependent upon political and economic power. Means replace ends, whereas theories of objective reason 'aimed at evolving a comprehensive system, or hierarchy, of all things, including man and his aims. The degree of reasonableness of a man's life could be determined according to its harmony with this totality' (Horkheimer 1974: 4). The disenchantment of the modern world described by Weber is not merely a matter of the disappearance of myths and the sacred, which were themselves products of reason. It is the unity of the world that has been lost. Human beings have to recover the positive freedom that Hegel and Marx dreamed of, and must not be content with the negative freedom defended by Locke and Kant and which protects individuals against the encroachments of power. Positive freedom means the ability to act in accordance with the universal rules of reason or, as Horkheimer puts it in 1942, the Greek *polis* without slavery. In terms that prefigure Michel Foucault, Horkheimer denounces the modern tendency towards subjectivation: 'The awakening of the self is paid for by the acknowledgement of power as the principle of all relations' (Horkheimer and Adorno 1973: 9). Philosophies of the Subject lead to resignation; nothing is more dangerous than the claims of an individualism which pays no attention to the organization of society and forces us to choose between an abstract morality and violence. A fully developed individual is the accomplished perfection of a fully developed society.

The history of modernity is the history of the slow but inevitable divorce between individual, society and nature. Augustinianism eventually triumphed over Thomism and Christianity, then based itself upon the triumph of the personal Subject and exploited it to establish its own moralizing power, and to subordinate the individual to society. In this modern society, individuals who have been isolated by the breakup of the family are at the mercy of social powers, just as cinema-goers are manipulated by the culture industry, whereas the theatre appealed to reason. According to Horkheimer, intellectual activity consists in understanding the order of the world and not its evolution. The cinema destroys the distance created by great drama and by music, and its main goal is to integrate the individual in to the crowd. It is, however, true that Leo Lowenthal takes a more qualified view in his essays (Lowenthal 1961) and recognizes that the cinema and mass culture do offer a taste of happiness. But all the Frankfurt School philosophers regard mass culture as a tool for repression and therefore enslavement, and not as a form of sublimation.

This way of thinking does not merely result in a general critique of modernity; it is also the history of a gradual rejection of Marxist optimism. Until 1933, Horkheimer, like Marx, still believed that labour and production represented the triumph of reason, as opposed to capitalist profit, and that political history was therefore the history of the removal of social obstacles to the triumph of reason. Having seen the impotence and liquidation of the German labour movement, and having then realized that Stalinism had replaced Nazism as the agent for the destruction of historical actors, he rejected the very image of the realm of freedom and devoted his intellectual energies to the realm of necessity. His re-enunciation of the realm of freedom is the defining feature of his critical theory, which he refuses to turn in to a positive theory of liberty and liberation. Horkheimer's work represents the end of historicism and its faith in our progress towards happiness and freedom. Being reluctant to abandon the hopes placed in the light of reason, he takes the view that, whilst it may have set individuals free, it is also destroying them by subordinating them to technological developments, and that the reign of instrumental reason has destroyed subjectivity. Habermas criticizes Horkheimer and Adorno for retreating in to pessimism and for reducing reason to instrumentality, but Horkheimer's central experience is not that of the success of technocracy: it lies in the triumph of the totalitarian powers that reduce society to a building site, and then a labour camp. The identification of reason with technology and absolute domination is the central principle of Horkeimer's thought and, differences between individual members notwithstanding, it is central to all the work of the Institute. Thought itself is the only possible defence against the dominance of technocratic power. Neither ethics, law nor art escape the decay. Only thought, defined as the ability to problematize (*Denken*) or as experimentation or the controlled reproduction of phenomena (*Mimesis*), escapes the grasp of power. Which leaves no hope for those who are not protected by their intellectual abilities.

Let us trace the two main strands in this critique. According to the first, industrialization leads to society's domination not only by Taylorism, but by Nazism and Stalinism, which transform society in to one vast factory and impose a discipline modelled on that of the shop floor upon everyone and every aspect of life. Horkheimer and Adorno often mourn the old world of trade in which economic activity was based upon computation and forecasts, or in other words on a rational activity and not the domination of actors. As it becomes more advanced, capitalism increasingly eliminates both rational thought and feelings of pity and compassion. Sade's *Juliette* provides the model for modern society: woman-nature is dominated by a man-reason who has foresaken love for *jouissance*, and whose goals are purely instrumental.

I find it astonishing that these ideas have been so widely accepted. Taylorist and Fordist production methods have been used in the United States and the Soviet Union, in France and in Nazi Germany. In all cases, they subjected wage-earners to domination in both social and professional terms, and thus provoked the spontaneous resistance of the workers' movement. They are not, however, responsible for the existence of authoritarian political regimes, as they have been used by very different types of regime. The idea that society has become a huge factory and that the consumer is controlled and manipulated to the same extent as the worker is a moralistic theme which no sociologist can accept.

It is impossible to accept these aristocratic criticisms of mass society, as though majority access to production education and consumption led to a general fall in standards and as though it also automatically produced authoritarian regimes. Historians and sociologists long ago pointed out the mistakes of those who believed that Nazism could be explained in terms of the rootlessness of an urban and industrialized mass society. On the contrary, the dictatorship's most enthusiastic supporters came from categories with strong roots in society.

We have to reject the idea that industrialism is responsible for the chaos and violence of the twentieth century. It is essential to challenge the idea of progress with a critique of industrial society but it is a mistake to assume that all elements in a historical society are totally interdependent. It is the absence of historical actors capable of transforming one of the important aspects of this society that explains the development of a purely critical school of thought and, above all, the idea that modern and industrial society is to be rejected as a whole. In a study of Goethe's *Elective Affinities*, Walter Benjamin writes: 'It is only for the sake of those without hope that hope is given to us' (cited, Marcuse 1964: 201). This is a terrible and dangerous idea. Do we have to accept that workers, colonized peoples and the defenceless poor have nothing to hope for and cannot be actors in their own history? And do we therefore have to argue that intellectuals can act on their behalf? This is the formula that revolutionary vanguards and intellectuals used to speak in the name of people who were supposedly too alienated to be able to express themselves. If the workers really are no more than victims, then democracy is impossible and we have to place our trust in the absolute power of those who have a mission to understand and act. The Taylorism that divorced hand from brain is child's play compared to the creation of an infinite distance between the people and those who supposedly interpret history.

The second basic idea behind this critique is that the appeal to subjectivity necessarily subordinates the individual to society's masters. It suggests that if individuals were left to themselves, and were deprived of the support of God or the Logos, they would be like putty on which the dominant forces could print messages corresponding to their own interests. Yet why reject the idea that individuals can be something other – and something more – than consumers, that they can at once seek freedom and attempt to relate to other individuals on an affective and intellectual basis? I readily accept that these expressions create more problems than they solve. It is the idea that individualism can be reduced to passive consumption and manipulation that I cannot accept. Human beings have often been forced to submit to those who spoke in the name of God, reason or history. By what right can those who regret the disappearance of these metasocial references assert that individuals cannot become Subjects who create their Egos through various relations with self and others? Horkheimer is in mourning for a lost historicism, for his lost faith in Hegel and Marx; he sees in modernity only the sound and the fury, and turns to Being and to the objective reason that once preserved the world order. He objects to modernity because it is destroying Being by involving it in a mobility which is not even a process of becoming. This deep pessimism is obviously the result of the destruction of hopes which, because of the tragedy of Nazi Germany, could never be fulfilled. When he claims that Freud's scorn for human beings is not more than a manifestation of the despairing love which may be the only love left to us, Horkheimer is talking about himself.

The Frankfurt School had and has considerable influence, as a society dominated by mass production, mass consumption and mass communications does tend to reduce individuals to playing roles defined for them by others. This modern form of dependency is quite different to that of the traditional societies which subordinated individuals to rules and rites, but it is just as fearful. It does, on the other hand, have to be said that it is less restrictive and that the image of a machine-society subject to strict determinants corresponds to old rather than new representations of science. The pessimism of Horkheimer and his friends reflects the disappearance or perversion of historical actors during a period in which it was impossible to speak of a German workers' movement and when it was obscene to describe the Kremlin's dictators as 'guiding' the proletariat. If that is the case, is not the image they give of society simply its dark side? Is it not an image of a society without social actors, social movements and democracy? And, rather than rejecting technological civilization, should we not be pursuing the critique of social domination and making a truly *political* critique of the destruction of democracy?

Horkheimer mourns not so much the great hopes of Hegelian historicism as the stability of a bourgeois world whose order was based upon faith in reason and science. The critical theory developed by the Frankfurt School subsequently became an intellectual support for many who challenged the dominance of big capitalism, and especially of what the Germans call late capitalism (*Spätkapitalismus*), in which there is an increasingly close connection between economic and political power. But the conflation of the social critique and the cultural critique is based upon a serious misunderstanding. There is almost no trace of a social critique in Horkheimer's thought, but the cultural critique is everywhere. This is even more pronounced in the writings of Adorno or the work of his contemporary, Thomas Mann. The spirit of the Enlightenment, which closely associated individualism with reason, and freedom with intellectual rigour, has been destroyed, and the world has collapsed in to chaos. Max Weber worried about the effects of secularization, but he remained above all a modernist and a liberal. Horkheimer lost the faith in instrumental reason that Weber retained, and he lived in a world that was ablaze, whereas it was only at the end of his life that Weber witnessed the great upheaval of the First World War and the rise of revolutionary movements in Germany. The Frankfurt School's pessimism is an indication of a profound understanding, on the part of these German Jewish philosophers, of the collapse of a civilization to which emancipated Jews had free and full access for the first time and in which they flung themselves wholeheartedly in to the eminently universalist pursuits of science, art, law and philosophy.

The members of the Frankfurt School are now of more interest as witnesses than as analysts. Their nostalgia for a well-tempered rationalism simply convinces us that the world to which they aspired is indeed a thing of the past and that there can no longer be any principle to guarantee the unity of man and world, of the order of nature and the evolution of history. As industrial society came in to being with its technologies, its mass participation and its communications systems, it experienced both tragic difficulties and spectacular successes. Many great European intellectuals – from the Germans who fled to the United States during the Hitler period to the French thinkers of the 1960s and 1968 – reacted to the social problems it created by straying far from the highway to industrialization and challenged modernity by arguing that the decline of reason was leading to the triumph of absolute power. Having found no credible solution, their one consolation lay in aesthetic experience or in an appeal – and it was aesthetic rather than political – to the excluded, who were seen as the only forces to have escaped the rot introduced by modernity or its forms of domination. The extraordinary power of the philosophy that was applied to social thought in the mid twentieth century stemmed from this disjunction between thought and social action. It compensated for the disappearance of a militancy which became impossible because of the triumph of Stalinism, and for the transformation of so many liberation movements in to oppressive governments. So long as the problems of industrial society were masked by those of totalitarianism and colonialism, the voice of critical theory was convincing and could denounce the cowardice of those who, in the name of the proletariat or oppressed peoples, had become accomplices of the new dictators. This antimodernism does not, however, provide any real analysis of modern society, and sociology has been paralysed by a radicalism which pays no attention to the study of social practices. For decades, society has been depicted as being totally dominated by the logic of the reproduction of a social order in which institutions of social and cultural control are all-powerful; after a long period of purely critical theory, we now find that the landscape around us has been completely transformed by the presence of new problems, new debates and new social movements. In a world which is supposedly devoid of actors, we see actors reappearing everywhere, together with their utopias, their ideologies, their anger and their debates. The public space which the Frankfurt philosophers and the young Habermas believed to have been closed is now more open than ever. This settles no debates and solves no problems, but it does mean that we can no longer accept an antimodernism which is obsessed with its nostalgia for objective reason.

The dissociation we have noted is obviously the result of the way intellectuals were coming under fire. The heirs to the clerics who spoke in the name of God spoke in the name of reason and history. When the international public space was expanded to an unprecedented extent, when totalitarianisms replaced the brutal but limited despotisms of old, and when the crowds made their voices heard and when mass movements were being organized, the intellectuals, like the clerics before them, lost the key to their oligarchic power. They resisted the mass production, mass consumption and mass culture that denied them a monopoly on speech and deflated the elitist pretensions behind which they developed their arguments and waged their struggles. After the French Revolution, there could be no more Voltaires. At the end of the twentieth century, there can be no more critical theory because, whenever the domain of social practices and the field of actions available to social actors expand, it becomes increasingly difficult to address society from outside, or to perch on a branch of the tree of creation, reason or history, not least because it has its roots in heaven and not on earth. Twentieth-century German and French intellectuals are in mourning for the heaven where they were born. They are still nostalgic for it because it made them different to other people. Living in the absolute and in Being gave them a higher essence, whereas ordinary mortals were being tossed about by waves of accelerating change.

The intellectuals' protests against the loss of their role as secularized clerics must be both listened to and rejected. They must be listened to because, as Nietzsche understood better than anyone else, the main threat is utilitarianism and because, as the Frankfurt philosophers rightly remind us, power now speaks the language of needs. They must be rejected because there is no justification for the idea that we live in a closed world where power spreads without meeting any resistance, like a poison gas. That twentieth-century Europe has been dominated by the experience of concentration camps and totalitarian regimes does not give it the right to mistake a mass consumer society for a totalitarian regime. Critical theory is of limited value in that it contributes nothing to our understanding of modern societies and their forms of power, or of what is at stake in democracy.

This weakness is most apparent in the late works of Herbert Marcuse, whose analysis of Freud (Marcuse 1955) is, on the other hand, worthy of our attention.

The central thesis of *One Dimensional Man* is that 'advanced industrial society . . . obliterates the opposition between the private and public existence, between individual and social needs. Technology serves to institute new, more effective, and more pleasant forms of social control and social cohesion' (Marcuse 1964: 13). Marcuse adds that technology dominates capitalist society and communist society alike, and is creating similarities between them. There is no denying that technology permits the extension of social controls. But by what right do we move from this banal observation to the untenable assertion that technology is imposing increasingly total controls and that nothing can resist it? Why not accept, like Edgar Morin, that an increase in social density, to cite Durkheim, goes hand in hand with both greater complexity, increased controls and increased indeterminacy or greater potential freedom?

The image of a society in which power is so diffuse as to be coextensive with all social practices is far removed from the reality of societies which are simultaneously influenced by powerful States, disciplined public bureaucracies, living systems of political representation, interest groups and social demands, firms, financial centres and juridical institutions. The image of a totally unified society in which there is a perfect correspondence between technology, firms, the State, and the behaviour of consumers and even citizens could not be further removed from observable reality. Rather than bathing modernity in the light of reason, this image plunges it in to the half-light of technocracy, and thus obscures the central fact that is the theme of this section: in both culture and society – which, in this sense, have been post-modern for the last hundred years – the shattering of modernity coexists alongside nostalgia for Being. Commodity consumption, the power of firms and the rise of nationalisms all coexist together.

It is understandable that intellectuals who wallow in nostalgia for

Being should elaborate a negative image of modern society in which the other three components are so strongly welded together that they form a monstrous being which is poised to devour thought and freedoms. The danger is real, but there are no grounds for the claim that mass consumption, the development of industrial capitalism and nationalism are the three heads of the Cerberus that Marcuse calls society. 'Society is indeed the whole which exercises its independent power over the individual, and this society is no unidentifiable "ghost". It has its empirical hard core in the system of institutions' (Marcuse 1964: 153–4). What are we talking about? The State? Then we have to admit that State and Society have been separated, which contradicts the central thesis. The Law? Then we have to argue that social law, legislation on social security, and the texts that protect individual liberties, are all designed solely to promote social integration and the power of society. Yet the only proof to have been put foward is a handful of doctrinaire formulations. This Society is a myth, and the characteristic feature of modern societies is that the word 'society' can no longer be written with a capital 'S', that all forms of functionalism, conservative or critical, are inapplicable to social situations in which the promotion of mobility is at least as important as the maintenance of order. As liberals on both the right and the left have accurately noted, neither planning nor political repression is centrally controlled.

Finally, how can anyone fail to notice that Marcuse's book was published in 1964, the year in which the student movement first exploded with the Free Speech Movement at Berkeley, and at the beginning of a decade which, in both the United States and other countries, was to be dominated by campaigns for black civil rights, and women's equality, by protests against the war in Vietnam and by great student uprisings? The fact that these movements turned to critical theory or to structural Marxism, to Marcuse or Althusser, does not alter the fact that their actions, which were often in contradiction with their consciousness, proved that a mass society had not finally eliminated social actors. It was the rapid collapse of these student movements that led to the triumph of schools of thought which deny that social actors can intervene in society.

The history of social ideas has no difficulty in analysing this particular moment and the role played within it by the ideas of writers like Marcuse. The destruction and exhaustion of the workers' movement had left an immense vacuum in the centre of the social scene. Social-democratic reformism, which had no great principles and was bogged down in the slow and technical process of modifying forms of authority and laws, was unattractive to intellectuals, who therefore turned to a total and radical critique which led them, like many French students in May 1968, to doubt their ability to act on their own: they were privileged bourgeois and it seemed to them that only the proletariat was strong enough to take up the banner of revolution. The facts immediately belied this false consciousness, as it is the student rebellion and not the workers' strike, long and massive though it was, that lingers in the collective memory. Marcuse's argument was one of the student movement's ideological resources, but it also made it quite impossible for it to control the consequences of its own action. The intellectual critique mobilized Marxist fundamentalism; it did not enable it to explain why the new protest movements had appeared in the cultural rather than the economic field. Still less could it explain the social nature of the student uprising, as its base obviously did not correspond to Marcuse's description (Marcuse 1964: 200):

> Underneath the conservative popular base is the substratum of the outcasts and outsiders, the exploited and persecuted of other races and other colours, the unemployed and the unemployable. They exist outside the democratic process; their life is the most immediate and the most real need for ending intolerable conditions and institutions. Thus their opposition is revolutionary even if their consciousness is not.

If we examine the facts, the reverse is true. The opposition of the excluded is not usually revolutionary even if their consciousness is. Even if they are supported by radical proclamations from intellectuals, movements created by the unemployed or prisoners are rapidly transformed in to pressure groups with limited objectives. And, after his death, the extremely radical thought of Frantz Fanon, who inspired Ben Bella in Algeria, was transformed, both in France and other countries, in to a fundamentalist-type call that led ultimately to Islamism rather than revolutionary action.

Whilst the revolutionary idea is based upon the conviction that power can only be destroyed by its own contradictions and not by a social movement, we have to accept – as Marcuse admits later in the text – that the revolutionary crisis is alien to democracy, and that it leads, by definition, to an antidemocracy. It leads, that is, to the integrating absolute power against which the leftists rebelled. They are the unwitting agents of what Thomas and Merton call a self-fulfilling prophecy: the denunciation of supposedly absolute power creates an extreme crisis which results in the creation of an absolute power where none existed.

Social and politial critiques of Marcuse's ideas tend, however, to miss the main point, which pertains to the cultural domain. According to this careful reader of Freud, modern culture is above all sublimatory: it produces a sexuality which is completely immersed in sex and dedicated to a quest for the immediate and direct satisfaction of needs. All distance, as Brecht puts it, and all 'two-dimensionality', as Marcuse puts it, tends to disappear. Hence the triumph of the death instinct and the death of art in industrial society. 'The Pleasure Principle absorbs the Reality Principle; sexuality is liberated (or rather liberalized) in socially constructive forms. This notion implies that there are repressive modes of desublimation' (Marcuse 1964: 69). What is more, the destruction of the environment leads to the disappearance of the romantic image of a nature that exists in harmony with love. In short, the libido becomes fused with aggressivity, whereas Freud's thought is based upon the opposition between the two. Modern society refuses the 'great refusal'. Negative thought is replaced by exercises in instrumental thought. 'In the one remaining dimension of technological rationality, the *Happy Consciousness* comes to prevail' (Marcuse 1964: 74).

Although it is not demonstrable, this assertion lies at the heart of any critique of modernity. I accept it to the extent that it reveals that the classical rationalist conception of modernity is now exhausted because, in a technological civilization, there is no place for the idea of a world order or of guilt, which is an expression of the feeling that the world order and human experience are out of joint. Social life no longer has any metasocial guarantors. Are we therefore to conclude that our hyper-modern society is no more than instrumentalism or hedonism?

We first have to note that any assertion to that effect is contradicted by a second radical assertion, namely the thesis that social life functions in accordance with the logic of power. It is impossible to prove that the logic of the consumer and the logic of power converge, as they constantly come in to conflict, both in the factory and the office, and in political debates about the State budget or macroeconomic policies. Secondly, and more importantly, Marcuse's deeply pessimistic stance means that we have to look elsewhere for something that can limit the triumph of instrumentality. We cannot look to the will of God or the laws of reason, but we can look to the will to freedom and personal and collective responsibility. And that means that we have to abandon the idea of a system without actors and accept the return of the actor and the birth of the Subject, against which social thought has mobilized all its forces for so long. If Marcuse's formulations are worthy of attention, it is because of their extreme nature. With Marcuse, whose work has been very influential, the decay of modernizing rationalism is complete.

Marcuse's theses do at least have the virtue of reacting against the pansexualism of Freudo-Marxists like Wilhelm Reich, who argues that social regulation means no more than the repression of a sexuality which should, on the contrary, be set free. Such an extreme conception inevitably contrasts an artificially constructed nature with culture, and thus makes the historical construction of ethical norms impossible.

Our conclusions must be historical rather than philosophical. The mid twentieth century did not witness the intellectual triumph of what Jean Fourastié (1950) called 'the great hope of the twentieth century'. On the contrary, the dominant intellectual mood was an obsession with crisis. At a time when intellectuals felt that they were caught between fascism and communism and when very few resisted the attractions of one or the other, the Frankfurt School was an exceptional centre of resistance against both these perversions of the meaning of history. After the brief upturn of the Liberation, when Jean-Paul Sartre developed a philosophy of freedom, intellectuals felt themselves threatened by the triumph of a social practice without a theory, and by an accumulation of wealth whose only cultural model was utilitarianism. Within the space of a generation, the Frankfurt School's rejection of fascist and communist dictatorships had given way to a vague distrust, to a general resistance to a modernity which seemed dangerous because of what it promised rather than of what it rejected. No individual, intellectual or not, living in the West at the end of the twentieth century can escape the fear of a total loss of meaning, or the fear that private life and the capacity to be a Subject are being invaded by propaganda and advertising, by the degradation of society in to a crowd, of love in to pleasure. Can we live without God? For several hundred years, we believed that we could reduce God to reason. Then Nietzsche and Freud taught us to replace God with life or the law. Those lines of defence crumbled in their turn, and modernity's criterion for the evaluation of behaviour – the social utility or functionality of individual modes of behaviour – seemed to invade everything. Is recognition of a supra-human or metasocial principle such as God, the Logos or Life the only way to fight this invasion? Twentieth-century thought is torn between the need to pursue secularization to its logical conclusion, and the need to defend itself against the moralization and social utilitarianism which has often received support from sociology. It is now either retreating in to a quest for Being or stubbornly clinging to a great refusal. As it has no model for transforming society and no hope, it can sustain that position only when the threat seems to be imminent. For a long time, the difficulties of decolonization, and above all the continued existence of the Stalinist and then the Maoist system, made it possible to justify that 'great refusal', but for very different purposes. The collapse of the Communist system, the absence of a new fascist threat and the strengthening of democracy means that we must abandon it. We then find ourselves defenceless against the world of consumption, to which many of us surrender because it allows us to satisfy desires that have long been frustrated. But why lose our heads? Why not make up for lost time and analyse the new social and cultural problems that force us to reject certain modes of management or organization, rather than society as a whole? As the century draws to an end, thought is slowly and painfully being weaned away from a nostalgia for Being which is no longer sustained by a justifiable rejection of an unbearable present. We must analyse, criticize and transform our present society, which is more flexible and more diverse than the author of *One Dimensional Man* believed it to be.

Michel Foucault: Power and Subjects

The weakness of almost all thinking about modernity stems from the presupposition that one central power, either that of the State or the ruling class, is all-powerful. This comes very close to being a very superficial conspiracy theory of history. It is common knowledge that the central power is much less visible in so-called democratic societies than in other societies. In some cases it is invisible. Democratic societies are tolerant or even liberal. In other words, they do not subject individual behaviour to a social representation of the truth. One of the strengths of the thought of Michel Foucault is that it rejects the idea of generalized repression and manipulation, and even the idea that there is one central power which sits like a spider at the centre of a web of functionaries and propaganda agents. The central tendency in Foucault's thinking in this area, and it is this that gives it its originality and explains his influence, is his rejection of the idea that the central power constantly becomes stronger and more condensed. On the contrary, the exercise of power increasingly merges in to the categories of practice itself. In a modern liberal society, power is thus everywhere and nowhere. Foucault's main point, however, is that, far from being governed by technical rationality, social organization is governed by the exercise of power. This is an extreme form of the critical thought which challenges the very idea of modernity. If social utility is the criterion by which good and evil are to be judged, is it not a criterion which refers to society rather than its members, and does it not therefore strengthen the social system's hold over its functional elements? To reduce Michel Foucault's thought to its simplest expression, power means normalization. The whole of society constantly sets this mechanism in motion, and therefore produces an ever-wider divorce between the normal and the abnormal, the healthy and the pathological, the permissible and the forbidden, the central and the marginal. Power is not a discourse pronounced from on high; it is a set of utterances which are produced autonomously in all institutions, and they are all the more efficacious in that they appeal not so much to some supreme will, as to objective observations or even science. A similar argument had already been introduced by Tocqueville in the second part of his *Democracy in America* (Tocqueville 1835–40): a modern democratic society which has been freed from absolute monarchy is in danger of becoming a slave to public opinion, to a majority which is naturally conservative and which distrusts both innovations and minorities or ideas and modes of behaviour which threaten the established order.

Foucault adds a coda to this general argument. It both changes its meaning and reveals his central concerns. He does not simply criticize the real nature of liberalism. His prime concern is to detect the presence, throughout history, of the Subject and the increasing importance of ethics, which *The Use of Pleasure* defines (Foucault 1984a: 251) as 'the elaboration of a form of relation to self that enables an individual to fashion himself in to a subject of ethical conduct'. He discovers in the concern with sexuality, which was so slow to recognize itself for what it is, 'the study of the modes according to which individuals are given to recognize themselves as sexual subjects' (Foucault 1984a: 5). He completes this definition by referring to 'the practices by which individuals were led to focus their attention on themselves, to decipher, recognize and acknowledge themselves as subjects of desire' (1984a: 5). The period between the end of the classical Greek period and the end of the Roman Empire saw the emergence of an ethical asceticism which rejects pleasure in the name of the control the Subject exercises over himself and the care for the self the Greeks called '*epimelia heautou*', and which the Romans called '*cura sui*'. The same asceticism can be found almost intact in Christian culture, which will give it a more repressive content and at the same time strengthen the appeal to subjectivity, whereas the ancient model is still that of an individual who exercises self-control so as not to squander the energy he should be devoting to society.

Having identified the rise of *subjectivation*, Foucault's principal goal is to demonstrate that it is an effect of the initial and decisive extension of 'governmentality'. The appearance of the Subject, or subjectivation, is primarily a matter of subjection. The constitution of the Subject is a product of 'the whole technology of power over the body that the technology of the "soul" – that of educationalists, psychologists and psychiatrists – fails either to conceal or to compensate, for the simple reason that it is one of its tools' (Foucault 1975: 30).

There are two sides to the objectification of human beings, and therefore to the birth of the human sciences. On the one hand, the abnormal individual is marginalized, rejected or confined; on the other, he or she is classified as a particular case and individualized. Punishment, for example, takes in to account the motives of the lawbreaker and tries to rehabilitate him either through work or through an isolation conducive to the workings of his conscience. The effects of normalization are therefore not purely repressive and destructive, as most critics of modernity are content to claim. Foucault rejects that thesis, just as he rejects the idea that the nineteenth century and capitalism repressed and concealed sexuality. On the contrary: 'Surely no other type of society has ever accumulated – and in such a relatively short span of time – a similar quantity of discourses concerned with sex' (Foucault 1976: 33). Foucault is attempting to demonstrate that the subject is created by power, or in other words by all the mechanisms of the micro-physics of power, and therefore by the objectifying mechanisms of normalization.

Objections can be addressed to both stages in this argument. Firstly, can power be identified with normalization? The most influential book from the second period of Foucault's life, namely *Discipline and Punish* (Foucault 1975), refutes this thesis. The society which confines delinquents in prison, pupils in boarding schools, patients in hospitals and workers in factories is not a network of normalizing mechanisms. It works – and here Foucault is still directly influenced by Marxist research – to the advantage of a ruling class. The ruling class calls for what Jean-Paul de Gaudemar (1982) calls a *general mobilization* and transforms society in to an industrial army under authoritarian command. This is not simply a matter of normalization alone; it also involves repression and the primary purpose of prisons is, according to Foucault's own analysis, to remove delinquents from the social body. A distinction has to be made between this logic of repression, and the logic of marginalization, which corresponds more closely to the work of normalization. Pupils or workers who are too slow are separated from the rest, and are thus marginalized and doomed to being unemployed before being, in some cases, locked up in specialized establishments which label them as abnormal. Yet this is the logic of a liberal society or even a mass society which is introducing more – and increasingly powerful – integrating mechanisms, and thus producing a residue which it finds more and more difficult to assimilate. This does not, however – and this is not a minor detail – create a closed world. It creates a margin from which many can, when circumstances are right, return to the mainstream. Studies of marginal urban cultures in Latin America clearly show that the frontier between the formal and the informal sectors is porous, and that it is often crossed. The distinction between confinement and marginality is a vital one. Marginality corresponds to the workings of an open system; confinement to that of power and, more generally, of institutions which simultaneously eliminate and try to produce autonomous subjects capable of acting on themselves and their environment, of self-control and of being guided by their 'conscience'. The same cultural and social model of repression also provokes rebellions and revolutions which in turn inspire the idea of the Subject and speak of freedom and justice.

Foucault is right to begin with the objectification which gives society more power to control its members, but whilst this objectification is associated with individualization – of both consumers and of 'social cases' – it does not result in subjectivation. On the contrary, a technologically-based and adminstrative society transforms human beings in to objects, as is suggested by the word 'bureaucracy', as used in its most ordinary sense. We can speak of the Subject only when power intervenes, as it is the appeal to the subject that constitutes actors who define themselves in opposition to the ascendancy of apparatuses.

The normalization and objectification of human beings produce the Self whereas the I is constituted through resistance to power centres which are perceived as repressive.

A situation in which the orders of objectification and subjectivation merge is a situation in which power is identified with rationalization. This is the case in enlightened despotisms and, in our century, in communist regimes, which are truly totalitarian in that they establish their power over subject-objects and use the word 'progress' to mask the particular interests of the Party-State. Foucault's analysis is acceptable as a critique of totalitarian regimes, but it does not apply to situations in which State and civil society are separated, and where, more importantly, normalization in the name of power is not the same thing as power in the repressive sense.

In *Discipline and Punish*, Foucault states (1975: 194) that the individual is 'a reality fabricated by this specific technology of power that I have called "discipline"'. This presupposes that the Subject can be identified with reason. Discipline requires the application of reason to a nature which reacts only to immediate pleasure. Yet this conception contradicts the very thing that Foucault himself analyses so well: the appearance in Greece and Rome, and even more so in Christianity, of a conception which does not identify the Subject with the universal value of reason, but with the transformation of individual characteristics in to a life history, in to personalization. Personalization can take the form of salvation or a vocation for business, and it transforms the individual in to an actor capable of modifying the world of rules, norms and impersonal principles. Foucault could have given much more importance to the idea of the Subject, but he was so anxious to eliminate the idealist vision of the Subject and history that dominates his earlier work, and especially *The Order of Things* (1966), that he gives the central role to the theme of power, which is, in his view, the only thing capable of destroying the image of the Subject. Why reduce social life to the mechanisms of normalization? Why not accept that cultural orientations and social power are always intertwined, and that knowledge, economic activity and ethical conceptions therefore all bear the mark of power, but also the mark of opposition to power? Why not accept that all power – with the exception of totally despotic power – is the implementation of cultural orientations which are not in themselves reducible to instruments of power. Foucault's passionate loathing for what he calls the Subject leads him to resist the very themes that his remarkably far-seeing historical gaze brings in to our field of vision.

In the afterword to Dreyfus and Rabinow's study of this work, Foucault formulates (Dreyfus and Rabinow 1982: 226) his ideas very openly:

> In effect, between a relationship of power and a strategy of struggle there is a reciprocal appeal, a perpetual linking and a perpetual reversal. At every moment the relationship of power may become a confrontation between two adversaries. Equally, the relationship between adversaries in society may, at every moment, give place to the putting in to operation of mechanisms of power. The consequence of this instability is the ability to decipher the same events and the same transformations either from inside the history of struggle or from the standpoint of the power relations.

He concludes by defining the central object of his research as 'the locking together of power relations with relations of strategy and the results proceeding from their interaction'. This text, which was written towards the end of Foucault's life, is far removed from the crude idea that the practice of power produces the subject. It is the social struggle that brings the individual-object in to conflict with the individual-subject, and only the triumph of power and the crushing of protest struggles can leave the field open for a representation of the individual as an object that can be examined and manipulated. Not everything is power, and only absolute power succeeds in desubjectivating human beings and in confounding the almost universal will and capacity to act as a subject. Foucault's most extensive descriptions are devoted to what I term *social antimovements*; and social movements which introduce the defence of the Subject against an apparently technocratic power are no more than evoked in passing. Foucault constantly clings to a purely critical vision, and denounces the Subject as an effect of power, but he does not have total control over the meaning of his own work and it is too rich to be doctrinaire. My reading suggests that, in its final phase, it reaches the limits of its own ideology, to the point where Foucault has to recognize that the Subject lies at the heart of debates about modernity. Foucault's importance and his superiority over his doctrinaire contemporaries stems from the fact that he comes increasingly close to the very things he rejects, rather like a religious artist whose work is most successful when he is painting or sculpting sinners who have been cast in to hell. Foucault's work can, despite Foucault himself, be part of a rediscovery of the Subject.

These comments on Foucault's work are in a way similar to the serious criticisms addressed to it by Marcel Gauchet and Gladys Swain in their study of the asylum as institution, and more specifically of the work of Pinel and Esquirol (Gauchet and Swain 1980). According to Gauchet and Swain, the great confinement of the mad that developed between the sixteenth and the nineteenth centuries is inseparable from what I am defining as modernity, namely the creation of a self-centred society which is divorced from both the human world, nature and the gods. The mad were once believed to be possessed by a divine force and to be dominated by nature. Nature was divorced from culture, but there was no complete divide between the two. When society came to be defined solely in terms of its actions, there was no room for the mad. The mad were not, however, excluded. They were confined, which is almost the opposite of being excluded. Society took the view that the mad had to be resocialized, and their alienation was indeed defined as a breakdown of sociality. This thesis overlaps with Foucault's in that it recognizes that, in this society, it is the State that becomes 'humanist'. It is the changing representation of madness that leads to its intervention. Gauchet and Swain go further than this, as they assert that confinement leads inevitably to the resocialization of the mentally ill. The process began with the early work of Esquirol, which centres on the assertion that the alienated never leave the world of meaning – and, what is more important still, that the mad can only be brought back in to society when the non-social element within them is no longer a matter of gods and nature, but reappears, thanks to Freud, in the form of the unconscious, or as the Id. This corresponds to the idea that I am defining as the decay of modernity, which, by destroying the self-sufficiency of rational action, makes it possible to see mental illness as something other than an illness. Mental illness has to be seen as a breakdown of the relationship between the social and the non-social, between the Id and the Super-Ego, and that relationship is basic to the formation of the personality. From *Madness and Civilization* (1961) to *Discipline and Punish*, Foucault demonstrates admirably how power over human beings develops, but he divorces it to a dangerous degree from the overall transformation represented by modernity. The state is certainly its main agent, but modernity has a much broader sociological and even anthropological meaning. Foucault's lasting contribution is the idea that modernity implies the omnipotence of a State whose ideal of rationalization has produced the worst forms of repression, and that the crisis in modernity is therefore also a liberation.

In his afterword to the above-mentioned study by Dreyfus and Rabinow, Foucault comes close to recognizing that there are limits to the controls exercised by mechanisms of normalization, and therefore to recognizing the constant presence of a protesting or rebellious Subject. He evokes the new social movements that are defending the Subject against the State. And his work contains many pages – notably the last page of *Discipline and Punish* – in which we hear the grumble of rebellion in social life. Yet one cannot at the same time depict a conflict-ridden society and identify power with social practice as though power had become impersonal and completely objectified. Either one struggles inside society against an identifiable social or political adversary, or one struggles against society, in which case struggle means simply 'refusal' or is debased to meaning marginality. I quite understand the need, in a society of apparatuses and techniques, to move away from a representation of power which puts it in the hands of a personal God or a king, but an apparatus is still a centre of power and it is still defined by a social relation of dominance. Such a relation can exist only within a society and especially a culture, just as the conflict between capitalists and wage-earners developed within an industrial society or culture whose orientation was not only accepted but actually demanded by both parties. If we destroy, in the name of a radical critique, the triangle made up by adversaries, issues and conflict, we end up with the same vision as an integrative functionalism. There are no longer any forces in conflict. All that remains is marginality or a counter-culture, and neither has anything in common with a social conflict. We therefore have to disagree rather than agree with Foucault, and conclude that the formation of the Subject takes place in struggles against increasingly impersonal powers which claim to have some technical authority.

Foucault's thought corresponds to a period when there were no oppositional social actors, to a period in which the old social actors, and especially the workers' movement, had been transformed in to apparatuses of power, and in which the new social movements had more to do with a counter-culture than with social conflict. That is why, even though it eliminates any possibility of understanding social movements and the Subject, Foucault's work does draw our attention to these themes and, in doing so, paves the way for a renaissance in social thought, even though Foucault himself distrusts it and accuses it of being part of a policy of normalization and labelling.

Foucault's conflation of antithetical aspects of social life is not restricted to the analytic level. It also has very obvious practical implications. Like Marcuse, Foucault believes that only the excluded and dropouts can challenge a normalizing society in which there is no place left for classical social conflicts. That is why he attaches such importance to the prisoners' movement. The actors of a social movement, however, are never defined in terms of their exclusion, marginality or confinement. Prisoners no more constitute a social movement than the unemployed. Their situation may force society to ask questions about itself and may give it a bad conscience, but in themselves they constitute, at best, a pressure group putting forward demands, violently or otherwise, to the adminstration in the hope of winning concrete concessions. This has nothing to do with challenging power relations. Those who define themselves in terms of a non-relation, and their adversary as society as a whole through its institutional apparatus, cannot be the main actors of society and its history.

The quality of Foucault's work is such that it can be read against the grain, and his radically critical intentions are not in doubt. His last books, from *Discipline and Punish* (1975) to the first volume of the *History of Sexuality* (1976) can be seen as a discovery of the Subject, which seemed to have been completely eradicated by *The Order of Things* (1966). This almost unexpected return to the Subject occurred during the period when Foucault was teaching at the Collège de France. His books reveal his gradual discovery that Christianity and the modern economy cannot be accused of enforcing asceticism and forbidding the pleasures of paganism. This is the main conclusion of his study (1984a) of 'the use of pleasure' and of pederastic love in Ancient Greece: history shows that there was a transition from citizen to Subject rather than from pleasure to self-punishment. Yet Foucault will not accept the implications of his own observations. That is why he tries to see subjectivation as a byproduct of governmentality and moralization. The hypothesis is unacceptable, even though one has to admire the power and intelligence that went in to the attempt to prove it.

From the Frankfurt School onwards, critical intellectuals have devoted all their energies to the struggle against the idea of a Subject. Now that the most intelligent and daring assault on that idea – that made by Michel Foucault – is over, it is time to clear the battlefield and to admit that the Subject, which has survived every attack and every insult, is the only idea that allows us to reconstruct the idea of modernity. Anyone who doubts this has only to recall how rapidly a purely critical vision of modernity became a total rejection of the very idea of modernity and then self-destructed when it became post-modernism. Jean Baudrillard provides a classic example when he attacks Foucault (Baudrillard 1977) in order to explain his own transition from critical leftism to post-modernism. Conversely, it is possible to find in Foucault's failure reasons for believing that the Subject is back.

Clerics against the Age

Intellectuals introduced the notion of progress in to a society that was still steeped in customs, tradition and privileges, and as Daniel Roche's study of eighteenth-century France shows, they readily found allies amongst the nobility and the bourgeoisie (Roche 1991). Throughout the long nineteenth century which lasted until the First World War and the Soviet Revolution, they placed more and more emphasis on their progressivism, or in other words on the critique they made of society in the name of a future that was necessary in both the ethical and the scientific senses. The communist movement and then national liberation movements filled them with enthusiasm, even though they felt that they were themselves being challenged by revolutionaries who rejected both the freedoms constructed by the West and the power of the bourgeoisie and the colonial powers. The goals of advancing knowledge and defending tolerance and liberty seemed to them to be related to the goals of social revolution and anticolonial wars. Even when it was not explicitly evoked, the idea of modernity provided a link between struggles which seemed unrelated only because of the planetary divide between rich and poor, between colonizers and colonized. For a long time this progressivism resisted reality and stubbornly refused to see it for what it was.

On the other hand, the experience of totalitarianism, which has dominated the twentieth century, explains the reaction of the many intellectuals who, being intelligent enough and brave enough to refuse to be the fellow travellers of totalitarian parties, came to the conclusion that the only way out of the contradictions that threatened them was the adoption of a generalized critique. They broke with the progressivist hope that history could be reconciled with freedom; they turned their back on Hegelianized, or even Christianized, Marxism, on all forms of historicism and all philosophies of history. Louis Althusser provides the most political, and therefore the clearest, expression of an antihumanism that was designed to deny political power's right to speak in the name of man and to impose a repressive politics as a result. If the role of governments were restricted to administering things in the name of science and historical necessity, their role would be to renounce their privileges, and there would no longer be any danger of their being transformed in to Churches or Inquisitions. Hence the emergence of a rationalist fundamentalism which did away with any reference to the Subject because of its distrust of totalitarian indoctrination. Perched on the rock of science, it was able to condemn both totalitarian regimes and consumer society. The history of ideas demonstrates not only the vigour of the intellectual movement I have just described, but also its success and even its power in the intellectual world and in the academic world, as well as in publishing and the media.

The second half of the twentieth century has been dominated by the divorce between theory and practice. With progressivism in ruins, there was a parting of the ways between those who became the servants of business and government and those who were looking for success, and those who saw modern society primarily as an increasingly powerful system of social controls. Marcuse denounces the tolerance of Western societies as a manipulative system which is as repressive as the taboos of totalitarian regimes. Increasingly, a society based upon mass production and mass consumption is becoming divided in to two sectors. These are not social classes, but qualitatively different social and cultural worlds. On the one hand, we have the world of production, instrumentality, efficacy and the market; on the other, we have the world of social criticism and the defence of the values or institutions that resist the intervention of society. The dichotomy between the techno-economic and the socio-cultural sectors is not simply a socio-professional one. It tends to become more general than that, as the former tends to vote for the right, and the latter for the left. What is more, men tend to belong to the technico-economic sector, and women, to the socio-cultural sector. With the rapid development of a mass system of higher education, the history of ideas acquires a new dimension and a new meaning. The intellectuals are no longer a small and influential group; they have been turned in to a broad intelligentsia. Some magazines and major publishing houses address this intelligentsia, which are their most important audience, just as the French Socialist Party cannot ignore the fact that its most solid support comes from the socio-cultural sector, and particularly from teachers. Hence the relative isolation of those who attempt to think about contemporary society: they are trapped between thinkers who are critical of modernity, and actors who are completely immersed in modernity. Sociology almost succumbed to this two-pronged attack and in most countries has been weakened by the almost total fragmentation of the social thought bequeathed it by the nineteenth century.

There are two kinds of possible intellectual and political reactions to this, and the combination of the two set the tone for the May 1968 movement. On the one hand, social thought reacted effectively against the mawkish optimism of the ideologues of modernization. It preserved the negative space without which the formation of new actors and new social movements would have been impossible, and it tried to work out the meaning of the new demands that were being put forward. It concentrated on the women's movement, the critique of Jacobin centralism and the ecologists' refusal to countenance the destruction of the environment. Antipositivism and antiproductivism led to the re-awakening of a society which seemed to have been reduced to an absurd market in commodities and services. Yet at the same time intellectuals became increasingly trapped in to their 'leftist' critique of a society they described as a manipulative machine. The critique was now out of step with reality. Whilst modern society may well be an increasingly dense network of signals, it must not be forgotten that those signals are less imperious than norms and that their socialization effect is less powerful. The conventions and rules of the game do not impose such strict constraints as the articles of a catechism or forms of direct personal dependency.

The triumph of this mode of thought was spectacular, but it also proved to be short-lived. The mood of the times changed quickly, not because things backfired when some leftists went over to postmodernism, but mainly because the international economic conjuncture changed in the 1980s. The so-called crisis that was created or triggered by the breakdown of the international monetary system and by sudden rises in the price of oil was followed by a new period of prosperity, first in the United States and Japan, and then, many years later, in France. The 1980s were the years when practice took its revenge on theory. The technico-economic sector took its revenge on the socio-cultural sector, and success on criticism. At this point, critical thought, that enfeebled heir to the progressivism of old, gave way to the neo-liberal and post-modernist thought which completed the destruction of the classical idea of modernity.

Can we go on oscillating between rejecting modern society and worshipping the market, as though the political action exerted by societies upon themselves were by definition an object of hatred? Our distrust of both reforms and social innovations is blocking the formation of new social movements, which quickly lapse in to either banal moralism or short-sighted pragmatism for want of adequate intellectual preparation. When it comes to dealing with both its own internal problems and the problems of the world at large, our society seems to be lacking in both ideas and imagination. Outside the most privileged countries, the absence or weakness of intellectuals is still more tragic. Led by the Brazilians and Chileans, the Latin American intellectuals who for so long celebrated the cult of a revolution with no roots in the popular masses, are now back in touch with reality, but they have been weakened by the economic and social crisis of the 1980s. In the Eastern bloc countries, and especially in Poland, intellectuals played an admirable role in criticizing and overthrowing the communist regimes, but they soon found themselves being stifled by reconstruction programmes which sacrificed everything to the market economy. In the Islamic world, intellectual critics have been almost totally silenced by the rise of fundamentalist movements which destroy intellectual life when they achieve power.

Intellectuals do not have sole responsibility for the situation to which they have fallen victim. Political power's increasing reliance on ideology, together with the invasive presence of the most utilitarian forms of knowledge, has transformed much of the land which once sustained intellectual life in to military training areas and shopping malls. But why has intellectual life allowed itself to become so locked in to a rejection of modernity and in to a critique which is so far removed from the observable facts? Why do intellectuals pay so little attention to what is being said on the street, and why do they interpret it so badly? I can think of only one explanation. Intellectuals identified so completely with the rationalist or enlightenment image of modernity that, having triumphed when it triumphed, they are now a declining force as that image loses its influence on social and cultural modes of behaviour throughout the world. A new definition of modernity will not simply be useful to modern societies or societies undergoing modernization; for intellectuals, it is also a way of escaping the loss of meaning that makes them see technological civilization purely in terms of controls and repression, and deny the existence of social actors in a world that is alive with problems and innovations, projects and protests.

5

Leaving Modernity

The idea of modernity dominated thought only until such time as industrial society was actually constructed. The struggle against the past, the Ancien Régime and religious beliefs, and absolute faith in reason gave the image of modern society a strength and coherence which quickly vanished when the new society became a reality and not simply the obverse of the society that had to be destroyed or transcended. The history of modernity is the history of the emergence of social and cultural actors who increasingly lost their belief that modernity was the concrete definition of the good. The intellectuals were the first to follow Nietzsche and Freud in rejecting that belief, and the most influential current in modern thought, from Horkheimer and his friends in the Frankfurt School to Michel Foucault, has been the pursuit of a critique of modernity which has resulted in the complete isolation of intellectuals from what they scornfully describe as a 'mass society'. At the same time, nations and their passion for their independence, their history and their identity, took on such importance that the twentieth century was to become, at least in modernized countries, the century of nations, just as the nineteenth had been the century of classes. At times, this development had something in common with the intellectual critique of modernity; usually, it did not. Thanks to a later development, companies, first in the United States and then in Japan, became actors and acquired a power that sometimes exceeded that of Nation-States as they became centres for political decision-making rather than mere economic agents. The United States, then Europe and finally Japan experienced the explosion of mass consumption, followed by the mass communications which made public the desires, the imaginary and, more simply the body that modern rationalism had rejected, repressed and confined. Yet so long as instrumental rationality could weave its web of relations between these social and cultural actors, modernity was still in place, and it was possible to speak of industrial society, or even neo- or hyper-industrial society. The most modern societies feel threatened with fragmentation, but technology is so important a part of their workings that they can react by combining technical education with the defence of a certain asceticism. Their strongest defence was the educational system which, especially in France, saw itself as the defender of Enlightenment rationalism until it was outflanked by the return of what had been eliminated by the post-revolutionary bourgeoisies during their long occupancy of power.

At what point did the shattering of modernity become total rather than partial? At the precise moment when the world of instrumental rationality became completely divorced from the world of social and cultural actors. Eros, consumption, companies and nations were then free to drift freely in the way that icebergs can drift when the pack ice breaks up. They drift away from one another, collide and sometimes join up. To put it in still more concrete terms, we left modernity when we ceased to define a mode of behaviour or a form of social organization in terms of its position on the tradition–modernity axis or the underdevelopment–development axis. We have been more or less conscious that we were leaving modernity since at least 1968. We no longer explain social facts in terms of their place in a history which supposedly has a direction or meaning. Spontaneous social thought, ideologies and the mood of the times have jetisoned all reference to history. That is the primary meaning of the theme of post-modernism, which is above all a post-historicism.

There are two possible responses to the crisis affecting the classical idea of modernity or the modernist ideology. The first, which is that of the post-moderns, is to assert that its decay is irreversible; the second is that modernity can and must be defended, or even extended. That is Jürgen Habermas's view and it is also, in different terms, the idea that I will be defending in part III below. But before we go in that direction, we must first of all retrace the road that leads from the classical idea of modernity to its crisis, its decay and, finally, its demise.

The Market and the Ghetto

The crisis of modernity reaches its paroxysm when society abandons all principles of rationalization, either because it functions as a market or because it defines itself purely in terms of a cultural identity, and when its actors' references are purely cultural, communitarian or individual. Should we in fact be still speaking of modernity at this point? Does not modernity, as defined at the beginning of this study, tend increasingly to divorce the system from actors, and is not its history that of the increasingly complete destruction of any principle that could unite them? The breakup of the sacred world has been followed by the destruction of the rationalist worldview, and by the exhaustion of the idea that society is the locus for correspondences between institutions and actors socialized by the family and the education system. As we move from Christian dualism to bourgeois individualism, and from a post-revolutionary romanticism to a youth culture which is implacably hostile to every aspect of the culture of big companies, we see the great dissociation which both completes and abolishes modernity. For a long time we hastened the destruction of the integrated world in which human beings had a place in nature, which may or not have been a divine creation. What frightens us now is not the closure of a world which is too immobile and whose laws are too imperious; it is the disorder of a society in which the world of techniques and organizations clashes so violently with the world of desires and identities. Various post-modern currents shed light on different aspects of this fragmentation, but it has to be described in its historical reality before we look at how it has been reflected in modes of thought which are themselves as fragmented as the world they interpret.

We must begin by looking at economic actors rather than at conceptions of man.

The central intellectual role has in fact been played by the sociology of organizations. Functionalist or institutional sociology described organizations with economic, administrative or social goals as applications of instrumental rationality which could establish a correspondence between functional rules and individual or collective modes of behaviour. The sociology of organizations has destroyed that image. It sometimes does so by speaking in terms of a social critique, as when it paints a less than flattering portrait of 'the organization man' (Whyte 1956). It usually does so in a more productive way by demonstrating that an organization's rules and even its observable workings are no more than a fragile and unstable compromise between a great number of pressures and constraints, and that an efficient organization is not one which is open, solid and transparent, but one which can handle complexity, conflict and change. The idea of strategy thus comes to replace that of management. Peter Drucker provides a clear account of the change. At a more theoretical level, the work of Herbert Simon and James March in the United States, and that of Michel Crozier in France, show that there has not been a crisis in instrumental rationality. On the contrary, it can be revitalized, provided that it abandons all reference to the idea of a social system or society, and wholeheartedly adopts the theme of social change. The company thus ceases to be the basic cell of modern industrial society; it becomes the warrior who, either in its own name or that of a national society, fights in international markets and struggles to transform new technologies in to production processes and to adapt to a constantly changing and unpredictable environment. Simon speaks of limited rationality, and Crozier of controlled uncertainty. These remarkable analyses describe companies as strategists who are not blinded by so-called scientific management, but open to both the outside world and the internal human problems of a complex organization. The cult of the strong simple organization has given way to the celebration of a weak, flexible and complex organization. This conception is both richer than the functionalist modernism it replaced and more modest, as it is prepared to abandon the central principle of classical sociology, namely the notion that there is some correspondence between institutional rules and modes of behaviour. Strategy may centre on a Japanese-style company loyalty based upon relations which are at once authoritarian and participatory. Alternatively, it may simply introduce in to the company the market constraints and incentives that define the so-called Silicon Valley model. It is also possible to imagine a very different company strategy which both integrates individuals in to the company and encourages personal projects. Companies may also attempt to maximize participation in both their productive activities and their adaptation to the market. All these images of the company are clearly outward-looking, even though their primary concern is to mobilize both human and technical resources.

If we extend this conception from the company to society as a whole, we have to conclude that we no longer live in an industrial society dominated by central social conflicts, but in a constant flow of change. We are navigating a sea or a dangerous river, and we are expected to respond rapidly to incidents that are largely unpredictable. Some win the race and others drown. The idea of society has been replaced by the idea of the market, and the change has taken a dramatic turn with the collapse of the communist system. The principal leaders of the countries concerned have reached the conclusion that their system cannot be reformed, that they have to launch themselves in to the rapids of an unknown river despite the atrocious conditions. Come what may, they must establish a market economy. In both East and West, we now belong to a society made up of three groups: a small group of helmsmen who are not in command, but who react to market and environmental incentives; passengers who are both consumers and crew members; and the losers who have been swept overboard by the storm or thrown in to the sea because they are non-productive or surplus to requirements. The liberal society that is replacing the class society created by social democracy or other forms of the Welfare State, is replacing exploitation with exclusion and, more importantly, a functional model with a strategy for change, a synchronic vision with a diachronic vision.

These images of *liberal* society are very attractive to many of those who have been disappointed by the most voluntarist and revolutionary forms of political action. This explains the enthusiasm with which so many former leftists fling themselves in to extreme liberalism, and sing the praises of the void or the ephemeral, the liberation of private life and the end of the limitations and constraints imposed by voluntaristic social models. We then see the emergence of what the Americans call libertarian liberalism. It should not, however, be forgotten that a society which has been reduced to instrumentality, change and the strategies of its leaders, is also a savage society in which society's rejects are less and less likely to be able to get back in to the race. Social inequalities are increasing despite the dangerous conditions. The only people who are not part of this society are members of minority cultures, whose relationship with the majority culture is unequal and diglossic.

The conflict between these minorities and a majority which includes the masters of production, consumption and communications gives a new meaning to the right–left dichotomy. The right no longer defends the people at the top, but rather those who are in front, and it relies upon good strategists to reduce the social costs of change. The left defends the excluded rather than those at the bottom, and is more aware of the growing inequalities between North and South, of threats to the planet and of the exclusion of so many social and cultural categories. Even so, the spirit of the left encounters many difficulties, as it now speaks in the name of minorities and not the majority. The American Democratic Party had great difficulty in escaping a traditional definition which condemned it to defeat.

This extreme liberalism was once the vanguard of modernism, but it has already gone beyond that stage and is now building the type of economic society in which post-modernist culture develops. As we reach the end of the twentieth century, it is now the dominant mode of social management.

As society comes increasingly to resemble a market in which there are no more ideological or even political issues at stake, all that remains is the struggle for money or the quest for an identity. Social problems have been replaced by non-social problems, and individual problems by global problems which extend far beyond the social and political field and thus destroy much of its content. This is a society which rejects analysis, which distrusts the big ideas and great discourses that disturb its pragmatism or its dreams. The greatest strength of this liberal vision is that it seems to offer the best protection against attempts to seize power on the part of ruling elites, and especially those who claim to speak in the name of humanity and society. Money appears to be the least personal and therefore the least brutal of masters, whereas people with convictions that involve grandiose projects always try to impose their faith and powers on others.

The obvious criticism of this vision is that it is a victim of its own instrumentalism. It reduces society to a market and a constant flow of change, but it cannot account for modes of behaviour which escape its reductionism. It cannot explain either the defensive quest for identity or the desire for stability. It understands neither national passions nor the culture of the excluded. It is, in a word, the ideology of the elites who control the changes that are going on and who feel so in touch with things that they would rather be on the move than standing still, on the offensive rather than on the defensive. They prefer the impersonality of communications systems to subjectivity. And their ability to sway the silent majorities should not be underestimated.

Liberalism corresponds only to one aspect of our shattered modernity: action and change. It is divorced from its other aspects: an identity cut off from all social action, the suffocating subjectivity of nationalities and ghettos, of aggressive gangs and the gestures that inscribe walls and metro trains with an indecipherable and truly anonymous identity.

No society is simply a market. But there are countries in which the market exists alongside the ghetto, in which innovation and mobility surround pockets of exclusion. For a long time, the United States was the fascinating and disturbing model for these fragmented societies, but the countries of Europe are very quickly catching up, despite their solemn declarations about integration in to the Republic, exemplary social security systems and the need to fight social inequality. The model takes on a much more tragic form when there is no great wealth to allow the poor to survive and in some cases to get out of the ghetto. The underdeveloped countries and even countries which, like most of Latin America, are in an intermediary position, seem to have been caught up in an accelerating dualization. Poverty is increasing, and the poor are increasingly isolated from the categories that are involved in the world economic system. Such societies have been described in pathological terms, as they are characterized by their poor or declining capacity to act upon themselves. We therefore are no longer talking about social systems, but about internally divided societies where the poor live in a world that is increasingly different to the world of the rich, and where the coexistence of closed communities and zones that have been opened up to the world economy makes both political intervention and social protest impossible.

This vision of a purely mobile society cannot be contrasted with the rationalist model of the early modern era. That model represented an overall vision, even though the crisis of modernity does tend to fragment it. The liberal vision, in contrast, describes only part of society, just as tourist guides show us around only part of a city, namely the rich areas. The same criticism also applies, *mutatis mutandis*, to the vision promoted by the communitarian life of the ghettos or of excluded groups.

Those who are excluded from the constant process of innovation and decision-making no longer have the support of a class culture or a working-class or popular milieu. They are no longer defined by what they do, but by what they do not do. They are defined by their unemployment or marginality. The excluded are sometimes destroyed by their anomie, and sometimes drift in to crime. Increasingly, they are integrated in to local or ethnic cultures. This has long been the case in the United States and Great Britain. Anyone who is no longer defined by their activity soon constructs or reconstructs an identity based upon their origins. The phenomenon takes on increasing importance if we look at it on a world scale, but our analysis here will be restricted to those industrial societies which have become post-modern societies. These are dynamic and liberal societies because they are embarked upon a process of change that will permanently transform all modes of sociality and modernity, but they are also societies with communities and ghettos. When the economy is no more than set of business strategies, and when actors are no more than non-actors – the unemployed, immigrants or school students worried about their futures – the divorce between system and actors is complete. There is no link between the objectivity of the market and the subjective quest for an identity which, unlike that of a peasant or worker, can no longer be a socio-professional identity. This dualization has much more serious implications than the 'two-speed' economy that is so often denounced in both the industrial countries and the Third World.

In the space of a few years, industrialized Europe has lived through the death of the workers' movement, which either became perverted by its involvement in communist totalitarianism or was incorporated in to the economic and political decision-making system and therefore reduced to being a 'social partner'. This gave it an important role within the political system, but not in the central debate about the direction society should be taking. Social life has become a marathon. Some are fighting to win the race, and the majority are struggling to keep up with the pack. A certain number are voicing fears about being outdistanced and left behind, whilst others bite the dust and give up because they are exhausted. We have moved from social conflicts to the hopes and fears associated with increasingly rapid mutations, from the problems of a social structure to those of a mode of change. The youth movements that were seen in France in 1990 are typical of this new social conjuncture. The *lycéens*, and especially those from the suburbs, took to the streets because many of them came from a background in which the previous generation had not enjoyed the same level of education, and they were afraid that they would be denied access to the immense middle class of urban consumers. They were joined by young people from the new suburbs on the outskirts of Paris and Lyon who became involved in serious incidents. They looted shopping centres and set fire to cars, in some cases because one of their number had died as a result of brutal police intervention. Unlike the *lycéens* they no longer had any hope of being integrated in to society. They were motivated by an anger fuelled by society's inability to integrate them rather than by its refusal to do so. Yet, just as the actions of the so-called dangerous classes of the nineteenth century did not become the cradle of the workers' movement, neither of these reactions provided the starting point for a new social movement. They point to a crisis in a system which discourages collective action rather than encouraging protests. It has long been obvious in the United States that exclusion from the world of production and consumption encourages ethnicity, or in other words an awareness of ethnic identity. The same thing is now becoming obvious in Europe. Those who are no longer defined by the work they do, largely because they are unemployed, define themselves in terms of what they are and, for many of them, this means their ethnic background. These counter-cultures are embodied in gangs, and often in forms of music with a high ethnic content. They become rallying points for a population which has been marginalized but which still wants to be part of the world that has rejected it. What we are seeing in parts of New York, London and, to a lesser degree, Paris, is no different to the divide between rich nations and poor nations, and that divide is growing year by year. The day when Alfred Sauvy could call these proletarian nations the 'Third World' and could predict that they would have the same future as the Third Estate which overthrew the Ancien Régime in France, is long gone. We now speak of a fourth world in order to emphasize that frustration has replaced hope, and that marginality has replaced the prospect of involvement in production and consumption. The outcome is the decay of collective action, which is no longer capable of challenging the social appropriation of the means of production. Collective action now means falling back on an increasingly mythical identity or succumbing to the fascination of the bright lights of consumption.

Post-modernisms

The post-modern situation is defined by the complete divorce between instrumental rationality, which has become a strategy to be used in unstable markets, and communities which are locked in to their 'difference'. Modernism asserted that the advance of rationality and technology had the critical effect of liquidating beliefs, customs and privileges inherited from the past, and that it also created a new cultural content. For a long time, modernism asserted that reason and pleasure were complementary. It did so in libertarian and aristocratic fashion in the seventeenth century, in bourgeois fashion in the nineteenth, and in popular fashion in the twentieth as standards of living rose. Freed from the guilt instilled by religious thought, modern individuals could reconcile bodily pleasures with those of the mind, and even with the emotions of the soul. They were at once skilled and sensuous, sensuous and intellectual. True, this image of what the Greeks called *kalos kagathos* is hardly convincing, as it reveals a shocking indifference to the real living conditions of the majority. Yet the idea that there is a direct link between rationalization and individualism was rarely challenged, even by critics of social inequality and economic exploitation. It was simply claimed that everyone had a right to enter the modern world, or in other words a world which was productive, free and happy. It is this all-encompassing image of modernity that has been shattered, after having been cracked by the attacks of all those who brought about a crisis in the very idea of modernity from the second half of the nineteenth century onwards.

The preconditions for economic growth, political freedom and individual happiness no longer seem to us to be analogous and interdependent. The divorce between economic strategies and the construction of a type of society, culture and personality came about very quickly, and it is this that names and defines the idea of *post-modernity*. Whereas modernity associated progress with culture, contrasted traditional cultures or societies with modern cultures or societies, and explained all social or cultural facts in terms of their position on the tradition–modernity axis, post-modernity dissociates elements that were once associated with one another. If it is the realism of the strategist and not the rationality of the engineer that is rewarded with economic success, and if success is the result of the talent of the financier or the boldness of the games-player – in the sense in which one speaks of games theory – and not of the protestant ethic or devotion to the national cause, then we have to abandon the heritage of both Weber and Condorcet. We therefore have to stop referring to the spread of rationalization and leave the domain of historical action. Gianni Vattimo regards two transformations as basic to the definition of post-modernity: the end of European dominance over the whole world, and the development of media which give 'local' or minority cultures a voice. They signal the disappearance of the universalism that gave central importance to the social movements which eighteenth- and nineteenth-century Europe assumed to be fighting for or against reason and progress. Society no longer has any unity, and no individual, social category or discourse has a monopoly on meaning. The multiculturalism which then emerges defends many different achievements. On a different register and as we have already noted, the anxiety generated by the divorce between production, consumption and political life, and therefore by the disappearance of society, as conceived by Western thought, coincides with an awareness that there are no more historical subjects. At the same time, the individual subject's decay is such that Erving Goffman reduces it to a series of presentations of the self (Goffman 1959). These are defined by their context and interactions, and not by projects or action plans. The Self is therefore reduced to a state of great weakness.

As the twentieth century draws to an end, the destruction of the Ego, society and religion begun by Nietzsche and Freud seems to be complete. Its destruction is finally completed by the systems theory of Niklas Luhmann (1984), who rejects the idea of actors and subjects, which was still present in Talcott Parsons's functionalism, and centres his analysis on the system itself. Actors and subjects are no more than an environment for increasingly differentiated subsystems, just as social life is now no more than an environment for the political system.

It is easy to criticize the variety of meanings that are given to post-modernism, but such criticisms miss the real point. Post-modernism, which I have just defined and whose main tendencies I am about to describe, is much more than an intellectual fashion. It is a direct extension of the destructive critique of the rationalizing model that was inaugurated by Marx, Nietzsche and Freud. It is the end-product of a long intellectual tradition. The tradition in question has almost always challenged technical and economic modernization. The last hundred years has not produced any major interpretation of modernization, with the possible exception of the work of Dewey, which is steeped in Darwinism. Post-modernism in all its forms is obviously incompatible with the essential features of the social thought bequeathed us by the last two centuries, and especially with the notions of historicity, social movements and the subject which I will be defending against post-modernist thought in part III below.

Post-modernist thought is a combination of at least four intellectual currents, each of them representing a break with the modernist ideology.

1. The first defines post-modernity as a *hyper-modernity*, just as Daniel Bell (1976) defined post-industrial society as 'hyper-industrial'. The tendency towards modernity accelerates constantly. Avant-gardes become ever more ephemeral and, as Jean-François Lyotard (1979) rightly points out, all cultural production becomes avant-garde as its consumption of signs and languages speeds up. Modernity abolishes itself. Whereas Baudelaire (1863) defined modernity as the presence of the eternal in the instant, and therefore as a challenge to the idealism of cultures which attempted to rescue eternal ideas which had been distorted and tarnished by practical life and feelings, a hundred years later modernity seems to be the prisoner of the instant. It is caught up in the increasingly complete eradication of meaning. Post-modernity is a kaleidoscopic culture. It does not abandon modernity, but reduces it to the introduction of technological innovations which draw attention only because of their novelty value and their technical sophistication, and they are quickly superseded.

2. Even though the two are complementary, there is a critique, not of technical modernism, but of the social and political modernism which invented societal counter-models representing such a complete break with the past that their realization would have required the intervention of an absolute power. As I have said from the outset, the idea of revolution has always been closely associated with that of modernity. The intellectual success of post-modernism at the end of the 1960s was a direct effect of the crisis in revolutionary leftism. The neo-liberalism that triumphed in economic and political life during the 1980s and cultural post-modernism are both products of the decay of leftism. Leftism was an extreme form of modernism, especially for the Trotskyists who, from the very beginning of the Soviet Revolution, cultivated the utopian dream of the central machine, which became the central plan and, more recently, the central computer. It was supposed to transform the government of human beings in to the administration of things, and to liberate human beings from the evils of Stalinist or Hitlerian political subjectivism. In France, Jean Baudrillard (1978) is the most resolute exemplar of the transition from the leftist critique to the post-modernist critique of leftism, or even to the negation of the social.

Have we entered the era of the dissolution of the social? Many people, from Baudrillard to Lipovetsky (1983, 1987), regard this as the real meaning of the decay of modernity and claim that the idea of post-modernity indicates no more than a break with an intellectual and cultural tradition. The *post-social* situation is a product of the complete divorce between instrumentality and culture. Instrumentality is managed by economic or political companies which compete in markets; meaning has become purely private and subjective. Tolerance is therefore the only principle that can regulate social life. In his *L'Ere au vide*, Lipovetsky (1983: 46) writes: 'All tastes and all modes of behaviour can coexist without being mutually exclusive. Everything can be chosen at leisure: both the simple ecological life and a hypersophisticated life in a devitalized time where there are no stable points of reference and no major co-ordinates.' This divorce between the private and the public can be seen everywhere. Politics no longer claims to be able to 'change life' and parliaments no longer represent social demands. They are no more than sites for the ever more pragmatic definition of a power base for a managerial and, above all, financial executive. Actors have ceased to be social actors. They have become introverted, and are dedicated to a narcissistic quest for their identity, especially if they are not integrated in to a middle class defined in terms of profession and consumption rather than modes of social behaviour. Although some, myself included, thought that May 1968 and the new social movements that came in to being at that time prefigured a new social world of actors, issues and conflicts which would be more integrated and more central than those of industrial society (Touraine 1968), analysts of the post-social situation see only desocialization. This has more far-reaching effects than the demise of ideologies. In this post-social situation, the 'social question' is, finally, replaced by what Serge Moscovici (1981, 1988) calls the 'natural question', or in other words the question of the survival of a planet threatened by the destructive effects of pollution and of the proliferation of technologies that are divorced from both culture and society.

The three major tendencies of the day – the triumph of an instrumentality which has become strategic action, the withdrawal in to private life and the ecologicial globalization of the problems caused by technology – thus combine to form a post-social field in which there is a divorce between truly social relations oriented towards other social actors, and relations with the self and nature. Sociologists themselves feel embarrassed by the word 'social', as though it referred simultaneously to all forms of normalization, as well as to campaigns against drugs, ghettos, poverty and racism. The word 'social' suggests clichéd noble sentiments and minor powers, or the clear conscience of a middle class surrounded by the non-social forces that alone are capable of modifying behaviour and organizing collective mobilizations. Calls for integration and solidarity seem quite derisory when the decomposition of social life is advancing apace on all sides. In the poorest and most fragile regions it results in chaos and violence, but in the richest societies it is experienced as an Arcadian idyll, as a relaxation of constraints and rules. It is as though scarcity alone brought about the concentration of power and the rigidity of rules, and as though the evolution of a rich society were self-regulating and required almost no intervention from the centre.

Although I find it difficult to control the irritation this vision arouses in me, I have to admit that, by destroying modernist ideologies, the notion of the post-social has delivered us from the fascination that even the most repressive 'progressive regimes' had for so many intellectuals, even though they were very fond of their own freedoms.

3. Both the hyper-modernist and the antimodernist approach make a complete exit from the field of modernity, but they leave it in opposite directions. Most thinkers leave modernity by breaking with historicism, or by replacing a sequence of cultural forms with a simultaneity of forms. In both our imaginary and our museums, works which had a powerful religious and social meaning in non-differentiated societies must be hung alongside purely formal constructs, direct expressions of feeling or works with a commercial or political meaning. Not because they all make us think of eternal ideas, but because we have no criteria for choosing between experiences which must, according to Habermas, all be accepted because they have a certain authenticity. This cultural pluralism or this return to a combination of polytheism and atheism is an extreme form of an idea Weber derived from Kant: if modernity is based upon the divorce between essences and phenomena and if technical and scientific action belongs within the latter domain, our political and cultural space is of necessity polytheistic, as the uniqueness of rational explanations of phenomena has been dissociated from a world of gods which no longer has any unifying principle. Post-modernism now becomes *post-historicism*. That is its primary meaning, and that is what gives it its importance. It is quite in keeping with the experience of our contemporaries, who travel through space and time by going on holiday, visiting museums, reading books, looking at art and listening to records and cassettes which sensitize them both to works to which they are materially close, and to works from which they are separated by hundreds of years or thousands of kilometres. Taking up Ernst Bloch's theme of the simultaneity of the non-simultaneous (Bloch 1962), Jean Cazeneuve (1980) emphasizes television's ability to make something that is far away in time and space appear close at hand in time and space. It thus destroys the idea, which was obvious for so long, that a culture is a unity, and strengthens the idea of cultural pluralism. Claude Lévi-Strauss (1971) was brave enough to admit that cultural pluralism implies a certain defensive closure of individual cultures. Without that closure, all cultures will sooner or later be destroyed by either one dominant culture or by the action of purely technical and bureaucratic apparatuses which are alien to the world of culture. Post-modernism feeds directly in to a cultural ecologism that challenges the universalism of the modernist ideology which, especially in its conquering phase and in those countries which, like the hegemonic France of the Revolution and the modern United States, identified most strongly with modernity and universal values.

4. Now that cultural works are divorced from the historical ensemble which produced them, their value can be defined only by the *market*. Hence the

new importance of the art market, whereas for a long time, works of art were chosen either by princes or by connoisseurs representing the cultural demands of the aristocracy or the bourgeoisie. This brings us back to our analysis of the liberal society in which two fragments of our shattered modernity – the company and consumption – triumph over Eros and the Nation. In other words, mobility and change triumph over Being.

The post-modernist movement thus takes to extremes the destruction of the modernist representation of the world. It rejects the functional differentiation between domains of social life – art, the economy, politics – and its corollary, namely the ability of every domain to make use of instrumental reason. It therefore also rejects the divorce between a high culture – which can be social and political as well as aesthetic – which refers to the social order's metasocial guarantors (reason, history, modernization or the liberation of the working class), and mass culture. Hence the 'anti-aesthetic' slogan, whose importance is stressed by Fredric Jameson (see especially his contribution to Foster 1983). At a deeper level still, what is being rejected is the construction of images of the world, to use what Heidegger calls the most significant word in modernity. Post-modern thought no longer puts man in front of the world so that he can watch it and reproduce it in images. It places man in the world and abolishes the distance between the two, or rather replaces distance, which implies that the object already exists, with the construction of a communications network, with a language shared by the painter, the artist or the architect, and their objects. The painter Jean Dubuffet refers (Dubuffet 1991: 228–9) to a reality that lies behind the artificial constructs of culture:

> Basically, our mind can only apprehend individualized objects, or in other words *forms*; it then plays with those objects as though they were a deck of cards, shuffling them and collecting kings and queens in the same way that musicians play with their twelve notes on their little pianos. The absolute content of things, the substance of things is, naturally, quite different to their forms (our forms); there are no forms in the absolute. Forms are an invention of the mind. Our mind turns to them because it needs forms to think and therefore sees everything through its window, its totally falsifying, totally falsified window.

With Dubuffet and others, post-modernism rediscovers an antihumanist naturalism which is the complete antithesis of the philosophy of the Enlightenment and of the thought of Locke in particular. This attitude results in the violent rejection of the ideological discourses and the clear conscience of our civilizations. Jean-François Lyotard's celebrated statement (1979) about the end of grand narratives has a similar meaning. It is not simply the content of ideologies, but the narrative conception of human experience that is being rejected. Its rejection actively destroys the idea of the Subject. Hegel's Subject no longer exists. Neither modernity nor the future of the world will bring about the emergence of a rational Subject that has been liberated from traditional beliefs. Neither the Ego nor culture have any unity of their own. Western culture's claims to unity and universality must be rejected, as must the notion that consciousness or the Cogito can create an Ego. Jameson takes the critical anaysis still further and defines post-modern culture in terms of pastiche or schizophrenia. It is a pastiche because the absence of any cultural unity leads to the reproduction of the styles of the past. It might be said that the late twentieth century breaks with the modernism of the nineteenth and twentieth centuries by imitating the eighteenth, and especially its aristocratic libertinage, its fascination with language and its liberal-libertarian conception of the critique of power. It is schizophrenic, or narcissistic as others would put it, because its confinement within a perpetual present abolishes the space that makes it possible to construct the unity of culture.

Post-modernism marks the completion of the task begun by Nietzsche: the destruction of the reign of technique and instrumental rationality. Experience and language replace projects and values. Neither collective action nor the meaning of history have any existence. Post-modernism reveals that contemporary hyper-indus-trialization does not lead to the formation of a hyper-industrial society; on the contrary, it leads to a divorce betweeen the cultural world and the technical world. And it thus destroys the idea on which sociology has, until now, been based: the interdependence of the 'modern' economy, 'modern' politics and 'modern' culture.

It seems that nothing is capable of reuniting things that have now been divorced for a hundred years. That is why political and social ideologies have disappeared and have been replaced only by moraliz-ing declarations which are momentarily moving, but which soon come to look laughable, hypocritical or even manipulative. This destruction of modern ideology reached its high point when advertis-ing agencies were put in charge of the celebrations to mark the bicentenary of a French Revolution which has lost all meaning and become a piece of kitsch. Those who called for a return to great causes and great values, who wanted to restore some meaning to history, or even to identify their country – be it France, the United States or some other country – with that meaning and with universal principles, looked like retarded ideologues when what had once been a foundational event was officially reduced to being a pure spectacle, a product of mass culture whose content is as disparate and as ephemeral as the programmes on television.

The multiplicity of definitions and the confusion of most analyses are not sufficient grounds for rejecting the idea of post-modernity. The most important periods recognized by cultural history, from romanticism to structuralism, were not defined in clearer or more stable terms. But in the case of post-modernism, a more serious obstacle has to be overcome, as the name itself is contradictory: a historical definition – *post* – is used to name a cultural trend which breaks with historicism. We are encouraged to look to the state of society for an explanation for a cultural ensemble which tries, like a text, to define itself in its own terms. The most important thing of all is the transition from a productivist society based upon rationalism, asceticism and a belief in progress, to a consumer society in which individuals are part of the workings of the system not only because they work or think, but also because their desires and needs determine what they consume. Those needs are no longer mere attributes of a position within the system of production. This turns the individual–society relationship upside down. Individuals were once the producers and creators of a historicity. They no longer transform nature from the outside; they have been fully incorporated in to a cultural world, in to a set of signs and languages which no longer have any historical referents. This appears to destroy completely the idea of a Subject, which has always been associated with the idea of creation, and usually with that of the work of reason. Everything from our individual personalities to social life is becoming fragmented.

This idea destroys classical social thought, which believed that the triumph of reason made possible or necessary a correspondence between the norms of the social system and the motives of actors; human beings were therefore primarily citizens and workers. The divorce between system and actors is now complete. The lengthy triumph of the modernist modes of thought that dominated Western thought from the philosophy of the Enlightenment to philosophies of progress and sociologism is coming to an end. The success of the post-modernist critique does not, however, obviate the need to look for a new definition of modernity based upon the relative autonomy of society and its actors. For it is impossible to accept unreservedly that their dissociation is complete, as the *fin-de-siècle* coexistence of neo-liberalism and post-modernism might suggest. Neo-liberalism describes a society reduced to the state of a market with no actors (or one in which behaviour can be predicted on the basis of the laws of rational choice), and post-modernism describes actors without a system who are trapped in to their imagination and their memories.

The consequences of such a break are much more serious than the words we have been using might suggest. What is an actor who is defined without any reference to rational action? Someone who is obsessed with identity, and who sees others only in terms of their difference. At the same time, in a society which is no more than a market, everyone tries to avoid everyone else, or relates to them only through market transactions. The other easily comes to look like an absolute threat: it is us or them. They are invading our land, destroying our culture, forcing us to accept interests and customs which are foreign and threatening. The absolute separatisms and the unrestricted multiculturalism that we can observe in vast regions of the world and which, in the best American universities, sometimes take the form of ideological pressure to declare and enforce an absolute. Multiculturalism that bears the seeds of and wars of religion. It replaces society with a battlefield fought on by cultures which are totally alien to one another, where Whites and Blacks, men and women, the followers of different religions or even non-believers, are no more than one anothers' enemies. The social conflicts of past centuries, which were always limited as the social classes involved shared the same values and were fighting for their social implementation, are giving way to culture wars. They are all the more violent in that this kaleidoscope of cultures is also hostile to the cold, impersonal power of apparatuses of domination. They are like the spaceships we see in films and video games for adolescents. They are commanded by mathematical systems and an implacable will to power. Trapped within their own cultures, actors are opposed by the armoured might of the civil and military productive forces. The prospect of war between them is bleak in the extreme.

The End of Modernist Ideology

The crisis affecting the modernist idea was born of the refusal, first on the part of Nietzsche and Freud and then on the part of social actors, to reduce social life and the history of modern societies to the triumph of reason, even when it was deliberately associated with individualism. And that refusal itself was born of a fear of power, meaning both the power of despots and the power of a mass society which identifies itself with rationality, and which represses, exploits or excludes all the social actors it regards as irrational. It expels from individual life, and from collective life, anything it cannot use, anything that does not help to reinforce its power. The refusal inaugurated by Nietzsche and Freud also received support from the more aggressive critique voiced by the very actors of modernization when they appealed to life or needs, to the company or the nation, none of which is reducible to a form of rationalization. As the processes of modernization accelerated and multiplied, it seemed increasingly impossible to define them as being endogenous, or in other words to regard them as a product of modernity itself. The State, national and religious movements, companies' will to profit and the power of conquerors had taken charge of a modernization which was never a task for technicians alone.

The contemporary world which once seemed to represent the triumph of rationalism, now seems on the contrary to be the site of its decline. The idea of objective reason triumphed in Greek thought and in the Christian thought that drew on Aristotle. It asserted that the world was created by a rational god, and thus facilitated the victories of the scientific spirit. Hobbes and Rousseau taught us that society itself could be reconstructed on the basis of rational and freely-made decisions. From then onwards, the idea of modernity was complemented by the emergent idea of a modern society. The triumph of reason gave way to the transition from the rationality of ends to the rationality of means, which, in its turn, was debased to meaning technique. This left a value-vacuum which some saw as the liberation of everyday life. The majority, however, saw it as a vacuum that had been filled by a social power which was permeating every part of social life thanks to either charismatic appeals, the rebirth of nations and religion, or violence and the disappearance of order.

How can we fail to be convinced by the convergence of all these critiques of modernity? How can we fail to see the weaknesses of the language that so obstinately and so ineffectively tries to defend the conquering image of modernizing rationalism? Given that real societies are far from being rationally run companies or public services, rationalism falls back on education. But it does so in vain, as there is an increasing demand for an educational system that takes in to account the child's entire personality – family relations, cultural origins, personal characteristics and personal life history. Perhaps because their profession is on the decline in a society with rising educational standards, some teachers' representatives resist the demand for this model of education and for children's rights, and even the demands of children themselves. They wish to remain, or become once more, clerics who mediate between children and reason, who have a responsibility to remove children from the oppressive influence of their families, their social background and their local culture, and to introduce them to the open world of mathematical ideas and great works of culture. Their noble language cannot conceal the weakness of an approach which gives the school an increasingly repressive role. If their proposals were accepted, education would result in increased inequality, as its goal would be to divorce universals from particulars in the same way that the chaff is divided from the wheat. This conception simply increases the divorce between instrumental reason – meaning classes and examinations – and the personality of children or young people – an expression of a desire for life, preparation for work, and a cultural, national or religious identity – and youth culture. How can we speak of a successful education system when we have, on the one hand, teachers who have been reduced to transmitting knowledge with an accepted use-value and, on the other, children and young people who live in a cultural world that is completely divorced from the world of education? Fortunately, when it comes to individual activities, many teachers turn their backs on the conceptions they often defend as members of a collectivity. The failure of this discourse on education reveals the decline of a rationalism which has to be rejected because, on the one hand, it masks the power of a rationalizing elite and because, on the other, it has been overtaken by all the things it despised and rejected. They now dominate the scene of collective and individual history so completely that the liberating call of reason – and one would have to be insane not to heed it – is in danger of being ignored. The classical conception of modernity, which equated modernity with the triumph of reason and the rejection of particularisms, memory and emotion, is so worn out that it can no longer supply any principle that could unite a world where there is a confrontation between religious mysticism and modern technology, basic science and advertising, personal power and policies for accelerated industrialization.

The twentieth century has been the century of the decline of modernism, even though it has also been a century of technological triumphs. Intellectual life today is dominated by the belated, and therefore all the more violent, rejection of the communist model which was – if anyone cares to remember – the great hope of the century, not only for militant workers and anticolonial movements, but also for a great number of intellectuals. It is also dominated by the rejection of any notion of history, and of any analysis of historical actors, their projects and their conflicts and of the preconditions for a democratic conflict between them. Intoxicated with its political and ideological victory, the Western world is slipping in to liberalism. It is beginning to exclude actors and to resort to universal regulatory principles known as, depending on the level of education and occupation of those concerned, self-interest, the market or reason. Intellectual and even political life is now divided between those who are trying to define new actors and new issues for both what might be called post-industrial societies and for the developing countries, and those who appeal to a purely negative freedom, or in other words to the institutional rules and economic methods that afford protection against the abuses of power. For some, this rejection of any sociology of action takes the form of a return to economic individualism; they are attempting to show that individuals are primarily motivated by self-interest and that collective action, which often seems to be an essential means to defend individual interests is, as Roberto Michels predicted almost a hundred years ago, in danger of becoming an end in itself. For others, it takes the form of an appeal to the constraints and proofs of reason: they are the only possible principles of social unity, the only effective defence against the pressures exerted by churches and sects, minorities and irrationalism.

This defensive attitude is all the more pronounced in that, despite its victory over the communist system, the West feels threatened by the demographic and political pressures exerted by the Third World. When the dominant image is one of famine and urban violence from Calcutta to Bogota, the West remains unmoved, or limits its response to reassuringly philanthropic campaigns. But when the Third World comes to the next neighbourhood or to a housing estate inhabited by people who feel that they belong to modern society, they are quick to reject it. In the case of those who, like the poor whites, as they used to say in the post-bellum Southern states, feel a direct threat, the rejection is immediate and is expressed in both political and social terms. In the case of those who are protected from this penetration by their level of education and income, it is sublimated and takes the form of the assertion that Western society is the guardian of universalism, and that defending it against all particularisms is a matter of duty rather than self-interest. After a hundred years of campaigns for the rights of this or that category, calls for their extension now arouse suspicion and fear rather than support. Western society no longer feels capable of the openness and integration that allowed nineteenth- and twentieth-century Britain and France to become cosmopolitan societies and countries that welcomed immigrants. It feels swamped by the numbers, the poverty and the growing cultural distance between the new arrivals and host countries which are increasingly disrupted and disturbed by them.

At a more abstract level, we find that sociology too is being rejected. Sociology has always been a disturbingly critical analysis of modernity, but it was also a positive critique. This was as true of Durkheim and Weber as it was of Tocqueville and Marx before them, and it was also true of Parsons and the Chicago School. Sociology talked about industrialization and social classes, about political institutions and social conflicts; it asked how economic innovation could be reconciled with majority access to the fruits and sources of growth. Nowadays, the most pressing question seems to be not the management of growth, but the struggle against despotism and violence, the preservation of tolerance and the recognition of the other. Being one of those who believe that cultural issues and social actors provide the answer, I have to admit, before indulging in more personal considerations, that the liberal response to the ravages of totalitarianism is more convincing than the sociological response. It too is under threat, albeit in a different way, from communitarian movements, especially when they are based upon a religious faith or a national consciousness.

We have to be patient and wait for social thought to re-emerge from the darkness. Just as we had to wait for a long time after the triumph of the financial and mercantile bourgeoisie to see the formation of a worker's movement, for the recognition that there was a 'social question' and for the appearance, after a century of growth and poverty, of signs announcing an industrial democracy. A quarter of a century ago, when sociologists, myself included, began to write about post-industrial society (Touraine 1969), it was difficult to get away from the image of a gradual transition from one society to the next. It was as though the new society would both complete and transcend the old. We now know that one mountain ridge does not lead directly to the next, that we have to go down in to the valley, traverse the scree and lose sight of the next peak. We are no longer in danger of losing a belief in an illusory continuity, but we are in danger of refusing to believe in the existence of mountains we cannot see, and therefore of assuming that we have reached the end of our journey. I unreservedly accept that historicism has to be rejected and that sociologies of progress are in a state of crisis, but I also believe that it is as dangerous to surrender to the obsession with individual or collective identity as it is to surrender to a rationalist fundamentalism.

We have to admit that, whilst the materialist conception of modernity still has an emancipatory power, especially at a time when 'fundamentalisms' are on the rise, it no longer has the capacity to organize a culture and a society. The decay of the idea of modernity, which has been the theme of part II, is generating increasingly dangerous contradictions. Public and private life are divorced from one another. The field of social relations is breaking up and giving way to a direct confrontation between particular identities and world trade flows. On the one hand, everyone is retreating in to subjectivity. At best we forget the other; at worst we reject anything foreign. On the other hand, trade flows constantly strengthen the central countries and groups, and lead to a greater dualization at both the national and the international level. These contradictions are more serious than the social conflicts that tore apart industrial society. Increasingly, sexuality, consumption, the company and the nation are separate worlds which either clash or ignore one another rather than forming an alliance. The public space between them is becoming empty, or is no more than a piece of waste ground where rival gangs clash and where violence is unleashed.

How can we reconcile the decay of the classical rationalist vision, which we know to be inevitable and even liberating, with the organizational principles of social life that guarantee the continued existence of justice and freedom? Is there any way of escaping both a dominating universalism and a multiculturalism that leads to segregation and racism? How can we avoid both the destruction of the Subject, which leads to the reign of self-interest and might, and the dictatorship of subjectivism, which has given birth to so many totalitarianisms?

Whilst there are those who are rash enough to claim that the world is being unified around the 'Western' values which have triumphed over fascism, communism and third-world nationalism, the world today is in fact the site of a rift between the objective world and the subjective world, between system and actors. We can see the two coming in to conflict. The logic of the world market is in conflict with the logic of powers that speak in the name of a cultural identity. For one, the world seems global; for the other, there appear to be no limits to multiculturalism. These complete rifts have to be seen as a twofold threat to the planet. Whilst the law of the market is crushing societies, cultures and social movements, the obsession with identity is trapping them in to a political arbitrariness which is so complete that only repression and fanaticism can sustain it. It is not only that our knowledge of the history of ideas obliges us to redefine modernity; the naked clash between two cultures and two kinds of power obliges us to reunite worlds that have been divorced without surrendering to nostalgia for the lost unity of the universe. If we do not succeed in defining a different conception of modernity – one which is less haughty than that of the Enlightenment but which can still resist the absolute diversity of cultures and individuals – the storms that lie ahead will be still more violent than the storms that accompanied the fall of the *anciens régimes* and industrialization.

Part III

Birth of the Subject

1

The Subject

Return to Modernity

Everything forces us to go back to this question: can modernity be equated with rationalization or, to put it more poetically, with the disenchantment of the world? We also have to learn from critiques of modernity, given that we live at the end of a century that has been dominated by so many repressive or even totalitarian 'progressivisms', as well as by a consumer society which is consuming itself in an ever more ephemeral present and which remains indifferent to the harm progress is doing to both society and nature. Yet in order to do that, we have to go back and investigate the nature and birth of modernity.

The triumph of rationalist modernity rejected or forgot anything that seemed to resist the triumph of reason, or else confined it in repressive institutions. Yet what if the arrogance of statesmen and capitalists did not promote the cause of modernity? What if it destroyed part of modernity – perhaps the most important part – just as revolutionary avant-gardes have done more to destroy popular liberation movements than their social or national enemies?

We have to close roads that lead to nothing but the wrong answer. Let us begin with that of antimodernity. The contemporary world accepts modernity by an overwhelming majority. Only a handful of ideologues and despots appeal to a tradition-bound notion of community, and to traditional forms of social organization or religious belief. Almost all societies have been penetrated by new forms of production, consumption and communication. Eulogies of purity and authenticity are becoming increasingly artificial, and even when leaders denounce their country's penetration by the market economy, the people welcome it, just as poor workers in Islamic countries are drawn towards the Gulf's oil fields, just as the semi-unemployed of Central America are drawn towards California and Texas, and just as those of the Maghreb are drawn to Western Europe. The pretence that a nation or social category has to choose between a universalist and destructive modernity and the preservation of an absolute cultural difference is too crude a lie for it not to be a means of concealing vested interests and a strategy of domination. We are all embarked on the adventure of modernity; the question is whether we are galley slaves or passengers with luggage who travel in hope, as well as being aware of the breaks we will have to make. Simmel saw the foreigner as the emblematic figure of modernity. Its emblem today is the emigrant, a traveller full of both memories and hopes who discovers and constructs himself in his daily attempt to connect past and future, a cultural heritage and membership of a socio-professional category.

The second path we have to ignore is signposted by the image of 'take-off'. This image suggests that we make our entry in to modernity by being violently wrenched from the ground of tradition. After a dangerous period of turbulence, we then reach cruising speed and a stability that allows us to relax, to forget both where we have come from and where we are going, and to enjoy our release from normal constraints. This idea is now very widespread, rather as though every country had to endure a hundred years of hard work and social conflicts before it could enter the tranquility of affluence, democracy and happiness. The first countries to industrialize are now out of the storm zone; new industrial countries like Japan or other countries in Asia are still struggling to escape it, whilst many countries are waiting impatiently to enter the purgatory of modernity. This optimistic view of the stages of economic growth does not stand up to a more realistic assessment of the contemporary world, which has been in upheaval and torment for the last century. Death by starvation is the only growth sector.

The third path also leads to a blind alley. It equates modernity with individualism, or with the breakdown of what Louis Dumont calls holistic systems. The functional differentiation of subsystems, and in particular the divorce between politics and religion, or between the economy and politics, and the formation of the worlds of science, art and private life, are indeed preconditions for modernization, as they destroy the social and cultural controls that guaranteed the permanency of an order and resisted change. As Brecht demonstrates so forcefully in *The Life of Galileo*, modernity identifies with the spirit of free research and always comes in to conflict with the doctrinaire spirit and the defence of established apparatuses of power. It is, however, worth repeating that there are no grounds for identifying modernity with a particular mode of modernization, such as the capitalist mode, which is defined in terms of the extreme autonomy of economic action. The history of countries as different as France, Germany, Japan, Italy, Turkey, Brazil and India demonstrates that, on the contrary, the State almost always plays a role in modernization. Subsystems are certainly separated out, but general mobilizations do occur. Individualism did play a major role in industrialization, but so too did the will to unity or national independence. Can we regard the protestant idea of a *servum arbitrium* and of predestination as an instance of individualism? The image of the solitary businessman who took risks, innovated and made a profit triumphed in the United States and in new countries with open borders. But outside the centres of the capitalist system, modernization was a more co-ordinated and even more authoritarian process.

The debate is not simply one about successful industrializations; it is of still greater concern to countries that are trying to emerge from the ruins of a statist voluntarism that was long ago transformed in to either authoritarian or bureaucratic power or a client system. In the post-communist countries, many Latin American countries, Algeria and many other areas, the market economy is the only thing that will get rid of the planned economy and the privileges of the *nomenklatura*. Yet whilst the introduction of a market makes everything possible, it settles nothing. It is a necessary precondition for modernization, but not a sufficient precondition. It represents the negative process of destroying the past, but not the positive process of building a competitive economy. It may lead to financial speculation, to organized shortages or to a black market, or simply to the formation of foreign modern enclaves in the midst of a disorganized national economy. The transition from the market economy to the action of a modernizing bourgeoisie is neither automatic nor simple, and the State has an essential role to play in all cases. We therefore have to conclude that there can be no modernization without rationalization, but that modernization also means the formation of subjects-in-the-world who can take responsibility for themselves and for society. Modernity must not be confused with the purely capitalist mode of modernization.

We therefore have to go back to the idea of modernity itself. It is a difficult idea to grasp as it is hidden behind a positivist discourse, rather as though it were not an idea but a mere statement of fact. It is because modern thought always refused to be confined to lived experience or to a mystical or poetic participation in the world of the sacred, that it became scientific and technical by asking *how* and not *why*. The idea of modernity defines itself as the antithesis of a cultural construct, and as the unveiling of an objective reality. That is why it appears in a polemical mode and not a substantive mode. Modernity is an antitradition. It overturns customs and beliefs, abandons particularisms in favour of the universal and foresakes the state of nature for the age of reason. Liberals and Marxists placed the same trust in the exercise of reason and concentrated their attacks on what they both saw as obstacles to modernization, meaning, respectively, private profit, and arbitrary power and the dangers of protectionism.

The most obvious image of modernity is now that of a fluid economy, of a power with no centre, of a society based upon exchange rather than production. The image of modern society is, in a word, that of a society without actors. Can we apply the term 'actor' to an agent who acts in accordance with reason or the direction of history, and whose praxis is therefore impersonal? Wasn't Lukács caught in a complete paradox when he refused to regard the bourgeoisie as a historical actor because it was introverted and concerned with its own interests, and not, like the proletariat, with the rationality of historical development? Conversely, can we apply the term 'actor' to a financial or even industrial operator who adjusts himself to a conjuncture and to market indicators? According to modern thought, consciousness is always a false consciousness and French state schools, which are a late and extreme manifestation of the modernist ideology, quite logically emphasized scientific knowledge rather than the development of the personality. In its militant phase, the French school system dreamed of cleansing the minds of children of beliefs and family influence, but, having failed to achieve that goal, it rapidly settled for an armed truce with the private world of religions and families, in the expectation that belief would eventually fade away thanks to the impact of science and geographical and social mobility.

The things that are rejected by the idea of modernity and its refusal to define itself tell us where we have to start digging. Is modernity to be defined in negative terms? Does it mean no more than liberation? It is this self-representation that gives it its power. And it also explains why it so rapidly became exhausted once the world of production had obviously won its battle against the world of reproduction. We therefore have to try to define it in positive rather than negative terms, in terms of what it asserts rather than what it rejects. The idea of modernity does not have to be purely critical and self-critical.

Subjectivation

Can we rest content with an image of reason dispersing the clouds of irrationality, of science replacing belief and of a productive society taking the place of a reproductive society, and with a vision which predicted that the finalism imposed by the image of an omnipotent divine creator would be replaced by impersonal systems and processes? Yes, if we are talking about our representation of the world and our mode of knowledge. For centuries there have been no grounds for calling scientific knowledge in to question. But that is only half of what we call modernity or, more specifically, the disenchantment of the world. If we look at human action rather than nature, the picture changes completely. In traditional society, people are subject to impersonal forces or a destiny over which they have no control; what is more important, their action has to conform to an order which is, at least in Western thought, seen as a rational world that they must understand. The sacred world is both a world which has been created and brought to life by a god or a large number of deities, and an intelligible world. Our modernity did not destroy a world which was at the mercy of the favourable or unfavourable intentions of hidden forces; it destroyed a world which was both created by a divine subject and organized in accordance with rational laws. It destroyed a world in which man's most noble task was to contemplate creation and to discover its laws, or to discover ideas behind appearances. Weber said that modernity meant the disenchantment of the world, but he was also aware that this disenchantment was not reducible to the triumph of reason. It meant, rather, the destruction of the correspondence between a divine subject and a natural order. It is because he revealed this dualism that Descartes is both the emblematic figure of modernity and the heir to Christian thought. The further we enter in to modernity, the greater the divorce between subject and objects, which merged in to one in pre-modern worldviews.

For too long, modernity has been defined solely in terms of the efficacy of instrumental rationality and the mastery of the world that comes from science and technology. This rationalist vision must certainly not be rejected, as it is our most powerful critical weapon against all holisms, all totalitarianisms and all fundamentalisms. It does not, however, give us a complete idea of modernity, and conceals half of it: the emergence of the human subject as freedom and creation.

There is no one figure of modernity. Modernity has two faces and they gaze at one another: *rationalization* and *subjectivation*. Gianni Vattimo cites these lines from Hölderlin:

> *Voll Verdienst, doch dichterisch wohnet*
> *der Mensch auf dieser Erde*

> (Full of merit, yet poetically,
> Man dwells on this earth)

The success of technical action must not make us forget the creativity of human beings.

Rationalization and subjectivation appear at the same time, as do the Renaissance and the Reformation, which complement rather than contradict one another. The humanists and the followers of Erasmus resisted this divide and tried to defend both knowledge and faith, but they were swept away by the great rupture that defines modernity. From this point onwards, the world was no longer unified, despite scientism's repeated attempts to reunify it. Man was certainly part of nature and the object of positive knowledge, but he was also a subject and a subjectivity. The divine logos that haunts the pre-modern worldview was replaced by the impersonality of scientific laws, but also – and simultaneously – by the I of the Subject. Knowledge of man became divorced from knowledge of nature, just as action becomes distinct from structure. The classical or 'revolutionary' conception of modernity remembered only the liberation of rational thought, the death of the gods and the disappearance of finalism.

What did the term 'subject' mean? Primarily the creation of a world governed by rational laws which could be understood by human thought. The shaping of man in to a subject was therefore equated with the acquisition of rational thought and the ability to resist the pressures of customs and desires. The subject was governed by reason alone. The school curriculum is a good example. Similarly, historicist thought viewed historical development as a march towards positive thought, Absolute Spirit or the free development of the productive forces. This was what Horkheimer called the world of objective reason. This is the world for which he was nostalgic. How could he, and many others, fail to take a pessimistic view of the modern world, when modernity was so closely identified with the decline of objective reason and with the divorce between subjectivation and rationalization? Our modernity's tragedy is that it developed in the course of a struggle against half of modernity itself. The subject had to be driven out in the name of science. The entire heritage of Christianity, which lived on in Descartes and through him in to the following century, had to be rejected. The heritage of the Christian dualism and the theories of natural right that had given birth to Declarations of the Rights of Man and the Citizen on both sides of the Atlantic had to be destroyed in the name of reason and the nation. What we go on calling modernity therefore meant the destruction of an essential part of modernity. Although modernity can only exist because of the growing interaction between subject and reason, between consciousness and science, we became convinced that we had to abandon the idea of a subject in order to permit the triumph of reason, that we had to stifle our feelings and our imagination to see reason free, and that social categories identified with the passions – women, children, workers and colonized peoples – had to be crushed under the yoke of a capitalist elite identified with rationality.

Modernity does not mean a transition from a multiple world with a proliferation of deities, to the unitary world revealed by science. On the contrary, it signals the transition from the correspondence between microcosm and macrocosm, between world and man, to the rupture brought about by Montaigne's *Essays* and then Descartes's Cogito. The breach was soon made wider still by the irruption of sentiment and bourgeois individualism in the eighteenth century. Modernity triumphed together with science, but it also began to triumph when human behaviour was governed by a conscience – sometimes, but not always, known as a soul – rather than an attempt to conform to the world order. Calls to serve progress or reason, or the State which is their secular arm, are less modern than calls for freedom and the right to take responsibility for one's own life. Modernity rejects the ideal of conformity, except when the model in question is that of freedom of action. The figure of Christ is exemplary in this respect. He submits to his father's will, but leaves Being and enters in to existence, leads a life history and teaches that we must all love our neighbours as we love ourselves, and not as though they were the law or a world order.

Those who insist on equating modernity with rationalization alone refer to the subject only so as to reduce the Subject to reason and to enforce depersonalization, self-sacrifice and identification with the impersonal order of nature or history. The modern world, in contrast, increasingly abounds with references to a Subject. That Subject is freedom, and the criterion of the good is the individual's ability to control his or her actions and situation, to see and experience modes of behaviour as components in a personal life history, to see himself or herself as an actor. *The Subject is an individual's will to act and to be recognized as an actor.*

Individual, Subject, Actor

The three terms 'individual', 'subject' and 'actor' must be defined in relation to one another. Freud was the first to define them thus when, especially in his second topography, he analysed the Ego both as the final product of the Super-Ego's action on the Id and as part of the Id. Pre-modern man sought wisdom and felt impersonal forces, such as his destiny, the sacred and love, coursing through his veins. A triumphant modernity tried to replace this surrender to the world with social integration. Man had to fulfil his role as worker, parent, soldier or citizen. He had to take part in a collective task and, rather than being the actor of a personal life, become the agent of a collective project. This was in fact a semi-modernity which tried to give the old rationalism of those who watched the skies the new form of the construction of a technical world which repressed with greater severity than ever anything that helped to construct the individual subject. The emergence of the subject did not mean that reason had to triumph over the senses, to use the language of the classical age. On the contrary, the individual had to recognize within himself both the presence of the Self and the will to be a subject. Modernity triumphed when man was no longer part of nature, when he recognized that nature existed within him. The subject can be produced only to the extent that life persists within the individual, rather than being seen as a demon which has to be exorcised. Life has to be accepted as meaning libido or sexuality, and it must transform itself – rather than being passively transformed – into an attempt to construct the unity of a person. And that unity must transcend the multiplicity of lived time and space. The individual is no more than a particular unity where life merges with thought, experience with consciousness. The Subject is the transition from Id to I, the control that has to be exerted over the lived experience if it is to have a personal meaning, if the individual is to be transformed in to an actor who is inserted in to social relations and who transforms them without ever identifying completely with any group or collectivity. An actor is not someone who acts in accordance with the position he occupies, but someone who modifies the material and, above all, social environment in which he finds himself by transforming the division of labour, modes of decision-making, relations of domination or cultural orientations. Both left and right functionalisms speak exclusively of the logic of the situation or the reproduction of society. Yet society is constantly being transformed. Indeed, it is now being transformed so rapidly that what they call a situation is usually a political construct rather than an expression of an impersonal economic or technical logic.

The idea that a material base determines political and ideological superstructures, which was so widely accepted in the social sciences when, from Karl Marx to Fernand Braudel, they were studying the triumph of liberal capitalism, is inappropriate to a century dominated by political revolutions, totalitarian regimes, welfare states, and a huge expansion of the public space. It is therefore quite natural that the social sciences should have gradually abandoned their old determinist language, and have begun to speak increasingly in terms of social actors. I believe that I had something to do with this transformation, as I have always spoken of *social actors* and replaced the idea of 'social class' with that of *social movements* in my own work. The idea of a social actor is inseparable from that of the subject. For if an actor is no longer defined in terms of his usefulness to the social body or of his respect for divine commandments, what principles do guide him, if not his own constitution as a subject and the defence and extension of his own freedom? The notions of subject and actor are inseparable, and together they resist the individualism that privileges the logic of the system over that of actors by reducing them to a rational – and therefore calculable and predictable – pursuit of their own interests. In modern society, the subject's production of an actor may end in failure. Individual, Subject and Actor may drift apart. This is civilization's new discontent, and we are often affected by it. On the one hand, we are the creatures of a narcissistic individualism; on the other we are in the grip of a nostalgia for being or the subject, defined in the old sense of the term, and give it new aesthetic or religious expressions. At the same time, we also 'get on with the job', play our roles, and consume, vote or travel in the manner expected of us. We lead several lives and we have such a strong impression that this Self is not our identity that we flee it by using drugs or simply by surrendering to the constraints of everyday life.

The Subject is no longer the presence within us of a universal, no matter whether we call it the laws of nature, the meaning of history or divine creation. It is a call to transform the Self in to an actor. It is an I, an attempt to say I, in the full knowledge that personal life is dominated by, on the one hand, the Id and the libido and, on the other, social roles. The Subject never triumphs. It may be under the illusion that it does so, but that is because it has suppressed the individual as well as sexuality or social roles, and that it has once more become the Super-Ego, or in other words a Subject projected beyond the individual. The Subject abolishes itself as it becomes the Law and identifies with its extreme externality and impersonality.

Subjectivation occurs when the Subject penetrates in to the individual and transforms – to some extent – the individual in to a Subject. What was once a world order becomes a principle which can govern behaviour. Subjectivation is the antithesis of the individual's surrender to transcendental values. Man once projected himself on to God; in the modern world, man becomes the basic value. The central ethical principle now becomes freedom. Freedom is a creativity which is its own end and which resists all forms of dependency.

Subjectivation destroys the Ego, which is defined by the correspondence between personal modes of behaviour and social roles, and which is constructed by social interactions and the action of agencies of socialization. The Ego shatters in to the Subject on the one hand, and the Self on the other. The Self is a combination of nature and society, just as the Subject is a combination of individual and freedom. As Freud teaches us, the Subject – which he tended to confuse with the Super-Ego – is bound up with the Self and the Id, but not with the Ego, the goal of analysis being to destroy the Ego's illusions. The Subject is not a soul as distinct from a body, but the meaning the soul gives to the body, as opposed to the representations and norms imposed by the social and cultural order. The Subject is at once Apollonian and Dionysiac.

Nothing could be more antithetical to the Subject than the consciousness of the Ego, introspection or that most extreme form of the obsession with identity: narcissism. The Subject destroys clear and bad consciences alike. It inspires neither guilt nor self-satisfaction; it urges the individual or the group to seek their freedom in endless struggles with the established order and social determinisms. This resistance is positive to the extent that it is rationalization, as Reason too is an instrument of freedom; it is negative to the extent that rationalization is dominated and used by masters, modernizers, technocrats or bureaucracts who employ it to impose their power on those they transform in to instruments of production or consumption.

The divorce between the I and the Self has constantly been resisted, not only by norms and definitions of social roles, but also by self-consciousness, which tries to reconnect the I with the Self in order to prevent it from returning to the world of the gods and to stop the Self sinking in to the Id. Ever since the beginning of the sixteenth century, humanism has identified with this search for a compromise between the gods and nature, faith and the Church, the subject and science. The work of Montaigne is its most noble expression. That lesson in prudence and wisdom cannot, however, prevail against the breaks that have to be made. Nor can it prevail against the quest for self as Subject that leads modern individuals to challenge the established order on a permanent basis. The day when the Subject is debased to meaning introspection, and the Self to meaning compulsory social roles, our social and personal life will lose all its creative power and will be no more than a post-modern museum in which multiple memories replace our inability to produce anything of lasting importance.

As we have already noted, Michel Foucault sees an element of subjection in subjectivation. The inner or so-called 'psychological' man had to be constructed to allow social control to penetrate more deeply, to get a hold on the heart, the mind and the genitals and not merely the muscles. Yet this perversion of subjectivation can in no sense be a substitute for the birth of the subject, and nor can it be its primary meaning. Whenever totalitarianism is established, the main source of resistance is the appeal to the subject and to the ethics of conviction, which may or may not take a religious form. It can produce either a Solzhenitsyn or a Sakharov. A hundred years ago, Max Weber hailed the triumph of the ethics of responsibility over the ethics of conviction. We now tend to admire those who refuse to be good workers, good citizens or efficient slaves, as well as those who rebel in the name of religious convictions or human rights. This resistance to repressive modernization cannot be purely modernist; it is not enough to say, like the socialists of the early industrial period, that, thanks to the workers' movement, modernity will triumph over the irrationality of capitalist profit. If we are to resist total oppression, we must mobilize the total subject, the religious heritage, childhood memories, ideas and courage. Max Horkheimer formulated one of the most profound ideas of the century when he said, with reference to the inability of German intellectuals and political militants to halt the 'resistible rise of Arturo Ui', that reason alone cannot defend reason. This sentence, which Cardinal Lustiger adopts as a motto in his memoirs, marks a break with the over-confident optimism of the Enlightenment. It is a reference to the subject, a refusal to give central importance to the traditional–modern dichotomy. Nietzsche and Freud were the first to rediscover this when they found in man the oldest myths and beliefs and refused to divorce their rationalism from an attack on the pseudo-modern – or at least proto-modern – view that human beings and society were conscious, organized beings. Having recently lived through the catastrophes brought about by the authoritarian modernization forced upon us by totalitarian States, we now know that the production of the subject – the emblematic figure of modernity – is only possible when consciousness does not divorce the individual body from social roles, or the old figures of a subject that was projected in to the world in the form of God, from the modern will to construct oneself as a person.

The idea that the subject is an ethical principle is a challenge to both the idea that reason should control the passions, which is a constant from Plato to the 'rational choice' ideologues, and to the idea that the good means performing one's social duties. These three contrasting conceptions could even be described as successive stages in the history of ethical ideas. First of all, we have the idea that there is a world order. The main variation on this theme is the idea that the world order is rational. The noblest form of behaviour is therefore one which allows the individual to live in harmony with the world order. Secularization undermines this conception by reducing objective reason to mere subjective reason. At this point, the social utility of modes of behaviour, or their individual contribution to the common good, becomes the measure of their value. And it is only when this social moralism has been denounced by critical thinkers, and especially the followers of Marx and Nietzsche, that the affirmation of the individual as subject can come to the fore. It is, however, more likely that central importance will be given to the individualism which claims that the only ethical principle is the right of all to live in accordance with their individual desires. This naturalist position leads to the abolition of all norms and therefore all sanctions. If it were applied – if murder and rape were no longer punished – it would lead to violent reactions, and would thus demonstrate the artificiality of appeals to nature.

This evolutionist vision is inadequate, and even dangerous. It overlooks the fact that the modern appeal to the subject takes up, in secular form, the old idea that all human beings are equal and have the same rights because they are the creatures of God. That idea lies at the origin of natural right. Conversely, it also overlooks the fact that the idea of living in harmony with the world can take a modern form and at the same time remain a hierarchical social principle. Only its content changes, as scientists and businessmen replace priests and warriors at the top of the hierarchy. It is therefore preferable to introduce a permanent dichotomy between the ethics of order that is associated with a hierarchical vision of both society and the world, and an ethics of human rights which can appeal to both the idea of divine grace and the idea of a human subject.

The important thing is to contrast these conceptions of ethics. It seems to me that Charles Taylor (1989) fails to do so when he defines modern ethics in terms of respect for human rights, the notion of a full and autonomous life and the dignity of all in public life. I find that these three principles diverge rather than converge, as the first leads to the idea of a subject and the third to a social ethics which constantly contradicts that idea, whilst the second leads either to an extreme individualism or the idea of a life governed by reason and of the need to control the passions. The divergence becomes greater as a result of a major transformation. As Taylor rightly notes, for the moderns, ethics no longer defines the life of a higher category of individuals: it defines the ordinary life of all. This idea takes up the Christian theme of 'neighbours' and leads us to admire, not heroes or sages, but the ordinary individuals who respect, understand and love others, and who sacrifice their social success or intellectual prowess to those demands. The idea of a subject asserts the superiority of private virtues over social roles, and of a moral conscience over public opinion.

The idea of a subject cannot be a central 'value' that inspires institutions. The reliance upon values that is so pronounced in societies which, from the United States to Islamic countries, claim to be based upon religion, is in open contradiction with the idea of a subject. The idea of the subject is a *dissident* idea which has always upheld the right to rebel against an unjust power. It is an ethical demand that can never be transformed in to a principle of public morality, as there can never be any correspondence between the personal subject and social organization.

The Religious Origins of the Subject

The modern spirit was defined primarily by its struggle against religion. This was particularly true in countries which had been marked by the Counter-Reformation. It is not enough to allow this discourse to die a natural death because it has lost all its mobilizing power, or to point out that in, for example, Chile or Korea churchmen fought against dictatorships with greater courage and conviction than many free-thinkers. We must openly reject the idea of a break between the darkness of religion and the light of modernity, for modernity's subject is none other than the secularized descendant of religious expression of the subject.

The demise of the sacred destroyed both the religious order and all forms of social order. It set free a subject that had been embodied in religion, just as it set free the scientific knowledge that had been imprisoned in a cosmogeny. Nothing could be more absurd or dangerous than a rejection of secularization or secularism, but there is no justification for throwing the baby out with the bathwater by rejecting both the subject and religion. Given the increasing dominance of technical apparatuses, markets and States – which are all products of the modern spirit – we urgently need to look to both old religious debates and new ethical debates if we are to find a non-social principle for the regulation of human conduct which is irreducible to either the collective consciousness of a community or to the link between the human world and the universe.

This is why I adopt with such enthusiasm the idea of natural right, which inspired the 1789 Declaration of Rights. Its goal was to place restrictions on social and political power, to recognize that the right to be a subject was more important than the order of law, and that the organization of social life must reconcile two irreducible principles: the rationalization of production and the emancipation of the Subject. The Subject is not merely consciousness and will. It attempts to reconcile sexuality and programming, individual life and involvement in the social division of labour. This presupposes both that every individual has the greatest possible autonomous space and can stand back from things, and that restrictions are placed on the ability of the law and the State to control minds and bodies. The return of religions is not simply a matter of mobilizing communities thrown in to turmoil by an imported modernization; it also implies, especially in industrialized societies, a rejection of the conception that reduces modernization to rationalization and therefore leaves the individual defenceless against a central power with unrestricted means of action. This return to religion does not hand power back to Churches; they continue to decline as rapidly as the ideological parties which wave the flag of a modernizing and antireligious rationality. It does not necessarily announce any return to the sacred or to religious beliefs in the true sense of the word. On the contrary, it is precisely because secularization is so solidly established that it is possible to see in the religious tradition a reference to a subject that can be mobilized against the power of economic and political apparatuses as well as that of the media. 'Ethics' has replaced religion as a source of morality, but ethics has to find in religious traditions references to the subject that must not be rejected by our secularized culture. The central importance that is now accorded to human rights and to moral choices stems from the decline of socialist or third-worldist political philosophies of history, but it is also in part the heritage of Churches and established religions. This is probably as true of the Islamic or Judaic worlds as it is of the Christian world despite the presence, in all three cases, of neo-traditionalist, quietist or mystical tendencies.

The expansion of political powers and movements which reject secularization and attempt to impose a religious law on civil society is frightening. Yet whilst the general trend towards the return to the subject is based upon a rejection of 'fundamentalisms', it is also inspired by the tragic failure of the modernizing policies bequeathed us by enlightened despotisms. They allowed ideological and police power to permeate everywhere, even in to the mind. And they did so in the name of reason. No one principle defines modernity and it is no more reducible to subjectivation than it is reducible to rationalization. It is defined by the increasing divorce between the two. That is why, after centuries of domination by political ideologies which were convinced they were the agents of progress, and after even longer periods dominated by great civilizations with a religious basis, we now live in a fragile world. There is no higher power and no arbitrating agency capable of affording effective protection to the essential interdependency of the two faces of modernity.

The idea of a subject, as defined and defended here, seems to go against the grain of modern thought. Many take the view that it is also dangerous, as it is the masters of power who appeal to the notion of Man in a bid to extend their domination over our minds. The entire content of part III is a response to these criticisms, but they are so fundamental as to require a more direct response.

Modernity supposedly marks the transition from subjectivity to objectivity. Science developed because it became materialist, because it discovered physical and chemical explanations for sensations, opinions and beliefs. Even in the moral domain, the ethics of responsibility has replaced the ethics of conviction, and the morality of duty has replaced the morality of intentionality that characterized those religions which are furthest removed from the idea of modernity. This general representation of modernity is consonant with the general idea of secularization and disenchantment. Natural facts no longer reflect the intentions of a Creator; they reflect laws that define relations between phenomena without speculating about Being and Nature. There is no denying that the sacred is in decline, but the survival or resurgence of irrational beliefs or magical practices may give cause for concern. There are, however, no grounds for reducing modernity to the triumph of rational knowledge and action. To say that the sacred no longer exists and that the realm of laws is now divorced from that of values is one thing; to proclaim the triumph of the positive era is quite another. The idea of a subject divorced from the idea of nature opens up two possibilities. The idea of the subject can be identified with Society and, more directly, with Power. Alternatively, it can be transformed in to a principle of personal freedom and responsibility. The choice between a religious and a positivist worldview is an artificial choice. We all find ourselves forced to choose between being the subject of society, just as we were once the subjects of a king, and being a personal subject defending an individual or collective right to become the actor of our own lives, ideas and conduct. Those who describe themselves as positivists often, like Auguste Comte himself, become devotees of the cult of society, and there are numerous secularized versions of the eschatology that gave birth to cults of the nation, the proletariat or morality.

Modern man is constantly threatened by the absolute power of society, and it is because our century has been tarnished by totalitarianism that it is more inclined than earlier centuries to recognize that the idea of the subject is the central principle which allows us to resist authoritarian power.

Modern society was born of the breakup of the sacred world order and saw the divorce between rational instrumental action and the personal subject. It also discovered that they were interdependent.

When rationality ignores the subject, it replaces it with the cult of society and of the functionality of behaviour; conversely, when the subject rejects rationality, it degenerates in to the cult of an individual or collective identity.

There is, however, another and more acceptable way of rejecting the dualism which, in my view, defines modernity. I refer to *liberal* thought, which is centrist in the literal sense of the term and which tries to bring together or even fuse the world of nature and that of human action. It takes its inspiration from the less rigid vision of naturalist determinism elaborated by modern systems theorists and from models derived from physics, chemistry and biology. This rejection of dualism has many virtues, not least in that it takes us away from an outdated conception of determinism which has always provoked a spiritualist response. On the other hand, Henri Atlan (1979) rightly points out that an over-synthetic approach can lead to misunderstandings, and stresses the continued need for dualism. Modelling and hermeneutic interpretation are extreme forms of that dualism. Even the work of Edgar Morin, who has done so much to establish a continuity between the natural sciences and our under-standing of human beings, demonstrates (Morin 1981) the need to go back to the subject when we analyse mass society.

It is essential to prevent one element of modernity from absorbing the other. This can only be done by recalling that the exclusive triumph of instrumental thought leads to oppression, just as the exclusive triumph of subjectivism leads to false consciousness. Thought is modern only when it rejects the idea that there is such a thing as a natural and cultural world order, and when it combines determinism and freedom, the innate and the acquired, nature and subject. This must lead to the recognition that there is an essential difference between the natural sciences and an understanding of society. But it should not be forgotten that, given that human beings are both nature and subject, the natural human sciences do exist.

Modernity Divided

Some may say that there is no reason to describe as 'modern' a conception that could be more accurately described as 'post-modern'. Their reaction may seem acceptable, as I have myself placed the thought of the last hundred years, which is inspired mainly by Nietzsche and Freud, under the sign of the crisis and decay of modernity. This is not in fact an acceptable criticism, as the critique of *modernism*, or in other words of the reduction of modernity to rationalization, must not lead to an anti- or post-modern position.

On the contrary, it allows us to rediscover an aspect of modernity that was forgotten or repressed by triumphant rationalization. If we remember both Descartes and the idea of natural right, as well as the contemporary concern with the subject, modernity can spread its wings and occupy the space of subjectivation as well as that of rationalization. Verbal quibbles aside, we have to assert the modernity of the theme of the subject, and reassert that it is bound up with the accelerated creation of an artificial world which is the product of human thought and action.

It is impossible to take an optimistic view of modernity's contemporary situation. It is because contemporary human experience is indeed shattered in to fragments that I have dwelled so long on the fragmentation and decay of modernism. This is an effect of the 'globalization' of social realities, which so many sociologists rightly stress. This is its real meaning. To say that new communications techniques have brought us closer together and that we are all aware that we belong to the same world may be superficial and banal, unless we immediately add that every form of mobility is accelerating and that our world therefore looks increasingly like a kaleidoscope. We all belong to the same world, but it is a broken and fragmented world. If we are to be able to speak once more of modernity, we must find a principle that can integrate this contradictory world and put the pieces back together again.

One part of the world is preoccupied with a defensive quest for its collective or personal identity, whilst the other part believes in nothing but permanent change, and sees the world as a supermarket which always has new products on display. For some, the world is a company or a productive firm; others are attracted to the non-social, which can go by the name of either Being or sex. In the midst of these fragments of social life and conflicting values, a swarm of human ants pursue goals set by technical rationality. Everything conspires to stop operatives, employees and technicians, whatever their rank, from concerning themselves with the ends of the actions. It is impossible to run the film backwards and to rediscover the irremediably lost unity of the world of Enlightenment and Progress. We therefore have to look for ways to reunite life and consumption, nation and company, and to relate them to the world of instrumental rationality. If that reconstruction proves impossible, we would do better to stop talking about modernity.

Does the idea of a subject and, more concretely, the tendency towards subjectivation, make it possible to reunite what has been scattered, and can it be the unifying principle for a new modernity? The answer has to be negative: it is impossible to conceive of a society with subjectivation as its central principle, primarily because the figure of the Subject is always divided in two. The idea of the subject is now emerging with such force because we are reacting against the demonic pride of the totalitarian, or merely bureaucratic, States that have devoured society and speak in its name. They are ventriloquist States which pretend to give society a voice when they have in fact swallowed it. Nietzsche, the Frankfurt philosophers and Michel Foucault have taught us that it is necessary to resist social power, and our resistance must be based upon the least social element in human individuals and upon supra-social forces that resist the orders of political power. It must be based upon sex and history, on the individual and the nation. We can all see quite clearly that an immense gulf separates Western youth, which rejects social controls over sexuality and which is fascinated by the assertion of individual identity and freedom, and the collective mobilizations of cultures and religions threatened by an exogenous modernization. Yet the recognition that this gulf exists must not be divorced from the discovery that the subject is attracted towards both sexuality and communality. Because it provides the link between the two and between the Id and the We, the subject allows us to resist both the State and the company. Both sexuality and communality are forces of resistance and revolt. Just as natural law could resist historicism, they can prevent social power from dominating our personalities and culture. Whereas the great project of the functionalists, and above all Talcott Parsons, was to unify the study of society, culture and the human personality, we know from Nietzsche and Freud that they have to be contrasted. We now have to go further still by asserting that the appeal to the individual and to individual desire, and the appeal to the nation and its culture, are complementary messages sent out by a single subject and that they enable it to resist the power of 'active society' on two fronts. It follows that the idea of the subject cannot reunify the fragmented field of modernity. Only *a combination of subject and reason* can perform that task. On the one hand, we live in a mass society made up of production and consumption, companies and markets, and it is governed by instrumental reason. It is a flux of change and a set of strategies that allow us to adapt to an unstable and poorly controlled environment and to take the initiative. On the other hand, our society is concerned with individual desire and a collective memory, with life and death instincts and with the defence of a collective identity. Auguste Comte, who was the prophet of modernity and of the religion of humanity, claimed that society was the creation of the dead rather than the living and, to pursue that idea, we might say that the modernity of a society can be gauged by

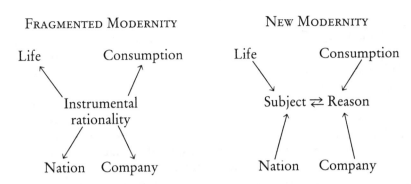

Figure 3

its ability to reappropriate human experiences that are far away in either time or space. The reconstruction that is taking place can be schematically represented as in figure 3.

The new modernity – and it is indeed a modernity – unites reason and the Subject, each of which combines two of the cultural elements of our fragmented modernity. Modernity, which repressed and suppressed half of itself by identifying with a triumphal and revolutionary mode of modernization – that of the *tabula rasa* – can at last be one again. It can only be defined as the link and the tension between rationalization and subjectivation. Indeed, the fact that the two principles are not integrated is essential to the definition of modernity. Modernity rejects the idea of society. It destroys it and replaces it with that of social change. Pre-modern societies believe that there is such a thing as a social order which, because of the pressure of causes that are beyond the control of actors, must be transformed in to a new order. They therefore look for an explanation for the transition from Antiquity to the Middle Ages, from *polis* to State, or from trade to industry. Today, historicity is no more than a secondary attribute of a society. Philosophies of history were the first to say so, but they still located real societies within a history, be it that of Spirit, Reason or Freedom, or in other words the history of a non-historical principle. The reason why, at risk of being misunderstood, I constantly focus my remarks on the idea of *historicity*, is that social life can no longer be described as a social system whose values, norms and forms of organization are established and defended by the State and other agencies of social control, and that it must be understood as action and movement. Social life is therefore a set of relations between the social actors of change. That is why the way in which the unity of the social field is constructed completely rules out the idea of *society*. Ridding the social sciences of that idea is a matter of urgency because, in so far as it is modern, social life is marked on the one hand by the innovations of a system of production and consumption and, on the other, by its openness to the desires of the Id, by the subject's insistence on defending a traditional culture and by the assertion of the subject's freedom and responsibility.

The subject must not be seen as a means of reuniting the scattered elements of modernity (life, nation, consumption and company), but it does connect them by weaving a dense web of relations of complementarity and opposition. The idea of the subject reconstructs a shattered cultural field which, after the critiques made by Marx, Nietzsche and Freud, can never again have the clarity and transparence it had during the Enlightenment. The subject is by no means a self-contained individual and Alain Renault (1989) gives a forceful demonstration of the difference between what he calls the monadological tradition inaugurated by Leibniz and continued, in his view, by Hegel and Nietzsche, and what he too calls the subject. The subject therefore has to be regarded, not as a superior ego modelled on a father or as a collective consciousness, but as an attempt to reconcile personal desires and needs, with an awareness of belonging to a company or nation, or the offensive face of human actors with their defensive face.

We have some difficulty in getting away from the view that society or the Ego is a system united by a central authority, or that it is a social body ruled by a brain or a heart. Modernity is constantly under attack from forces which, whilst they may come in to conflict with one another, all refer to a single principle. That principle is so often religious or national. In other cases, it is technical rationality or even the market; in the past, it was a global historical project entrusted to one party or a government vested with unrestricted power. Modernity, in contrast, is defined primarily by the transition from a centralized conception of social life to a bipolar conception, and to the management of the complementary and contradictory relations between subjectivation and rationalization.

This is why the idea of a subject cannot be identified with any of the shattered fragments of modernity. Every subject merges in to a community, nation or ethnic group. There is no such thing as a company-subject. The subject cannot be reduced to sexuality and, above all, the subject cannot be simply identified with the freedom of a consumer in a well-supplied market. This is not merely a matter of avoiding reductionism. What we call the consumer society is not a technical or economic system. It constructs social reality in accordance with a model diametrically opposed to the subject-model. It therefore destroys the subject by replacing meaning with signs, the depths of psychological life with the surface of the object, and the serious business of love with the games of seduction. The consumer society is a humdrum landscape swarming with stereotypical characters. Does anyone believe that a secularized world with no transcendental principles is purely a world of appearances and decisions as to what to buy? In the wealthy commodity society of the West, the subject is constituted in opposition to mass society, and forms of consumption which are both standardized and hierarchical, just as, elsewhere in the world, it is constituted in opposition to the nation. Only an appeal to the subject allows us to distance ourselves sufficiently from the market to formulate an ethical judgement, and to reconstruct what the consumer society breaks down. Weber defined capitalism and modernity as worldly asceticism. This does not imply a hypocritical rejection of the consumer goods everyone desires, but it does mean that the individual has to be sufficiently distanced from them to acquire the density and duration of a subject, rather than being dissolved in to the immediacy of consumption.

When rationality is reduced to technology and instrumentality, only the search for efficacy and profitability binds together the shattered fragments of modernity. Everyone constructs a world which is foreign to others; we speak of the corporate culture in the same way that we speak of the consumer society or national or religious fundamentalism. The characteristic, or even the defining, feature of the subject is the attempt to reunite what has been separated. It is the antithesis of an appeal to an otherworldly principle or a metasocial guarantor of the social order. The subject constitutes a field of action and freedom by bringing opposites together, by broadening its experience and by rejecting all the Ego's illusions, and all forms of narcissism. The subject combines a delight in life with an entrepreneurial will, the diversity of lived experiences with the serious business of memory and commitment. It requires the Id to break down the defences of the Super-Ego, and to remain faithful to a face or a language. The force of both desire and communication, the appeal of consumption and travel, and that of research and production, all free the subject from the roles and norms imposed by systems that objectify the subject so as to control it. The idea of the subject therefore revives the creative utopia of the humanism which foresaw modernity but could not enter in to the Promised Land because there could be no real modernity without the rift between the Renaissance and the Reformation. The modern subject is the heir to the contradictory heritages of both Erasmus, Rabelais and Luther. It at least recognizes that they are in part complementary and that its own *raison d'être* is to give them all a new lease of life through a combination of knowledge of the world and Self-knowledge, and personal and collective freedom. It is this never-ending but happy task of constructing a life as though it were a work of art constructed out of disparate raw materials, that best defines the subject.

Women Subjects

Society therefore centres on what I call *social movements*. The most important are those which attempt to strengthen one tendency within society at the expense of the other. In our society, the most conspicuous, and by far the most powerful, cultural movement is the attempt to make production and consumption hegemonic. Like any cultural, social or economic movement, it identifies with modernity and calls for the removal of obstacles to change and for permanent modernization. With the support of industrialists and businessmen, organizers and advertisers, it raises the banner of liberalism and even individualism. The only opposition its representatives face comes from interest groups hostile to changes which threaten their vested interests. Yet the antithetical cultural movement, which defends subjectivation, claims to be just as modern as its enemy.

Which concrete actors support this cultural movement? The most important actor to do so is the women's movement which, in the name of modernity, demands the recognition of women's desire and their bio-cultural identity. It throws down a twofold challenge to a society based upon technico-economic innovation. There are certainly powerful trends within feminism that reject this cultural movement and demand nothing more than equal opportunities for women, arguing that women's roles in economic or administrative life should not be defined by their sex (gender), but by their professional abilities alone. In France, this movement is illustrated by Simone de Beauvoir and Elisabeth Badinter, and it has had a sympathetic hearing from the government, not least because women's so-called gains are merely an effect of their appearance *en masse* on the labour market. The consumer society encourages the mass transfer of women from the non-commodity personal service sector to the market personal sector, and especially health and education. This feminism, which is inscribed within the dominant cultural movement, should not, however, be confused with the *women's movement*, which is fighting for subjectivation and against rationalization. It is a weak and divided movement because, just as it is easy for mass producers and consumers, or industrialists and merchants, to form a united front, it is difficult to reconcile the sexual liberation of women with their cultural identity. Sexual liberation implies a rejection of the roles to which society confines women, whilst their cultural identity, according to Freud, defines women, as well as men and children, in terms of relationships. Yet the influence of a movement which seemed to have exhausted itself in internal disputes, continues to spread and to promote references to the sexuality and cultural role of women throughout the female population. With such success that it now has more male supporters than enemies.

The Other

Is the subject the only judge of the appeal to the subject? It is impossible to answer that question, as to do so would mean confusing the I with the Ego, and the idea of a subject obliges us to divorce the two. If it is to escape consciousness and its traps, the subject must assert itself by recognizing the other as subject. This is a traditional notion and, ever since the Sermon on the Mount, Christianity has given it a central importance: we must love our neighbours because they are God's creatures, and we must love God by loving our neighbours. The modern conception of the subject refuses, however, to take the view that human beings are noble because God created them in his own image. The theory of natural right and the Cartesian dualism to which I have referred so often are historically important forms of the idea of the subject, but modern thought no longer finds them acceptable because they are based upon a religious worldview which has been destroyed by secularization. We are no longer willing to see in the other, or even in our relationship with the other, the presence of Being or of the Infinite, just as we no longer see love as a deity or an arrow that suddenly pierces the heart. Recognizing the other as subject does not mean recognizing God within the other. It means recognizing the other's ability to reconcile the Id and the I. What we call love is a combination of desire, which is impersonal, and a recognition of the other as subject. The individual asserts him or herself as a subject by combining desire with empathy, without surrendering to the temptation to identify one with the other, as that would reduce the I to the Ego, which is effectively its antithesis. The subject therefore asserts its presence in this interpersonal relationship – friendship or love – rather than in the experience of solitude which meant so much to the romantics, but which is too close to nature, or in the social experience to which functionalist thought and its essential conformism always returns.

Contemporary popular culture, and especially popular songs and the videos that accompany them, are spreading this idea, which may seem far removed from lived experience. At its most successful, it shows an encounter between eroticism and tenderness, a meeting between people who are both free and attracted to one another without ever losing their individuality. And these relations of desire and love are strong enough to exist outside any real social integration, place, time or social milieu because they belong to the world of the subject and not the world of social life and its rationalizing models. Our culture divorces the private and the public worlds so completely, not because it is narcissistic or because political ideologies are dead, but because it makes a distinction between rationalization and the reference to the subject, which had been merged for centuries, by gradually abolishing all links between the two realms, and especially anything that gave interpersonal relations a social content.

Women's action, which has resulted in official recognition of the distinction between reproduction and sexual pleasure, played a decisive role in this rediscovery of the subject, provided that we add that the subject cannot exist unless it reunites desire and intersubjective relations. The history of feminist movements is to a large extent the history of the rediscovery of the mother–child relationship, after an initial rejection of traditional female roles and a rather more hesitant rejection of relations with men. Just as the modernist ideology deemed interpersonal relations to be less important than involvement in collective undertakings, and therefore labour, so the return of the subject is characterized primarily by the central importance that is given to love relationships and eroticism. Private life is no longer confined to the hidden – and female-dominated – realm of social reproduction and of the transmission of heritages. It is becoming public to the extent that our culture accords as much importance to the affirmation and freedom of the subject as to technical and economic progress and to the ability to manage social changes collectively.

Similarly, studies of children, and especially the work of Winnicott and Erikson, give a central role to communications between the child and the person, usually the mother, who provides it with security and self-confidence by guaranteeing it a protected space in which it is able to take the initiative.

The theme of being-for-the-other plays an essential role in contemporary ethics because it breaks with an obsession with totality that found its most demanding expression in Marxism, and in the work of Lukács in particular. His rejection of that obsession leads Emmanuel Levinas (for example, 1972) to recognize the other as an infinite distance rather than a relational object. Respect for the other is the essential precondition for justice, and therefore liberation. Levinas defines the other as a face, but the face allows him to understand the infinite even as he takes responsibility for it. Levinas speaks like Aliocha Karamazov. He describes woman as the Other and defines woman in terms of secrecy and modesty because, in his view, what is at hand must remain distant if it is to resist all relationships and be truly Other. Levinas is suspicious of relations, which are so often contaminated by power, and strives to preserve the authenticity of the other, or in other words the other's involvement in the infinite and in Being. Levinas has learned from Husserl that consciousness is always consciousness of something, but adds 'of someone', and thus frees us from both individualism and collectivism, and makes ethics, or behaviour towards others, basic to philosophy. This vision offers protection against power's manipulations by showing how the subject is constituted through recognition of the other. This subject means the contemplation of being, of God through the other rather than communication with the other. Levinas's thought places less emphasis on the ethical relationship with the other than on the attempt to grasp the infinite that frees us from the limitations and fetters of reality.

Levinas is a philosopher of liberation rather than of relationships. For him, recognition of the other is a way of delivering God from the consoling, or even utilitarian, representations of religion, and of making God the principle behind a politics based upon 'the right of the other man'. Paul Ricoeur gives relations with the other a more positive meaning when he speaks in his contribution to *Sur l'Individualisme* (Birnbaum and Leca 1982) of the promise made to the other. He thus introduces the notion of solidarity and the image of a society which is not simply capable of resisting evil, but which can transform an ethical principle in to institutional rules. Levinas's thought, on the other hand, has all the power of a religious rejection of an invasive power which seeks to impose a model for identity, participation and homogeneity. It contrasts this standardization and reduction of society with a crowd, with the non-social character of relations with the other and, one is tempted to add, respect for strangers.

The notion of the subject is in permanent danger of being transformed in to a principle of social integration and moralization. We have been deafened with the appeals to comrades, citizens and even fraternity that totalitarian powers have used to infiltrate consciences and institutions. Nothing can resist this collectivism as effectively as recognition of the other, as the negative consciousness of the other, as the prophetic consciousness which sees in the other the hidden presence of the absent god whose coming it awaits. The idea of modernity can be constructed around the idea of the subject only if it simultaneously burns all the idols established powers would have us worship; it is inseparable from resistance to power, from the right to be different, or even the right to be alone in a mass society.

The distance and the psychological non-relation created and preserved by religious thought and eroticism alike, must not, however, be completely divorced from the communication that allows two beings to recognize one another as subjects and to transform their relationship in to the basis for a fragment of social life. One such fragment is the family, which is so often seen as an agency for the transmission of an economic and cultural heritage and as a place for the imposition of norms. Yet since Freud, we have slowly and with great difficulty learned to see it as a place for the formation of the subject and, more recently, as a site of resistance to authoritarian pressures. This means that we have to revise the classic dichotomy between the conservative family and the progressive school. The family is the site of subjectivation, just as the school is the site of rationalization. It is vital not to divorce the two and, *a fortiori*, not to regard the subject as a conservative illusion, as an equivalent to a closed society which must be laboriously opened up by the power of reason to the light of reason and the social order.

It is, however, the love relationship that brings us directly to the theme of the subject. With the fading of the old image of a god of Love whose arrows pierce hearts and enflame desires, love ceases to be a *de facto* state that we can observe and declare in the way that we declare our income or an illness. The touching thing about Marguerite Duras's *The Lover* (Duras 1984) is the absence of love. Although the reader knows that she has lived through a great love, the woman speaks no words of love and expresses no feelings of love. The telltale sign is the simultaneous dissociation and association of desire and the encounter with the other. The absence or the disappearance of the controls exercised by the Ego and by social norms are the signs that allow us to recognize the existence of a subject who feels committed, over and beyond the limits of what is permitted or forbidden, to someone or something whose loss would destroy the meaning of life and produce a feeling of self-loss. This twofold experience of the loss of the Ego and of accession to meaning takes different forms in different societies, but it always reveals the presence of the subject, be it a divine, natural or human subject.

It is because self-consciousness cannot reveal the subject that the emergence of the subject within an individual is so closely bound up with relations with the other. Self-consciousness, in contrast, conceals the subject. The individual is no more than the site for the encounter between desire and the law, between the pleasure principle and the reality principle. That encounter results in repression and reduces the subject to its antithesis, namely the impersonal language of the unconscious that psychoanalysts decipher. Self-consciousness reveals the antisubject. The quest for what is most personal and most subjective inevitably leads to the discovery of something very impersonal. It is only when the individual forgets himself and speaks to the other, not as a role or a social position, but as a subject, that he is projected out of his own self and his social determinations, and that he becomes freedom.

The love relationship does away with social determinisms, and gives the individual a desire to be an actor, to invent a situation, rather than to conform to one. Above all, it results in a commitment which is too absolute to be merely social. Such a commitment leads to the rejection of the patterns of consumption and adaptation that are so pronounced in interpersonal relations which have not been transformed by love or friendship.

A militant commitment is of the same nature as a loving commitment provided that it does not degenerate in to loyalty to an organization or party, and provided that it helps to free others, defined in either social, national or cultural terms. It is thanks to a relationship with the other as subject that individuals cease to be functional elements of the social system and become their own creators and the producers of society.

The Return of the Subject

This book is a history of the disappearance and reappearance of the subject. The philosophy of the Enlightenment eradicated Christian dualism and the world of the soul in the name of rationalization and secularization. The philosophers of history tried to overcome the dichotomy between spiritualism and materialism by constructing an image of history evolving towards Spirit, the satisfaction of needs or the triumph of reason. This monist vision reflected fantastic economic transformations and the triumph of historicism, or the hope that improved production would lead to greater freedom and the realization of universal happiness. It remained valid until we discovered that society's power over itself could be as oppressive as it was liberating, and that our belief in progress left us defenceless against the damage done by progress, to adopt the title of a book published by the CFDT union (CFDT 1977). It is this identification of social life with progress and rationalization and, conversely, with the resistance they encounter that is being challenged by historical experience and which must be challenged even more directly by social thought.

Some are content with a limited vision of these mutations. They think that, after a long and painful period of take-off during which the infrastructure of industrial society was constructed, industrialized societies have finally entered the consumer society. The construction of railways, weapons production and heavy industry dominated the construction of industrial society or its proto-industrialization phase. We have supposedly now entered a mature industrial society in which personal consumption plays a central role and in which an increasingly high proportion of the domestic budget is devoted to the purchase of goods and services which are not so much utilitarian as symbolic or culturally significant: leisure, information, education, health, fashion, etc. The triumph of consumption is so complete as to pose a threat to community facilities and social security systems.

This argument is not false, but it does distort and underestimate the meaning and the importance of the transformations that are taking place. It reduces them to meaning the triumph of individualism and the consumer society. Now, consumption can be better defined as the acquisition of signs of real or desired social status than as the self-assertion of a free individual or subject. The meaning of such expressions is so confused that they readily lend themselves to all kinds of ideological rationalizations. The changing conjuncture which has in the space of a few years taken Western Europe from a social-democratic to a liberal model must not be confused with the return of the subject.

Can we at least take the view that a civilization based upon individual consumption is more conducive to the return of the subject than a society which is mobilized by collective social and political projects? This idea is unacceptable too. The return of the subject is as difficult in a purely liberal society which relies upon the impersonal mechanisms of rationally calculated self-interest, as it is in a statist and *dirigiste* society which enforces total integration and destroys individualism along with all reference to a personal subject defined by a resistance to that integration. This must not lead us to search for an alternative to both individualism and collectivism. We know only too well that such quests lead to the most dangerous confusion as well as the greatest hopes, and the 1930s provide many examples of how the call for personal freedom can become contaminated by authoritarian and nationalist ideologies.

At a time when the barriers between Eastern and Western Europe are coming down, we cannot go on complacently believing that the people who were destroyed by Communist regimes are finally going to gain access to the freedom and happiness offered them by the West. We know that those who live in the East want to acquire the consumer goods they have been denied, but we also know that this world produced isolated dissidents or collective movements like Solidarity, and that they elevated the idea of the subject far beyond the hedonism that is celebrated by Western advertising.

A totalitarian regime certainly represses the return of the subject more actively than any other. Yet the subject is not reducible to affluence and consumption, which goes hand in hand with the increasingly complete marginalization of all those who enjoy neither. The return of the subject signals the demise of the State, market and every other principle that could unify social life. The commercialization of every aspect of life can do as much as the propaganda of a single party to destroy the public space (*Oeffentlichkeit*). If it becomes confused with individualism, the idea of the subject self-destructs. It cannot be divorced from the idea of rationalization. The two go together, and we therefore have to go back to a dualist vision of man and society, and deflate the pride of a reason which thought it necessary to destroy feelings and beliefs, collective loyalties and individual history.

This return of the private and of the subject that lies at its heart may lead to the breakup of social life. We often have the impression that our lives are divided in to two halves: a working life and a life of free time, a life of collective organization and a life of personal choice. We feel that individual personalities are on the edge of fragmentation, especially when the fulfilment of social and family roles goes hand in hand with freedom from violence and repressed desires. But it is better to run that risk rather than to succumb to dangerous dreams of reconstructing a culture which is unified by one central principle.

Modernity as Production of the Subject

Modernity must never be reduced to the birth of the subject. That is the best way to destroy the subject and to transform it in to its antithesis, namely the Self or an actor defined only by the expectations of others and controlled by institutional rules. The Self is what Robert K. Merton calls a role set, and its only unity is that of the logic of the social system, described by some as rationality and by others as power. Sociology has been too complacent about the notions of status and role, and fails to see that these are forms which actively destroy the subject. Similarly, individualist ideologies which seem so close to the idea of the subject are in fact designed to destroy it, to dissolve it in to the rationality of economic choices. The subject can be defined only in terms of its complementary and contradictory relationship with rationalization. It is in fact the triumph of instrumental action which makes possible the appearance of the subject by disenchanting the world. The subject cannot exist whilst the world is still magical. It is when the world loses its meaning that the re-enchantment of the subject can begin.

If we are to describe modernity, we must introduce the theme of the birth of the subject, as well as the themes of production and mass consumption. Our theme develops out of monotheistic religious thought and leads to the contemporary image of the subject. It has often been promoted by new social movements and taken the intermediary form – bourgeois or working class – of the affirmation of the subject which created civil society, as opposed to the State. We have to go back to Weber, who recognized that the spirit of capitalism was based not upon a transition from asceticism to a will to acquire and consume, but upon the transition from an otherworldly asceticism to a worldly asceticism, and therefore to an internalization of the process whereby the individual is transformed in to a subject. The demise of the metasocial guarantors of social action does not lead to the triumph of utilitarianism and functionalist thought. On the contrary, it leads to the appearance of creative human beings who no longer adapt to a divinely created nature, but who seek and find themselves thanks to their ability to invent and construct, and thanks also to their will to resist the logic of technical objects, instruments of power and social integration. Modernity means the permanent creation of the world by human beings who are endowed with the power and ability to create data and language, and also to defend themselves against their creations when they turn against them. That is why the modernity which destroys religions liberates and reappropriates the image of the subject, which had previously been imprisoned in religious objectivations, or in the conflation of subject and nature. It transfers the subject from God to man. Secularization means the humanization, and not the destruction, of the subject. It does not simply mean the disenchantment of the world; it also means the re-enchantment of human beings. It leads to an increasing divorce between their various aspects: their individuality, their ability to be subjects, their Ego and the Self that is constructed from the outside by social roles. The transition to modernity is not a transition from subjectivity to objectivity, from self-centred action to impersonal technical or bureaucratic action; it leads from adaptation to the world to the construction of new worlds, from the reason that discovers eternal ideas to the action which, by rationalizing the world, liberates and recomposes the subject.

The good is now defined in terms of respect for the subject. No individual or group should be regarded as something to be used for purposes of either power or pleasure. Evil is not the supposed impersonality of tradition, which tends to conflate individuals and universals. Evil is the power which reduces the subject to the status of a human resource for the production of wealth, might or information. Modern morality does not value reason as an instrument for bringing human beings in to harmony with the world; it values freedom as a way of making human beings ends and not means. Unlike misfortune, which results from human impotence in the face of death, illness, separation or poverty, evil is therefore something that is done by human beings.

We can no longer understand why religious thought found it so difficult to explain the presence of evil in a world created by an infinitely good God. The supreme will and the finalism of Creation no longer exist. The only things that exist are the human actions that construct man, and other actions which destroy man. And they are indeed actions, even when they seem or claim to be the internal logic of economic or political systems. Evil means man's domination over man and the transformation of human beings in to objects or their monetary equivalents. There are such things as neutral, technical and routine modes of behaviour which escape the logic of both good and evil. But good and evil appear when a mode of behaviour is social, or in other words when it is intended to modify the behaviour of other actors and to increase or diminish their capacity for autonomous action.

A Controlled Dissociation

The crisis of modernity marks the divorce between things that had been united for a long time: man and the universe, words and things, desire and technique. It is pointless to go backwards and to look for a principle of absolute unity. Some would like the world to be the creation of a geometer-god; others would like a liberated desire to make man part of nature once more. Yet nothing can put an end to continental drift, and nothing can prevent the world of production and power from drifting away from the world of individuals, their needs and their imaginary. And it is not enough to try to reconcile everything by resorting to a pure tolerance which constantly relaxes rules and taboos so as to accept a greater complexity. This solution, which is all too attractive, reduces social life to a set of markets under the benign surveillance of the old liberalism's nightwatchman-State. Do we have to choose between the quest for the One and acceptance of complete fragmentation, between a return to the Enlightenment

and a self-destructive post-modernism? Are there no intermediary
territories where thought, collective action and ethics can find a
home? If we have to gauge modernity, our criterion must be the
degree to which a society tolerates subjectivation. Subjectivation is
inseparable from a stable balance between two complementary and
contradictory tendencies: on the one hand, the rationalization that
allows man to dominate and master both nature and himself; on the
other, the personal and collective identities which constantly resist
the powers that implement rationalization. The technology that
creates change frees the subject from tribal law; memory protects the
subject from regimentation. Whenever these three forces become
divorced from one another, and especially when one of them claims
to be hegemonic, the world is in crisis, and suffering from a deadly
illness. Cultural fundamentalism is deadly. Technocratic and military
pride is deadly. And the narcissism of a subject with neither tools nor
a memory is just as deadly.

One of the grand narratives of modernity describes how secularization led from the enchanted world of the gods to the disenchanted
but knowable world of things. I am telling an almost totally different
story about the breakup of the sacred world and the growing distance
between nature and its laws, between the subject and the affirmation
of the subject's freedom. If we allow this separation to become a
complete divorce, there will be a break between the inside and the
outside, between a society identified with a market and social actors
reduced to drives or traditions. And that would destroy all principles
for social intervention against violence, inequality, injustice and
segregation. We must reconstruct a general representation of social
life and human beings so as to found a politics and to make it possible
to resist the extreme disorder of absolute power. This representation
can only be based upon the idea that the subject is born and develops
amidst the ruins of an Ego that has been objectified and transformed
in to a Self by those who hold power. The Subject is the individual's
will to produce and not simply consume an individual experience and
a social environment. The best definition of modernity is neither
technological progress nor the growing individualism of consumers,
but the demand for freedom and the defence of freedom against
everything that transforms individuals in to instruments, objects or
absolute strangers.

2

The Subject as Social Movement

Against the Establishment

The subject is not a reflection on the Self and on live experiences. On the contrary, it challenges what one is initially tempted to call social roles, though they in reality mean the construction of a social and personal life by power centres which do at least as much to create consumers, voters and a public as they do to respond to social and cultural demands. If he or she does not constitute him or herself as a subject, the individual will be constituted as a Self by power centres which define and sanction roles. The latter are neither neutral nor technical, and they are not constituted by the technical division of labour or by the functional differentiation of different institutions. Those who consume society rather than producing and transforming it are subordinate to those who are in charge of the economy, politics and information. The language of propaganda and advertising constantly tends to mask this central conflict, and to promote the idea that the organization of society is a response to 'needs', whereas it is the organization that constructs needs which, whilst they are certainly not artificial, do conform to the interests of power.

An individual can become a subject by abandoning the Self only if he resists the logic of social domination in the name of a logic of freedom and free self-production. It is this critical rejection of an artificial image of social life as a machine or an organism, not in the name of transcendental principles – God, reason or history – but in the name of free self-production that leads to the assertion of the subject and of the subject's rights in a world where human beings have been transformed in to objects.

This position is far removed from the rationalism which removes individuals from their particular situation in order to identify them with universals, but it is equally far removed from the liberalism of

Isaiah Berlin (1969) or Richard Rorty (1989). Their liberalism is based upon the acceptance of a plurality of values. We can refuse to choose between freedom and equality, or between personal creativity and social justice, only if we define individuals purely in terms of their particularity. Now that definition applies only to geniuses, and therefore cannot satisfy a sociologist. A sociologist is only too aware of the illusory nature of individualism in a mass society where behaviour is increasingly determined by decision-making centres that can predict what the population will like, demand and purchase. So much so that the only possible purpose of individualism is to protect an elite which has such abundant resources that it does indeed have a great range of choice.

When I speak of the Subject, or in other words of the construction of the individual as actor, it is impossible to divorce the individual from his or her social situation. On the contrary, we must contrast the individual who consumes social norms and institutions with the individual who produces social life and the changes that occur within it. At the level of the consumption of society, it may be possible, in the least harsh societies or situations, not to choose between freedom and equality, but in most cases we do have to choose: a goverment can either cut taxes or expand public social services. In most cases, of course, there is no need to make extreme choices, but choice there must be. There must, that is, be a quest for fairness and justice, and the terms of that quest have been best defined by John Rawls (1971). Similarly, at the level of the production of society, the defence of the subject must be reconciled with rationalization. And as was the case in industrial society, the two can be reconciled only if they enter in to an alliance against the reproduction of privileges and the element of irrationality that is always present in the exercise of power. The Subject has to be defined in terms of social actors and conflict. The Subject is neither a supra-social principle nor the individual in his particularity; like instrumental rationality, it is a mode of constructing social experience.

I have already made this point by analysing both subjectivation and rationalization as social movements. Like the Renaissance and the Reformation, modern societies are driven by two conflicting tendencies: on the one hand, the creation of a naturalist, materialist or illuminist visions of human beings and the world and, on the other, the discovery of a subjectivity that strengthens the ethics of conviction, as opposed to the traditional and religious ethics of contemplation and imitation. We now have to ask ourselves if one of these cultural tendencies, or the preference given to one of the poles of modern culture, is also a social movement. Is it, that is to say, the work of socially defined actors who are fighting not only a cultural tendency, but also a particular social category?

The Subject and Social Classes

My analysis suggests that this is indeed the case. The subject exists only in the form of a *social movement*, of a challenge to the logic of order, no matter whether it takes a utilitarian form or simply that of a quest for social integration.

Rationalization reinforces the logic of social integration and therefore increases an enlightened power's hold over members of society, who are in that sense the subjects of new princes or new ruling forces, as Michel Foucault might put it. Subjectivation thus becomes divorced from rationalization, and there is a danger that this will destroy a relationship without which there can be no modernity. The central history of modernity is that of the transition from the subject's struggles against the sacred order, in which the subject and rationalism were allies, to the subject's struggle against rationalizing models. In this second struggle, it sometimes falls back upon a self-image elaborated by monotheistic religions in a bid for better protection against the totalitarian pride of a modernizing power intent upon transforming society and human beings from top to bottom.

Subjectivation was initially – and for a long time – a matter for the leaders of society. It was initially, at least in societies marked by Christianity, a matter for priests, as it was Christ in person who brought the subject down from heaven to earth and who introduced the divorce between the spiritual and the temporal in to social life. The divorce between the two was the rock on which our modernity was built. This did not prevent the Church, or the Churches, from attempting for centuries to subordinate human action to a clerical interpretation of the divine law. As a result, they became the prime enemies of modernizing rationalism and were doomed when secularization triumphed. Subjectivation then became a matter for the bourgeoisie. We can use the term 'the bourgeoisie' to designate the actors of the civil society's autonomy from the State, and more specifically of the functional differentiation of the economy from politics, religion and the family. This basic act defines the 'great transformation' that liberated modernity. The *bourgeois* was the central figure in Western modernization because he was the agent of both rationalization and subjectivation. There was in that sense a great difference between the bourgeois and Weber's *capitalist*. The capitalist's great strength was his ability to eliminate all reference to the subject in the name of an acceptance of predestination which swept away all loyalties and feelings and replaced them with labour, production and profit.

The capitalist played such a central role that he might be contrasted with the bourgeois in that he was devoted to private life, conscience, family and piety. Edward Leites (1988) paints a much richer picture of the puritans of the American colonies of New England and Pennsylvania than that bequeathed us by Weber. These puritans did not reject private life, and especially not sexuality. On the contrary, their pastors were the first sexologists. They reconciled the quest for pleasure and happiness with a respect for the divine law. They extolled the virtues of constancy, and therefore conjugal fidelity and family happiness, but they did not obey St Paul's harsh injunction to regard the things of this world with indifference. As Philippe Ariès (1960) and Elisabeth Badinter (1980) in particular have demonstrated, the bourgeois of the second half of the eighteenth century gave a new importance to feelings and especially to relations with children, whilst women won a position in both the family and society which they would lose only when a rationalizing capitalism triumphed thanks to the industrial revolution. It was the bourgeoisie, and not capitalism, which defended property and human rights by making the right to own property the most important right of all. The negative aspect of the bourgeois spirit, namely the importance of inheritance and the correlative debasement of labour, has rightly been denounced with such force that we tend to forget its positive aspect: the restrictions it placed on political and social domination. In its battle against the absolute monarchy, the bourgeoisie founded modern individualism, which it associated with a social struggle against the established order and its religious foundations. There is a great continuity between Locke's defence of property, the Constituent Assembly in France and the workers' movement which, a hundred years later, would defend crafts and jobs because they, like property, are principles that lead people to resist an established power. The return of the subject is in part a return to the bourgeois spirit, and to that of the workers' movement, and a movement away from the totalizing spirit which, from the French Revolution to the Soviet Revolution, dominated two centuries of history. It is now more important to create an alliance of anti-totalizing thinkers than to reproduce the discourses that defended the world of labour against the bourgeois world by making it and its praxis the incarnation of the historical totality. We therefore have to abandon ambiguous notions like *praxis*, which, as we have seen, is closely associated with the notion of totality in Lukács. Sartre, in contrast, defines praxis in terms similar to those I am defending here when he writes (Sartre 1960: 30n.): 'Class consciousness is not simply the lived contradiction that objectively characterizes the class under consideration; that contradiction has already been sublated by praxis, and has therefore been both preserved and negated.' This praxis is a liberating action and not an identification with history, whereas during the French Revolution, as Eric Weil points out, moral practice became a historical practice, and its subject was no longer the solitary individual, but humanity. For both the bourgeoisie and the workers' movement – which was a social movement – it is the individual who exists in a network of concrete social relations, and not humanity – which is a pseudo-social image of the totality – that has to be defended, if need be against what we call society. This is because society imposes its greatest constraints on protesters and the dominated, and it usually does so in the name of social utility and the struggle against its eternal and internal enemies.

It was when this proto-modernity was complete, when rationalizing models triumphed in politics with the French Revolution and in the economy with the industrialization of Britain, that the unity between rationalization and subjectivation was destroyed, and that both culture and society became bipolar. As the bourgeoisie became capitalist, and then a vast managerial class, the reference to the subject disappears from a dominant world which believes only in profit and in social order and which comprises a ruling class and a dominated class. The reference to the subject is displaced in to the world of modern society's subordinates, who were soon renamed 'the working class'. Denis Poulot's book *Le Sublime* (Poulot 1869), which was republished by Maspero in 1980 with a long introduction by Alain Cottereau, indicates its presence in the workshop. Poulot, a small entrepreneur, establishes a typology ranging from the 'simple sublime' and the 'true sublime' to the 'Sons of God' and the 'sublime sublime'. He describes them as highly skilled workers who were at once troublesome and heavy-drinking, violent, revolutionary and delinquent. Value judgements aside, his analysis coincides with that given here. The subject rejects social roles by appealing to both life, sexuality and community.

We now have to complete Poulot's analysis by adding that the two faces of the subject are united by and through the struggle against a social enemy identified with progress and rationalization. In my *La Conscience ouvrière* (Touraine 1966) and then in *Le Mouvement ouvrier* (Touraine, Wieviorka and Dubet 1984), I demonstrate that the workers' movement, or in other words the presence of a social movement within working-class action, was defined by the defence of the workers' autonomy against scientific management, which soon came to be known as rationalization. The workers' movement did not

simply demand better working conditions and conditions of employment, or even the right to negotitate and sign collective agreements.
It called for the defence of the worker-subject against rationalization.
It did not reject rationalization itself, but it did refuse to allow it to
be identified with the interests of the employer. From the end of the
nineteenth century onwards, talk of social justice became a way of
stressing the need to reconcile the two principles of modernity,
namely rationalization and the 'dignity' of workers. It is true that the
workers' movement was almost always subordinated to political
action and to socialist, social-democratic, labourist or communist
parties, but that triumph of political action was no more than a ruse
on the part of the spirit of rationalization. It attempted to force its
logic on the workers' movement and to reduce it to a 'mass action'
led by a party which could easily be transformed in to a dictatorial
power that flung the organizers of working-class action in to prison.

The workers' movement succeeded in winning its independence
from political parties for only brief periods. It did so during the
period of direct-action syndicalism at the turn of the century, and,
more recently, on the eve of its demise during the 'Hot Autumn' in
Italy and the Lip strike in France, which occurred shortly after the
movement of May 1968. This type of workers' movement, which was
attacked by the political leaders of the left and the capitalist world
alike, must be recognized as the first great collective action to have
transformed subjectivation of a collective project in to a social
movement. At this point, the workers' movement also abandoned the
struggle between modernity and tradition, between religion and
reason. It located its struggle within modernity and revealed the
conflicts between the quest for productivity and respect for workers
who were usually treated as objects, or as mere labour-power.

The thought of Serge Mallet was extremely influential in the 1960s
because the idea of a 'new working class' (Mallet 1963) expressed the
workers' movement's great hope that it would become independent
of political parties. It hoped to become its own master and to defy
the Leninist conception by taking responsibility for the meaning of
its own actions. It is now difficult to understand what the workers'
movement was, as trade unionism has been able to retain its power
and influence only by being transformed in to a truly political force,
as in Sweden and Germany. The workers' movement was the complete antithesis of a social partner, not because it was revolutionary –
in most cases it was not, and when it was, it became more dependent
upon political parties – but because it was attempting to free workers
from scientific management and to defend them against the logic of
productivity. It tried to interpret their spontaneous attempts to resist

so-called scientific management, to establish an informal system of production and to construct a compensatory power at both company and shop-floor level.

Do we have to pursue this analysis to its logical conclusion and identify rationalization with capitalism, and subjectivation with the workers' movement? No, because a social movement is an attempt on the part of a collective actor to gain control of a society's 'values' or cultural orientations by challenging the action of an adversary with which it is linked by power relations. Because they are the two major cultural themes of modern society, rationalization-subjectivation is the issue at stake in the struggle between what are, in industrial society, known as social classes. Classes are defined by their position within social relations of production. Even though they are in conflict, the capitalist movement and the workers' movement are in fact referring to the same cultural values, namely rationalization and subjectivation. The workers' movement, and especially socialist thought, are openly historicist and naturalist, just as industrialists and financiers are self-confessed social Darwinists who believe that technology and investment will bring about world-wide affluence and happiness. Conversely, both sides believe in labour, hard work and the ability to save and to plan. Sociologists refer to this as a deferred gratification pattern, and in its name both workers and bosses impose a puritanical education and a rigorous ethics on both themselves and their children. Workers do so because self-control is essential if they are not to sink in to alcoholism and poverty; capitalists, because it is essential if they are to save and invest.

From Classes to Movements

The conception of social movements which I am applying here to industrial society breaks with the Marxist idea of class struggle, even though both analyse the same historical phenomena. The Marxist conception identifies the action of workers with nature and historical development, and capitalism with the construction of an artificial and irrational world of profit which is concealed by the pseudo-positive categories of political economy and the fog of religious thought. The necessary triumph of the labour movement will be the realization not of Spirit, as Hegel said of modernity, but of human nature. That is why class consciousness and classes do not exist 'for themselves'. According to Marxists, the class-consciousness that exists for itself is not equivalent to a working class that has achieved self-consciousness; it is equivalent to the interpretation, by revolutionary intellectuals, of

a working-class situation which signals the contradictions of capitalism and of their necessary and possible transcendence.

When I describe the labour movement as a social movement rather
than as class consciousness, I do so in order to avoid any confusion
with Marxist thought. I am referring to a collective actor whose
primary goal is the defence of the subject and the struggle for the
rights and dignity of the workers. That is why revolutionary thought
so often speaks of the proletariat, or in other words defines workers
in terms of what they do not have: property. Historians and sociologists of working-class action like myself have demonstrated on the
contrary that the workers' movement was the creation of skilled
workers who were defending labour and its autonomy, that their
action was positive rather than negative and that they were inventing
a different world rather than merely criticizing capitalism and scientific management. A *social movement* is at once a social conflict and a
cultural project. This is as true of dominant movements as it is of
dominated movements. The goal of a social movement is always the
realization of cultural values as well as victory over a social adversary.
A struggle which puts forward demands is not in itself a social
movement, though it may well defend corporate interests, exploit the
conjuncture on the labour market, or even exert political pressure. If
it is to become a social movement, it must speak in the name of the
values of industrial society and must defend them against its enemies.
There can be no social movement in industrial society as long as the
workers are opposed to industrialization, break machines or resist the
introduction of new technologies, even if they do so for important
and legitimate reasons, as when the technologies in question are a
threat to their jobs. There can be no social movement unless trade
union action has the positive goal of giving workers greater autonomy
and, more specifically, unless it fights the brutal assertion of Taylorist
employers that 'You are not being paid to think.'

I am not suggesting that a collective action with an essentially
economic rationale must also have an ethical content. The idea of a
social movement is a challenge to both historicist and utilitarian
concepts of working-class action. My analysis centres on the idea that
a society – defined as a collectivity implementing a certain level of
historicity and therefore modernity – is neither a body of values
which permeates every aspect of social life nor a latent civil war over
the social use of cultural values at the level of either production, ethics
or knowledge. A modern society revolves around a struggle between
rulers and ruled over the implementation of rationalization and subjectivation. Nothing must be allowed to divorce cultural values from
social conflict, and our analysis must resist both the ideologies of the

masters of society, who conceal their power by identifying them-selves with modernity and describing their adversaries as mere obstacles to progress, and the ideologies of dependent workers who, being unable to identify with a dominant system of production, claim to be the living incarnation of the principle of modernity, namely labour. The latter speak in the name of an energeticist conception which contrasts the creativity of directly productive labour with the wastefulness of a capitalist system that generates crises, unemploy-ment and poverty.

All social movements are internally divided, as none can serve both rationalization and subjectivation at the same time and in the same way. André Malraux's *Man's Hope* (Malraux 1937) is one of the major literary works of the twentieth century because it is constructed around the contradictions of collective action. It describes the conflict between the Party spirit, which is efficient but may lead to a totalitarianism as dangerous as the totalitarianism it is fighting, and an anarchistic rebellion inspired by an ethical protest which collapses as a result of internal struggles and an inability to organize. It might be said that the idea of totality always reflects the ascendancy of a class, whereas the idea of the subject provides consolation when there is a lull in historical action. During the phoney war of 1940, Georges Friedmann, Communist fellow-traveller and author of *La Crise du progrès* (Friedmann 1936), wrote in his *Journal de guerre* (1987) that a just social cause is not enough to inspire resistance. Moral qualities are also required. It is in moments of solitude and desolation, and in the face of a seemingly inevitable future that the consciousness of certain individuals comes to feel itself responsible for the freedom of others. This has nothing to do with moralism, and it results in a personal struggle against an unjust order. The political models con-structed by our century inspire horror rather than hope. We therefore have need of a theory of freedom or of non-commitment rather than a theory of commitment, which has often become so perverted as to mean the militarization of collective action in an era when the red flag of the labour movement has more often flown over troops repressing popular movements than at the head of processions of striking workers. The darker the conjuncture, the greater the tendency to fall back on the defence of the subject. When liberation struggles are more likely to succeed, the identification with history or reason reappears, but our analysis has a duty not to divorce – or, *a fortiori*, contrast – commitment and non-commitment, collective hopes and self-defence, modernization and protest.

The defence of the subject or subjectivation can generate social movements because a society's cultural orientations are not above it, like the sun in the sky. They are inseparable from the social form they are given by the state of social conflicts. Their form can vary from complete identification with the interests of the ruling class to extreme autonomy. Subjectivation means that rationalization cannot be equated with the interests of the ruling class. The subject is a social movement because it adopts the critiques of modernism inaugurated by Nietzsche and Freud. It insists that, as a society becomes more modern, it tends increasingly to be reduced to a rationalizing model, to a system of techniques and objects or to a technostructure. It is therefore essential to evoke the idea of the subject if we are to break the bars of what Max Weber called the 'iron cage' of modern society.

This analysis is so powerful and its attacks on technocratic and *dirigiste* illusions are so effective that it must be defended at all cost, but it must not lead to the apparently similar but unacceptable idea that modern society is merely a rationalized and ideological expression of the interests of either the system itself or its rulers. The evocation of the subject is a challenge to the established order, but it is also more than that, and it is therefore not to be confused with the creation of the counter-cultures or micro-societies that the Germans describe as 'alternative'. Such responses to modernity have no real importance except in totalitarian-type situations which refuse to tolerate anything that does not conform to the central logic of the system and the interests of its rulers.

The defence of the subject is no more subordinate to rationalization than it is incompatible with it. It does not dream of going back to a natural order, and nor is it the motor behind all institutions. Moralistic thinking has to be rejected as firmly as purely critical thinking. Both are incapable of recognizing the duality of the principles that constitute modernity. Yet this must not prevent us from recognizing that the defence of the subject immediately comes in to conflict with the positivism and the technocracy of modern society and its management and control apparatuses. We therefore have to emphasize the anti-establishment content of the idea of the subject rather than the modernizing content of the idea of rationalization.

The idea of the subject is always an anti-establishment idea. It is because modern society tends to deny its own creativity and to see itself as a self-regulating system over which social actors and their conflicts have no control, that the idea of the subject is always a challenge to the establishment. Just as the theocratic or merely clerical tendency always carried more weight than the appeal to faith in Christian societies, both technocratic and liberal conceptions tend to be more closely associated with established power than with the freedom of the subject in modern society. That is why the idea of the subject is primarily a challenge to the establishment, and that is the justification for the extreme formula used as the title of this chapter: *the subject as social movement*. The idea of the subject obviously cannot occupy an extreme position, as its importance is too central, but nor can it simply be central to the analysis. It is the combination of rationalization and the subject that defines the cultural orientations of modern society, and not the idea of the subject alone. The idea of rationalization usually tends to combine cultural centrality and involvement in the management of the established order; the idea of the subject also tends to centre on culture, but it is associated with an anti-establishment social content. Rationalization tends to be closely bound up with the action of the ruling forces, whereas subjectivation has often been the central theme of the social movement of dominated categories.

The notion of *social class* was congruent with historicist thinking. It explained the contradiction between rulers and ruled in terms of that between society and nature, or past and future. Today, we have to replace notions which define actors in terms of a non-social situation with notions that analyse situations in terms of social actors or social relations. That is why the notion of *social movement* must replace that of 'social class', just as an analysis of action must take the place of an analysis of situations. This does not mean replacing facts with opinions, or the objective with the subjective, but it does mean recognizing that whilst it cannot be reduced to the actors' awareness of it, the meaning of an action is by no means independent thereof. A social movement is not a current of opinion, as it challenges a power relation which is very concretely inscribed in institutions and organizations. It does, however, pursue cultural goals by working on power relations and relations of inequality. One of the important roles of the social sciences, especially since Marx, has always been to discover the social relations that exist beneath the impersonal categories of economic, administrative or even theoretical analysis. And that role is even more important today than it was in the era that gave birth to industrial society.

The Programmed Society

It is impossible to defend the idea of modernity unless our general reflections are closely bound up with an analysis of a particular historical situation which is itself defined as a stage within modernity. But how can we both reject historicism and speak in concrete terms of post-industrial society? Simply by recognizing that historicism is

the self-perception of a certain form and a certain stage of modernization, and that the following stage, which we have already entered,
does not think of itself in terms of historical development. Nor did
the previous stage, which saw the emergence of classical political
philosophy. Unlike the nineteenth century, the eighteenth century
spoke of happiness and not progress. Why shouldn't the characteristic
discourse of a post-industrial society speak of the subject?

Our modernity was originally equated with our emergence from
traditional society, yet it was still bound up with Christian dualism.
As we have seen, this meant that there could be no real unity to what
is known as the Enlightenment Spirit. Then came the great attempt to
integrate the two phases of modernity in to both idealist and
materialist philosophies of history. Historicism was above all the will
to reconcile rationalization and subjectivation. A more lively conception of our historicity is now associated with a critical awareness of
the dangers of productivism and modernism, and with the return to a
dualism that places as much emphasis upon the contradiction between
rationalization and subjectivation as on their complementarity.

Defining post-industrial society means explaining the reasons for
this new dualism. Conversely, this dualism cannot be understood
outside the historical situation in which it developed, and that
situation is determined by the rapid growth of the culture industries.
I apply the term *programmed* – the term 'programmed society' is
more precise than 'post-industrial society', which is defined purely in
terms of what went before it – to a society in which the production
and mass distribution of cultural commodities plays the central role
that belonged to material commodities in industrial society (Touraine
1969). The production and distribution of knowledge, medical care
and information, and therefore education, health and the media are to
the programmed society what metal-working, textiles, chemicals and
even the electrical and electronics industries were to industrial
societies.

Why 'programmed'? Because in this society, managerial power
consists in predicting and modifying opinions, attitudes and modes of
behaviour, and in moulding personalities and cultures. Rather than
remaining in the realm of utility, it is therefore directly involved in
the world of 'values'. The new importance of the culture industries
replaces traditional forms of social control with new mechanisms for
governing human beings. To invert the traditional formula, we might
say that the transition from an industrial society to a programmed
society is a transition from the administration of things to the
government of men. The phrase, 'the culture industry', which was
coined by the Frankfurt philosophers, captures it well.

In the programmed society, resistance to managerial power can no longer be based upon a naturalist philosophy of history; it can be based only upon the defence of the subject. In the most highly industrialized societies, no theme arouses more passion that those of education, training and especially health. The object of conflicts in these domains is to defend a certain conception of freedom, and the ability to give a meaning to life, by resisting apparatuses dominated by a neo-liberal will to adapt to change, a desire for social control or technico-bureaucratic arguments.

Should a hospital, in particular, be an organization ruled by a combination of professional, financial, administrative and corporate logics, or should it be patient-centred, so as to ensure that a patient is not simply an object of medical care, but also an informed subject with projects and a memory who has a voice in deciding what treatment he or she should receive and how it should be applied? This debate has not led to the emergence of organized actors or patients' unions. But it is present in everyone's mind and is often aired on television. The medical programmes which have the greatest impact are those which deal most directly with the theme of patients' responsibilities and rights in the context of euthanasia and palliative care, artificial insemination, or the treatment of serious illnesses. French public opinion was horrified to learn that patients had been infected as a result of being given transfusions of what the authorities knew to be HIV-contaminated blood.

The debate about the goals of education is less focused both at the level of public opinion and at the institutional level. *Lycée* and university students are, on the other hand, acutely aware of the tension between the vocational training that prepares them for work or transmits school culture, and an education that takes into account both the personality of individual pupils or students and the realities of class. The French school students who launched a major protest movement in 1990 were worried about their professional future and the threat of unemployment, but they also wanted a school culture which was not alien to their youth culture or cultures. Similarly, the students interviewed by Didier Lapeyronnie (1992) were trying to defend their personalities against what they saw as a disorganized and aggressive academic world. They were not interested in the pursuit of their own interests or pleasure, but they were seeking an authentic way of life in the situation in which they found themselves. Their reaction did not lead to any collective action, as they were very suspicious of parties and unions. It did, however, lead to an acute awareness that there was a general conflict between the goals of the educational apparatus and their personal projects.

The debate over television, which is the most important of all the media, is the least organized of all, but attitudes towards it are extremely ambivalent. Television channels turn everything in to entertainment and are often concerned only with improving their market share, but they also bring in to every home faces, words and gestures which turn human beings from distant lands in to our neighbours. Whatever the content – politics or current events – mass communications, by their very nature, prioritize communication and impact rather than the message. McLuhan (1967) was the first to voice an idea that is very clearly understood by television professionals, irrespective of whether or not they approve of the transformation of their medium in to an end in itself. Yet there are no grounds for believing that viewers are interested in nothing but violence, money and stupidity. The appeal of the least demanding programmes, which reduce viewers to being consumers, is, fortunately, not great enough to overshadow the ability of the best to ask questions to force us to look at and become part of issues that are both close to home and far away.

Whereas the social movements of old, and especially the trade unions, degenerated in to being either political pressure groups or agencies for the corporate defence of sectors of the new wage-earning middle class rather than the defence of the underprivileged, the new social movements are already revealing a new generation of social and cultural problems and conflicts, even though they are unorganized and do not have any capacity for permanent action. The conflict is now not one over who controls the means of production, but one over the goals of cultural productions such as education, health care and mass information.

Totalitarian or authoritarian powers which rule minds and manners as brutally as they organize production, and which concentrate every form of political, economic and cultural power in to their own hands, generate more complex and more visible forms of rebellion. The most powerful figure to have emerged in recent decades is that of the *dissident*. The dominant image of anti-Nazi resistance was that of political resistance and, especially in France, the resistance of Communist or Gaullist militants. The dominant image of resistance to post-Stalinist totalitarianism is a solitary individual. It is the *zek* and the free and courageous conscience of a Sakharov, a Solzhenitsyn or a Bukovsky, amongst many others, that has become the symbol of a freedom which calls not for commitment but for non-commitment, not for the courage to storm the Bastille but for the courage to say no to a power which has no qualms about using every form of repression.

To adopt a rather different perspective, Gandhi can be seen as one of the century's central figures. His call for non-violence mobilized cultural and national convictions as well as social interests. The greatest challenges to the establishment now have an ethical basis, not because collective action is powerless, but because domination now affects bodies and souls rather than labour and juridical status, and because totalitarian propaganda and repression are the most serious sicknesses of a world which claims to be modern.

What Charles Tilly (1986) calls the 'repertoire' of the social movements of the industrial era – mass demonstrations, violent slogans and the idea of seizing power – is disappearing before our very eyes. In May 1968 in Paris, I witnessed the clash between the old repertoire of the general strike, which was used mainly by the CGT, and the new repertoire created by the students and interpreted with such political skill by Daniel Cohn-Bendit: it concentrated on self-mobilization rather than the enemy, and used the tactic of peaceful sit-ins imported from the United States. One important change has been the new role played by women in these new social movements. Most of the active participants are now women, and they have introduced themes which are as much social as they are cultural, such as the call to defend the subject that found its most conscious and most highly organized expression in collective actions to defend the right to contraception and abortion.

These new social movements now fill the public space, even if some see only their political weakness. Despite the influence of the revolutionary fundamentalism of leftist sects or, at the opposite extreme their exclusive concentration on non-political themes and the combination of very broad statements and highly specific objectives, it has to be recognized that these new challenges to authority are not trying to create a new type of society. Still less are they attempting to set free the force of progress and the future. They are trying to 'change life', and to defend human rights, be it the right to life of people threatened by hunger or extermination, or the right to free speech and the right to have a personal life-style and life-history. These new social movements are of course taking shape in industrialized countries, but they also make their presence felt in the defence of the poorest and most exploited. Hence their internationalism, which is much greater than that of the pre-1914 workers' movement. Almost no other theme inspires so much emotion in young people as that of solidarity with the poorest of people and with the victims of segregation and intolerance. The ethical consciousness which lies at the heart of these new social movements has much more to do with the defence of the identity and dignity of those who are fighting extreme oppression or poverty than with the socio-political strategies of trade unions and pressure groups, which are not part of the decision-making process in rich countries.

This great shift from political action and economic themes to personal and ethical themes is not restricted to the most organized forms of mobilization. On the contrary, it is most conspicuous in the fears, opinions and attitudes that are expressed in everyday life. So much so that many people are disaffected with political institutions and social ideas. When industrial society first developed in Western Europe, the formation of a brutal capitalism and utopias which were at once social and ethical seemed to be the only alternatives, and it took a very long time to develop political mediations between these extremes. Similarly, we are now witnessing the decay of the political and social forces we inherited from industrial society. They no longer express strong social demands and are being transformed in to agencies for political communication, whereas the new social movements are mobilizing both principles and feelings. The dawn of a new utopian period is not, however, the sole explanation for this decline of political passions. Political *parties* which once represented historical necessity rather than actors are now in a state of crisis and are on the verge of extinction. The totalitarian regimes of the twentieth century originated in great mass political parties; the new social movements want to distance themslves as far as possible from the model provided by fascist and communist parties. Truly political forces are therefore becoming weaker as the public space becomes more open and more active, and as public opinion comes to play an increasingly important role precisely because it is flexible and fragile, and much more in touch with social demands than great political machines which have every confidence in themselves and their historic right to represent a people they rapidly reduce to the lowly status of a 'mass'. The new social movements speak of self-management rather than the meaning of history, of internal democracy rather than the seizure of power.

It would be a mistake to conclude that all the forms of individualism and ethical judgement that are spreading so quickly in the most highly industrialized societies are expressions of the subject and, more specifically, of new social movements. They are not, just as not all manifestations of trade union action were an expression of the workers' movement. Every society functions at a number of different levels. A country which belongs predominantly to a given societal type or system of historical action, is also marked by its mode of modernization, which may be either liberal or statist, depending on whether change is brought about by capitalists or by the State. Despite this dual principle of internal differentiation, any system of historical action is defined by the existence of a certain set of cultural orientations – historicity – and of social conflicts over the appropriation of models of the self-production of society. Evolutionism was industrial society's dominant epistemological model. Energy, labour and self-control provided its ethical model, and the reference to the subject was drowned out by the philosophy of history. The mutational crises that bring about the transition from industrial society to a programmed society threaten to destroy our consciousness of historicity and therefore the very idea of modernity. Yet it is the distorting influence of such crises that allows the idea of the subject to escape from historicism.

The modern world is not simply living through the collapse of voluntarist modes of development, the end of socialism and, in a word, the triumph of the market economy. It is also making the more important transition from industrial society to the programmed society, and therefore from the fusion of rationalization and subjectivation characteristic of philosophies of history, to their separation and complementarity. This mutation affects the whole world, so great is the effect of the domination of societies which have already entered the post-industrial stage and whose ideas and ways of life are now to be found everywhere. It is highly unlikely that the liberal methods the contemporary West is using to enter the programmed society will be used everywhere. These methods are now triumphing in both post-communist Europe and post-populist Latin America, but it is likely that they will be found intolerable or will be modified in many countries, and that other modes of State or popular intervention will develop. It is probable that they will reproduce in a different form the types of reforms European social democracy achieved in the first half of the twentieth century. Not all roads lead to liberalism.

All roads do, however, lead towards a programmed society, even though not all of them reach it. We are so impressed by the collapse of socialist regimes and the disintegration of socialist ideas that we are tempted to see these contemporary historical changes simply as the revenge of capitalism, if not as the complete triumph of the one best way: liberalism. We are making the dangerous mistake of confusing a mode of development with a type of society. The important thing is to recognize that a new culture and new social relations are taking shape as material industries are replaced by culture industries. Forms of social and political organization, and personal and collective modes of behaviour vary, depending on whether we take the liberal road to the programmed society, a different and more interventionist road, or one which is more influenced by popular social movements. Specific historic differences aside, we still find that the societal model and the new system of historical action known as the programmed society, does have its own unity. And that model is best defined in terms of the return of the idea of the subject, rather than the appearance of new technologies. That the return of the subject should sometimes produce anti-modernist effects is understandable, but to argue that the transcendence of historicism implies a break with modernity indicates an inability to see the forest for the trees.

This vision of a new system of historical action, or of the programmed society, with its actors, its social movements, and its struggles and negotiations over cultural issues, is far removed from today's dominant images of our society. Those images are associated with the idea of post-modernism. We therefore have to specify the differences between that idea and the idea of the post-industrial or programmed society. Post-modernism asserts that there is a complete dissociation between system and actor: according to Luhmann (1984), the system is self-referential or *autopoietic*, whereas the actors are defined not by social relations, but by cultural difference. I am not saying that these statements are completely out of step with a reality, but they are as distorting as early-nineteenth-century descriptions of industrial society as the reign of money and commodities. What had yet to become the working class was represented as the other world or the 'sublime's' world of the *faubourg*, the workshop and the grogshop; in capitalist society, the world of money and the world of labour seemed to be quite alien to one another. It was only with the appearance of trade unions and socialist ideas that it became possible to discern relations of production behind these extreme differences. Society's historicity, is now so great that it is possible that culutral differences will leave no space for social conflict. The reverse is, however, more likely to happen. We speak of our society as though it were an information society, just as we once spoke of industrial society or a mechanical society. How long will it take us to discover the human beings and social relations behind the technologies? How long will it take us to realize that there is a universal conflict over socially different ways of using information and organizing communications? They can, that is, be used 'abstractly' so as to increase flows of data which are also flows of money and power. Or they can be used 'concretely' so as to further a dialogue between speakers who are unequally situated in power or authority relations.

I regard post-modern ideas primarily as a superficial sociological interpretation of transformations which call for an analysis which has much more in common with the type used in industrial society. I regard the phenomena emphasized by post-modern thought as crisis situations rather than as lasting innovations. The extreme differentiation of the political system and the social system described by

Luhmann (1984) defines a crisis in political representation which we can all recognize. It will not be resolved until new social demands are organized and until our democracies are once more representative. Similarly, talk of absolute difference is no more than a panic reaction when it is divorced from a recognition of social conflicts and the cultural issues at stake in them.

We are living through a transition from one society to another. Virtually the whole of the nineteenth century was taken up by the transition from a mercantile society to industrial society, and from the republican spirit to the workers' movement. Luhmann rightly points out that a society can be defined simply in terms of one of its dimensions: industrial, capitalist or democratic. That is true today, but it was also true yesterday.

The main interest of this debate is to remind us that the idea of the subject cannot be divorced from the idea of social relations. In a programmed society, the individual is reduced to being a mere consumer, a human resource or a target, and individuals challenge the dominant logic of the system by asserting themselves to be subjects, by resisting the world of things and the objectification or commodification of their needs. That is why the idea of the subject cannot be divorced from an analysis which describes contemporary society as post-industrial or programmed rather than as post-modern. Post-modern theories describe the decay of the subject, but also the increasingly vocal demands of minorities and the development of cybernetic systems. Rather than concentrating exclusively on the differences between them, we should be stressing that these two worlds are in conflict. Neither can define itself in its own terms as being either technological or cultural. Both have to be defined socially, or more specifically, in terms of their mutual opposition. This is the main difference between the idea of a subject and that of identity or consciousness: the subject is a challenge to an established order, just as the image of society as market is intended to weaken the resistance of cultural defences. Our consciousness may well still be estranged, but public opinion, if not organized political life, is already giving expression to new conflicts and to the call for the complete transformation of a society whose cultural orientations are accepted by the social movements which are opposed to their social and political implementation.

At the Crossroads

What is known as post-modernism is, as I have already stressed, an extreme form of the decay of the rationalizing model of modernity.

It provides a good definition of what the subject is challenging. The impersonal language of the drives and especially of everything that the law and the Super-Ego repress in to the unconscious, are no longer purely individual; they are visible everywhere in a so-called consumer society which therefore replaces social demands with an aggressive withdrawal in to a culture, and the new power uses it as a language.

Above all, this post-modern culture rejects depth, or in other words the distance between signs and meaning. This is why it takes to extremes the suppression of the subject and substitutes the object – Andy Warhol's Campbell soup tins and Coca-Cola bottles – for the subject, which can, like the same artist's *My Marilyn*, become an advertising image. This consumer culture now constitutes the field in which the subject expresses its demand, just as industrial society constituted the field in which the workers' movement took shape. This gives a new contemporary relevance to Marx's critique of the categories of life and economic analysis, and to his attempt to discover the social relations of production that lay behind them. We can follow Marx's example if we adapt it to a profoundly new situation. In a world of images, it is pointless to evoke use-values in the same way that it was once possible to evoke the necessary liberation of the productive forces from the irrationality of social relations of production. The way to resist this world of signs is to look for a meaning which refers not to nature, but to the subject. Relations between the subject and consumer objects are as conflictual as the relations between capital and labour that characterized earlier types of society. This means that both the affirmation and the negation of the subject are bound up with the replacement of a productive society by a consumer society, and that our image of the subject has nothing in common with the rationalizing and ascetic subject described by Max Weber. It is impossible to define a social conflict unless we can also delineate the cultural field in which it occurs. It is that field that is at stake in the attempt to give society a different form. The consumer society and the subject are actors who are in conflict, and the conflict between them defines the form taken by post-industrial society, which is therefore not post-modern, but hyper-modern.

The increasing importance given to the idea of the subject represents a challenge to visions which completely eliminate the subject, either by reducing it to its market demands, by finding within the subject structures that cannot be perceived by the actor and his consciousness, or by pursuing the work of critical theory and a sociology inspired by Althusser and looking for the logic of a system of domination that is masked by false consciousness. In a transitional period in which the social practices of collective action are too weak or too disoriented to be self-analytical, intellectuals attached great importance to modes of behaviour and explanations that rejected all reference to the subject. They were the main victims of their own analysis, as no society is devoid of actors, and by insisting on being purely critical or attempting to replace a historical sociology with an ahistorical anthropology, they rendered themselves incapable of explaining new practices and eventually created a State within the State, a guild within society. And the rejection of the subject was its native language.

In order to find the real meaning of the changes they observe, intellectuals, and above all sociologists, have only to go back to the great tradition of their profession: discovering what is hidden, and forgetting themselves and their background so as to re-establish the distance that allows the historian or the ethnographer to construct an analysis. Isn't it already too late to be arguing that we have entered a 'post-social' and 'post-historic' period, or a society of pure simulacra in which actors are permanently dissolved in to a kaleidoscope of images? Are we not seeing, rather, the reconstruction and the attempted self-transformation of the societies that were once ruled by the communist system? And are we not at the same time seeing previously unknown modes of personal and collective behaviour spreading rapidly throughout Western societies, whilst part of the Third World is sinking in to poverty, ethnic struggles and corruption? This is not the time to announce the decline of industrial society and to dream of a new equilibrium after a period of great transformations and accelerated growth. The night is coming to an end. Since 1968, we have gone through every stage of social change. We have seen the demise of industrial society and of post-historic illusions, and the emergence of the purely liberal project of reconstructing a new society; it is high time we learned to describe and analyse the cultural modes and the social relations and movements that give them a form. It is time to analyse and describe the political elites and the forms of social change that are changing what momentarily looked like a world beyond historicity. If we are to rediscover the idea of modernity, we must begin by recognizing the existence of a new society and new historical actors.

3

I is not Ego

The Disciplines of Reason

The spirit of the Enlightenment aspired to being liberating, and it was; it has often been defined as being individualist, but it was not. The reader will recall the contrast, which was discussed at the beginning of this book, between the ode to reason and empiricism which characterizes the spirit of the Enlightenment, and the Christian and Cartesian dualism which appears in the Declaration of the Rights of Man and Citizen. Submission to the demands of rational thought freed humanity from superstition and ignorance, but it did not liberate the individual. It replaced the reign of custom with that of reason, and, according to Weber, traditional authority with legal rational authority. Modern rationalism distrusts the individual, and prefers the impersonal laws of science, which apply to human life and human thought alike. So-called modern thought claims to be scientific. It is materialist and naturalist, and dissolves the individuality of the phenomena it observes in to general laws. In the social order, social utility becomes the criterion of good, and education must therefore train selfish adults and especially children to become altruists. They must become men and women with a sense of duty who fulfil their roles in accordance with the rules that seem most likely to create a reasonable and well-tempered society.

The view that education means socialization and an apprenticeship in reason has not vanished, and is still conspicuously present in the schools of many countries. Children must be both disciplined and stimulated by rewards. Repression and punishment will teach them self-control, and will inculcate both the rules of life in society and rational thought processes. The goal of education and its constraints is to enable every individual to resist the material, and especially the intellectual and ethical, difficulties he or she will encounter in life.

Individuals must be able to retain their self-control, as well as to display courage and a willingness to make sacrifices. Education is an apprenticeship in duty, and it is no coincidence that the word *devoir* refers to both the tasks or homework a schoolteacher sets a child and a constraint, and *discipline* to both an instrument of punishment and a domain of knowledge. One can take either an optimistic or a gloomy view of this conception, but it is difficult to define it as individualistic. Education mediates between the individual's demands and their socially acceptable satisfaction by introducing sublimating mechanisms which are outside the individual's control and which are as universalist as possible.

In its early stages, industrial society was regarded as a general mobilization. The working class was an army of labour, and factory discipline was often enforced by military men. Whilst we can readily agree that this image is too brutal or too partial, it does contain enough truth to demonstrate that modern society did not accept that individualism was appropriate for the majority of the population. And nor was it appropriate for the ruling elites, who were subject particularly to the harsh constraints that made them servants of profit or industry and members of a class or profession who hid their individual personalities behind uniforms or conventions. Hence industrial society's liking for allegories which depict social roles but ignore the particular characteristics of the men and women who play them. For women, the loss of individuality was even more complete, as they were reduced to the role of wife, mother or mistress. The struggle against individualism developed still further and became the object of taboos and campaigns to sway public opinion when modernization came to be associated with the rebirth or creation of the nation. Appeals were then made to the heroism of all. Individual happiness and individual interests had to be sacrificed to the conquest of the independence or the greater glory of the nation. Companies used a more measured version of the same vocabulary.

What is individualist about this modern society? So-called traditional ethics was centred on the individual, even when it attempted to free individuals from the grip of the passions; so-called modern ethics is primarily a set of rules which have to be obeyed in the interests of society, which can only prosper if individuals sacrifice themselves for its sake.

And how, finally, can we forget that modern society can also be defined as a mass society in which production comes first and communication comes second, and that it is therefore impossible to call it individualist? Modern societies claim that they are strong because they have replaced particularisms with universalism, and

sociology abounds in binary oppositions which stress this characteristic of modernization: community and society, reproduction and
production, status and contract, individual and group, emotion and
calculation.

The ubiquitous appeal to rationalization and to the motor role of
science and technology once had a powerful appeal in both the East
and the West. And yet it now inspires fear rather than enthusiasm.
This is primarily because the universalism of reason is a formidable
device for destroying individual lives which are made up of a trade,
memories and skills, as well as science, projects and incentives.
Progress once required the sacrifice of a generation. As it accelerates,
it now requires the sacrifice of the greater part of humanity on a
permanent basis. Is it still possible for late-twentieth-century Europe
to believe, as it believed when Eisenstein made *The General Line*,
that the triumph of technology and people's power will free humanity
from ignorance, irrationality and poverty? Above all, we have seen
that, whilst reason is eminently respectable when it is merely a
matter of basic science, it is increasingly identified with powers,
apparatuses and individuals. Totalitarian powers speak enthusiastically of progress, Man and modernity. Even in societies which have
been made more humane by decades of the Welfare State, we feel
ourselves to be prisoners of public or semi-public apparatuses which
claim to speak in the name of reason or the general interest they
represent. Yet they know nothing of reality, or reduce it to meaning
the decisions they take. The discourse of States, and sometimes of
private apparatuses – especially when they have a monopoly – is
steeped in voluntarism. Their voluntarism extends far beyond the
scientific spirit or any concern for the common good. There is an
increasingly blatant contradiction between their discourse and a
reality which frequently indulges itself by contradicting the discourses
of the mighty.

In the social domain, critical thought has destroyed the naïvely
proud Ego of States, just as Freudian thought has discomfited the
illusions of consciousness in the individual domain. In all these cases,
we quite rightly speak of the destruction of the Ego and of consciousness. Yet such critiques often mistakenly claim that they are destroying the Subject. They are right to destroy all principles which identify
human action with the world order, irrespective of whether they are
referring to a religion or reason, meditation or science. When,
however, they destroy an individual or collective Ego whose power
is based upon the laws of nature, they, like Descartes before them,
liberate both a scientific spirit which is constantly threatened by

finalism, and the idea of a subject born of resistance to the power of apparatuses.

It would, however, be pointless to dwell at length on conceptions that reflect the rise of the rationalizing model, as it is not critical thought which weakened them, but a social transformation which was almost unexpected – or at least long delayed – in the industrializing Europe of the nineteenth century: the birth and rapid expansion of the *consumer society*. It was the consumer society, and then the information society, that gave birth to the individualism that now challenges the idea of the subject much more effectively than the old absolute power of reason, and it is therefore worthy of our critical attention.

Individualism

We can no longer simply endorse representations that were elaborated at a time when the large-scale industrialization of the late nineteenth century was triumphing with even more force in Germany and the United States than in Great Britain and France. We have to look at the very different image that has become dominant in our consumer societies, and which seems to be spreading from the United States to the whole world. The idea of modernity is now associated with the liberation of desires and the satisfaction of needs, rather than with the reign of reason. The rejection of collective constraints, religious, political or familial taboos, and freedom of movement, opinion and expression are basic demands which reject as 'outdated' or even reactionary all forms of social and cultural organization which hinder freedom of choice and behaviour. A liberal model has replaced the technocratic and mobilizing model. Images of youth, in particular, are mostly images of the liberation of desires and feelings. This liberalism defines the subject – and democracy – in negative terms. Democracy now means the rejection of everything that stands in the way of individual and collective freedom. The binary oppositions we have just mentioned must therefore be replaced with a new dichotomy, and Louis Dumont's description of it immediately gained classic status: holism and individualism.

Non-modern societies – even recent ones – define individuals in terms of the positions they occupy in a set which constitutes either a collective actor or a corpus of impersonal rules created by a mythical form of thought referring to divine creation, a primal event or an ancestral heritage. Individualism has no content of its own, as a norm can only emanate from an institution, and has collective regulatory effects. The only restrictions on individual freedom are those imposed by the freedom of others. This implies the acceptance of rules in social life. They are pure constraints, but they are also necessary if we are to use a freedom which would otherwise be destroyed by chaos and violence. It is not the individual who must be guided and led; it is society which must be civilized. This idea completely contradicts the classical notion of education, which subjected children to a strict discipline to ensure that reason and order would triumph over the passions and violence. The rules of social life have been redesigned to expand the space available to individual freedom. This liberal model can only be defined by a very general appeal to freedom of initiative, whereas the more directive models for education and organization were infinitely complex and produced a casuistry exemplified by the confessors' manuals of our Middle Ages, which have been analysed so well by Jacques Le Goff and others. Observation of contemporary mores – and especially those of young people, or at least of the majority faction who feel that they are part of this modern liberal society – demonstrates that individualism is closely associated with tolerance and a refusal to exclude any social or national category. Hence the success of the negative campaigns waged by the feminist movement over the right to contraception and abortion, and hence too the weakness and failure of the positive actions of the 'women's liberation movement'. This is also why racial discrimination and apartheid are rejected as firmly as authoritarian and totalitarian regimes.

Modernity means the disappearance of all models and all transcendence, and therefore of religious, political or social forces which create civilizations defined by the imperious norms of ethics. Our conception of modernity, or in other words of modern history, is dominated by the idea that the inertia of social systems and agencies of social control – the family, education, the Church and the law – was overcome only by the combination of the two factors that set society in motion: the opening up of the frontiers of the system and the formation of a central power which destroyed the mechanisms of social reproduction.

The first theme is that of the creative role of trade and, therefore, of the superiority of maritime States like Athens, Venice or modern England over continental States like Turkey or Russia. Contemporary Europe gives this theme a central importance: the main stages of its construction are known as the European Payments Union, the European Coal and Steel Community and the Economic Community. The construction of Europe is rarely defined in positive terms, and almost always in terms of the removal of frontiers. The act which best symbolized the fall of communist regimes in Europe was not the first election to be held in a communist country – Hungary – but the demolition of the Berlin Wall. The free circulation of people, ideas, commodities and capital appears to be the most concrete definition of modernity, and makes customs officers look like figures from the ancient world.

The second theme is that of the modernizing role of the State. A society does not modernize itself: the same does not become the other. Everything resists change, especially the values and motivations that come in to being when individuals internalize them. The State is not part of society, and can therefore transform it either by opening it up to trade and by conquering distant lands, or by destroying traditional forms of social organization and local powers, as did the kings of France, especially at the beginning of what is therefore known as the *modern* era.

The social cost of these economic and political mechanisms for development is very high. They destroy in order to create. They mobilize economies and armies which divide, challenge and conquer before they integrate and convince. Large-scale modernizations in both Europe and the Americas usually relied on violence rather than reason, and imposed slavery, forced labour, deportations and proletarianization. Such were the origins of modern society, which produces its own modernization not through the constraining force of reason and the institutions that implement it, but through the proliferation of supply and demand, through freedom of initiative and the expansion of the market. In the economic order, liberal societies replace positive rules with negative rules; similarly, in the political order, the democratic State has rolled back its own frontiers by encouraging free associations of producers, consumers and tenants.

As a result of these transformations, the power of judges replaces the power of both the State and Churches or families. Private and political life, which were both loci for principles, powers and secrets, are dissolved in to public life, which is a combination of codes and calculations. This conception derives its strength from its elimination of all references to the subject, but it does not resort to coercion. Our society tends not to speculate about the subject and often loudly asserts that mores and laws are modern only if they eliminate all reference to the subject, which is regarded as a disguised form of the divine substance. Modernity is, it would seem, by definition materialist.

Such is the meaning of what might be termed liberal thought, though it is by no means merely an economic or political doctrine. It restricts State intervention to the creation of conditions and rules that encourage the free circulation of people, goods and ideas. It does not make moral pronouncements about how individuals should behave, except when they pose a potential threat. It relies upon reason as an individualist principle and therefore as a principle for resisting the pressures of all particularisms, and especially religious, national or ethnic particularisms; it separates State and civil society, not to mention Church and State, and does all it can to tolerate minorities. This vision of collective and personal life obviously now seems 'normal' to those who live in rich democratic societies where there are almost no collective movements calling for a different type of society or a revolution. This liberalism gives rise to criticisms of two kinds. Some denounce it for applying good principles badly or inadequately. They want greater freedom and tolerance, more mobility and fewer barriers and taboos. Others recognize, usually with some embarrassment, that these principles cannot be applied to all the world's inhabitants, either because many of them have not been sufficiently modernized, or because the rich countries are preventing the poor countries from developing. Although they have very different connotations, the two arguments are still very similar in that they refer with equal conviction to the same central model.

The theme of social life as permanent change and as a network of strategies accords central importance to the *market* which ensures that companies are in touch with the consumer. Companies use marketing to adapt production to consumer demand, as expressed in the market. This transition from an ordered society to an unstable and changing society sheds light on an important aspect of modernity. All the characters on the human stage are in pieces: the Ego, the Law and the will of the Prince, individual or collective. The transition also allows us to understand the countervailing movements that are attempting to reintroduce a community spirit in to a society which is now more than a series of changes. They became increasingly powerful when nations which had demanded the right to embody modernity began to feel threatened by it and increasingly to define themselves in terms of a cultural tradition that had been destroyed by the abstract universalism of modernity, which is always resented because it is 'foreign'. They have dominated the twentieth century because they provided the base for the totalitarian regimes which have marched through it, from Nazi national-racism to Stalinist national-communism and then the cultural and military imperialisms of the Third World, and the Islamic world in particular. The mention of these antiliberal regimes means that we have to reject the over-facile attitude which condemns Western consumer society as roundly as it denounces totalitarian regimes. These finely-tuned scales weigh only words. We have to accept that, like almost all those who are in a position to choose, Eastern Europeans are looking to the West, whereas very few Western Europeans now see any light in the East. Our century has seen too much persecution and extermination and too many arbitrary acts not to prefer the weaknesses and stress of a highly mobile society to the institutionalized violence of societies which appeal to community, history, race or religion. Yet this choice, which we have to make with our eyes open, merely means that, in a world where modernization – which is rarely endogenous – is accelerating, the greatest threats are those posed by the destruction of both traditional and modern society at the hands of an authoritarian and modernizing State. That only the market offers any effective protection against the arbitrary power of the State does not mean that it must be the principle behind the organization of social life. Social life will always involve power relations, and they demand something more than a liberal or authoritarian response. This implies a study of relations between social groups and political forces.

Hence the importance of the crowd or 'mass' psychology which, from Le Bon to Freud and the Frankfurt School, played such an important role in the social thought of the nineteenth century and which has recently been rediscovered by Serge Moscovici (1981). If we define modern society solely in terms of the dissolution of hierarchies and norms, and if we see it solely in terms of consumption and competition, we generate the complementary and inverted image which contrasts the irrationality of collective and especially political life, with the apparent triumph of science, technology and administration. All those who, from the philosophers and politicians of the socialist left to those of the fascist right, have studied mass society have been fascinated to discover a collective life whose laws seem to contradict those of nature. Whenever the image of modern society is reduced to that of a market, and takes no account of either social relations or individual or collective projects, the terrifying image of a mass society reappears. We now find the media more worrying than political agitators, but the dichotomy between strategic action and political or cultural manipulation has not changed. Whenever the idea of the Subject is destroyed, we go back to the dichotomy between pure instrumental rationality and the irrational crowd, and both its components are artificial. The only way to get away from this over-superficial interpretation of modern totalitarian regimes is to abandon the reductive image of modern society. It is by no means an individualistic society. The hierarchical order which, as Louis Dumont rightly says, is typical of traditional societies, has been replaced by organic solidarity and, above all, by relations for the production and management of social resources. Just as integration in to the communitarian order was complemented by access to the mystical world and the individual's attempt to establish a direct relationship with the sacred, involvement in the social relations of production is now complemented by a relationship with the self, by the assertion of a subject defined by a demand to be an actor and therefore to resist the domination of things, techniques and languages that are distributed on a mass scale.

In proto-modern society, a mode of social functioning merged in to a mode of historical development, and civil society therefore merged in to the State. The characteristic feature of modern or hyper-modern society is that it divorces the two. This means that modern society is irreducible to either the market or State planning, which are modes of development. If we make individualism the general principle that defines modern society, we reduce it to the liberal-market mode of modernization. We therefore overlook the realities of labour, production, power and politics. It is possible to accept that, as almost everyone now agrees, the market is better than a planned economy, and at the same time to refuse to reduce society to a market. Modern society is neither holistic nor individualistic; it is a network of relations of production and power relations. It is also the site for the emergence of the subject. The subject does not emerge in order to escape the domination of technology and organization, but to demand the right to be an actor. The dichotomy between the modern and the traditional now gives way to a certain continuity. Just as the subject is involved in both rationalization and an attempt to escape the dominance of commodities and techniques in a productive society, the subject is not completely swallowed up by roles and ranks in an ordered society, because the individual attempts to escape the social world by entering in to as direct a contact as possible with the world of Being. The dichotomy established so forcefully by Louis Dumont is primarily an expression of the worries of the many moderns who fear that they will be drawn in to a purely fluid society characterized mainly by anomie and social disorganization. That is why I am defending both a 'liberal' conception of development and a conception of the subject that is diametrically opposed to the individualism which describes man as a non-social being. That is also why I establish a close connection between the idea of the subject and that of a social movement, and therefore the conflictual relations that constitute social life.

The individualism that is based upon economic rationality is primarily associated with an optimism that now means very little to us. When he uses the term 'risk society' to describe a society in which nuclear energy has a central symbolic role because of its statistically unlikely but potentially devastating effects, Ulrich Beck (1982) inverts the traditional vision which saw the individual as the locus of the irrational, and the economic system as a product of reason and progress. Isn't it now the reverse?, asks Anthony Giddens (1992), who speaks of a search for trust in a risk society and of a subject who relies on himself and on interpersonal relations, on his 'reflexivity' and loving relations for protection against the uncertainties of *fortuna*. Early descriptions of industrialization depicted society as a machine with a regular output; it would be more accurate to describe our society as a spaceship heading in an uncertain direction. An individual is no longer someone who rationally pursues his interests in the marketplace nor a chessplayer. Such figures now seem very impersonal, and will one day be replaced by 'smart' systems. An individual is an affective and self-centred being who is concerned with what Giddens calls self-fulfilment.

Modernity and Self-Identity (Giddens 1992) develops the ideas introduced in *Consequences of Modernity* (Giddens 1990), and its themes often seem similar to those I am developing here. This is primarily because Giddens stresses the complementarity between the globalization of social facts and the rise of individualism that leads to the emergence of a 'self-identity'. The breakup of restricted communities and their stable and explicit codes leaves the individual free to choose his life-style, but it also encourages reflexivity, or in other words the ability to modify behaviour on the basis of an understanding of behaviour. Psychology, sociology, consulting and all forms of therapy play an increasingly important role in that understanding. But, according to Giddens, the individual is originally constituted in a defensive mode; in the early stages of life he places his trust in those who take care of him, and then defines himself by 'integrating life experiences within the narrative of self-development' (Giddens 1992: 80). As Giddens recognizes in his discussion of lifestyle sectors, this 'care of the self', as Foucault (1984a) terms it, has no unifying principle. It is indeed a matter of self-consciousness, or in other words of the behaviour expected by others and which the individual attempts to unify. This is an endless task, and it involves a high degree of narcissism. This image is one of cocooning, the mirage of an Ego taking itself in hand and withdrawing from the threatening social relations in which it is involved. This is the complete antithesis of what I call the Subject. The subject does not imply the care of the self, but the defence of the ability to be an actor, or in other words to modify one's social environment by resisting the norms and forms of social organization through which the Self is constructed. The self-identity explored by Giddens is a psychological reality or a form of individual reflexivity, whereas the Subject, as I define it, is a dissident, a resistance fighter. The shaping of the Subject is not a matter of the care of the self, but of defending freedom from power.

A generation after David Riesman, Robert Bellah (1985) depicts American mores in a way that is reminiscent of the tradition of Tocqueville. He demonstrates the limitations of extreme individualism and its 'culture of separation'. Middle-class Americans now find a 'culture of coherence' equally attractive, both at work, in local life and in interpersonal relations. Witness the rise of social ecology. Self-discovery can, in other words, take as many different forms as the lifestyles described by Giddens and Bellah. Individualism breaks up the hierarchical and communitarian traditions of old, but it does not constitute the dominant type of personal and social life. It would therefore be to mistake the subject, or a principle which defends the human person in its conflicts with apparatuses of power, with the disparate and changing images of individualism which, as Robert Bellah rightly says, are so many different ways of adapting to a changing environment. The rugged individualism of the Americans of legend is far removed from both the parochialism of small-town conservatives and from the cocooning of the 1980s. It is pointless to attempt to relate this type of behaviour to a general model. The idea of the subject should not be confused with an account of how mores vary from country to country and generation to generation.

All these images of the individual fail to grasp the implications of the destruction of the Ego, which was completed by Freud. Even when he believes he is acting in accordance with his desires, the individual is increasingly an effect of the system and its objectives. Which means that we have to make an even clearer distinction between the I, or the principle that resists the logic of the system so stubbornly, and the Self, which is an individual projection of the demands and norms of the system.

The idea of the subject does not contradict the idea of the individual, but it is a very particular interpretation thereof. On a number of occasions, Louis Dumont stresses the need to make a distinction between the individual as empirical singularity, and the individual as ethical notion. The first sense is purely descriptive, whereas there are several ways of constructing the individual as ethical notion. According to one view, the quest for utility or personal pleasure must be the organizing principle behind social life. For those who see society as a set of apparatuses for making decisions and influencing people, the individual is primarily a demand for personal and collective freedom. Others take the intermediate view that individuals are to be defined by their social roles and, in particular, by their roles in production. Like Marx, they therefore regard the individual as a 'social' being. Liberals do all they can to reduce the individual to the rational pursuit of self-interest. Because of the importance I attach to social movements and especially to those I termed 'new social movements' after 1968, I use 'individual' in the second sense, whereas Marxism – and many other schools of sociology – emphasizes the third view. I am reluctant to adopt either the first or the third because nothing could be less individual – or more statistically predictable – than rational choices, whereas critical theory has demonstrated the individual is to a large extent either acted upon by the system and by the functional categories imposed by those who hold power, or controlled in more subtle ways because of the dominance of the whole over its parts. Yet whilst we can replace the notion of 'the individual', which can mean so many different things, with the more sharply defined notion of the subject, modernity cannot be completely equated with the birth of the subject. That is why I define it in terms of the increasing divorce and tension between rationalization and subjectivation.

The Dissolution of the Ego

Rationalist thought is overtly anti-individualist because one cannot appeal to a universal principle – truth as demonstrated by rational thought – and at the same time defend individualism, unless, of course, one defends everyone's right to seek and expound the truth. Rationalist thought is therefore a powerful weapon against intellectual and political oppression. The theme of individualism which, as I have tried to demonstrate, is confused and even non-existent, conceals the greatness of rationalist modes of thought which call upon human beings to submit to a principle, namely truth, that elevates them above the distractions of diversion and the stirrings of the passions.

The term 'individualism' is also inapplicable to the Nietzschean and Freudian discovery of the Id or, more concretely, to the importance given to sexuality by contemporary culture and thinkers influenced by philosophies of life. This is the antithesis of the liberation of the individual: the Ego is dissolved and reduced to being the locus of an unstable and conflictual equilibrium between the Id and the Super-Ego. It might also be added that, despite the self-image it likes to promote, consumer culture too is one of the weapons that destroys the Ego. The destruction of the Ego can therefore be regarded as one of modernity's great tasks.

The Ego, which once meant the presence of the soul, or in other words God, within the individual, has become a set of social roles. Its triumph was therefore restricted to the beginnings of modernity, when it appeared to be a principle of order associated with reason's triumph over the passions and with social utility. Early modernity coincided with the cult of portraiture, particularly in the heartlands of modern civilization in Holland and Flanders, but also in the Italian cities. The portrait, which first appeared in Rome, signals a correspondence between an individual and a social role. The emperor, the merchant or the donor is individualized, and the viewer's pleasure derives from a perception of the violence, avarice or sensuality that is concealed beneath the uniforms of the bourgeoisie, the aristocracy or the clergy. The most important thing of all, however, is the social role, firstly because it is this that explains the very existence of a portrait commissioned by a dignitary, and secondly because a successful portrait demonstrates that a role can no longer simply be equated with a rank or function, as it was in pre-modern society. A social role is an activity which calls for strength and imagination, and which mobilizes ambition and faith. Early modernity was the moment of the triumph of both individualism and the bourgeois spirit. As a result of a long century of critiques of rationalist modernity, our culture has shattered the portrait. It has revealed impersonal desire, the language of the unconscious and the effects of organizations on the individual personality, and references to the Ego thus become meaningless.

Given that the subject appears only when the correspondence between Ego and world disappears, the Ego can be neither a character in a novel nor a 'subject' for a painter. The decay of the novel from Proust and Joyce onwards leads to the development of writing about the subject. Writing in *Le Monde* (8–9 September 1991), the painter Pierre Soulages states: 'Painting is not a means of communication. I mean that it does not transmit a meaning; it makes sense in itself. It makes sense for the viewer, but its meaning is determined by what he is.' Creative man no longer identifies with his works, which have acquired such autonomy that the creator himself needs to stand back from them. God existed within the world he created, and early modern man tried to imitate him and take his place. His pride led him in to a trap and he agreed to be imprisoned in the name of freedom. He therefore had to go back to the divorce between subjectivity and objectivity. What is more, he can now grasp his freedom only in an oscillation between commitment and non-commitment.

This shattering of the Ego increasingly distances the Self from the I. The Self is the self-image the individual acquires through linguistic exchanges with others within a collectivity. The determinant factor here is the socially determined relationship with others. It is that which defines a role and our expectations of a role. As Taylor puts it (Taylor 1989: 35), with reference to Wittgenstein's principle that any language presupposes the existence of a language community, 'One is a self only among other selves. A self can never be described without reference to those who surround it.' The Self therefore exists within a world of communications, whereas the Subject or the I exists at the centre of the world of action, or in other words of the modification of the material and social environment.

Of all the social scientists of the twentieth century, it is George Herbert Mead (1934) who provides the most fully worked out expression of the view that the personality is the internalization of models of social relations. This is why he finds it difficult to make a distinction between the Self and the Ego or the Me. 'The "me" is the organized set of attitudes of the other which one himself assumes' (Mead 1934: 175), whereas the Self is constituted through the complementary recognition of the Other to whom the I reacts. The Me and the Self combine to produce the personality, and Mead's central thesis is that 'the content put in to the mind is only a development and product of social interaction' (1934: 191). The difference between the I and the Me is that the I is free to react either negatively or positively to the social norms internalized by the Me. Why it resists the injunctions of a 'generalized Other' (1934: 154) is, however, unclear; it seems that the very existence of individuality explains the frequent discrepancy between individual actors and general norms. Mead speaks of the creative and transforming role of men of genius (1934: 217), but certainly does not share the idea of the Subject, as outlined here. 'A person is a personality because he belongs to a community, because he takes over the institutions of that community in to his own conduct' (1934: 162). More specifically, 'One attains self-consciousness only as he takes, or finds himself stimulated to take, the attitude of the other' (1934: 194). Mead therefore comes close to endorsing the classical view that the personality is defined by social roles and that individuality becomes stronger as the personage internalizes social norms.

The idea that the Self and the subject are increasingly divorced and that identity, which is associated with the Self, and the I are contradictory, destroys the unity of what is vaguely referred to as the personality. It does not impose a radical interpretation, but it does react violently against all attempts to establish a reciprocity of perspective between the subject and social roles. On the contrary, it is the discrepancy between question and answer that ensures the permanent transformation of society. And it is the ability to manage that discrepancy that defines the efficacy of an institutional system.

At this point, I have no option but to retrace the argument of part II. The shattering of the rationalist image of modernity and of objective reason revealed the existence of the four separate forces which, when combined, define contemporary society: sexuality, commodified needs, the company and the nation. The shattered Ego is projected to the four corners of this shattered world. It is traversed by sexuality, moulded by the market and the social hierarchy, integrated in to the company and identified with the nation, and it appears to recover its unity only when one of these forces defeats the others. The mask then sticks to the skin and the individual feels at one with himself only when he is under arms, at work, in his sexual desire or when he is a consumer who is free to buy what he likes. In the richest societies, the consumer is the most important figure of the individual. The importance of the consumer is heightened by an insistent ideological discourse whose poverty and artificiality rivals those of the discourses of companies, nations or erotic literature. At this level, the only reality is the individual, as the individual is the locus where impersonal and mutually hostile forces meet and mingle.

Intoxicated by its victory over the empires of the East and the nationalist dictatorships of the South, the West is now enthusiastically embracing a liberalism that knows no limits. There is no longer any need to define either the Good or the steep road that allows us to approach it. It seems that we can abandon everything to self-interest, the 'blossoming' of the individual and the expression of desires simply by getting rid of absolute powers and their ideologies. This libertarian liberalism can be found right across the political spectrum, and it unites the libertarian far right with the far left class of 1968. Defining the Good seems to be too dangerous. It has been reduced to authenticity and is no longer seen in terms of liberation struggles. Individualism is triumphant, and only Evil can be clearly delineated. Evil means the subordination of individuals and their interests and desires to the omnipotence of a State which appeals to community, denounces everything foreign and is suspicious of all intermediary bodies. Communist regimes have become almost perfect images of Evil, and we can be sure that we are on the right road when we extol what they condemned. Contemporary culture rejects symbolism because it refers to a supra-human world. It replaces it with signs of immediate experience, effort, desire, solitude and fear, and can do without the idea of the subject because the only things that matter are living, expressing oneself and communicating. There is no point in self-reflection or in regarding oneself as anything other than an object to be exploited to one's greatest possible advantage.

This enjoyment of unbridled consumption is not to be scorned; it is a reaction to the stifling triumph of collectivist ideologies which spoke only of mobilization, conquests and construction. It does, however, have obvious limitations, as the individual is the very opposite of what he believes himself to be. As soon as he was freed from authoritarian constraints, the individual began to disintegrate. On the one hand, the individual is determined by his position in a system of social stratification and mobility: the individual who thinks he is expressing his personal taste makes choices typical of a social category. His freedom seems artificial because his behaviour is eminently predictable. On the other hand, the individual is governed by the unconscious Id, and the analyst can therefore once more justifiably denounce the illusions of the Ego. Those who speak of nothing but the individual are in reality those who believe in the logic of systems and the most active opponents of the idea of the subject. If human beings are motivated by self-interest, we can understand their behaviour without referring to their personalities, their culture or their political positions. The idea of the subject reappears only when we become aware that the personality is being affected by a kind of crisis. Liberal society is synonymous with the pursuit of self-interest, but it is also full of holes and tears. And in their depths, we hear not the voice of the subject, but the screams or even the silence of those who are no longer subjects: the suicidal, the addicts, the depressed and the narcissists. It is as though society were a motor racing circuit, with a hospital for the accident victims in the background.

The idea of the subject is far removed fom that of submission to the Law or the Super-Ego. And nor is the subject an Ego, which is why I am suspicious of the idea of the 'human person': it implies what I see as an unreal coincidence between the Ego and the I. The subject is a conscious will to construct individual experience, but it also implies an affection for a communitarian tradition. It is a form of self-enjoyment, but also a form of submission to reason. It does not replace the shattered world of postmodernism with an omnipotent principle of unity; it is a 'weak' notion which is not so much a central affirmation as a network of relations between commitment and non-commitment, individuality and collectivity.

The decay of the Ego goes in parallel with the dissolution of the idea of *society*. Society was once defined as a collective Ego to such an extent that, long before Freud, it was commonly identified with the image of the father and the Super-Ego. Contemporary sociology has clearly demonstrated the illusory nature of this representation.

Society is no longer an avatar of the Church, the community or the sacred; and nor is it the shaping or organization of rationality. A national society, a company, a hospital, an army, or any other form of society or organization is never anything more than a changeable space which is poorly integrated and badly controlled. It is a screen on to which we can project a number of different logics and therefore sets of relations, negotiations and social conflicts. Sociologists who, like Michel Crozier, study organizations have demonstrated that the reference to the norms of a social system must be replaced by an analysis of strategies for managing changes which are to a large extent uncontrolled. Companies that claim to be defending their ego, personality or spirit, are being very naïve. Totally narcissistic companies are in great danger, as efficacy implies openness, an ability to adapt and change, pragmatism and calculation. At both company level, government level and the individual level, an obsession with identity results in paralysis and increasingly defensive behaviour.

Nothing can abolish the distance between the Subject and an Ego which, as Cornélius Castoriadis (1984) puts it, exists *For Itself*. To the extent that they exist for themselves, society, individuals and organizations are capable of finality, calculation and self-preservation, and can create a world of their own. The subject on the contrary is defined in terms of self-creation, of the deliberate transformation of self and environment. And this, according to Castoriadis, gives a central role to the imagination, or the capacity for symbolic creation.

The Mirage of Absolute Modernity

The consumer society has brought us at great speed to a place which was perceived by a restricted group of eighteenth-century intellectuals. The distance between what is and what ought to be, between desire and the law, seems to have been abolished as completely as the frontier between the inner man and his social behaviour, as David Riesman puts it in his rightly celebrated *The Lonely Crowd* (Riesman 1958). The world seems to have become as flat as a stage set or a page of writing. It is no more than a text, a montage of signs which is as weak and as non-directive as possible. This society's great dream is that of a spontaneous match between supply and demand, between the consumer's imaginary and the profits or power of companies involved in consumption and communications. Interpretations of this consumer society are not so much post-modernist as *low modernist*, to use a phrase coined by Marshall Bermann and adopted by Scott Lash and Jonathan Friedman (Lash and Friedman 1972). This in fact means an extreme and generalized or ubiquitous modernism. Thanks to a process analogous to the transformation of power, as described by Foucault, low modernism is initially concentrated in the higher reaches of society and then permeates the entire social body and everyday life. When we enter a shopping mall, are we in an internal space where repressed desires mingle, or in the service sector?

It is quite understandable that a situation in which both the subject and the objectivity of reason vanish in to a world of images should have caught the attention of almost all commentators – from those who are involved in advertising to those who work at the most abstract level – and that they should all be fascinated by a world which is the child of Marx and Coca-Cola, as Godard puts it in *La Chinoise*. Yet isn't the fusion of the individual and social organization with flows of consumption and communications something that occurs in the discourses of commentators rather than in our actual behaviour? Sociological observation and the discourses of the new social philosophy in fact take us in opposite directions. Sociological observation reveals the extreme divorce between the subjective world and the world of objects, between primary groups and the consumer society, as well as the negative effects of the dissolution of the subject in to an environment constructed by dealers in the imaginary. Michel Maffesoli (1988) is right to see tribes where we are supposed to be seeing individuals. In the peripheral suburbs that surround the great cities of the West, the shopping centres are indeed used and devastated by gangs, ethnic groups, communities and neighbourhood groups. No matter where we look, we see savage conflicts, relations between strangers and aggressivity rather than actors and a system which are fusing in to a consumer society.

It is true that the consumer–communications society is hyper-modern and that it is completing the destruction of essences and ascribed status that was begun by the classical period of modernity; but it is even more true to say that this society is no more than the culmination of the long process that secularized and disenchanted the world. The self-image it produces, and which is amplified by social philosophies, masks the rifts that reveal its true nature: the growing divorce between meaning, which is being privatized, and the signs that are invading public life, between projects and a market, and between the construction of democratic decisions and the freedom to consume. The defence of the subject against the consumer society is primarily a matter of denouncing the dominant ideology, and of discovering, in a supposedly flat and homogeneous world, relations or power and dependency, breaks and rejections, aggressivity and lack. Hyper-modern society is not something that lies beyond the subject and social movements; it strengthens the mechanisms that destroy them, but it also expands their field of action.

Although it is mistaken when it speaks of individualism, liberal thought does understand the general tendency to eliminate essences. Indeed, it does as much as the most radical critical theory to destroy the illusions of consciousness and interiority. That destruction has been underway for so long and is so complete, that one is almost tempted to identify modernity with its results. Surely we have to describe as 'modern' a culture and a society which have pursued secularization and empiricism to their logical conclusion by completely eradicating the appeal to central explanatory principles and to subjects, which used to be variously known as God, the Soul, the Ego, Society or the Nation? I accept these conclusions, subject to the proviso that we add that the birth of the Subject has nothing to do with the defence of the Ego, consciousness or the inner life and that *only the destruction of the Ego permits the emergence of the I*. And this goes hand in hand with the destruction of a humanized or anthropomorphic nature.

It was thanks to Cézanne that nature became nature once more, and ceased to be a human impression, sentiment or invention. As a result, art lost its unity. Whilst one school of painting, which includes both the surrealists and the cubists, eliminates the subject and reveals a structure, another school begins with expressionism, culminates in lyrical abstraction, and either becomes obsessed with or rediscovers the subject. The first school has enjoyed one success after another, as it has turned artists in to creators of languages, and some of them have demonstrated an almost boundless ability to create a whole series of languages. Even though they inspire less admiration, the works of the second school are more moving, especially when they explicitly associate the destruction of the Ego with the discovery of the subject. Giacometti is a case in point. His spindly figures, some of which would fit in to a matchbox, seem to be pure movement and to indicate the absence of any gaze, but if we look at them more carefully we quickly come to the conclusion that Giacometti is primarily a portrait-painter, with his brother Diego, Isaku Tonaihara and Elie Cantor as his favourite subjects. He himself says (Giacometti 1990: 245) of his work that:

> If I begin to want to paint, or rather sculpt it, the content of even the most insignificant head, the least violent head, the most shapeless head, or the head of an inadequate figure, all that is transformed in to a tensed form which always, it seems to me, indicates a tightly suppressed violence, as though the very form of the figure always transcended

what the figure is. But it is that too: above all, it is a sort of core of violence.

It is more important to demonstrate that the two schools complement one another than to contrast them. They are similar to the extent that they both break with the depiction of social roles and types, and completely eradicate allegory.

I against Self

The I exists only when it is invisible to its own gaze. It is a desire for Ego and never a mirror for the Ego. This principle obviously applies with even greater force to relations between the I and the Self, which is a set of social roles. The I can be shaped only if it breaks with those social roles and distances itself from them. The face and the gaze are hidden behind masks, but all too often we recognize only the masks. We identify with our masks. Our faces seem shapeless and our gaze seems empty, in the same way that the unemployed feel that they have lost their social existence as well as their professional existence. Contemporary liberal society can encourage the birth of the I because it offers a greater number of differentiated social roles and imposes increasingly complex rules and modes of behaviour on us in all our roles. If we play the game long enough, we realize that it is all make-believe. The result can be a narcissism which rejects all commitment and which flits from role to role and from situation to situation in search of an I that can escape all roles. It can also be the will to be a subject if, rather than escaping roles and breaking machines, we find the logic of a power or apparatus that forces us to defend the subject. Rom Harré's distinction between the person and the Self is unsatisfactory. According to Harré, the person is 'the socially defined, publicly visible embodied being, endowed with all kinds of powers and capacities for public, meaningful actions', whereas the Self is 'the personal unity I take myself to be, my singular inner being, so to speak' (Harré 1983: 26). This distinction presupposes, as Harré stresses (notably in chapter 4) that there is a correspondence between the social being and the inner being who is aware that he exists as an individual. The argument that there is a correspondence between the I and the me, to adopt George Herbert Mead's classic analysis (Mead 1934), is inadequate. It is precisely the non-correspondence between social roles, the self-images lent me or forced upon me by society, and my assertion of myself as a subject creating my existence that creates sociology's central problem: the opposition between determinism and freedom. Erik Erikson (1971) is more aware of the constrast between changing Selves and the Ego. He contrasts the formation of an identity with identifications that lead to an identity crisis.What I am calling the subject is an individual's ability to reflect upon his or her own identity.

The withdrawal from social roles, the limitations of socialization and the dissociation between social functions and personal projects are major facts. They distance us from the old idea of social integration and the Greek model of the man-citizen which our modern societies are trying to defend or revive – by speaking of workers rather than citizens – at a time when practices are rejecting them completely and when the affirmation of the Subject is increasingly bound up with a rejection of systems and their logic of organization and power, as André Gorz (1988) and Ulrich Beck (1982) have so forcefully explained.

Nothing must distract us from our central assertion: *the subject is a social movement*. It is constituted, not in self-consciousness, but in *the struggle against the anti-subject*, against the logics of apparatuses, especially when they become culture industries and, *a fortiori*, when they have totalitarian goals. This is why the consciousness of the subject is so constantly associated with a critique of society. This was already the case in Baudelaire's day, and even more so in *Une Saison en enfer* (Rimbaud 1873), which is the founding moment of the consciousness of the subject in contemporary culture. The I is revealed to itself only when it becomes detached from all personal and social bonds, only through the derangement of the senses or through a mystical experience. And this discovery of the I does not survive the return from hell. The subject is burned in the flames that lit it up, and henceforth Rimbaud will be exiled from himself. We hear the subject's demands in the testimony of the victims, the deported and the dissidents, and not in the moralizing discourses of those who speak of nothing but social integration. It is the gesture of refusal, of *resistance*, that creates the subject. It is the more restricted ability to stand aside from our own social roles, our non-belonging and our need to protest that allows each of us to live as a subject. And subjectivation is always the antithesis of socialization, of adaptation to a social role or status, provided that we do not become trapped in to a counter-culture of subjectivity and provided that we commit ourselves to the struggle against the forces that actively destroy the subject.

The idea of the *person*, in contrast, remains true to the main tradition of Western thought. Human beings are seen as transcending the individuality of their bodies and senses and as aspiring to reason, not because reason is universalist, but because it obeys only its own laws and because those laws are inscribed in the human mind. Kant spoke of 'personality', but he used the word in the sense in which many later writers speak of a 'person'. Even Emmanuel Mounier, who addresses very different themes, defines personalization as a commitment to general values which allow the human person to rise above the material world (Mounier 1949). I speak of a subject and not a person in order to distance myself from this tradition. The appeal to reason frees us from the passions, but does not constitute a subject, except in that initial moment when modern thought is still the heir to the Christian idea of a rational God who created the world. The triumph of reason is above all the triumph of industrial and state power. In ideological terms, that power can be referred to as 'society'. In a modernized world, the call for commitment and devotion to reason therefore means at best imprisonment in the iron cage of technology and, at worst, involvement in lethal activities carried out in the name of a rational quest for victory.

The essential inversion consists in linking the freedom of the subject to man as phenomenon, and not to man as noumenon, to adopt the terminology of the *Fundamental Principles of the Metaphysics of Morals* (Kant 1785) and to man-as-body. Not in order to reduce the subject to the individual, but in order to define the subject as the demand to be an individual, to lead a personal life. This usually means resisting the apparatuses and techniques of power, but it can also mean using the power of reason to resist arbitrary power or the hold of the community. The subject is not formed by abandoning the body and the Id or the world of desire, and modernity does not consist in crushing affectivity and interpersonal bonds in the name of reason. On the contrary, the subject is always a *bad subject* who rebels against rules and integration in an attempt to assert itself and enjoy itself, and it is by resisting power that self-assertion is transformed in to the will to be a subject. The subject is defined by its freedom and efforts to achieve liberation rather than by reason and rationalizing techniques. This does not mean that we have to contrast reason and the subject; as we shall see, they are interdependent. It does, on the other hand, mean that we have to divorce them from the outset by breaking with the idea that individualization and socialization are one and the same, and that personal freedom can only be won by submitting to the laws of reason. Yet the tragic consciousness of the subject, which is associated with the attempt to break free of social roles and to resist the pressure of groups, public opinion and apparatuses, cannot be reduced to a self-sacrificial consciousness, as it submits to no law and to no higher necessity, but only to human existence.

How can progress towards the subject not be immobile? How can it transform the transcendence of the norms of the Self and the illusions of the Ego in to the creation of an I and ensure that it is not a new image of a hidden God which introduces a new Jansenism and an ethics of rigour and renunciation? Those who criticize rationalist modernity try to find an answer in a return to Being through Life, eroticism or the contemplation of life. Art came in to existence in Germany at the end of the eighteenth century as a substitute for the sacred and the religious. And Nietzsche, Adorno or Barthes still look to art in their quest for an absolute without transcendence. If we are dissatisfied with this nostalgia for Being – and Michel Foucault's attempt to find it in Ancient Greece ended in disappointment – and if we have a clear awareness that the subject emerges only by resisting apparatuses, or even the total apparatus known as society, we have to conclude that the personal subject can be understood only in terms of a relationship with the other-as-subject. It is only when the other-subject addresses me so as to make me a subject for him or her, that I am indeed a subject. Just as being-for-others, or in other words the Self, destroys the subject by subordinating it to social norms and roles, so being-for-the-other is the only way in which the individual can experience himself as a subject.

No experience is more central than the relationship with the other which constitutes both I and other as subjects. Yet it would be artificial to contrast this private relationship with public life. All individuals are caught up in a network of roles. They exist for others, and the encounter with the other never takes place on open ground, as in films where two characters meet face to face on an empty set. External and internal obstacles always have to be removed; above all, recognition of the other as subject must lead us to support the other in his attempts to break free of the constraints that prevent him from experiencing himself as a subject. This solidarity cannot be purely individual because, whilst the subject is always personal, the obstacles to his existence are almost always social, irrespective of whether they are products of the family, economic and administrative life or political and religious life. There can be no production of the I without love of the other, and no love of the other without solidarity. Does it have to be added that there can be no solidarity without a real awareness of the real relationship between the situation in which I live, and the situation in which the other lives? It is, for example, only too easy for rich countries to send a billion dollars to poor countries when twenty or thirty billion dollars extorted from poor continents are piling up in banks in rich countries. Ethics is now more important than politics, at least in certain circumstances and in certain parts of the world, because we no longer believe that the individuals and societies who submit most fully to the laws of reason are the most modern. We see the affirmation of the freedom of the subject as the central principle – a non-social principle with multiple social effects – behind resistance to the pressures of social power, irrespective of whether it is concrete and in the hands of a despot, or distributed throughout the entire fabric of social exchange.

The oldest industrial countries, which lie at the centre of the programmed society, have seen the emergence of the image of a consumer society which transforms earlier conceptions of social roles. Whereas individual functions were once defined by a pre-existing ability, a trade, a skill or even a vocation, activity has been redefined in terms of communications. Skill now means the ability to encode, transmit and decode the most complex messages as efficiently as possible. This has given rise to an ideology which celebrates exchanges and therefore the mutual understanding without which no communication is possible. This is the ideology of ruling groups, and it promotes the idea that the best way for an individual to express himself is to become more fully involved in the process of data transmission. Day by day, we hear them singing the praises of the information society in which almost everyone receives more information – and more quickly – than the great men of this world received scarcely a hundred years ago. We have to react against this ideology by recalling that communication means both circulating information and giving individuals a communicative role, and that these two dimensions are contradictory rather than complementary. Similarly, advertising messages are most effective when the attitudes they are seeking to modify are less important to the receivers. We change brands of washing powder more readily than we change our religion, which explains why the most expensive advertising campaigns are devoted to the least important aspects of life. A good communications system is one which makes it possible to transmit more personal messages in which the pertinent information is less divorced from the whole personality, and especially from projects, and in which a greater quantity of noise is required if a complex message is to be understood. We are reintroducing ever more varied aspects of personal life in to technical activity. The divorce between public and private life, which was for so long identified with modernity, is becoming the sign of a primitive and outdated form of modernity.

This is why, after an interval of two hundred years, we are rediscovering the spirit of the Declaration of the Rights of Man and Citizen, even though the bourgeois figure of the subject is no longer appropriate to the society in which we live. Rather than interpreting society from top to bottom and from centre to periphery, as though practices were no more than particular applications of values, norms and forms of organization in general, we now begin with the individual's production of the I, with all the forms of the destruction of the Ego and the Self that are required for its production, and then try to make it compatible with the work of reason that gives birth to oppressive powers. The work of reason is also, however, always a liberating force.

Biology has done a great deal to facilitate, perhaps not the idea of the subject, which is none of its concern, at least the destruction of a representation which negated it. Models derived from physics long ago dissolved the particular in to the general, and man in to the laws of nature. This approach is so central to all the sciences that it cannot be ignored, but it is now complemented by the more historical vision of nature elaborated by the astrophysicists and the geologists who are attempting to reconstruct the history, not of the universe, but of this universe. It is further complemented by the concern for individuality which, as Francis Jacob (1970) demonstrates so forcefully, is central to genetics. Genetics studies the implacable mechanisms that create difference and which mean that, identical twins aside, there is no such thing in the world as two biologically identical human beings. This discovery is related to the discovery of the plasticity of the human organism. Tens of billions of neurones and hundreds of billions of synaptic relations produce such an ability to evolve and adapt that the dichotomy between innate and acquired has to be replaced by an innate ability to acquire. It is because the individual is no longer absorbed in to general categories that we can study the construction of the human person, the Ego, the Subject and the I, not as socialization, but as the work of the individual on the individual to assert his or her individuality.

Lucien Sève, who wrote the report on medical research and respect for human persons for the French Comité Nationale d'Ethique (Sève 1987), uses very similar notions to the ones I am describing here, and stresses that it is the subject, and not the person, who is a value. The subject is indeed defined by its assertion that the person is a value, and by its modification of social relations, and especially language. It tends, however, to constitute a subjective body or an Ego before it asserts the rights of the human person. A direct connection can thus be established between an absolutely singular biological individual, and the subject who demands the right to be a person, the right of the objective individual to transform himself in to a subjective individual rather than identifying with a general or even universal category that supposedly allows him to transcend his individuality. Modes of thought dominated by physics produced systems theories; modes of thought influenced by biology look more favourably on the theory of the actor and the politics of personalities. This is a concrete expression of the principle that only recognition of the other as subject allows the actor to be constituted as a subject and not simply as a Self. This principle signals a departure from the modernism which claims that the subject emerges only through the instrumental action of dominating nature. I fully agree with Habermas when he writes (Habermas 1985: 292–3):

> As long as we only take in to account subjects representing and dealing with objects, and subjects who externalize themselves in objects or can relate to themselves as objects, it is not possible to conceive of socialization as individuation and to write the history of modern sexuality *also* from the point of view that the internalization of subjective nature makes individuation possible.

The break with the transcendental foundations of the subject does not lead simply to the empiricism of science; as Novalis said, it also allows the subject to have domination over his transcendental ego and to be his 'own ego's ego'.

Social thought always resists ideas which deny that the social can, as modern thought claims, provide the basis for an ethics. In that sense, modern thought is the heir to Greek thought. Yet if sociology does not take the side of the subject against society, it is fated to be an ideological instrument promoting social integration and moralization, sometimes in a soft form, but sometimes in brutal form. And they will always inspire a quest for the forbidden subject.

The Absent Subject

The idea of the subject was for a long time so arrogant that scientific and critical thought had to make a frontal assault on it in order to discover the impersonal logic of classifications, systems of exchange and myths, language and the unconscious. It is now time to take the opposite path without returning to the starting point where the axis of the Ego was also the axis of the world, reason. Reason could teach human beings how to behave because it made nature intelligible, and therefore something that could be controlled and used.

In modern societies, which have a high degree of reflexivity and historicity, the destruction of the subject does not have the same meaning as in societies with a low degree of historicity. Its destruction is the result of a direct clash between the Id and the Super-Ego, between desire and the law, which partially represses in to the unconscious and thus prevents the individual from creating himself as a personal subject. As a result, psychoanalysts like Lacan quite justifiably begin to look for the subject of the signifier. This cannot be the naïvely triumphant 'popular and metaphysical subject', but nor can it be reduced to 'forces'. The subject is weak. Not only is it dominated by the apparatuses of power; it is also deprived of a large part of itself, as it has been transformed in to the unconscious. It can therefore manifest itself and act only by struggling for its liberation, and by expanding the internal space in which desire and the law are not contradictory. The subject is constituted through democracy and the politics of individual rights, through freedom and tolerance, through a partial abrogation of the law and through the transformation of the drives in to a desire for the other. The subject is never constituted by its transformation in to a complacent Ego or through a surrender to the narcissistic pleasure of introspection. It is constituted through its escape from the order of the law and the logic of the impersonal language of action.

The essential contribution made by psychoanalysis, from Freud to Lacan, is to have divorced the subject of the statement (the Ego) from the subject of the utterance. In my view, only the latter can be said to be a subject. Modern society is a society in which the decay of order and its languages makes possible both the extreme domination of the languages of power and the repression or marginalization that ensues, and the formation of a personal subject which both challenges authority and attempts to transform desires in to happiness. This subject never triumphs; it has no protected space, even when it thinks it has found it in a holiday village, in a sheltered private life or in a sect. And to reduce the subject to being the good life that is so readily on offer in rich countries would be an indecent surrender to their privileges. The subject asserts its existence only by negating impersonal logics, internal and external. And the social sciences must never divorce the lived experience of freedom from the threats that loom over it.

Sociologists and historians must be wary of ideologies and voluntarism, and must refuse to identify the subject with the social order. To put it much more simply, they must recognize the existence of hell and sin, even when they appear in everyday life. The strength of the great classics of social thought, irrespective of whether they take the form of sociology, history, novels, films, plays or paintings, is that they make visible the intervention of something that is absent, invisible or lacking. We have to reveal the observable effects of the subject's absence. It would be a mistake to see the reference to the subject as the upper story of modes of behaviour which are solidly based upon utilitarian foundations. Collective attempts to win greater political influence do not lead to the challenge to a society's general orientations that defines a social movement in the same way that a staircase leads from one floor to the next. That vision implies that, even if there is no upper story, the lower stories are still solid but have to use an ideological tarpaulin to protect them from the elements. The absence of a reference to the subject or to rationalization and social movements does not in fact leave the lower levels of the structure intact: it devours them. What the old literary psychology described as vices or passions can now be reinterpreted as an expression of a lack. Social psychology shows drug dependency to be a lack of a subject which destroys the individual's ability to be an Ego or Self, or in other words a social being. In his study of marginal youth, François Dubet (1987) attaches great importance to the *rage* of these young people. Their rage cannot be reduced to the effects of their marginality or even their social exclusion, as it destroys objects, others and selves. It is a manifestation of the absence of the I, which is destructive in itself. Similarly Michel Wieviorka (1988, 1991) has studied the ill-defined boundary between a social movement which has been inverted in to a social non-movement, and a pure terrorism which no longer has any real social referent. Castoriadis, Lefort and Morin (1981) interpret the movement of May 1968 as having opened up a breach. I would argue, however, that this description is inadequate and that we have to add that, as I argue in my *The May Movement* (Touraine 1968), the May movement held out the promise of new social and cultural movements which were fettered by an archaic political ideology and associated with authoritarian forms of action. The *lycéen* movement which developed in France in 1990, on the other hand, had no political capabilities and could therefore be manipulated by outside groups. It quickly collapsed and was accompanied by marginal acts of violence. The search for an identity, which is now so obsessional, is not a manifestation of the will to be a subject; it means the self-destruction of an individual who is, for internal or external reasons, incapable of becoming a subject. Narcissism is one of the extreme forms of this self-destructive search for an identity. Nature abhors a vacuum, whereas the subject is always the individual's indirect mode of relating to himself through the other and through resistance to oppression. If we fail to make this type of analysis, we will lapse back in to the kind of sociology this book is attacking. I refer to the sociology which takes social utility and functionality as a criterion for morality and which refers to forms of behaviour that upset the order of things as marginal or deviant.

The I manifests its presence in both a society's cultural model, which can range from a religious form to modern secularized ethics, and in movements of solidarity and challenges to various forms of domination. The analysis of the subject, social movements and rationalization is the base and not the superstructure. It is the starting point for a social analysis, and any sociology which claims to be more positive and more empirical because it deals only with the Ego and the Self and ignores the I, is actively supporting the forces of socio-cultural and ideological control which give the system its continued stranglehold on actors. These forces replace the subject with the individual consumer of commodities and norms, and historicity with the reproduction of established values, norms and forms of organization.

The reference to the subject is not an appeal for a supplement of the soul, and nor is it an abstract ethics that can limit self-interest and violence. It is a central principle that allows us to analyse all manifestations of individual and collective life. The I is not the Ego, but it does determine the Ego through both its absence and its presence.

Commitment and Non-commitment

The subject can manifest itself to the individual only if it escapes both social roles and the shattered fragments of modernity, which all destroy the subject in different ways. As the surrealists well knew, eroticism destroys the subject because it liberates unconscious desire. Consumption destroys the subject in a different way; it is both a quest for social status and a form of seduction which dissolves the subject in to a world of signs. In a very different way, the subject is also destroyed by its identification with the company or, more generally, with collective undertakings which attach more importance to loyalty, *esprit de corps* and military-style mobilization than to the relationship with the self. The nation calls for the greatest sacrifices of all, as it is made up of the dead and those who have yet to be born rather than the living. After two hundred years of commitment – both exultant and barbarous – we can no longer unreservedly say that human beings transcend themelves through commitment or by serving a cause, either political or religious. The subject manifests its presence when actors begin to distance themselves from their situation. Actors are not fully committed to their acts; they stand back from them, not in order to observe them from the outside, but in order to look inwards and to experience their own existence. They stand back in order to see what their acts mean for that existence rather than for society or the tasks they have been set. The cavalryman in Gericault's *Officier de chasseurs à cheval de la garde impériale chargeant* (1812, Musée du Louvre) is a good example. We see him at the height of the battle, sabre in hand. He is twisting backwards and his eyes are staring. As he stands motionless in the maelstrom of battle, he is thinking of his life and his death. Whilst it was, especially in Germany, a form of nostalgia for Being and Beauty and a fusion with nature, romanticism was also a return to self and solitude after the collective upheavals of the Revolution and the Empire, and although its tonality changes, the detachment it introduced became more pronounced as the nineteenth century progressed. No one has done more to fragment the personality than Fernando Pessoa, who invented his own heteronyms: the epicurean Ricardo Reis, the violent Alvaro de Campos and the old Alberto Caeiro, who is haunted by anguish. Borges imagines Shakespeare saying to God: 'I have created so many men in vain: I would like simply to be one man.' But God replies: 'I do not exist either. I dreamed my world, just as you dreamed your works, William Shakespeare. You come between the men that appear in my dreams, and you, like me, are many men and, like me, no one.' Pirandello provides the most powerful theatrical vision of this dispersal of the personality, which explains the appeal of literature, especially when the First World War destroyed, as Valéry puts it, the illusion that our civilization was immortal.

The decomposition of the Ego, defined as both consciousness and a person, is so obvious that we now have to be wary of going to the opposite extreme. Extreme non-commitment threatens to lead to the Subject being confused with the individual, to an increasingly suspicious egotism and, ultimately, to an inability to rise up to defend the freedom of the Subject when it comes under attack. It leads at best to a Camusian ethics (Camus 1947). Like Tarrou and Grand, Rieux, the doctor in the plague-stricken city, risks his own life by devoting himself to his patients. He has no faith in either God or man, is committed to no cause, but he responds to every request for human solidarity so as to be more than a mere victim and to face up to things. His active pessimism is all the more profound in that, before the plague, the city was mediocre and interested in nothing but money. And what is the value of an ethics which applies only in desperate cases?

It will be recalled that modernity's appeal to the Subject is not a substitute for objective reason and that it does not combine with rationalization to supply a principle of unity. The subject is neither a return to the self nor something that distances us from both Ego and Self. It is also the meaning that is given to the Ego's commitment. It appeals to the I through its commitments, and not despite them. This means that we have to understand that most forms of behaviour obey two logics, which are contradictory rather than complementary, and that we therefore have to argue against sociologies which see the individual and society, or its institutions, as sharing the same perspective. On the contrary, it is the discrepancy between these two logics that explains most forms of behaviour, their internal conflicts and their richness.

Discussions of loving relationships provide the clearest expression of this idea. Desire for the other and recognition of the other do not naturally go together, and this gives the theme of love even greater force. It commits the Subject to his desire. It is a combination of tenderness and eroticism. It makes the other both an object of desire and a Subject. It creates both fusion and distance. For a long time, we depicted love as a God whose arrows pierced hearts. When that image faded along with every other magical representation of the world, we identified love with desire. It no longer hits us like a bolt from the blue. It welled up from deep inside us. It is a drive rather than a feeling, an emotion rather than an idea. The change of imagery coincided with the triumph of individualism and the disappearance of all reference to the sacred. Yet desire is not everything, and the sufferings of separation and loss are not reducible to the absence of pleasure. Love is not something which is present only at the beginning of a relationship, or which triggers it. It is also something created by the relationship, the meaning it acquires – quickly or slowly – and which makes it possible to reconcile a desire to merge with the other, with recognition of the other as Subject. It is a union that is created or destroyed by a joint response to the separations, conflicts and ordeals inflicted by life. Love is not a static state of being. One comes to be in love, just as an individual is not a Subject, but can become one if he survives his ordeals intact. There can be no love without desire or without recognition of the other, but it is also true that there can be no love without a life-history, without resistance to adversity and loss. This is why love is associated with death, especially in the Western tradition. It is the antithesis of life because it exists beyond desire and transforms desire in to a desiring Subject. And in doing so, it may make desire impossible.

Love is one of the places where the Subject appears because it cannot be reduced to either consciousness, desire, 'psychology' or passion. It means abandoning social roles. It means forgetting oneself. It is also an experience through which the subject discovers himself and recognizes the other as both desire and subject. In an interpersonal relationship, as in collective relations, the subject is never at rest or in a state of equilibrium; the subject is in perpetual motion, as he moves from distance to fusion, from conflict to justice. The subject has no nature, no principles and no consciousness. The subject is an action whose goal is the creation of the subject throught a resistance which can never be completely overcome. The subject is self-desiring.

This tension between the Subject and commitment, either personal or collective, can be seen in all forms of social behaviour. The subject's commitment to the company is an increasingly dominant theme. Whereas the so-called Japanese model is based upon the absence of any reference – even a linguistic reference – to the subject, and defines both the Ego and the Self in terms of belonging and loyalty, it is increasingly being argued that efficiency at work improves greatly when personal work projects are combined with organizational rationality. This is especially obvious in the most up-to-date organizations, and especially in research centres and hospitals where researchers, teachers and clinicians must be both integrated in to a complex system of production and motivated by a commitment, not to the organization, but to 'public service', or the struggle against disease, ignorance or injustice. Unlike the discourse of advertising, which speaks of the company spirit or morale, the idea of being committed to both the company and to oneself gives concrete expression to the general theme of the necessary combination of non-commitment to social roles and commitment to social relations and collective activities.

It seems more difficult to reconcile commitment to the nation with the appeal to the Subject, as there appears to be too great an imbalance between the individual and a collective being, or the laws or authorities which regulate its activities. Yet those Western countries which were or are colonial powers force their nationals to have two dissociated experiences. They have an inner experience of their nationality, in which language, familiar landscapes and childhood memories all have an important role to play. But they also have a self-image which is forced upon them by those they colonize or colonized. To adopt a more modern vocabulary: they belong to the North, but they also have a self-image which is reflected back to them by the South. This is why colonizers do not always display total loyalty to the administrators, the army or the Church they serve. Some of them are the first to defend the colonized.

There is no equilibrium between these conflicting tendencies towards commitment and non-commitment. The disequilibrium between the two is, however, conducive to the real existence of the Subject, as the Subject is an unstable state. The Subject is not the strongest thing in the world. And nor is a statue of the Super-Ego that looms over the individual and his conscience. The Subject is at once extremely fragile and immensely demanding.

Ethics

It seems difficult to reconcile things as different as self-reflection and non-commitment to social roles, or transformational action and integration in to a collective labour unit. And yet the two faces of the subject must not be separated at all cost. What does have to be abandoned, and even rejected, is the attempt to find the subject in an identification with the meaning of history or the rebirth of the nation. We know that sacrifices made for great causes are fraught with danger; they pave the way for the formation of authoritarian powers and transform the other in to a foreigner and an enemy. This conception is all the more necessary in that, as technical and administrative activity expands, the greater the contradiction between the ideologies that serve great economic and political organizations, and the protests of beautiful souls. The increasingly necessary modern concern with *ethics* combats both these conflicting tendencies because ethics means the application of moral, and therefore non-social, principles to situations created by social activity. The ethical domain constantly expands as the domain of religiously inspired morality shrinks, and it becomes more visible as a technology which has been left to its own devices in fact surrenders to a technocratic power which abuses the rights of reason by conflating its authority with the force of scientific truth itself. Its defenders fight on two fronts. On the one hand, they fight against the reduction of society to an industrial company which sees everything in terms of the balance of trade, inflation and cash-flow; on the other, they fight against the return to a religious communitarianism. This requires a twofold critical analysis. On the one hand, labour must not be reduced to being an apparatus of production; on the other, the image of the Subject which is present in religious thought must not be reduced to a reactionary search for a communitarian morality.

The close association between the construction of both the personal subject and social movements is central to this book. It contradicts both the idea of praxis and the moralism of the clear conscience. The subject is constructed both in the struggle against apparatuses and through respect for the other as subject; a social movement is a collective action which defends the subject against the power of commodities, companies and the State. Unless it can become part of a social movement, the subject is in danger of being dissolved in to individuality; unless action on social life is based upon a non-social principle, the idea of a social movement succumbs to the alienating temptation to conform to the meaning or direction of history. There can be no subject without social commitment; there can be no social movement without a direct appeal to the freedom and responsibility of the subject.

The debate over education is the best example of how a vision centred upon society is being replaced with a vision organized around the personal Subject. We are now shocked to hear the goal of education being defined as the formation of loyal citizens, active workers and mothers and fathers who are aware of their duties towards their children. Self-esteem and self-respect are considered to be the driving forces behind education. Psychologists have observed that a child who is told 'You're a success because you've been lucky' is a poor achiever. What is more, self-esteem is not simply a matter of performance, but of resisting the pressure of the majority, unfair rules and discrimination. Yet involvement in a social movement has a positive meaning only if it is based upon self-esteem and virtue.

Unlike God, reason or history, the Subject is not an impersonal principle. Yet even when the religious experience takes the form of a religion of the incarnation and of grace, as in the case of Christianity, it has more in common with the Subject than with the subordination of the individual to the laws of reason or history. Which explains why the trend towards subjectivation is associated with an increasingly secularized interpretation of roles and traditions which were transformed by the transition from religious language to ethical language.

As modernity asserts its presence, the representations which equated it with the disappearance of the Subject begin to fade, in the same way that the sun takes the place of the moon in the sky. The idea of a subject cannot be divorced from that of a social actor. An actor, individual or collective, acts in order to introduce rationalization and subjectivation in to a network of social roles which tends to be organized in accordance with a logic that integrates the system and strengthens its hold over the actors. The actor is the antithesis of the Self. Rather than playing roles which correspond to a status or becoming locked in to self-consciousness, an actor reconstructs the social field on the basis of demands, including the demand for subjectivation which introduces a non-social principle in to society. There can be no actor without a Subject, but nor can there be a Subject without an actor to involve it in real social life, and to fight its cause against established equilibria and ideologies. When Talcott Parsons elaborated a vast general theory of action, he described as 'action' the workings of a social system governed by rationality in modern societies. The approach outlined here, and prefigured in earlier books like *Sociologie de l'action* (Touraine 1965) and *La Production de la société* (Touraine 1973a), could not be further removed from that vision. Action always goes against the logic of the system. Action presupposes a certain capacity to transform and produce a society which tends simply to reproduce itself. The 'institutional' sociology of Talcott Parsons and his disciples aspires to being modernist because it identifies action with modes of behaviour which are either functional or dysfunctional in terms of the system. I take as my starting point the critique or the decline of that modernism. I am attempting to rediscover ideas that were discarded two hundred years ago, and to reinterpret them in such a way as to incorporate them in to a new vision of modernity. This vision is more tragic than the classical vision. It is a non-integrated and bipolar vision of social life. On the other hand, it is suspicious of the tradition–modernity dichotomy, to which Parsons is as loyal as Weber or Durkheim. It finds in Christian thought and the idea of natural right forms of reference to the subject, and is looking for their modern equivalent.

It is difficult to break with transcendental representations of the subject. In an age when political power has become ubiquitous and omnipotent, it is tempting to think that religious convictions or faith in God are the only things that can resist it. In the best-case scenario this would lead to the 'Jewish' vision of history Paul Ricoeur (1990) expresses when he defines history as a divine promise and a human expectation that it will be fulfilled. Yet it is Paul Ricoeur himself who tells us to be wary of the temptation to place ethics above politics or to see it as an immobile moment of being that transcends the turmoil of social and individual phenomena. In a secularized world, the appeal to the beyond has difficulty in making itself heard. The presence of the Subject is not like the presence of the Sun that lights and warms the earth; we sense it only when individuals and groups protest against established powers, managerial apparatuses and technocratic justifications for the social order. Far from being the One that transcends a changing and diverse world, the Subject is glimpsed only in shouts, in fleetingly visible faces and in claims and protests. And its existence becomes intelligible only through a hermeneutic search for the inseparable unity and diversity of all the rifts in the established order, of all the calls for freedom and responsibility.

Can we organize the subject's appearance in to a history? To some extent, we can, because the growth of secularization increasingly forces us to look for the subject here on earth, and makes the nostalgia for Being that appeals to so many philosophers seem increasingly unrealistic. But we cannot really do so because the discovery of the

Subject is always a partial discovery and because, depending on the circumstances, we hear only one or another part of its call. We can only hear it if we first make due allowance for truly historical realities. We must, for example, hear the call of the Subject in the workers' movement of industrial society, yet that movement is also part of the historicist world and it believes in the natural development of humanity and in the growth of the productive forces. To put it in concrete terms, it is constantly confused with the socialist idea, and I have long tried to demonstrate that the two are fundamentally different. The more we concentrate on a historical analysis, the greater the importance we give to socialist action; it is when we move away from that type of approach that we discover a social movement which is similar to older and more recent movements, which also emerge from historical forces as characteristic of their era as socialism was of industrial society.

We now have an extreme image of the Subject. It is not a principle which can organize a culture or a society, and it is the antithesis of a religion, a philosophy or an ideology. The Subject can be glimpsed only in a social situation, only when it resists or appeals against an order or power. The Subject is not defined by institutions or ideologies. It is defined by both social relations and self-consciousness, and by the assertion of an I which rejects all the roles that go to make up the Self. It is difficult to see how an action, meaning the modification of a situation, can occur unless we distance ourselves from the established order, or without the lever that allows us to move it. If the appeal to the personal Subject becomes part of a collective mobilization, a new power will establish itself, and it will be more restrictive than its predecessor. Conversely, if the appeal to the Subject is no more than a protest, it will merely give birth to a counter-culture, and it will quickly be crushed by the weight of communitarian norms or torn apart by power struggles. The appeal to the subject is a combination of commitment and non-commitment, personal freedom and collective mobilization. Similarly, social movements are never mass mobilizations, but calls for the non-social to transform the social.

Is the Subject Historical?

I have often used the expression 'the historical subject' in my writings. I admit that it has historicist connotations and that it could be understood as implying that the subject should be identified with history, rather as though the proletariat, like the Prussian State or the French Revolution before it, were the realization of Spirit or the agent of the totality. A reading of the texts in question, and especially of the texts I have devoted to the workers' movement, should demonstrate that this misunderstanding ought never to have occurred, as I have always regarded social movements as actors, and even as subjects defined by a struggle to become actors. As I demonstrate in *La Conscience ouvrière* (Touraine 1966), the workers' movement is based on the 'proud consciousness' of craftsmen and not on a 'proletarian consciousness'. That is why I am still reluctant to abandon the expression 'the historical subject' as a way of describing, not history-as-subject, but the social movements through which a society's cultural orientations are given a social form which is constantly modified by conflicts and negotiations between adversaries. We do not have to choose between a historical subject and a personal subject. The subject is both historical and personal. The subject exists in a social situation. It exists in an interpersonal situation or in the relationship with the self that manifests the presence of a subject struggling to escape both the shattered form of modernity and the powers that reduce everything to the conditions of their own reproduction and reinforcement. We must always look for the *personal* subject, for the individual as subject, in *historical situations*, just as we now have to recognize that the problems of personal life, culture and the personality are central to public life.

We have to conclude by noting that there is an underlying unity to all appeals to the Subject. Religious faith has something in common with Rimbaud's revolt, and neither has anything in common with clerical power or market utilitarianism. And at a time when unbridled liberalism and the most naïve faith in the virtues of the market seem to have triumphed in the West, it would be absurd not to recognize and defend all manifestations of the Subject, no matter where they come from and irrespective of whether those who support them do or do not believe in heaven.

Rather than taking us further away from the past, progress towards greater modernity reinterprets the past and uses it as a defence against the power of systems and organizations. Intellectuals have usually sought refuge from the technological society in nostalgia for Being or aesthetic pleasure, but whilst this deliberate rejection of the modern world takes the critique of the rationalist conception of modernity to extremes, it has nothing to put in its place. It therefore results in a growing divorce between intellectuals and social actors. That divorce momentarily gave the impression that the influence of the intellectuals was growing, but their positions soon proved to be contradictory. The central importance of Jean-Paul Sartre is that his work reflects every stage in the rise and fall of the intellectuals. He created a committed individualism which combined a critique of the Ego with a social critique. As a defender of the anti-colonialist movement, he was able to give a positive historical content to his critique of both society and his own personality. Being a philosopher of freedom he asserts (Sartre 1946: 55) that 'Man is nothing but his project; he exists only to the extent that he realizes it; he is therefore nothing more than the sum of his acts, nothing more than his life.' Yet as Pierre Naville pointed out to him, this freedom appears to take no account of social determinisms. This subjectivism, and the absence of any reference to the Subject as social movement, or as a reaction to social domination, soon led Sartre to recognize the crushing weight of social determinisms and of domination, and to confine his vision to a purely critical analysis of the bourgeois order. As early as 1956, when the Khrushchev report was made public, he therefore turned to a supposedly unavoidable Marxism which, without ever completely destroying it, gradually modified his anti-Ego individualism and replaced it with a purely critical leftism that took him closer to terrorism and further away from social reality. This life history should be deemed neither a failure nor a deviation, as Sartre was constantly concerned with the Subject: witness his conception of collective action, which is based upon a voluntary oath and the destruction of the practico-inert. The intellectuals of the next generation became trapped in to an antimodernism that turned its back on Sartre's critical stance. The result was a divorce between intellectuals and society. The fact that Sartre never became divorced from society gave him an exceptional influence which will outlive criticisms of his errors of political judgement.

Now that the intelligentsia has lost its influence either because it adopts a purely critical stance or because it collaborates with post-revolutionary despotic powers, our primary task is to create a conception of modernity. It must be vigorously critical and it must place its trust in a Subject whose presence is made all the more obvious by the nature of the new forms of domination.

A conception of modernity which emphasizes the Subject's non-commitment rather than its commitment is so in keeping with a period in which post-revolutionary regimes are collapsing and in which individualism is on the rise, that an immediate and serious caveat is required. Firstly, it must be made quite clear that the Subject is no more to be confused with the-individual-against-powers than it is to be confused with the 'march of the people'. The Subject may be present in both these figures. It is also threatened or destroyed by both of them. On the one hand, it is destroyed by avant-gardes which speak in the name of the people and then construct a State power which devours the people; on the other, it is destroyed by the consumer society which gives the illusion of freedom at the very moment when social status is the most direct determinant of consumer choice.

This elementary but essential point having been made, it has to be stated that even the most personal demands are inseparable from collective action. The choice is not between the individual and the collective, but between the production and the consumption of society, between freedom and the social determinisms which, like other determinisms, operate both at the level of individual behaviour and at that of collective action.

The subject is not the consciousness of the Ego, and still less is it the recognition of a social Self. On the contrary, it means freedom from the image of the individual created by the roles, norms and values of the social order. The individual is released from that image through a struggle for the freedom of the subject. The individual therefore comes in to conflict with the established order, expected modes of behaviour and the logic of power. The release of the individaul implies recognition of the other as Subject. In positive terms, this means relations of love and friendship; in negative terms, it implies the rejection of everything – poverty, dependency, alien-ation or repression – that prevents the other from being a Subject. Anyone who claims to be a Subject and ignores his neighbours who are being reduced to silence or death, is deceiving neither himself nor anyone else. His behaviour is determined not by external causes, but by internal causes, as it is an expression of his self-interest and of the ideology that defends them. Conversely, a social movement is never reducible to the defence of interests or the conquest of power by a social group. A social movement always promotes personal freedom, and can claim as its own the motto of the French 1848 Revolution: Liberty, Equality, Fraternity. It is now easier than ever to perceive the close and constant link between the freedom of the Subject and collective liberation struggles, as the world seems to be fully preoccu-pied with the direct confrontation between despotisms and the market, between absolute power and total self-indulgence. Those who are demanding freedom and reponsibility for the Subject, and those who are trying to recreate social movements, are therefore destined to meet.

Hope

The presence of the Subject within the individual can be seen as both distancing the individual from the social order, and as an immediate lived experience. Religious texts abound in accounts of this absent presence. Literature often attempts to reconstruct that experience, as in the work of Bernanos, and especially in the works of an author who, together with Malraux, dominates French discussions of the century in which we live. I refer to Claudel's *Le Soulier de satin* (Claudel 1929). For Claudel the impossible love which has more to do with transcendence than possession, never means renouncing the world. It means living in a world whose splendour and triviality are illuminated by the light of God.

This language is not far removed from other languages which make no reference to God. Those who believe in the Subject and those who believe only in self-interest and social norms have less in common than the two images of the Subject, even when one believes in Heaven and the other does not. The presence of the Subject in all its forms is testimony to the satisfaction that comes of achieving a balance between what we expect of others and the possibilities opened up by the situation in which we all find ourselves. The idea of satisfaction is inseparable from the individual's submission to society, even when it is equated with happiness. Diderot, who was probably the author of the *Encyclopédie*'s article on 'Society', expresses this very clearly: 'The entire economy of human society is based upon this simple and general principle: I want to be happy.' Contemporary society, which has seen an expansion of commodity consumption, expresses it better when it speaks of 'pleasure', or even of a 'fun morality'. This taste for pleasure is liberating – nothing is more ambiguous than a puritanism that uses grand principles to enforce authoritarian integration in the name of a suffocating collectivity – but it is easily reconciled with the interests of shopkeepers who are quick to use their turnover as a yardstick for individualism.

Nor does the experience of the Subject remove the individual from the world. It does not mean that the Subject merges with a meaning that comes from the beyond, or that it merges in to the social. It is associated with a hope which introduces a feeling of distance, but also the expectation of possession. *Hope*, or the attempt to attain a happiness which is difficult rather than impossible, is a combination of joy and happiness, or rather a tense relationship between mobile forces and *jouissance*.

Modernity is inseparable from hope: hope placed in reason and its conquests, hope invested in liberation struggles, hope placed in the ability of every free individual to live increasingly as a Subject. Even though they do have a rationalist dimension, traditional societies generate an ethics of submission to order, and may even eradicate desire and individuality. Religions which promise salvation are also dominated by the idea of the Fall, and the Subject achieves self-awareness only through the guilt and consciousness of sin that gives

birth to the need for grace and redemption. It is only by identifying
with the Saviour that the sinner discovers that both reason and faith
allow him to be as one with God the Creator. Whatever the diversity
of its contradictory forms, the modern consciousness is an affirmation
of the hope it places in human beings and in the struggle to eliminate
guilt. This is a dangerous undertaking, as the hope for liberation has
more than once turned in to a mere desire to consume, and can easily
be manipulated by the power of money or force. Yet nothing can
restrain this vital effort to replace guilt with hope, and therefore
renunciation with liberation. Both the dominant and the dominated
give this hope a social form in their various ways. The former see the
individual in terms of energy and desire; the latter see the same
individual purely in terms of the constraints and fetters from which
they want to free him. Yet both believe that whilst action has the
power to liberate, it is also a matter of self-creation. This general
vision is at times optimistic and embodied in achievements and a great
trust in the power of reason. At other times, it takes the form of the
search for protection against forces of domination whose effects it
cannot dominate. The dark and light sides of modern hope are
inseparable. When there was no light and no hope of light, action had
no meaning. When there is no shade, time stands still and nothing can
disturb a perfect order. In traditional societies, it is isolation, ignorance and dependency that restrict action; in modern societies, it is the
turmoil, the proliferation of noise and the consumption of all the
consumer goods. In both cases, there is a lot of room for non-action
and non-hope. Yet the difference between action based upon guilt
and grace, and action based upon freedom and hope is no greater than
the difference between the empty time of penury and the accelerated
time of affluence.

During the intermediary period that separated the world of tradition from the world of modernity, men played at being gods. Their
games allowed them to assert themselves whilst ignoring the infuence
of God, and to imitate God by using their reason. They went on
believing that their reason was an attribute of the God who had
created an intelligible world. Man was so intent on becoming a god
that he became fascinated by his own power and identified with his
achievements until such time as this early heroism gave way to a
consumer demand. The fact that it mobilized and enriched a rapidly
increasing number of individuals and social categories made up for its
apparent mediocrity. If he is not to vanish in to the shifting sands of
mass society, modern man must now concentrate on himself once
more. He must discover mobility, but he must also become distanced
from himself. He must reconcile progress with freedom. This return

to the self brings to a close a century in which human beings committed themselves so fully to totalitarianism, war and mass society that they lost sight of one another in a night where the only light came from the stars that signified the world order and the intentions of God.

The Subject is back. This Subject is not merely a rejection of order, but also a desire for the Self, a desire on the part of individuals to take responsibility for their own lives. This implies both a rejection of roles and an unremitting attempt to reconstruct a world organized around a central void where all can enjoy freedom. The idea of the Subject is equidistant from individualism and the utopian search for a new community or a new society based upon integrative values. It is an appeal to human beings who are in this world rather than of this world, and who can transform a social situation in to a private life, just as they transform the reproduction of the species in to loving relationships and families, and just as they find in membership of a particular society a means of access to different societies and cultures. We have been asked to integrate, to identify, to make sacrifices and to repress everything personal for so long that we were initially tempted by a deceptive consumerist individualism. Yet the demand to be a Subject is constantly present. And it is growing stronger, because it is our sole defence against all the social order's strategies of domination.

This demand seems at first sight to be a search for a meaning to personal life, to individual histories. A successful life is one which has a meaning, one in which the conception of a great project results in its realization in either the private or the public domain. A successful life can be reproduced in a narrative. And yet this image, which is more in keeping with the idea of the human person, is dangerous rather than useful, as it reintroduces the dream of a correspondence between actor and system, between individual and history. The emergence of the Subject results from neither the unity of a life nor the construction of a Self. It results from the overcoming of constraints, from the call for freedom and from the attempt to piece together the shattered fragments of modernity in the form of an individual life. The decomposition of the Ego means that the Subject cannot surrender to the discreet charms of the Self.

4

Light and Shadow

Two Faces of the Subject

Is the Subject no more than a will to be uncommitted, to be distanced from artificial roles, and to be free to choose and to act? If it were, it would be merely another name for reason, or a principle for transforming the world. It would be the Prince of modern society. The defence of the Subject is not, however, reducible to the active affirmation of its freedom; it is also based upon resistance against the power of productive and administrative apparatuses. The Subject is both body and soul, a memory as well as a project. This is quite apparent in all social movements. The workers' movement is a will to social liberation; but it is first and foremost a defence of the autonomy of workers or of a craft, town or region. In Poland in 1981, one of Solidarity's first concerns was to erect monuments commemorating great moments or figures in the country's national history which had been written out of the history books or covered up by the communist regime. In the Soviet Union, the first breaches in the system were created by men whose religious convictions gave them the strength to challenge the regime directly. This does not detract from the critical thought of Sakharov, but it is a reminder that there have always been two complementary aspects to great struggles for freedom: the appeal to critical reason, and a resistance to absolute power that is based upon ethical convictions and social or cultural loyalties. The Subject escapes the roles given it by the social system both by turning to a community of origins and belief, and through 'care of the self' and the quest for personal freedom.

When the modern spirit is primarily concerned with upsetting the traditional order, reason seems to be associated with the will to individual freedom, but as the inherited order gives way to the organization of productive and managerial apparatuses, that alliance breaks down. At the same time, the association between the twin aspects of the Subject is strengthened: the defensive face and the offensive face, the reference to community and the appeal to personal freedom. When modernization is no longer endogenous, or when it is no longer the product of the application of reason to science and techniques, but of a social and cultural mobilization against the 'enemies of freedom' and obstacles standing in the way of the transformation of society and culture, the future is built by destroying the past. Progress is simultaneously seen as a return to more or less mythical origins. How can colonized or dominated countries not distrust a rationalization they identify with the history and culture of the powers whose might oppresses them? How can they not invoke their history and culture in order to resist a hegemonic power which identifies with modernity and reason, and which regards as universals forms of organization and thought that correspond to its own interests?

Just as an abstract universalism is unsatisfactory, there are, however, obvious dangers in appeals to difference and to a community which is so defined that its relations with other societies or cultures are based upon estrangement, rejection or aggression. Irrespective of whether we are speaking of individuals or nations, one conclusion is inescapable: only certain combinations of a universalist appeal to reason and the defence of a particular identity against the general forces of money and power allow the Subject to exist. The Subject is destroyed if the two are divorced either by an economistic or technocratic logic which appeals to reason, or by religious appeals to a community and to the values enshrined in it. Even before we begin to look for the forms that can reconcile these antagonistic forces, we have to combat both the opposing arguments with equal vigour. They are irreconcilable and the conflict between the two, in both the political world and the world of ideas, may render the formation of the Subject impossible.

The philosophy of the Enlightenment believed in human nature. Voltaire, in particular, attempted to understand the revelation of that nature rather than the way it was transformed through progress, whilst Montesquieu strove to identify the spirit of the laws. Historicism represented a break with this universalism, and the gulf between the two philosophers grew steadily wider. We are increasingly aware that economic change, like political systems or representations of society, can take many different forms. This by no means implies that we have to abandon all general definitions of modernity; it does mean that we cannot divorce general ends from the particular means or the different histories individuals and nations use to achieve them and give them a form. That is why there has been no contradiction between reason and nation since Herder, an enlightenment philosopher and disciple of Leibniz, equated the understanding of progress with the understanding of the spirit of a people (*Volksgeist*).

The nation can be a collective figure of the Subject. This is the case when it is defined by a will to live together in a framework of free institutions and by a collective memory. It has become customary to contrast the French conception of the nation, which is based upon free choice and a revolutionary and anti-royalist assertion of national sovereignty, with the German conception which views the nation as a community of destiny (*Schickalsgemeinschaft*). Nothing could be more artificial and even dangerous. It is dangerous because this collective will can easily come to mean no more than the absolute power of a minority which imposes its will on all in the name of the nation, especially when the nation is at war. Above all it is artificial, as the most forceful representatives of the French national consciousness – Michelet, Renan, Péguy, and General de Gaulle – are acutely aware of their country's physical and historical personality. For them, it is a combination of body and soul as well as a set of institutions, a country as well as a Republic. They are right, as a Subject is always both freedom and history, a project and a memory. If it is merely a project, either individual or collective, it merges with its achievements and vanishes in to them; if it is merely a memory, it becomes a community and is dominated by the guardians of tradition.

This is why it is so difficult and so important to integrate newcomers in to the nation. It is not enough for them to acquire the norms, life-styles and rights of citizens through social integration, cultural assimilation and naturalization. They must also become part of a memory, and must then transform it through their presence. It is as wrong to demand that they acquire a memory in which they have no part, as it is to expect them to be satisfied with a multiculturalism which has no real content. If it is to integrate newcomers rather than giving them an intangible history lesson which has become a nationalist mythology, a collective memory must be a living memory that is constantly being transformed.

The modernist tradition that began with the Enlightenment has often deliberately rejected the spirit of the nation in favour of the free circulation of ideas, people and commodities. This has helped to create increasingly violent conflicts between a universalism which is too obviously linked to dominant nations, and a defensive nationalism which can sometimes take the extreme form of racism. Pierre-André Taguieff (1990) is rightly critical of the dangers inherent in a universalism which is as aggressive as the racism it seeks to combat. It is because the personal Subject no longer exists independently of the collective Subject or of a combination of a free collective will and a historical memory, that the national consciousness now has such global importance. The assertion of the personal Subject is strongest in those countries which are best able to combine these elements, even if it means resisting the pressures of both a national identity and all social loyalties. There can be no democracy when there is no national collectivity because it has been segmented in to regions or ethnic groups or because it has been destroyed by civil war. The nation must exist if civil society is to be able to free itself from the State, and if individuals are to be able to win their personal freedom within that society. The Subject, both collective and individual, is both body and soul, and it is a very narrow conception of modernity that identifies the Subject with the mind as opposed to the body, or with the future as opposed to the past. Modernity comes in to being when the two are integrated.

The Return of Memory

As modern societies' hold over their own existence grows stronger as a result of accelerated economic development and social change and of ever more mobilizing policies, the relationship between rulers and ruled is inverted. In societies entering modernity, the Third Estate was defined by its activity, and the higher orders by privileges which were either hereditary or associated with non-economic religious or political functions. In the most highly modernized societies, in contrast, the rulers are captains of industry or public sector managers, but the ruled are no longer defined solely as workers. They are increasingly defined in terms of, on the one hand, natural character-istics, individual or collective, and, on the other, in terms of member-ship of a cultural community, ethnic group or gender. As the field of society's organized interventions constantly expands, what had been private is incorporated in to public life. Social relations and conflicts which were once restricted to paying feudal dues to a lord or king, and then to professional activities, now include consumption, and therefore the whole of culture and the whole personality. This contradicts the widespread idea that social relations and conflicts are being increasingly reduced to restricted fields. The two ideas are not, however, contradictory. As Weber states, modernity is indeed defined by an increasing differentiation of social functions, but it also gives decision-making centres a greater hold over the lived experience of individuals and groups. Our involvement in modernity is becoming increasingly complete, and we are therefore subject to the initiatives and power of the directors of a modernization which is transforming every aspect of social organization.

This leads to an apparently paradoxical situation. Ascribed status has never been more important than it is in this society, which defines itself in terms of achievement. The idea offends those who cling to the classical image of modernity as rationalization. It is, on the other hand, rejected by liberal feminists, radical or moderate, whose principal goal is the emancipation of women, or in other words the rejection of any notion of female nature. Emancipation is a necessary precondition for equal opportunities. Yet the success of this movement cannot conceal the fact that, as is obvious from research in to the position and action of women in both culture and society, more and more women are clinging to their difference, both in the women's liberation movement itself and in public life. Similarly, age categories play an increasingly important role in public, political and cultural life, but this obviously does not imply that all young or all old people have the same income or level of education. It is, finally, also obvious that the appearance of the Third World on the international political scene has resulted in an increasingly constant reference to ethnic, national or religious identities. Whereas we once tended to speak of capitalism, the working class or socialism, we now speak of Arabs, of nations which were ruled by the Soviet Union, of Islam, of the Basques and the Irish. Merely registering the fact provides no answer to the burning question of the dangers inherent in this return to communities, age categories, gender categories or ethnicity, but it does mean that we cannot regard them as a relic of the past which is doomed to disappear. That was the rationalist illusion: Enlightenment would dispel the shadows or even the darkness, cast by the family, the nation and religion. Our experience of modernity is very different: it involves body and soul, reason and memory. So much so that in modern societies the public field now seems to include preoccupations which extend so far beyond social and political realities that the latter seem to have lost the decisive importance they once had. The most important of those preoccupations relate to sexuality on the one hand and to the environment on the other.

The fact that the theme of sexuality is not synonymous with that of woman's estate or man's estate justifies the English distinction between *gender* and *sex*, which has not caught on in French. As we have already said, Freudian thought, which is in this sense close to Nietzsche, breaks completely with the classical view that the Ego is a will enlightened by reason or a form of individual self-government. The modern concern with sexuality introduces the sacred – or something that lies beyond or exists prior to the social – into the field of speech, whereas religion, and especially revealed religion, kept the sacred at a distance.

The concern for the environment and the increasing importance of ecologist parties is an even more spectacular demonstration of how ideas and feelings have been inverted. Ecologists often seem to be actually hostile to modernity, rather as though, having achieved a successful take-off, the most modern countries should at least be replacing the increasing destruction of the environment with stability and equilibrium, and as though latecomers to modernity should be wary of imitating a mode of modernization as predatory as that adopted by the richest and most powerful countries. This formulation is of course superficial, but it is a good description of the reasons that lead many people to join environmentalist or ecological campaigns. It establishes a dichotomy between nature and human action, whereas ecology itself and, at a more general level, biology tend to find similarities between the two. Early modernity contrasted the two and celebrated man's dominance over nature. The tendency is now to agree with the scientifically trained ecologists who insist that, whilst human beings do have the ability to transform the world, they must also take in to account the various effects their actions have on even the most distant parts of the system. The more human beings assert their creative abilities, the better their understanding of their conditions and limitations. To an increasing extent, they therefore define culture as an interpretation and transformation of nature, and not as its repression or destruction.

The definition of modernity as the triumph of universals over particulars should now be a thing of the past. Countries which played an eminent role in the creation of modernity tended to identify with one or another form of universalism. This is as true of Great Britain as of France or, more recently, the United States, and it helped to strengthen the colonial vocation of these countries. France gave this conviction a highly political form by identifying with the principles proclaimed by the French Revolution – a privileged moment when a nation was in direct communion with universally valid principles. Even though we can still understand why that belief arose and why it was so strong, it is now obvious to all that it is artificial and ideological. The reason why Weber's essay on the relationship between protestantism and capitalism had such an impact is that to some extent it gives the lie to the classical conception which saw the Enlightenment as something which rose out of the ashes of religious belief. From Herder onwards, German thought has often tried to reconcile the quest for modernity with the defence of a culture or a people which had apparently been marginalized by history. Neither claims to having a monopoly on universality nor pretentions to absolute specificity or insurmountable difference can be allowed to triumph. Rationalization is bound up with the emergence of a subject which is both a demand for freedom and an affirmation of a personal and collective history. Hence the influence of Jews in particular. Whilst some merged in to the population and whilst others clung to an extreme orthodoxy, the majority were remarkably successful at reconciling the universality of thought, science and art with a very strong sense of identity and a historical memory.

The Pitfalls of Identity

This defence of a cultural tradition is very different to the assertion of an identity defined solely by opposition to a foreign threat and fidelity to a social order. Such assertions are more common amongst those who are dominated than amongst the dominant, who tend to identify with universals. Those who feel threatened, whose collective and individual attempts at upward mobility have ended in failure, and who feel that they are being invaded by a foreign culture or foreign economic interests, tend stubbornly to defend the identity they have inherited. They are its guardians rather than its creators. Yet this assertion of an identity is artificial. The dominated are attracted by the dominant world, just as workers from poor countries emigrate to the rich countries which can give them jobs and higher wages, even though they have to accept that, when they enter those societies, they will be rootless, poor, exploited and frequently rejected. The claims of identity tend to be voiced by the political leaders and ideologues of dominated countries rather than by the majority of the population. They are used to justify nationalist policies which despise rather than defend the interests of majority categories. Similar policies are often used to conceal the omnipotence of a militarized State. The State takes the place of society, which loses its capacity for autonomous action and is transformed in to a crowd or mass. Antidevelopment can take this statist and militarized form, but it can also take the very different form of a political or religious populism. Populism is not equivalent to a national consciousness, and still less is it equivalent to a national will to development; it subordinates the goal of modernization to social and cultural integration. This does not imply a rejection of modernization, but it does make it difficult or restrict it, as any process of modernization leads to a break with the past, and therefore to borrowing from other societies. Populism is always inspired by the idea of a rebirth or a return to origins. It is based upon a foundation myth, and believes in neither progress nor the economic determination of culture.

In his *La Revanche de Dieu*, Gilles Kepel demonstrates (Kepel 1991) in greater detail the simultaneously contradictory and complementary relationship between, on the one hand, the Islamicization from above which triumphed in Iran when Khomeini came to power, and which failed in countries with a Sunnite tradition, and, on the other, Islamicization from below. The latter's most powerful political weapon is the missionary-style 'proclamation' (*tabligh*) of Islam. It was imported from India, and its most radical political expression is the Algerian Front de Salut Islamique. These forms of Islamicization are based upon a combination of accelerated economic modernization, especially in oil-producing countries, and very inadequate social integration, usually as a result of the concentration of resources in the hands of an antidemocratic power elite. It is not reducible to neo-traditionalism, which is usually swept aside by both the excesses of modernization and popular movements. As Farhad Khosrowkhavar (1992) demonstrates, the overthrow of the Shah in Iran did represent the victory of a revolutionary movement involving both the poor and rootless masses of southern Tehran and the modernizing younger generation. This liberation movement found no support in a country where the bourgeoisie of the bazaar had been removed from power by the fall of Mossadegh. It soon came under the leadership, not of the clergy, but of Khomeini, who was almost the only religious leader to have been involved in the political struggle against the Shah. Religious neo-communitarianism was inseparable from the social movement. Neo-communitarianism defended the social movement in its initial phases, but it then became the basis for the formation of a theocratic dictatorship. The alliance between the deracinated and proletarianized masses and students with no prospects of employment produced an antimodernist pietism, a greater emphasis on communitarianism and even an Islamicist political mobilization. As in other cases, the return of the religious resulted from the failure of social integration, combined with the diffusion of the products of growth and the impotence of the 'progressive' political forces, which were crushed by the nationalist State. Cultural and political movements of this type lead to a struggle against all forms of individualism. Yet, just as it is dangerous to draw a veil over the closure and the authoritarian cultural controls represented by such movements and the regimes that are based upon them, it is impossible simply to contrast them with the rationalist socio-cultural model. That model is too closely associated with the relations of domination that helped to bring about the disintegration of societies already affected by exogenous modernization.

As the twentieth century draws to a close, the world appears to be being torn apart by these conflicting forces. On the one hand, subjective instrumental reason traps the richest in to a logic of desire as well as a logic of might; on the other, a defensive appeal to identity paralyses dominated or poor nations. A divorce which has destructive effects on both parties is clearly not acceptable, as it gives rise to an inexpiable antagonism between the poor and humiliated, and the wealthy who either patronize or despise them. At a time when the clash between capitalism and socialism is coming to an end as a result of the victory of the market and the collapse of the command economy, and when the market's victory is being hailed by those who believe that the era of great conflicts and historic choices is over, an even more serious conflict is breaking out. This time it is both a cultural and a socio-political conflict between technology and religion, or between what Tönnies, writing at the end of the last century, called society and community. Society is associated with rationalization; community with the defence of values identified with forms of social organization.

We should not, however, over-simplify the rationalization–community dichotomy, as the religious defence of a community is merely the most extreme form of the cultural defence of a collective Subject, and it therefore cannot be completely dissociated from a personal affirmation of freedom. Similarly, it is only in extreme cases that the defence of a community can really be contrasted with the will to modernization. The open conflict between technology and religion must not be allowed to conceal something still more important, namely the interdependency of rationalization and the two faces of the Subject: personal freedom and community. Whilst there is always a conflict between the two, just as there is always a conflict between freedom and community and between the social system and the personal or collective Subject, it is dangerous to hope that one theme will be victorious over the other. A purely rationalist society destroys the Subject, and debases freedom to choosing between what the market offers consumers. A communitarian society is suffocating and can be transformed in to a theocratic or nationalist despotism, whilst a society dedicated to subjectivation would lose all economic and ethical cohesion. The most helpful contribution made by the image of a clash between technology and religion is the idea that the only mediation between these diametrically different modes of organization will come from the Subject-as-freedom, and that Subject is inseparable from both the rationalization that protects it from a suffocating socialization, and the cultural roots which guarantee that it will not be reduced to being a manipulated consumer. The two faces of the Subject must always be present together if it is to resist both modes – and although they are different, they are equally dangerous – of its destruction by the social order, which may have been either created or inherited, the order of technology, or the order of religion.

The ambiguity of appeals to identify means that they can readily move from being a recognition of something that was brutally eliminated by capitalist modernization to meaning suffocation at the hands of a cultural particularism and the authoritarianism of the political power which claims to be defending it. The same ambiguity can be seen in movements which try to defend the *environment*. Once again, it is very tempting to eliminate the Subject completely and to take a purely external view of human beings, or in other words to regard them as part of a system which functions in accordance with laws that have nothing to do with the intentions of actors. Justifiable criticisms of this new naturalism must not, on the other hand, mask the positive character of movements which refuse to identify human beings with their works and which, whilst they recognize the constraints and limitations of growth, challenge the 'progressive' philosophies of history we have inherited. They pave the way for the new discovery of a Subject which is neither outside the world nor the centre of the world, which is both threatened, liberated and strengthened by its works. When it avoids the pitfalls of generalized hostility to growth, political ecology has a major contribution to make to the transcendence of the historicism of the worker's movement and, especially, of socialist thought. Logically enough, political ecology is defended by a growing fraction of public opinion, and its defenders have a higher than average level of scientific training. For whilst the appeal to reason allows us to resist the threats posed by extreme communitarianism and environmentalism, it also allows us to establish a link between the Subject as freedom and the Subject as community, or in other words a Subject which is aware of being part of a natural environment.

Rationalizatiom must be seen as an essential ally of the spirit of freedom in its struggle against the constraints of community. Reason and freedom are not entirely interdependent, as the subject is not reducible to the critical and instrumental work of reason, but it is also true to say that critical reason protects personal freedom against communitarian immobility. So-called Westerners are right to contrast the new, and often totalitarian, despotisms that have replaced social and national liberation movements in the communist world and the Third World, with the openness of their own society, whose technical efficacy is based upon the market economy. The market economy is the best defence against arbitrary power, clientelism, corruption and sectarianism. This defensive conception of freedom is very limited, but it is also too precious to be abandoned or subjected to harsh criticism.

Religion and Modernity

Relations between Christianity and modernity were, especially in France and in countries with a Catholic tradition, trapped in to a crude ideological representation. Religion meant the past and obscurantism; modernity was defined in terms of the triumph of the light of reason over the irrationality of beliefs. Rural society was often a narrow world. It was more concerned with continuity than change, and the Church – which drew most of its support from women – was anxious to maintain its cultural hold over minds which were disturbed by the attractions of the city and progress. This caricatural vision was reinforced by a clerical–secular clash which was in fact largely a clash between traditional France and the rising middle and working classes. This picture is based upon undeniable realities, but it interprets them badly. It would be more accurate to say that the resistance of rural societies – and urban societies – to economic and cultural change was based upon beliefs, as well as upon forms of property or social participation, than to claim that religion, by its very nature, plays a conservative role and that the spirit of the Enlightenment, in contrast, always encourages greater social involvement. We have to break with the simplistic evolutionism that defines modernization as a transition from the sacred to the rational. Do I have to stress yet again that modernity must be defined as a breakdown of the correspondence between the subject and nature? The image of a sacred world which permeates everyday existence is antimodern, but the image of a rational world order created by either the logos or a rational Great Architect has more in common with religious representations of the world than with post-Cartesian thought, which is based on a dualism of the world of the subject, or of what Augustin calls the inner man, and the world of objects. As we enter modernity, religion shatters, but its component elements do not vanish. *When it ceases to be divine or to be defined as Reason, the subject becomes human and personal.* It becomes a specific type of relation of individuals or groups to themselves.

I have no intention of reiterating the central theme of this book here. We must, on the other hand, specify the other forms, positive or negative, in which the religious heritage can be preserved in modern society. I describe beliefs and modes of behaviour which continue to divorce the temporal and the spiritual as 'positive'. This is an essential aspect of Christianity, but historians and theologians also see it in Judaism, Islam, Buddhism and even Confucianism, which have developed an ethics of intentionality that is far removed from the ethics of duty. In contrast, I describe as 'negative' beliefs and institutions which sanctify the social.

The idea that social life must be based upon shared values, and especially religious references, is still powerful in the Western world. This idea acquires a particular strength in the United States, where the Bible is seen as providing the religious basis for the Constitution and where a sociologist like Robert Bellah (1985) can stress that social norms have a religious basis. This is a reminder that the political culture of the United States remains much closer to the eighteenth century and its deism than the cultures of Western Europe, which have been more influenced by nineteenth-century nationalism.

Modernizing rationalism associates reason with religion and there-fore contrasts normality with deviancy, which both have a religious and a social basis. At the opposite extreme, communities which are under threat experience modernization as an invasion. Christian peoples defended themselves against the Turkish invasion. The Polish nation identified with the Catholic church in order to preserve its identity from Prussian or Russian domination. What is more import-ant, part of the Muslim world, which has since the beginning of 'modern times' oscillated between relative dependency and under-development, simultaneously evokes social, intellectual and religious traditions to resist its colonial-style incorporation in to a world market in commodities and ideas which is dominated by the 'central' powers. As a result, the temporal is identified with the spiritual to an extreme degree, and religion is transformed in to a largely political force. Modernity is reduced to techniques that can be used for either defensive or offensive purposes. Criticism of this 'fundamentalism' is not confined to the laity. There are also those who think that a return to the Islamic faith is the best defence against Islamism.

In addition to the formation of the personal subject, modernizing moralism and neo-communitarianism, we also find a limited dissocia-tion between religion and modernity. It results in a dichotomy between a private religious life and a modern public life. This is one way of interpreting the emergence of sects in the world of the Christian tradition. It affects both Catholic and Protestant countries. Tech-nicians, professionals and office workers live their occupational lives in their offices or factories but share a collective religious experience, either outside ecclesiastical institutions or on their fringes. They pray together or await the coming of the Holy Ghost. Their behaviour is modern in that it shatters the unity of the human and divine worlds, which is preserved by highly institutionalized churches, many of them linked with political power. It is also antimodern, as it seeks to rediscover, on a limited basis, the all-encompassing communitarian experience and the direct presence of the sacred.

Religion thus gives birth to a set of cultural forms ranging from an openly religious neo-communitarianism to a modernizing moralism, a privatization of religious life, and a non-religious but post-religious affirmation of the personal subject. The crude dichotomy between religion and modernity seems very remote.

The fact that moralism has such importance in a country as highly modernized as the United States means that we have to abandon all evolutionism. The characteristic feature of a modern society is its reluctance to identify with any one system of beliefs and values. A modern society therefore generates both beliefs which encourage modernization and secularization, and beliefs which resist them. The most modern society is not one which is quite indifferent to religion or quite devoid of the sacred, but one which has extended the break with the divine world by simultaneously asserting the existence of the personal subject and resisting the destruction of personal and collective identities.

The Totalitarian Threat

It is only in the most central states that modernization is seen as the practice of reason. In their different ways, both the English and the Americans take that view. The French, for their part, take the even more forceful view that the progress of reason can be equated with a central will to modernize. This explains why their philosophers acted as advisors to the enlightened despots of Prussia and Russia in the eighteenth century and why, from the Revolution onwards, the French State was identified with reason and succeeded in convincing the majority of the population – and not least its civil servants – that it had a universalist mission.

Elsewhere and on the periphery, this identification of the workings of modernity with the forces of modernization did not look so convincing. Even when modernity was also defined in economic terms, the central role in modernization was played by non-rational political and cultural forces such as national independence or the defence or resurrection of a national language. Germany was the first and the most important focus for this national modernization, which has triumphed not only in Japan and Italy, but also in Turkey, Mexico, India and Israel, to mention only a few important contemporary examples. This national-cultural modernization is not dangerous in itself; indeed, it is essential wherever modernization cannot be entirely endogenous. It can, however, produce a regime which, rather than creating the preconditions for endogenous modernization, uses modernization as a mere instrument for political mobilization. Bismarck and Emperor Meiji used the State or the mobilization of a national consciousness to create modern societies and economies, but this type of society also saw a militarization of society which, in the cases of Italy and Germany, went hand in hand with a fascist populism. It is dangerous to contrast fascism only with the democracy of the central countries because, if we regard as legitimate only endogenous modernization and free relations between its actors, Leninism, fascism or various types of authoritarian regime are the only paths open to peripheral countries where modernization encounters major internal and external obstacles.

It is impossible to reduce all nationalist modes of development to totalitarianism. The causes that turn a mode of development in to *antidevelopment* have to be examined carefully. In the case of nationalist modernizations, the danger becomes greater when the distance between State and society increases. We therefore have to make a distinction between two types of rupture. Society may rebel against the crisis and the corruption, and adopt a populism which soon finds authoritarian leaders who are prepared to denounce its institutions. Alternatively, a central power with highly concentrated economic, political or military resources may impose its will on a society which is still poorly mobilized, fragmented, and entangled in local, family or tribal networks. In the first case, a single political will replaces a plurality of interests and opinions, and their ability to negotiate limited conflicts. The greater the mobilization, or in other words modernization itself, the greater the State's tendency to become *totalitarian* rather than merely authoritarian. The twentieth century has seen the mobilization of the entire planet, the globalization of processes of modernization and of the destruction of traditional societies. It has therefore been the century of totalitarianism.

Totalitarianism appears only in countries which are caught up in a powerful modernizing process and mobilized by mass industrialization, mass urbanization and mass communications. There is no room for either personal freedom or cultural traditions, or even for religious traditions which do not identify themselves with State power. Totalitarianism is no more religious than it is technocratic; it replaces the autonomous action of social actors and culture with the absolute power of the State. It devours civil society. Technology and science become servants of the State, just as individuals are torn away from their family, local or religious backgrounds and are mobilized in the service of the State, irrespective of whether it is secular or religious. It is not only personal freedom that is destroyed; so too are cultural loyalties. Totalitarianism destroys society and reduces it to being a crowd, a docile mass which obeys the words and orders of a leader. The triumph of the leader associates the defence of the community and its threatened identity with the will to modernize. Totalitarianism destroys a society which was once a network of relations organized around an increased productive capacity, and replaces it with the mobilization of an identity that serves the cause of its collective might. History replaces society. Past and present merge, crush the present and abolish the public space in which collective choices are debated.

The exclusive appeal to community produces a neo-conservative despotism; a voluntarist modernization leads to authoritarianism, and a combination of the defence of the community and authoritarian modernization produces totalitarianism. All the great national-historical movements which arose as new regions entered modern society and the modern economy were potential totalitarian regimes. And many of them did produce totalitarian regimes. The nationalities that arose as central Europe entered the modern economy and as the old empires broke up produced a variety of authoritarian nationalisms and fascisms. The Russian Revolution, which resulted from the crisis in the old regime rather than the action of the workers' movement, led to a Communist totalitarianism which, from Lenin to Stalin and Mao, proved to be the greatest political force of the twentieth century. More recently, Third World national liberation movements have given rise not only to more traditional despotisms or to corrupt regimes dependent upon the great powers, but also to communitarian totalitarianisms which resist modernization in the name of national and religious unification. They identify modernization with the loss of their collective identity and with the importation of foreign products and customs. Even when modernization is firmly rejected, the result is not the conservative despotism which still exists in Saudi Arabia, and which is based upon the preservation of traditional forms of social organization. On the contrary, it is a close alliance between modernization and nationalism that is hostile to tradition and personal freedom alike.

Communism was the most ambitious and most destructive form of the revolutionary modernizing State. It undertook the destruction of the old regimes in the name of science and the laws of history. The Jacobin Terror was too closely associated with a war situation, both at home and abroad, for it to stabilize and to resist self-destruction.

Because its goal was not the historical goal of development, but the political goal of order and transparence, there were no limits to its obsession with purity, or to the struggles it waged against factions and deviations. Communist regimes often faced the same difficulties and the same internal crises, but they succeeded in keeping themselves in power for a long time because they were so closely bound up with the idea of modernization. The Soviet regime was for decades defined by the general line of industrialization, and its worldwide influence was bound up with its successes in the fields of education, public health and production, and, in the case of the Soviet Union, with scientific and military feats like space exploration. It is the constant reference to scientific knowledge and to the Enlightenment spirit that explains communism's appeal to intellectuals, and particularly Western scientists. Communist regimes did not succumb to quarrels between their ruling factions because they succeeded in transforming themselves in to an autocratic and repressive techno-bureaucracy. Yet this modernizing State is experiencing the same forms of crisis and decomposition as the modernist idea itself. The appeal of consumption, and therefore a fascination with the West, an entrepreneurial spirit that tries to escape the stranglehold of the State, the resistance of private life and especially religious life, are all forces which had been attacking the communist model for decades. In 1980, however, a complete social movement finally emerged in Poland. *Solidarity* represented not only a breach in the Soviet system, but also a model which was diametrically opposed to the Soviet model. Less than ten years later, the Soviet system was collapsing, stifled by its internal paralysis, and exhausted by its military and political expansionism and its inability to keep up with the technological and economic progress of the West. Its symbol – the Berlin Wall – was destroyed.

For the purposes of the present analysis, the crisis in poorly modernized economies and societies is, however, less important than the exhaustion of the *revolutionary* model. In the Third World it is increasingly being replaced by nationalist models. The revolutionary idea, or in other words the alliance between economic modernization and social transformations, is giving way to the defence of an identity that is threatened by modernity. That identity may be traditional, but in most cases it is an identity that has been constructed or reconstructed. Islamist intellectuals are anti-traditionalists. They are Islam's reformers, but they are also hostile to modernization, even though they use its techniques. No matter where we look, we are witnessing the rebirth of a communitarian spirit opposed to foreign domination and the social upheavals provoked by uncontrolled modernization. A *social totalitarianism* is giving way to a *cultural totalitarianism*, just as

communism came in to conflict with the *national totalitarianism* of
Nazism. The idea of modernization is giving way to the idea of
tradition, of a return to a revealed law and above all to a rejection of
secularization. And its fundamental principle is the refusal to eman-
cipate women.

The appeal to community is not restricted to the Islamic world,
where forms of political organization are often either archaic, or in
other words incapable of inspiring involvement in the nation, or
similar to the enlightened despotism inaugurated by Nasser and then
adopted by rival and fraternal Ba'ath parties in Syria and Iraq. In
Latin America, it finds expression both in revolutionary movements
supported by Catholic liberation theology, and in mass support for
Pope John Paul II, who associates the defence of communities with
controlled modernization. As Central and Eastern Europe enter their
post-communist period, it may take the form of either the social-
democratic dream, or that of a national populism similar to that seen
in Latin America prior to the crisis of the 1980s.

Recognizing that there is a difference between the national mobilization needed for development and the totalitarian threat has been
an important task for twentieth-century intellectuals in all parts of
the world. They have often failed in their task, even though certain of
them committed themselves to the anti-totalitarian struggle with both
lucidity and courage. Many of them were fascinated by the vitalism
of Hitler's regime, and still more of them saw Stalin and his successors
as the heirs to a popular revolution or as the heroes of the war against
Hitler. Many intellectuals, especially those in the regions directly
concerned, refused to see Khomeini's regime as anything other than a
national liberation movement, or Saddam Hussein's militarism as
anything other than the expression of the Arab world's revenge. Their
tragic errors demonstrate that, far from being natural, the democratic
idea requires an active intellectual effort to resist the temptations of a
nationalism and a populism which can, when the threats intensify and
when there is a possibility of conquest, turn in to totalitarianism.

Totalitarianism is our century's most serious social illness. That is
why the appeal to the Subject is now so powerful. A totalitarian
regime subordinates individuals to its order with such brutality that
many of them make a direct and dramatic appeal to respect for human
beings and human rights because they cannot adopt 'social' objectives
such as growth or social equality. Some regard their goal as vague and
moralistic, but that is because they have enjoyed lifelong protection
against the greatest of evils, namely persecution, occupation by
foreign powers and loss of freedom. The experience of totalitarianism
has put an end to two hundred years of progressivism and historicism.

It means that we now often have to defend the man against the citizen.

We cannot, however, allow instrumental rationality and the communitarian spirit to drift further and further apart. We have been analysing the most extreme forms of their dissociation, and therefore of the crisis of modernity, in order to come to a better understanding of the need for a new analysis of modernity which can limit the divorce between the life of the mind and lived experience, between instruments and values.

Moralism

The totalitarian threat can lead us in to the trap of moralism, or of completely desocializing the subject in order to defend the Subject. This deviation is the antithesis of the deviation which has done so much damage in the modern era. After having accepted constraints and forms of slavery that were much worse than those of the past in the name of the necessary struggle for freedom, and after having installed an absolute power in order to rid itself of privileges, modern society is now defending human rights in such abstract terms that it can no longer name its concrete adversaries, and is replacing real struggles with campaigns designed to sway public opinion. Worse still, it is substituting the supposedly irresistible pressure of the money and the media of the richest countries for the active involvement of those who are most directly affected.

Such forms of action do nothing to change the life-style of a middle class which is accustomed to the consumer society and which can therefore buy a supplement of the soul at little cost in the hope that the dollars and songs it distributes will protect it from explosions that might otherwise disturb its rest. In most cases, such actions are merely grotesque, but they can also be dangerous. Humanitarian organizations themselves have put the charity business on trial. The most serious thing of all is that the argument is based upon the seeming inevitability of the division of the world. Those who so readily evoke the increasing gulf between North and South often believe that the two worlds are quite foreign to one another, and that they are as different as day and night. They thus abandon any attempt to take a critical view of their own world. They merely admit that it is selfish and think to themselves that, unfortunately, people are like that, and find it difficult to show an interest in anyone who is so different. Such comments are no more superficial than the apparently more radical arguments which explain the misfortunes of the South in terms of the wickedness, indifference and greed of the North, rather as though a lack of conciousness, will or capacity for action were natural characteristics of the poor.

Moralism can only be overcome when the call for freedom, which is so powerful in countries undergoing endogenous development, is bound up with the defence of identity, as that is the last resort of the oppressed. Moralism is dangerous because it flatters the good conscience of moralists, either because they have every confidence in their own society, or because they denounce that society in the accents of a man of justice who speaks in the name of something that transcends political, social or religious society. The defence of the Subject can never mean the defence of an ahistorical and asocial principle. It must avoid the tragic errors of historicism and rediscover the inspiration behind the British, American and French revolutions that founded the modern world, and not the inspiration behind otherworldly asceticism. This is possible only if we strengthen society and not the State, only if we give society the strength that comes from reliance upon the will to personal freedom, the defence of private freedoms, which are social conquests, and respect for the memory and culture of communities and groups of believers. The appeal to the Subject is not the last resort or the final defence against political or communitarian pressures. The Subject is not an external or higher principle which determines how we behave, and nor is it merely a secularized image of God and the soul. It is both committed and non-committed, as the production of the self presupposes both a non-commitment to social roles and a commitment to an action involving the intellect, desire or a relationship with others. That is why the Subject is both freedom and memory and why, most important of all, it is no substitute for rationalization, which is the principle behind modernity. Rationalization is essential if the unstable equilibrium of the Subject is not to be destroyed for the benefit of a communitarianism dedicated to the service of an absolute power.

Freedom, *community* and *rationalization*: the terms are inseparable. It is the combination of the three that defines modernity. There are tensions between them, but they are also complementary. The heirs to the philosophy of the Enlightenment believe that freedom is associated with rationalization alone. They make the mistake of forgetting that human beings are also creatures of desire and memory who belong to a culture, and almost all of them lapse in to the 'Republican elitism' which hands power to those who possess the abilities required to exercise it wisely, and who are, as Guizot put it, both educated and owners of property. Western history has been dominated by the elitist rejection of the non-rational beings – women, children, workers, and the colonized – whose rebellion provides the starting point for our discussion. The scorn with which they have been treated is not acceptable. It is true that the twentieth century has been thrown in to turmoil by a series of populist and nationalist reactions against rationalism and that they have confined the Subject within the supposed heritage of a race, a nation or a religion. Yet we do not have to choose between conceptions which are both born of a divorce between freedom, and tradition, which must always be united.

If we did have to choose and if the war between the two sides did leave no room for the many people who are striving in different ways to reconstruct the Subject, we should opt for liberal society. Liberal society is self-critical and aware of its limitations, whereas exclusive appeals to nation and culture replace criticism with repression, hypocrisy and escapism. No discussion of modernity can accept such a destructive break, or such artificial choices. *The subject has two faces*, and they must not be divorced. If we concentrate solely upon the freedom of the Subject, we are in danger of reducing the Subject to a rational producer and consumer. The best defence against this possibility is democratic openness, as only the financially privileged can behave as the model of *homo economicus* teaches us to behave. If, on the other hand, we concentrate on cultural loyalties and traditions, we leave the subject defenceless against powers which speak in the name of communities. The best defence against those powers is rationalization and its merciless critique of anything that claims to speak in the name of a totality.

Freedom and Liberation

The subject asserts itself in the face of the domination of political and social apparatuses; its freedom is bound up with membership of a culture. As with all social movements created by dominated categories, its defence takes the form of positive demands, and to that extent it is the heir to the movement that defended the rights of workers. We therefore now hear talk of the rights of patients, school students or television viewers. It can also take the more defensive form of an attachment to a culture which is threatened by the penetration of an external economic, political or cultural power. In classical terms, these two aspects of the defence of the subject correspond to the anti-capitalist and anti-imperialist struggles of the past, but they exist within national societies as well as at the international level. Demands of the first kind may be absorbed by the political system, and may lead to the neo-corporatism characteristic of so many industrial countries, or may be reduced to a set of pressure groups formed by consumers. Demands of the second type may, on the other hand, trap

us in to a general rejection of modernization, in to military adventur-
ism or a populism which is to a greater or lesser extent bound up
with leader-worship. Yet even though there is a danger of their being
debased, the assertion of the Subject is still closely associated with
both the defence of a culture and the assertion of a personal freedom.

Modernization requires a break with the past, but it also requires
continuity. Total discontinuity means that modernization is completely exogenous or imported through conquest, in which case it
would be more accurate to speak of colonization or dependency
rather than modernity. If, on the other hand, the continuity is
complete, the same does not become other. It remains immobile and
becomes more and more ill-adapted to a changing environment. Both
Western Europe and the United States provide convincing examples
of how change can be associated with continuity, and for a long time
social-democratic countries like Sweden were able to combine economic openness with the maintenance of national controls over social
and cultural organization. This interdependency of the personal
Subject and the defence of community define a mode of thought
which is diametrically opposed to the thought that once dominated
intellectual life, and which was the topic of part II.

Intellectuals have constantly sought to replace religion with another
version of the absolute: beauty, reason, history, the Id, or energy.
Following the example set by Marx and Nietzsche, whose influences
began to merge in the twentieth century, they contrasted the social
world they denounced with a higher world. They therefore contrasted
'petty bourgeois' subjectivity with the objectivity of being or becoming, the movement of spirit or the stirrings of desire, and the will to
power. According to this view, the social is dangerous, but the
cultural, defined in the ethnographic sense, is hateful because it is
particularly introverted, whereas the liberation of man requires him
to rise above particular cultures and societies and enter the domain of
the universal and the absolute.

As we have already said, this school of thought's answer to the
crisis of the philosophy of Enlightenment is to look to the past. It
takes the increasingly dangerous form of a nostalgia for Being and a
rejection of modernity. Modernity must, however, be seen as a
combination of rationalization and subjectivation. This is why the
subject is defined both in terms of a will to organize life and action,
and by the defence of a cultural identity threatened by dominant or
colonizing apparatuses. The Subject is not an absolute, and its content
is not the same as that of reason. But nor is the Subject reducible to
social, cultural or individual particularisms. The Subject is neither an
individual nor a collective Ego. The Subject and the I can assert

themselves only because there is a link between self-assertion and the defensive struggle against the apparatuses of production and management.

Modernity and Modernization

For a long time, modernity was defined in terms of what it destroyed. It was defined as a constant challenge to ideas and forms of organization and as artistic avant-gardism. But as the modernization movement gained strength, modernity began to affect cultures and societies which were incapable of adapting to it, or which underwent it rather than using it. What had once been experienced as liberation became alienation and regression. In many parts of the world, it led to first the triumph of the most exclusive nationalism and then to the confinement of societies in their discourses and their apparatus of political control, and finally to regimes which were identified with a nation, culture or religion. The West once believed that modernization was no more than modernity in action, and that it was the purely endogenous product of scientific and technical reason. The twentieth century, on the other hand, has been dominated by a sequence of increasingly exogenous modernizations which were enforced by either national or foreign powers. They were increasingly voluntarist and decreasingly rationalist. A century which began under the sign of scientism seems to be ending with the return of religions. The naïvely arrogant response of the American-dominated West is that history is 'over', that the rationalist model has won a total victory in both the economic and the political order.

This reaction is quite understandable. Throughout the century, the capitalist and liberal model has been the object of constant attacks, and its principal adversaries have been totalitarian regimes in the First, Second and Third Worlds. At a time when its victory was a foregone conclusion, how could the West fail to contrast political voluntarism with the gradual and delicate construction of the market, indoctrination with freedom of thought and expression, and ideologies with pragmatism? The wealthy West now has little faith in progress or the triumph of reason. It now adopts a more defensive attitude and, like Churchill, defines democracy as being a bad political system, but the best one we have. It defends reason as a critique, and capitalism as a market economy which prevents economic action from being invaded by ideology, the class struggle or patronage. This is the meaning of the new *liberalism* which, in the space of a few years, has spread throughout the social sciences and politics, and which promotes a rationalist vision of man and society in which self-interest plays the central role. In its most ambitious form, this new rationalism defends the West because it is attached to universal values which always liberate us from prejudices and communitarian loyalties. It contrasts the West with societies which deliberately and insanely concentrate on the quest for their differences and particularisms, and therefore condemn themselves to blindness and paralysis. Some go further still, and identify their own countries with universal forces. Republican patriotism can take on a great importance when it is combined with a real political mobilization.

This new liberalism is unacceptable because it cannot account for two sets of phenomena. Firstly, it cannot account for the growth of sectors which do not belong to the open society: the isolated poor, marginals, social or cultural minorities and ethnic communities. The characteristic feature of liberal societies which are functioning with maximum efficiency, or in other words which have a high capacity for social integration, is that they produce excluded or marginalized minorities. Those minorities become more and completely divorced from a vast middle class which it is easy to enter and where mobility and change are increasingly rapid, but where individuals are increasingly exposed to the risk of failure or accidents. Secondly, the exclusion of minority groups goes hand in hand with the exclusion of majority categories in a world where equality of opportunity improves as modernization comes increasingly to be as dependent upon cultural and political conditions as it is upon technical and economic conditions.

Now that the totalitarian regimes have been defeated, peripheral countries must as a matter of urgency reject false populist and militarist solutions. By the same criterion, the central countries must criticize the purely liberal vision which all too readily justifies the exclusions it produces and which naïvely identifies the history and culture of one country or region with universal values. The central countries have no cause to abandon their rationalism, but they must also attach equal value to a subjectivation which is negated or rejected by major tendencies within liberal thought. They must not destroy cultural traditions which are more alive than many people thought, especially in a changing world where the past mingles with the present, difference with continuity, and communities with society. For the greater part of this century, our world has become increasingly divided, and the wealthy countries of the West have seemed more than once to be under threat. They are triumphant today, but inequalities are on the increase and the most urgent task, for both the centre and the periphery, is to reject a divorce between rich and poor which is legitimized by communitarian movements and extreme liberalism alike.

The collapse of the Soviet system has done no more to unite the world than the fall of the Hitler regime half a century ago. After a long period of extreme social integration brought about by social-democratic and Keynesian policies, the countries of Western Europe are in their turn experiencing a growing divide between ethnic groups and social categories. The image that comes to mind is neither that of the end of history nor that of the triumph of the Western model. On the contrary, it is that of an increasingly divided world in which the forces that are being mobilized for modernization and independence have less and less to do with the instrumental rationalism that triumphed in capitalist countries. The collapse of communism and its model of the planned economy is leading to a direct confrontation between the economy and culture, the market and traditions, and money and speech, and no social or political conception appears to be capable of bringing them closer together or reconciling them. It is as though the world of light and the world of shadow had been dissociated. One hurts the eyes and dazzles them with the lights of the city; the other blinds those who have long been deprived of light. And these two worlds seem to be so foreign to one another, to be separated by much greater distances than the distances that separated social classes in the first industrial countries. Conflict therefore seems impossible. Conflicts have given way to a *war* between two camps which no longer recognize the same cultural values. They are not so much adversaries as strangers and competitors. Those who feel they are being invaded are calling for a holy war. Those who identify with modernity want to force their values on everyone because they regard them as universal and are no longer even surprised to see that they coincide so well with their own interests.

How can we get beyond this increasingly violent confrontation? Some argue that the violence will subside, just as the conflicts between social classes in the first industrial countries became less violent. They also argue that the new totalitarianisms which are defending cultures, nations or religions will run out of steam because, like Nazism before them, their only logic is the logic of war, which will inevitably lead them to exhaustion or suicide. Yet who can put all their trust in such cold calculations, and who can be confident that the exhaustion of these totalitarian regimes will solve the internal problems of other societies, rich or poor? Especially at a time when there is an increasing divorce between instrumentality and belonging, between an involvement in a changing society and withdrawal in to exclusion and marginality. Modern societies must revise their self-image. They must become capable of integrating most of those they have excluded, overlooked or despised. We therefore require a new definition of the

Subject. *The Subject must be redefined as a force that can, when supported by traditions and defined as an assertion of freedom, resist the apparatuses.* This critical stance is consonant with the ideas of those who, in the sectors or regions that are furthest removed from modernity, are trying to prevent the mobilization of their cultural resources, which is essential if they are to modernize, from turning against modernity in the name of an obsession with a lost or threatened identity. Together, we can attempt to destroy the walls that are being built at the very time when the wall between East and West is coming down.

Immigrants will never be fully integrated in to the central countries if those countries believe that the only solution is to deny newcomers any ability to transform the environment they have entered. Creolization or the mingling of cultures is already well advanced. Witness the work of Salman Rushdie or Kateb Yacine, who are being attacked by those who defend the divide between East and West, between Islam and the West. The divide between the two now appears in ideological discourses rather than cultural practices. There is no denying that integration and transformation make up a set of fragile cultural changes or that divorce is a possibility, but the complementarity between a Subject which is both freedom and culture and a culture of rationalization is the only appropriate response to a situation in which it would be presumptuous on the part of the rich countries to believe that the establishment of a new *limes* can still hold back the 'barbarians' who are threatening to invade the empire.

Throughout the world, the main political divide is no longer one between social classes or between wage-earners and property owners, but one between the defence of identity and the desire for communication. There is a growing obsession with difference and specificity in both rich countries and poor regions. The poorest define themselves in terms of a religion; the richest by appealing to a reason which is, they believe, exclusively theirs.

In Europe and the Americas, public opinion easily moves from one extreme to the other. On the one hand, the liberal call for an open society easily becomes cultural imperialism. On the other, the appeal to identity produces dangerous moral majorities and still more dangerous national fronts. It is also producing a new leftist theory of difference which recognizes no general truths and which demands histories written from the point of view of Indians, women or homosexuals, as opposed to what it denounces as written by and for white men. The best American universities have seen the development of a broad movement which is paradoxically defined as 'politically correct' when it is actually based upon fundamentalist tendencies that have nothing to do with democracy. France, where the left has been seriously weakened by the collapse of communism, faces a different threat: a combination of intolerant minorities and a truly reactionary loyalty to a universalism which rapidly results in a narrow particularism that is deaf and blind to different or new social and cultural demands.

A society which completely abolishes both past and belief cannot be described as modern. A modern society is a society which *transforms the old in to the new* without destroying it, which is able to ensure that religion becomes, not a communitarian bond, but an appeal to the conscience which destroys social powers and which enriches subjectivation. The period of nineteenth-century political and industrial revolutions was itself accompanied by a heightened historical consciousness; our highly modernized societies are rediscovering something more than a justifiable demand for equal opportunities, namely the specificity of women's experience and of childhood. Despite the existence of so many contradictory tendencies, they are giving more recognition than ever to both cultural diversity and the unity of the human condition. If the only result of the collapse of totalitarian regimes is to blind arrogantly triumphant societies to the limitations and dangers of their victory, the relief it brought us will be as short-lived as the relief that followed Liberation and the fall of Nazism. The necessary elimination of totalitarian regimes must go hand in hand with a redefinition of modernity on the part of democratic societies. Just as there can be no democracy unless social distances and barriers are lessened and unless a broader process of decision-making is introduced, there can be no democracy unless the ethics of reponsibility and the ethics of conviction begin to merge. There can be no democracy unless we transcend the frontiers between instrumental reason, personal freedom and cultural heritage, and reconcile the past with the future. Nor can there be any democracy if we do not challenge the oppression of women, young people and old people, of the poor and of nations threatened with decay and proletarianization. It should not, on the other hand, be forgotten that the parties concerned do have common goals as well as conflicting interests.

Alternatively

The world is now affected by more *radical* conflicts than those of the industrial era. The latter were confrontations between classes which were in conflict but appealed to the same values. Capitalist entrepreneurs accused workers of being lazy and conservative, and claimed to be the agents of progress; conversely, the workers' movement and socialist thinkers denounced the wastefulness of a capitalism which created crises and poverty, and saw the workers as championing the productive forces which had to be set free from irrational relations of production. The conflict is now not simply one between social actors. It is a conflict between cultures, between the world of instrumental action and that of culture and *Lebenswelt*. Mediation between the two is no longer possible. There is no longer any community of beliefs and practices. This why social conflicts have given way to the assertion of absolute differences and to the total rejection of the other. Those who, like Francis Fukuyama (1992), believe that a consensus has finally been reached, that history and the great ideological and political debates are over now that communisms have been as thoroughly eliminated and discredited as fascisms, are making the most serious mistake of all. Conflicts have never before been so global as to become international crusades and struggles to the death rather than politically negotiable conflicts. On the one hand, we have the assertion of the hegemony of a West which believes itself to be universalist and which is destroying cultures and nations along with species of animals and plants in the name of technology and techno-logical success. On the other, we have the rise of an anti-Europeanism which quickly becomes an aggressive and potentially racist and hate-filled notion of difference. The West's overwhelming military and industrial superiority must not lead to its identification with reason, and to the reduction of its adversaries to unreason and tradition. For too long, the West has been the home of nationalism, which can sometimes be the defender of a culture and a road to a modernity, but which is more usually simply a rejection of the other and a scorn for universalist values. It would be just as wrong to dismiss the movement that is rousing the Third World as a neo-traditionalism, when it is in fact an attempt to create a new alliance between modernization and cultural traditions – often in dangerous forms. The next century will be dominated by the *national question*, just as the nineteenth century was dominated by the social question. Many countries in Western Europe and North America are now experienc-ing nationalist, social and political reactions to the opening up of society, the arrival of immigrants and insertion in to a European or world community. Conversely, so-called global or world culture and companies are too often Americanized not to constitute elements of a power policy or even a hegemonic policy. Throughout the world, there is an open conflict between an arrogant universalism and aggressive particularisms. The main political problem is and will be to limit this total conflict, to re-establish values that are shared by conflicting interests.

The possibility of reconstructing society seems to many people to be no more than an intellectual fantasy, and it certainly cannot be reduced to a search for ideological solutions which could easily lead to populism or fascism. Yet these criticisms are weaker than the theories they are attacking, as we are no longer talking about ideological constructs or State forms. Liberal society dissolves the Subject in to needs or networks of relations; neo-communitarian societies imprison the Subject in a bloc of beliefs and powers. It is therefore difficult to perceive the Subject behind the visible and organized form of social life on either side. The call of the Subject can, however, be heard, usually together with other noises, in the gaps in the system and in the empty spaces that social controls cannot remove. In liberal societies, the Subject manifests its presence inter-mittently in the maelstrom of consumption, and in particular in the musical culture of the young. It manifests its presence, in other words, in places that are far removed from the centres of production and power where the Subject is sacrificed to the logic of the system. Places where the lust for life merges with real protest supply the clearest image of the Subject to be found in Western society. Similarly, in neo-communitarian societes the Subject makes its voice heard when the political order is rejected in the name of community, but it cannot become visible unless this great refusal is combined with a rationally-based assertion of personal freedom. It is not easy to reconcile the two modes of dissidence – Solzhenitsyn and Sakharov, for example – but liberation will be impossible unless the liberal critique and the nationalist critique become allies in a common struggle. The impov-erished young people who are society's main victims are also divided amongst themselves. Some want access to the consumer society, whilst others fall back upon a collective identity, an age cohort, a gang or an ethnic group. Yet the movements which are founding a new political field are, like those of May 1968, those in which the two modes of behaviour come together.

The idea of the Subject is always in conflict with the belief that society can be based on a model. We can no longer have faith in a social or political regime. It is not only that very few people wish to make the transition from capitalism to socialism. Those who – and there are many more of them – want to make the transition from socialism to capitalism wish to be free of the constraints of authoritar-ian regimes rather than to support a different social model, and their critique leads them to try to find themselves by plunging in to the economic competition rather than a new ideological militancy. That is why I am not looking here for an alternative to both East and West or North and South. On the contrary, I am trying to show that the demand for subjectivation is a worldwide development.

It is obvious that we have come a long way from historicism. The idea of constructing the society of the future – a fairer and more advanced society and a more modern and freer society – is a thing of the past. It has been swept away by successive waves of totalitarianism. The temptation now is not to dream of a radiant future, but to dream of living *differently*, of hiding away in a counter-society or an 'alternative' culture. The sectarian spirit is now stronger than political mobilization. But the two have more in common than it may seem. Both rely upon the image of a perfect utopian model which remains unchanging through time and space, and which is therefore so full and so homogenous that there is no room within it for the freedom of the Subject. Forces that challenge the establishment are always similar to the forces whose domination they are fighting, just as socialist industrialization aspired to being an improved and still more rationalized version of capitalist industrialization. For similar reasons alternative cultures, like neo-communitarian regimes, exert stronger cultural controls than the cultural industries of liberal society: propaganda is better at constructing needs than advertising. We have to distrust all models of perfection.

5

What is Democracy?

The representation of democracy has been inverted since the eight-eenth century. We initially defined it in terms of popular sovereignty and the destruction of an *ancien régime* based upon heredity, divine right and privileges. Democracy then became confused with the idea of the nation, especially in the United States and France. In the nineteenth century, however, fear of a revolutionary national dicta-torship modelled on the French Terror and above all the increasing dominance of economic problems over political issues led to the idea of popular sovereignty being replaced by that of a power serving the interests of the largest class. The idea of the nation was replaced by that of the people, which was then in its turn transformed in to the idea of the working class. In more general terms, democracy became representative and its main theorists, from Benjamin Constant to Norberto Bobbio (1984), have defined democracy primarily in terms of its representativity. This introduced, alongside the universalist principle of freedom and equality, the principle of respect for the rights of workers who were being crushed by capitalist domination. For a long time democratic politics made the idea of modernity, and even rationalization, and the defence of class interests part of the central theme of progress. Lenin himself called for a combination of Soviets and electrification.

This equilibrium between universals and particulars, between reason and the people, eventually broke down in its turn, and our image of democracy now tends to be more defensive. We speak of human rights, of the defence of minorities and of the restrictions that should be imposed upon State power and centres of economic power. The idea of democracy, which was initially identified with that of society, thus comes closer to that of the Subject, and tends to be the political expression of the Subject. This explains why my analysis of the Subject in modern society ends with some considerations on democracy.

From Popular Sovereignty to Human Rights

The individuals who came one day to regard themselves as citizens, who discovered that power was a human creation and that its form could be transformed by collective decisions, have ceased to believe unreservedly in traditions and divine right. The sovereignty of the people and human rights seemed, in that founding moment, to be twin aspects of democracy: people asserted their liberty through a claim to citizenship, and the creation of the Republic in both the United States and France provided the most solid guarantee of individual rights. The history of democracy is, however, the history of the gradual divorce between the principle of popular sovereignty and that of human rights. The idea of popular sovereignty tended to be debased to meaning a popular power which paid scant regard to legality as it took on revolutionary aspirations, whilst the defence of the rights of man was all too often reduced to meaning the defence of property.

'Popular' State power has now acquired such might, and has destroyed so many social movements and so many public freedoms, that it has become quite impossible to defend 'popular' democracies against 'bourgeois' democracies, or 'real' freedom against 'formal' freedom. We therefore believe that democracy can only be strong when it forces political power to respect rights that are defined in increasingly broad terms. Whereas we once spoke simply of civil rights, we now also speak of social and even cultural rights. The idea of human rights is gaining strength because the main objective is no longer the overthrow of a traditional power, but protection against a power which is identified with modernity and with the people, and which leaves less and less room for protests and freedom of initiative.

As it comes to mean the defence of rights, and above all the right of the governed to chose who will govern them and abandons the unifying idea of popular sovereignty, democracy has to fight on two fronts rather than one. It must fight the absolute power of both military despots and totalitarian parties, but it must also place restrictions on an extreme individualism which threatens completely to divorce civil society from political society, and to abandon the latter to either games which easily lead to corruption or to the invasive power of adminstrations and companies.

Few would now dare to defend the unanimist or popular concept of democracy which has so often been used to disguise authoritarian and repressive regimes. Many would, however, like to see the withering away of not only the State but also the political system. They place all their hopes in the market, and would like political decision-making to be ruled by market forces. We have to avoid both these extremes and admit that as both clerical and secular theorists of natural right asserted in the sixteenth, seventeenth and eighteenth centuries, democracy is now based upon the freedom to chose leaders and the restriction of political power by a non-political principle. The fact that power is the hands of the people does not guarantee individual rights, and can be used to justify both nationalist and revolutionary dictatorships. Nor are individual rights guaranteed by the fact that everyone is free to choose what the market offers, as the market cannot guarantee equal opportunities for all and cannot direct resources in such a way as to satisfy the most pressing needs. Nor can it further the struggle against exclusion. Democracy must therefore be combined with integration, or in other words with citizenship, and this presupposes freedom of political choice and respect for identities, needs and rights. There can be no democracy without a combination of an open society and respect for social actors, without the combination of cold procedures and the warmth of convictions and loyalties. We therefore have to abandon both popular and liberal conceptions of democracy.

Democracy is above all a political regime which allows social actors to emerge and to act freely. Its constitutional principles are the very principles that govern the existence of social actors. There can be no social actors without an internalized consciousness of personal and collective rights, or without a recognition of the plurality of interests and ideas. It must be accepted that there is a conflict between rulers and ruled, and that everyone has a responsibility towards their common cultural orientations. In the realm of political institutions, all this gives rise to three principles: the recognition of *basic rights*, which political power must respect; the social *representativity* of leaders and their policies; and an awareness of *citizenship*, of being a member of a collectivity founded on rights.

We must now describe in more detail these three principles, which define a mode of political action more broadly than any institutional rules.

Negative Freedom

The twentieth century has been dominated by regimes which suppressed freedoms in order to bring about or preserve the independence and economic power of the nation. The principal adversaries of democracy are therefore no longer the *anciens régimes*, but the new totalitarian regimes, be they fascist, communist or nationalist-third-worldist. The positive view that freedom means the realization of popular sovereignty therefore gives way to a negative conception, and democracy is defined and defended as the regime which, according to the definitions put forward by Isaiah Berlin (1969) and Karl Popper (1957), prevents anyone from taking or holding power against the wishes of the majority. Liberal thought has replaced the revolutionary movement so completely as the defender of democracy that it seems more appropriate to define it in terms of respect for minorities rather than majority rule. Democracy is now seen as being inseparable from the market economy. In Eastern Europe, the communist regimes collapsed when they no longer enjoyed the protection of Soviet military might, and priority must now be given to the difficult task of replacing a command economy with a market economy. In the East, democracy is best defined as a regime which puts an end to the dominance of the political power of the *nomenklatura* over the economy, rather than as a regime which guarantees the free represen-tation of interests. The unifying principle of popular sovereignty is being replaced by that of the separation of powers, and even of social subsystems. Religion must be separated from political power, which must be separated from both the management of the economy and justice. The government should intervene in private life only in order to protect freedom, or in other words in the name of tolerance and diversity, and not in the name of social integration and homogeneity. This political liberalism is an essential defence against both the militarisms of the Third World and regimes which attempt to enforce respect for a faith, and the communist dictatorships which still rule China, Cuba, Vietnam and North Korea. Having once placed our hopes in political action, we are now so convinced that political despotism – in both its traditional absolutist guise and its totalitarian or authoritarian guises – is the greatest obstacle to freedom and modernization that we distrust anything that establishes too close a connection between political action and social life, and anything that defines democracy as a type of society and not simply as a political regime. Our passions are no longer political, and we tend to take a wary view of politics rather than being enthusiastic about it. At times, the very word 'democracy' seems so tarnished that we are reluctant to use it. If the 'people's democracies' were no more than a mask for dictatorships imposed by a foreign army, does not the very idea of democracy imply the possibility of its perversion? And is it not clearer and more honest to speak simply of freedoms and to distrust all conceptions of power? Claude Lefort (1981, 1986) suggests that this is indeed the case when he defines democracy, not in terms of popular power, but in terms of the absence of any central power. It is more important to do away with the throne than to enthrone a new Prince, or to replace a king with a people whose power threatens to be even more absolute.

The inversion of the idea of democracy, or the transition from the conquest of popular sovereignty by force to respect for freedoms and minorities, is too faithful a reflection of the political dramas of the twentieth century for it not to be acceptable. But it has to be accepted as a starting point, and not as a point of arrival.

It is a starting point because there can be no political freedom unless power is restricted by a higher principle which prevents it from becoming absolute. For a long time, religions supplied the principle for the restriction of power. In both Christendom and Islam, they also ensured that the population submitted to the established power. In secularized countries, religion has lost its twin function of restricting and legitimizing power. The religious idea has been secularized and has become an appeal to human rights and respect for the human person. That it is not possible to construct democracy unless it is based upon a non-political principle that places restrictions on political power is as true today as it was yesterday. This idea is resisted by all those for whom modernity means the gradual naturalization of society, or in other words a process which must result in the transparency of institutions and the free activity of individuals and collectivities. Yet who would dare to defend such an arrogant conception today? Who can forget that, whilst it may well be the precondition for freedom, man's power over nature and himself can also be the most dangerous obstacle to freedom, that it can turn society in to a machine, an army, a bureaucracy or a forced-labour camp? It is not only the collective will that must be respected. It is also personal creativity, and therefore the ability of every individual to be the subject of their own life, if need be by defying the instruments of labour and the organization and might of the collectivity. The negative conception of freedom, whose most articulate spokesman is Isaiah Berlin (1969), is the indispensable foundation for democracy. It is more important to restrict power than to give absolute power to a popular sovereignty, which never takes the form of a mere social contract or a free debate as it is also an administration and an army. Popular sovereignty is both a power and a juridicial legitimation of that power. It is now impossible to speak of direct democracy, of people's power or even workers' control without immediately conjuring up the very real figure of the totalitarian party, with its authoritarian militants, the arrogant mediocrity of its petty bureaucrats, and the suffocatingly ponderous calls for the unity of people and nation. Democracy, or in other words the freedom of the governed to choose those who govern them, can exist only if freedom enjoys an indestructible space, only if the field of power is more restricted than the field of social organization and individual choice. This, however, is a necessary but not a sufficient condition. Whilst power must be restricted, social actors must feel themselves to be responsible for their own freedom. They must recognize the value and rights of the human person and must not define themselves solely in terms of the collectivity of which they are born, or in terms of their interests. There can be no solid democracy without this responsibility. And whether this responsibility is nurtured or destroyed depends on educational agencies ranging from the family and the school to peer groups.

Citizenship

The second precondition for democracy is that the governed must want to choose those who govern them. They must wish to participate in democratic life, and must feel themselves to be *citizens*. This presupposes that they feel that they belong to political society, and that in turn depends upon the political integration of the country. If the country is fragmented in to estranged and mutually hostile ethnic groups, or if social inequalities are simply so great that its inhabitants have no sense of the common good, there is no basis for democracy. If democracy is to be strong, there must, as Rousseau said, be a certain equality of condition and a national consciousness. Just as the subordination of society to State weakens or even destroys society, the integration and unity of political society strengthens it. If citizens believe that public affairs have nothing to do with their own interests, why should they concern themselves with them? They readily accept political patronage and submit passively to constraints. As T. H. Marshall demonstrates (Marshall 1950), an awareness of being a citizen is the only thing that can re-establish the unity of society, which has been shattered by conflicts between social classes which are very distant from one another.

Do we have to go still further, and introduce the idea that a democratic society is necessarily based upon shared values, and especially on religious and moral values whose presence can place restrictions on political power? This idea is very widespread in American society, but much less so in European countries and in new nations where the national consciousness has a historical and political rather than a religious or ethical basis. But in both cases, the cult of the national society threatens democracy rather than supporting it. It leads to the rejection of the other, justifies conquest and excludes minorities or anyone who ceases to be 'one of us' by criticizing it. Citizenship is thus transformed in to the militant assertion of popular sovereignty that has given rise to so many authoritarian regimes. The idea of citizenship must remain secular, and must resist the cult of the political collectivity, be it the nation, the people or the republic. To be a citizen is to feel oneself responsible for the smooth workings of institutions which respect human rights and permit the representation of ideas and interests. This is no small demand, but it does not imply a moral or national awareness of belonging, which usually does exist without being a basic precondition for democracy. Norberto Bobbio (1984) rightly associates democracy with controls over violence, and points out that there has not been an armed conflict between two democracies in the last fifty years.

Representativity

This institutional awareness of belonging must not be divorced from an awareness of social relations and of the conflicts it seeks to resolve. Democracy can only exist if it is *representative*, if the choice between different governors corresponds to the defence of different interests and opinions. If democracy is to be representative, governments must obviously be freely elected, but social interests must also be *representable* and must have a certain priority over political choices. If the support a party receives determines the positions it takes over major social problems, the democratic system is weak, but it is strong if political parties provide answers to social questions which are formulated by social actors, and not simply by parties and the political class.

Democracy is especially strong in the industrial countries of Europe and North America because those countries experienced open social conflicts with a general import at a time when they were acquiring a relative social integration and a stong national cohesion. When class conflict increases, democracy is strong. This is particularly true of Great Britain, which is both a class society *par excellence* and the mother of democracy. Democracy is weaker in France because social actors have constantly been subordinated to political agents, both in opposition and in government. The revolutionary attitude does not encourage democracy. Rather than defining a social conflict amenable to political solutions or reforms, it posits the existence of insurmountable political contradictions and the need to overthrow and eliminate adversaries. It therefore dreams of a socially and politically homogeneous society, and takes the view that its social adversaries have betrayed the people and the nation. A truly social conflict, in contrast, is always limited, and it is when the limits disappear that social movements give way to political counter-cultures or violence. Democracy can only tolerate limited conflicts, but it is weakened by the absence of central and profound conflicts, as that is a major obstacle to the social representativity of political agents. Democracy therefore presupposes the existence of both a highly structured civil society and an integrated political society. Both must be as independent as possible of the State, which is defined as power. The State acts in the name of the nation, and has responsibility for war and peace, the country's position in the world and the continuity between its past, present and future.

Parties

The institutional forms of democracy are less fundamental. They organize the formation of political choices and are therefore concerned with political supply rather than social demand. These institutional forms do not include the freedom to choose who governs us, as that, as we have already seen, is the very definition of democracy. If that choice is to be functional, individual choices must be aggregated to allow citizens to choose their governors on the basis of the clearest possible understanding of the implications and consequences their choices will have in the principal domains of collective life. How can the governed freely choose those who govern them if the voters do not know in advance what the government's economic, social or international policies will be? If candidates represent nothing more than particular interest groups, how can we establish a link between those interests and global choices? Such a situation inevitably restricts the influence of voters who are confined to their local life and abolishes all controls over major decisions, which are taken either by the political elite itself or as a result of the pressure brought to bear by the most powerful economic interests.

We have grown accustomed to thinking that political parties are indispensable instruments for the aggregation of social demands and the formulation of general political choices. Yet the proliferation of lobbies and the crushing of social demands by ideologies and political apparatuses leaves little room for parties. The United States often suffers because its political parties are too weak, or are mere electoral machines. France is paralysed by ideological discourses which are often designed solely to perpetuate the hold of candidates and political apparatuses over social forces which are no more than a conveyor belt for a political will. When parties come to see themselves as the embodiment of social models rather than as mere instruments for the formulation of political choices, democracy is weakened and citizens become increasingly subordinate to party leaders. This weakness is as apparent in Spain or France as it is in most Latin American countries where, as Albert Hirschman (1979) demonstrates, the great popular parties come dangerously close to being the single parties found in truly totalitarian countries. Conversely, democracy is not strengthened when political society is weak and subordinate to economic interests or the demands of minorities. Citizenship presupposes a concern for the *res publica* and the greatest possible continuity between social demands and the long-term decisions of the State.

Liberalism is not Democracy

As the twentieth century draws to an end, it may seem that democracy has won some great victories, but that is too optimistic an interpretation of the collapse of the totalitarian regimes. Democracy has in fact won few victories and has taken part in very few battles. The most glorious were those fought by Solidarity in Poland in 1980–1 and by the Chinese students in 1989. If we turn to the other Communist countries, the fall of the Berlin Wall can rightly be seen as the most important event. The joy that accompanied it was not a cry of victory but a sigh of relief at the end of a long confinement. There was talk of a democratic revolution in Romania, but it did really happen and still belongs to the realm of possibility. In Latin America, military dictatorships agreed to hand over power to the civil authorities in Brazil, Uruguay, Chile and even Paraguay, whereas in Argentina it was military defeat and not a popular uprising that brought a democratic regime to power. The euphoria created by the collapse of regimes that were as odious as they were ineffective was accompanied by a strange absence of discussion about democracy, which was defined simply as the absence of authoritarian or totalitarian power. In the post-communist countries of Central Europe, political ideas and projects soon ran out of steam and the return to a market economy has in every case determined all other changes. There has been no serious discussion of either education or social justice; the only issue that arouses any passion is where the capital and entrepreneurs will come from in countries which have produced neither. Intellectuals are not playing a major role in the establishment of a new democracy, whereas they did play the most important role in the struggle against dictatorship.

In Western countries, interest in democracy has been on the wane for a long time. After a long period during which the political was dominant, these countries are now finding that the economic is dominant. The goals of political management are international competitiveness, a trade surplus, a sound currency and the ability to develop new technologies. In other respects, we are content to be protected against political monopolies, State bureaucracy, the rhetoric of politicians and the excesses of intellectuals, many of whom have shown more interest in terrorism both at home and abroad than in legally-guaranteed freedoms. Democracy is considered to be just as natural as the market economy or rational thought, and it is therefore assumed that it must be protected rather than developed or organized.

This view is unacceptable, even if its historic importance does have to be recognized. It is true that a rich liberal society does have a great capacity for integration and, above all, that it can restrict the voluntarist and therefore authoritarian interventions of the State. It is also true that, between the beginning of the nineteenth century and the end of the twentieth, the space available to freedoms has expanded considerably in central countries. It is true that well-being, education and the divorce between religious or political dogmas and civil society have replaced qualified democracy and republican elitism with a mass democracy which is the political expression of the new middle-class majority. Mass democracy has replaced the old pyramid of classes, and its configuration and organizational norms and forms are very flexible. Seymour Martin Lipset (1960) argues strongly that democracy is so closely associated with affluence that it can be defined as the political dimension of modernization.

Yet it is also true – as has been said almost constantly since the French Revolution – that the identification of democracy with liberal society (or in other words a society undergoing endogenous development and where modernizing action is synonymous with the exercise of modernity itself and with the application of rational thought to social life thanks to the greatest possible differentiation between subsystems – economic, political, judicial, religious and cultural) does not provide any answer to the domination of political life by the masters of civil society, notably those who have money. Nor does it prevent liberal society from being an exclusive society as well as a highly integrated society. It is at this point that Marcel Gauchet's answer to Michel Foucault takes on its full force (Gauchet and Swain 1980). Liberal society is by no means a mask for a repressive society; it is almost absurd to criticize it on those grounds when the victims of totalitarian and authoritarian regimes regard it as their only refuge. It is because liberal society is open and flexible, and because it can integrate that it can be so brutally exclusive. Hierarchical societies in which there was little or no mobility were, in contrast, like old houses which are full of protective corners and hiding places. By doing away with most of the marks and constraints of inferiority, modern liberal societies 'liberate' marginality. As our societies become more open and egalitarian, they accentuate the marginality and even the exclusion of those who refer to social or cultural norms other than those of the mainstream, and who accumulate personal and collective handicaps. This observation may not be fully applicable to Europe, which has been strongly influenced by a long social-democratic tradition, where social security accounts for as great (or even greater) a part of GNP as the State's own budget. It is, however, quite applicable to the United States, which is a country with a profoundly democratic culture. The cultural and social barriers erected in Europe by higher orders or upper classes for their own protection are almost non-existent, but this is also a country abounding in ghettos and extreme forms of poverty and social decay. It is because the liberal model spread so rapidly in Europe, and especially in France, that there is such an acute awareness that inequalities are becoming more pronounced. This awareness is, however, an inaccurate perception of the real divorce between the excluded and the middle classes, and of the breakdown of the mechanisms – and especially the social and political conflicts – which once meant that the underprivileged were part of society as a whole. Once, they were exploited. They are now becoming outsiders, and it is no accident that they often redefine themselves in ethnic or cultural terms rather than social and economic.

This growing divorce between those who are 'in' and those who are 'out' becomes more and more spectacular as we move away from the centres of the planetary economy. The opening up of countries to the world market, often by antipopulist authoritarian regimes, may lead to a return to democracy, but it can also go hand in hand with increased economic dualism. In Latin America, for instance, the debasement of national-popular regimes initially led to the triumph of military dictatorships in many countries. Protectionism was replaced by liberal policies in an attempt to gain a comparative advantage on the world market. Yet whilst this economic policy could easily be reconciled with a return to free elections, it did nothing to reverse the trend, which was dominant throughout the 1980s, towards increased marginalization and the growth of the informal sector of the economy. The poor became poorer. Broad sectors of the traditional middle class – teachers, civil servants, etc. – saw their situation deteriorate badly, whilst the rich maintained their position and profited from the large-scale export of capital, much of it in the form of foreign debts. This growing inequality, which PREALC's researchers call a 'social debt', marks the limits of democratization. How can we speak of democracy when real power is used for the benefit of rich minorities and to the detriment of poor majorities? There is a growing divorce between those who are in and those who are out both in countries where the 'in' represent 80 per cent of the population and in countries where they represent only 20 to 40 per cent, as in Africa south of the Sahara or in the Andean countries of Latin America. The purely liberal conception of democracy is simply unacceptable, even though it has to be admitted that endogenous development does provide the most solid foundations for democracy.

Jürgen Habermas's Theory of Democracy

Contemporary thought reacts to the inadequacy of the liberal conception, which comes up against the harsh reality of inequality, by going in the opposite direction and returning to the universalism of the Enlightenment. There can be no democracy unless citizens can agree on propositions that are acceptable to all, regardless of their individual ideas and particular interests. The scientific community, as described by Robert K. Merton (1979), can be regarded as democratic to the extent that personal power and rivalries between schools or institutions are subordinated to the search for the truth and the demonstration of the truth. This conception is quite alien to liberal thought, which does not believe in consensus, but merely in compromise, tolerance and respect for minorities. Liberals are agnostics, whereas the defenders of enlightenment are either rationalists or deists. They also argue that the spirit of the Enlightenment must not be confined to the domain of scientific thought. It must permeate social life, or in other words the domain of values and norms, and even that of the most subjective experience of all: taste and aesthetic judgement. This poses major problems and there is even a serious danger of lapsing back in to the authoritarian image of a rationalism which destroys or despises everything it sees as irrational. And the category of the irrational is broad enough to include loving relationships and religion as well as the imaginary and tradition. This is the difficulty that Jürgen Habermas is trying to overcome.

Habermas rules out two extreme solutions: reducing the human actor to scientific and technical thought or to instrumental reason, and, at the opposite extreme, resisting the constraints of rationalism in the name of the particularisms of the individual or community. Like Adorno and Horkheimer before him, he is critical of the dominance of what he calls strategic thinking, but he has an absolute horror of the appeal to popular – *völkish* – forces which produced Nazism in Germany. He believes that it is possible to find universals in communication between particular experiences steeped in the particularity of a lifeworld or a culture. We should not be content with the compromises offered by liberal politics, or even with the tolerance that juxtaposes partcularisms rather than integrating them. We have to accept that there can be no democracy without citizenship, and no citizenship without agreement about procedures and institutions, and about their content.

How are we to establish a connection between universals and particulars? Through communication and, more concretely, through discussions and arguments which will allow us to recognize what is most authentic in the other as being bound up with an ethical value or a universal social norm. Respecting and listening to the other seems to provide more solid foundations for democracy than a clash of interests that results in compromise and juridical guarantees.

But how can we make this transition from the lived experience to thought, from particulars to universals? How can we invert the dominant tendency within our modernity, which contrasts the universality of reason with the particularisms of faith, tradition and community? Habermas gives the problem of modern democracy a much greater import than it is usually accorded by political science. His goal is to found a coexistence and communication between positions, opinions and tastes which seem at first sight to be purely subjective and therefore resistant to all integration. Following Piaget, Habermas argues that modern society is characterized by a growing divorce between the objective, the social and the subjective. It no longer has any central unifying principle, and it requires a theory of communication which can provide a theory of mutual understanding and therefore of sociality. Habermas constantly reminds us that there can be no democracy unless we listen to and recognize the other, unless we seek universal values in the subjective expression of preferences. Democratic debate, both in parliament, in the courts and in the media, presupposes that we recognize that the position of the other does have a certain validity, except in cases where the other clearly or even deliberately steps outside the pale of society. Hence the classic assertion – which is common to Habermas and both Parsons and Durkheim – that moral and social judgements are a way of maintaining and reproducing cultural values, social norms and mechanisms of socialization. In the case of aesthetic judgements, communication is more complete than in moral judgements, as it refers to a human condition or to thought processes which have an almost universal nature, or which at least apply to something greater than a society, or to what is sometimes called a civilization. Habermas is therefore in agreement with the many theorists who view society not simply as a productive apparatus, but as a collectivity which requires social integration and the preservation of cultural values as well as production. To put it in more concrete terms, education and justice are as important as the economy and politics.

Whilst this is a powerful argument against the extreme instrumental position which reduces social life to technical action, to the clash of interests and to the compromises that are established between them, it is vulnerable to the criticisms that have been put forward throughout this book. It is especially vulnerable to our critique of the idea that there is a correspondence between institutions which instil respect for values and norms, and individuals socialized by the family, education or other agents of socialization. There is in fact a constant discrepancy between system and actors: the system's goals include the strengthening of its own power, whilst actors are in search of their individual autonomy, no matter how they define it. This means that Habermas's image of society is not acceptable. It implies a constant transition from the particular to the universal, with political life playing the role of a *Bildung* that helps individuals to rise above their own interests. Communication simply means listening attentively to the other. It means no more than a concerned debate as to the meaning of the common good. Communication is contrasted with everything that comes between individual consciousnesses, namely flows of information, languages and representations controlled by powers, and flows of money and decisions.

Habermas is right to point out that, unlike the relationship between a buyer and a seller in the market, social conflict is never an outright confrontation or a zero-sum game. There can be no social conflict unless both parties have common cultural references and a common historicity. There are therefore always three dimensions to a democratic debate: *consensus*, or a reference to common cultural orientations; *conflict* between adversaries; and the *compromise* which reconciles that conflict with respect to the social framework – and especially the juridical framework – which restricts it.

When it comes to the aesthetic experience, communication is of a different nature, and is still more limited. It involves both a shared reference to what Habermas calls authenticity, or the tangible presence of the aesthetic experience, and a cultural content representing a tradition or a history whose presence is disclosed by the hermeneutic method. The distance between it and other traditions is, however, insurmountable. Indeed, we now find it extremely difficult to relate the representational arts which triumphed together with modernity, and the contemporary arts, which tend to be either languages or forms of lyricism without any referential object.

It seems to me that this distance between particulars and universals, which takes different forms in ethical behaviour and aesthetic experience, can only be overcome by according a universal value to the free assertion of the Subject and seeing it as one of the foundations of modernity. Habermas should have no objections to this, as whilst he criticizes the idea of the Subject in the name of intersubjectivity, he defines the idea of the Subject in the same terms as Hegel and pre-Hegelian metaphysics. Whilst I am as reluctant as Habermas to refer to any such principle, I fear that he is too ready to agree that it should be replaced by the classical ideas of society and culture, which he reintroduces when he refers to the lifeworld. This takes away the dramatic but dynamic quality of social life. It is by willing ourselves as Subjects, by transforming the individuality imposed on us by our biological being in to a production of the I, or in to *subjectivation*, that we come closest to the universal and therefore to modernity. And this self-production can only come about in and through the struggle against apparatuses, systems of cultural domination, and especially the State when it dominates culture as well as political and economic life. The fact that the personal subject is constituted only through a recognition of the other further reinforces this central idea: it is the subject, and not the intersubjective, self-production and not communication, that provide the foundations for citizenship and give democracy a positive content.

A recent example illustrates this idea. In France, there appears to be a traditional debate over the definition of nationality between those who claim that it is a matter of the country where one is born and those who argue that it is a matter of residency. The former view tends to be dominant in Germany, whilst the latter is more readily accepted in countries with a tradition of immigration. The (French) Commission on the Reform of the Code of Nationality appointed by the government in 1987 quickly abandoned this classic dichotomy and, to everyone's surprise, reached an explicit consensus by adopting the proposition that nationality should be the result of a choice on the part of immigrants, that everything possible should be done to facilitate that choice and that France should adopt a policy of integrating rather than rejecting or marginalizing immigrants. This conclusion has very wide-ranging implications. By rejecting all definitions of either the majority or the minority in terms of a social nature or a cultural heritage which moulds individuals, it extends what has been termed the French definition of nationality – a will to live together – without asserting that, in order to be French, one has to have no other loyalties. Defying the argument that nationality is automatically determined by place of origin or birth, it asserted that national status should be the result of a choice, in so far as that is possible. I would have liked the Commission to have gone further still, and I would like everyone to be asked to make an explicit choice, whatever the national status of their parents or grandparents. Only this appeal to freedom can do away with all forms of racism, xenophobia and the rejection of minorities.

Democracy is possible because social conflicts occur between actors who, whilst they are in conflict, refer to the same values, and try to give them different social forms. Rather than relying upon a generalized rationalism or an attempt to go back to the reign of objective reason and to extend the spirit of the Enlightenment, we should be turning to the subject to find the principle that founds citizenship. We should be defining social conflicts as a debate about the central cultural issue of the Subject which involves contradictory and complementary social actors.

This appeal to the Subject cannot, however, be a new version of the appeal to reason or modernity that characterized the philosophy of the Enlightenment. The goal of Enlightenment philosophy was to escape particulars by turning to the universal. I believe that the appeal to subject means both involvement in social conflict and a cultural choice, and that the two things are inseparable. A society cannot be built on reason alone, and nor can it be built on the Subject alone. The second illusion might be even more dangerous than the first, which led to the catastrophes brought about by communist regimes. The Subject is not a principle that can determine the law and social organization in a direct or positive way; it is a defence against the might of apparatuses which claim to manage or even produce information. Habermas speaks of 'communicative action', but what is *communication*? If we agree that it consists in finding universals within particulars, we lapse back in to the rationalist illusion; if, on the other hand, we are talking about interlocutors who are locked in to completely different identities and cultures, the only possible relationship they can establish is one based on either love or hate. Conflict thus either disappears or becomes total and insurmountable. Communication in fact means both a direct encounter between interlocutors and the transmission of messages from one to the other. It is both a flow of information and a sign that each interlocutor is actively working towards subjectivation and attempting to recognize the other's attempts to do the same. The contribution made by the idea of communication is essentially a negative one: society is no longer based upon history, nature or the will of God. Society means interaction, exchange and, in a word, action. This is an extreme form of something that was already visible in industrial society. Industrial society spoke about labour, and the word introduced the conflict between working-class autonomy and industrial organization. When we speak of communication we must not eliminate conflict by restricting the discussion to labour. On the contrary, we must stress both, as communication is the antithesis of information, not to mention self-expression. If expression triumphs, it becomes trapped in to self-consciousness and self-assertion, with all the attendant dangers of culturalism and notions of absolute difference. If information triumphs, it subordinates individuals and groups to its power, which is no different to the power of money.

If democracy is to exist, social conflicts must be restricted by the higher values of modernity, rationalization and subjectivation, but there must also be representative political forces, or in other words forces capable of representing both sides of the consumer society. Democratic debate exists when social demands govern political life but are in their turn governed by cultural orientations: they are contradictory and complementary social expressions of those orientations. A central social conflict over cultural values that are shared by both adversaries is the basic precondition for democracy. Whilst the freedom to chose who governs us is essential, it does not in itself define democracy.

Habermas rightly takes the view that democracy is not reducible to compromise and that there can be no citizenship without a consensus, and he attempts to reconcile this Enlightenment tradition with Marxism. This is difficult because Marxism speaks of contradictions between classes and of a struggle to the death between the productive forces and the relations of production. In contrast, I am talking about conflicts and not contradictions. The conflicts in question involve all that is at stake in modernity. This means that no social actor can identify completely with modernity: neither the apparatuses which run the culture industries, nor the subjectivity of individuals and groups which simultaneously defend traditions or communities and assert the rights of the subject. I fear that Habermas underestimates the conflictual dimension of society, as he defends the independence of actors against the logic of systems in the hope that the particularity of their lived world can be incorporated in to the world of the Enlightenment and its universalism. This has a concrete meaning only within a liberal perspective, as the market is a greater respecter of diversity and complexity, but Habermas is not a liberal. Arguments and debates do not lead to the integration of perspectives and demands; they can only reveal the insurmountable conflict between the might of apparatuses and the freedom of the personal subject.

The difference between these two perspectives arises primarily because Habermas takes as his starting point the German experience of culture as a particular historical culture, as a *Völksgeist* or a *Zeitgeist*, whereas I define the subject not as an individuality or a community, but as a demand for freedom. That demand may have no ultimate content, but it does have a great capacity for defence, struggle and a will to freedom. Habermas attempts to rediscover universalism by studying particular cultures and personalities. I am trying, in contrast, to rediscover the creative freedom of the subject and its ability to resist the domination of individual or collective life by apparatuses in possession of money, power and information, or in other words its ability to challenge the logic of systems.

Habermas's idea of a lifeworld or *Lebenswelt* is highly ambiguous. On the one hand, it reproduces the idea of culture, and refers to the values and norms transmitted by language, as well as by monuments and institutions; on the other, its very existence negates the essential cultural idea of a correspondence between actor and system. It introduces the romantic image of a lived experience which can be contrasted with social norms, and the possibility of a retreat in to privacy or nature so as to escape the conventions or injunctions of social life. Yet it is precisely this divorce between the lived world and institutions that is being denounced by modern critical thought. It is that divorce which is giving birth to new social movements which cannot become organized precisely because they position themselves outside society rather than against power, and because they have more in common with a counter-culture than with positive demands. To see the lived world as the world of social and cultural organization means going back to the dream of objective rationality, whereas the idea of the Subject emerges only if we accept that there is a divorce between actor and system. Needless to say, this is not merely a theoretical debate. It contrasts the difficult quest of the new movements that are challenging the system with the revival of rationalist liberalism. The philosophical face of social thought is once more becoming a quest for the lost One, whereas socio-historical thought is more alert to the increasingly extreme forms of the breakdown of the world order.

Many people take the view that it is participation that defines democracy; I take the view that it is the creativity of individuals and groups just as, at the level of interpersonal relations, love is a recognition of the other as subject that transcends sexual desire and rejects the ideal of merging of individuals in to either universals, truth or the ethical law. We therefore cannot establish a dichotomy between universalism and particularism, reason and religion, or technology and community. Democracy is the political form which guarantees the compatibility and combination of elements that are all too often seen as contradictory and as a potential source of conflict between apparatuses of domination and dictatorships of identity. That would be a battle to the death, no matter who wins. The idea of the Subject obliges us to accept a certain pluralism of values, as defined by Isaiah Berlin, who attempts to resist both the arrogance of French Enlightenment thought and the dangers of German romanticism.

Democratization

Our discussion has taken us from an analysis of democratic institutions to an analysis of democratizing action. The initial analysis took as its starting point the importance of free elections, but then went on to consider citizenship and political participation. It is based on the idea that democracy is closely associated with endogenous development. In such a situation, conflicts between social actors are conflicts over rationalization. Both parties regard themselves as the agents of rationalization and as opponents of the egotistic and particular interests of their adversary. History clearly demonstrates that democratic regimes took shape thanks to the triumph of secularization and rationalization, even though the principal agent of modernization was initially an absolute monarchy. This type of analysis obviously cannot be dismissed. It is impossible to breathe life in to a democratic regime governed by the One, which can mean either the unity of a State religion, that of an absolute power or that of a culture defined by its hostility to other cultures. A society which defines itself primarily in terms of its identity cannot be democratic. Still less a society which defines itself in terms of its uniqueness. Such a society is too caught up in a logic that benefits only the State, which then reduces society to the nation and the multiplicity of social actors to the unity of the people.

This analysis can, however, lead to such serious misunderstandings that it has to be examined critically. We cannot accept without demur the idea that only countries which experience endogenous development can become democratic, and that all other societies are fated to have authoritarian regimes. It is true that there is an obvious correlation between a democratic regime and economic modernization. But, as we have seen, it is also true that the constituent elements of democracy – an awareness of rights, the representativity of political forces and citizenship – are more likely to be found in societies which have been highly integrated by advanced economic development than in societies which are subject to private violence, segmented in to tribes or ethnic groups and dominated by conquerors.

We can, however, advance the alternative hypothesis that, as we move away from endogenous development, we are more likely to find weak civil societies ruled by enlightened despotisms or more or less totalitarian dictatorships, and that the fate of democracy is bound up with the formation of social movements with a greater mobilizing power. This would bring us back to the idea of revolution, which this book has criticized on more than one occasion.

Is it possible to identify the social or even cultural forces that resist the authoritarian or post-revolutionary State? The German or Italian-style authoritarian modernizing regimes which emerged in Turkey, Mexico and Brazil were resisted by a social mobilization which often had revolutionary overtones. That mobilization contributed to the development of a civil society in post-Bismarckian Germany and in Japan, even though it was defeated by the triumph of extreme nationalisms during a period of imperialist expansion. Similar developments have been seen in South Korea in recent decades. And was it not this revolutionary and anti-capitalist or anti-imperialist tendency that gave Cardenas's Mexico its democratic content?

We cannot, however, leave matters at that, as the twentieth century has seen the emergence of increasingly totalitarian regimes – ranging from Soviet or Maoist communism to Islamic revolutions – which were originally based upon a social revolution, but which quickly transformed it in to a repressive totalitarian power. Do we therefore have to conclude that only cultural forces, which have even more power to mobilize than social or institutional forces, can resist these regimes and lay the foundations for a possible democracy? Soviet dissidence and the actions of the Chinese students and intellectuals who created the Democracy Wall and were then massacred in Tienanmen Square exemplify cultural rather than social resistance, and they fought in the name of values rather than interests.

There is little hope for democracy in a totalitarian regime where the protesters are isolated. The collapse of authoritarian regimes usually results from their internal decay rather than from the success of popular oppositional movements. Hence the almost passive victory of a democracy which has been reduced to meaning freedom of political choice. Its superficiality was quickly revealed by the low level of political involvement and the weakness of political parties, as in the Soviet Union after the failure of the attempted coup of August 1991. Even if they are on the whole weak, cultural liberation forces may, on the other hand, indicate the modern preconditions for the democratization of those countries that have been least influenced by the endogenous model of development. All the more so in that, even in the developed countries, moral and cultural protests are the most effective ways of resisting the hold of the consumer society which has absorbed most of the social movements of the earlier period. Cultural movements whose action provides the basis for democracy take shape in the name of the consumer and not the producer. They are, that is, cultural and personal rather than economic, and therefore challenge the culture industries that control information. It is difficult to formulate demands in these countries too, as, although it is non-violent, the stranglehold of the consumer society is comparable to that of totalitarian societies. It is, however, very efficient.

The parallel is not an artificial one, and it has always been obvious. Just as it was the partial alliance between anticapitalist movements and anti-imperialist policies that gave Marxism–Leninism its exceptional strength, the cultural critique of the consumer society now has something in common with the ethical and political critique of totalitarian society. Both forms of protest are calls for personal freedom and for the respect of a collective identity which has now been extended to include the whole of humanity.

It is pointless to go back to the soft liberalism that so easily tolerates the poverty and dependency of the greater part of humanity and luxuriates in a 'consumer' society where the human Subject is dissolved. If we wish to resist totalitarianism and at the same time avoid the reduction of society to a market, we must construct a democracy based upon social movements which can defend the human Subject against the impersonality of both absolute power and the rule of commodities. Eastern Europe now places all its hopes in the market. This is quite justifiable, as a return to a market economy is essential if the *nomenklatura* is to be eliminated. The elimination of the past is not, however, enough to build a future, and this absolute faith in the market economy and foreign aid will be short-lived. The protest movements that are already beginning to emerge may lead to dangerous developments and may take a populist or nationalist direction conducive to new authoritarian solutions. A consideration of the possible formation of new social movements capable of transforming anti-totalitarian resistance in to democratic institutions is therefore a matter of urgency. Similarly, in those Latin American and African countries that are rediscovering political freedom, the opening up of the economy to the world market will not in itself safeguard freedom, as it may lead to greater inequality and calls for authoritarian solutions. Both the call for freedom and communitarian defence movements must be mobilized to prevent the triumph of a democracy based upon property qualifications and the social exclusion and political manipulation of the majority.

The preconditions for democratization are therefore no more reducible to the principles whereby democracy works than modernization is reducible to modernity in action. Pro-democracy struggles become perverted when their goal is no longer the autonomy of civil society and its social actors, just as authoritarian modernization becomes catastrophic when it is regarded as something other than a transitional stage in the construction of civil society and self-sustaining growth. Are we incapable of resisting both the mirages of a liberalism which benefits the centre rather than the periphery, and the deadly threat of a revolutionary or nationalist power which pursues its own interests and not those of the people it has mastered?

The Public Space

There is no such thing as a politically transparent society in which the will to independence and liberation from internal constraints are completely transformed in to representative institutions. There is always a high level of tension between institutions and political liberation movements. The former tend to become oligarchical, and the latter can become authoritarian or populist. Hence the need for a political system which is as autonomous as possible from the State on the one hand and the actors of civil society on the other, but which is still capable of mediating between the two. Such a system is not simply defined by the existence of a set of democratic institutions or of mechanisms for reaching decisions that are recognized as legitimate. It must involve the entire public space. And it must take account of the influence of the media and of individual initiatives.

The role of journalists and intellectuals in a democracy is not to challenge the power of the State in the name of the will of the people, as it is in non-democratic regimes, but to reconcile the implementation of endogenous development, and especially the social conflicts over the social use of rationalization, with the mobilization of forces of liberation. It is not easy to reconcile liberty and liberation. Many political forces and intellectuals have failed to do so, but both social-democracy – in the contemporary meaning of the term – and certain intellectuals have facilitated the existence of that combination and the creation of very democratic public spaces. These are spaces in which public freedoms are well established, but they also generate a heightened awareness of citizenship. The great virtue of such intellectuals is that they fight with all their strength against a popular authoritarianism that is hostile to both political freedom and the defence of

individual rights and which, in various forms ranging from communism to third-worldist nationalism, seemed to dominate the world in
the mid twentieth century. Revolutionaries and liberals speak of these
humanists with equal scorn and violence. And yet it is the humanists
who are the realists. It is they who have done most to reconcile free
institutions and the collective will to participate – and that is a good
practical definition of democracy.

Their role is all the more important in that the problems of
democracy can only be posed at the international level, as international relations now have an increasingly direct influence on
national political regimes. We cannot congratulate ourselves on the
smooth workings of our democratic institutions and complacently
ignore the fact that our countries dominate other countries and are
therefore an obstacle to their democratization. The same arguments
also apply inside the frontiers of individual countries where, all too
often, 'enlightened' elites boast of their liberalism whilst their dominance and control over the mechanisms of exclusion are creating a
vast zone where democracy does not penetrate.

It is inadmissible to pride ourselves on living in the world of
freedoms without asking ourselves whether or not those liberties
require a high level of servitude elsewhere, just as the elegance of the
upper classes conceals the harsh living conditions of the disinherited
masses. It is just as dangerous to describe as 'democratic' the invasion
of spaces of freedom by popular masses who are quickly transformed
in to disciplined assault troops whose intervention simply brings to
power dictators who are even less liberal than the oligarchs of old. It
is impossible to choose between the defence of democratic institutions
and the popular demand for participation; the only solution is to
combine the two. Democratization means the subjectivation of political life. Just as the Subject means both personal freedom and
membership of a collectivity, democracy means both the institutionalized resolution of conflicts over modern rationality and a defence of
personal and collective freedom. The last century made the discovery
that democracy had to have both a juridical and an economic content;
we now know that it must have both a cultural and political content.

For far too long, democracy appeared to be a political formula that
allowed the bourgeoisie to free itself from the constraints of the State;
being suspicious of democracy, the popular masses awaited the
revolutionary or populist leaders and parties who would remedy
social injustices. The non-democratic left and right are now collapsing, and the goal with the greatest mobilizing power is democracy
and not revolution. Democratic institutions are therefore coming
closer to the democratization movement.

To explain the memorable events of 1989 – and they were the most exhilarating to have occurred since mid-1789– we must go beyond the dichotomy between negative and positive conceptions of freedom, of democratic institutions and the will to democratize. Perhaps the time has come to give the idea of democracy a central role in our political thinking. This may seem a banal objective, but it is not. Once we reject democratic unanimism, we soon discover the strength to resist both the liberalism that reduces society to being a mere political market, and liberation movements which are more concerned with defending the identity and homogeneity of a country than the freedoms of its citizens.

We must also resist the eighteenth-century temptation to identify Man with citizen. That great hope resulted in terrible catastrophes, as it led to the destruction of all the barriers that could restrict an absolute power. Rather than confusing Man with citizen, democracy should, like the Declaration of the Rights of Man and the Citizen, explicitly recognize that popular sovereignty must respect natural rights and must even be based upon those rights. The most democratic society is also the society which imposes the strictest restrictions on the hold political powers have over society and individuals. This is simply another way of saying that the most modern society is the society which quite explicitly recognizes that rationalization and subjectivation have equal rights, and that the two must be reconciled.

Democracy does not mean the triumph of the One or the transformation of the people in to a Prince. On the contrary, it means the subordination of institutions to personal and collective freedom. It protects freedom from politico-economic power on the one hand, and from the pressures of tribes and traditions on the other. It protects itself from itself, or in other words from the isolation of a political system that exists in the interstices between the irresponsibility of the State and the demands of individuals, or in a vacuum which it then fills with its own interests, its intestine struggles and its rhetoric. Given the urgent problems of modernization and of economic and military competition, the modern State inevitably exerts great pressure on society. Our priority is therefore to strengthen the Subject. Whatever their individual nature, our societies tend to submit to the law of either the Prince or the market; democracy demands that the spirit of freedom, independence and responsibility must resist both these principles of order. This gives an important role to what are, somewhat inadequately, termed agencies of socialization, and particularly to the family and education. Rather than simply socializing them, they must transform individuals in to subjects who are conscious of their freedoms and their responsibilities towards themselves. Unless individuals become subjects, democracy has no solid foundations.

The spirit of freedom also presupposes respect for the law in which it is inscribed. There can be no democracy in a society ruled by money, patronage, sycophancy, gangs or corruption. As those who defend the 'Republican' tradition in France rightly say – even though they do tend to forget democracy's representative dimension – this implies that the central power must apply the law rather than surrendering to the influence of local interests. When the law and elected representatives are rendered powerless by clashes between gangs and the police, or between ethnic groups fighting over a territory, it is no longer possible to speak of democracy, even if there are free elections and even if the defeated party does relinquish power. There can therefore be no democracy without social peace. In the absence of social peace, the weak are defenceless. Revolutions may well rapidly transform the nature of the ruling elite, but they are a threat to democracy and do nothing to strengthen it. Personal freedom is not reducible to *laissez-faire* policies which mask the power of the ruling economic groups. Nor is it reducible to the coming to power of the defenders of the people, who may form a new ruling elite that is beyond the control of the people. There can be no democracy without an organized will to make all institutions work for the freedom and security of all, and do all they can to reduce social inequalities. We should not divorce formal democracy from real democracy, but nor should we confuse the latter with the dictatorships that proclaim themselves to be people's democracies.

The Democratic Personality

In his attempt to understand Nazism, Theodor Adorno, who had a Marxist background, elaborated the notion of the authoritarian personality (Adorno et al. 1950). To some extent, he was influenced by Nevitt Sanford and other American researchers whose approach was closer to that of social psychology. According to Adorno, the workings of the Nazi regime and above all its capacity to mobilize, which are usually explained in terms of the historical conjuncture or even the personality of the dictator, were an expression of a general dimension of the personality, namely the *authoritarianism* which can also be seen in sexual behaviour, political life, relations with minorities and the education of children. This famous example suggests that we should look for the foundations of democracy not simply in a type of development – endogenous modernization, which explains only the presence of 'negative' freedom – but in a personality-type, in the ability of individuals to act as a Subject and not simply as consumers. We should also look beyond the political field for an explanation of why democratic regimes appear and survive. There can be no solid democracy unless the State and the established order are challenged by a will to personal freedom based upon the defence of a cultural tradition, as an individual who is completely cut off from tradition is no more than a consumer of material and symbolic goods who is unable to resist the manipulative pressures and seductions of those who hold power. That is why democracy has so often been associated with a religious faith which both voiced the demands of conscience and offered the support of a spiritual power capable of resisting temporal power.

Democracy is strong when this democratic consciousness is combined with an open society where the weakening of the forces of social control promotes a spirit of invention, enterprise and rationalization. The democratic personality and the open society complement one another. Sometimes, they develop conjointly; at such times, democracy is at its strongest. If the democratic personality develops in a society which is still closed and dominated by an absolute power or powerful mechanisms which reproduce the established order, the democratic spirit is embodied in active minorities who put forward demands in the name of the right to resist oppression or who may even lead insurrections.

When, on the other hand, society is open to the winds of change even though there is still wide acceptance of traditional or charismatic authority, the democratic spirit cannot breathe life in to democratic institutions, and liberal society cannot function through the people and by the people.

The suggestion that the open society and the democratic personality complement one another is no more than a new version of definitions of democracy which equate rationalization with subjectivation. It is not modernity that produces democracy; it is the ability to combine rationalization and subjectivation that defines modernity. That is why modernity originates from the spirit of freedom and the search for efficacy. But where do they come from?

As we have said more than once, the origins of the spirit of rationalization are negative. As liberal thought well understands, it originally stems from the decay of systems of reproduction and social control. Subjectivation, on the other hand, appears when positive demands for freedom and communality are being put forward, and when political power is actively restricted by a religious, or at least spiritual, call for freedom and by an awareness of belonging to a community, family, nation, or Church. These preconditions are directly complementary: democracy is strong when the political and social order is weak and framed by an ethics at one extreme, and a community at the other extreme. This notion totally contradicts the long-standing idea that democracy can be equated with participation, with popular power and with majority rule. We have recognized the importance of all these components, but we have suffered too much at the hands of authoritarian and totalitarian regimes which called for popular participation not to realize that, as liberal thought teaches us, democracy is based upon the restriction of central powers. We have to break off the debate between liberal thought and left-wing thought, as there can be no democracy unless we can reconcile the respective ideas they defend. An open society presupposes the restriction of power, and an awareness of citizenship. These seemingly contradictory ideas can be reconciled once we begin to focus our analysis on the idea of the Subject and its struggle against apparatuses of domination. Democracy is not simply a set of institutions or a personality-type. It is primarily a struggle against power and the established order, be it that of the Prince, religion or the State, and for the defence of minorities against the majority. It means both a commitment to these struggles and the non-commitment of a Subject which refuses to be reduced to being a citizen or a worker, which is not satisfied with being dissolved in to the ideological fog known as the idea of Humanity. Democracy is not simply a static political system. It is a permanent effort and battle to subordinate social organization to values which are not properly social: rationality and freedom. Democracy is not the triumph of the people, but the subordination of the world of works, technologies and institutions to the creative and transformational capacities of individuals and collectivities.

Points of Arrival

Images of Society

Sociology was not constituted as the study of social life – that definition is too general. It came in to being by defining the good in terms of the social utility of the modes of behaviour it observed. According to this classical sociology, the good was neither conformity to the world order or divine laws, or even the creation of an order capable of restraining passions and violence, but the contribution made by an actor – or, more accurately, an organ – to the workings of the social body. The life of a society is based upon the internalization of norms. There is a correspondence between the institutions which elaborate those norms and instil respect for them, and the institutions responsible for the socialization of members of the collectivity, and especially newcomers such as children and immigrants. Individuals are therefore defined by their status and by the corresponding roles, or in other words the behaviour expected of them by others. *Homo sociologicus* is motivated by what is expected of him and not by self-interest. A father is someone who behaves as his son expects him to behave, or hopes he will behave. A worker or a doctor is someone who fulfils a role in accordance with models inscribed in the law, a collective contract and, above all, the state of contemporary mores and ideas. When the French 1848 Revolution speaks of 'fraternity', it is dreaming of a society in which everyone acts in the interests of one great family. This functionalism presupposes that society is organized, not around traditions and privileges which are, by definition, particularist, but around reason, whose universalism guarantees that all members of society can be socialized. According to this mode of social thought, schools must strip children of their particular heritages and introduce them to reason, either through scientific culture or through as direct an acquaintance as possible with the great achievements of the human mind, or with philosophy and art. The German conception of *Bildung* and André Malraux's cultural centres in France represent different stages in a continuous attempt to combine an apprenticeship in reason and beauty with social integration. Writing in the mid twentieth century, Talcott Parsons produced the most highly developed form of this classical sociology (Parsons 1966). It is based on the twin ideas that modern society represents the triumph of reason and that functionality is the criterion of the good. The idea of *society* dominates sociology, but it is an explanatory principle rather than a mere definition of a research field. Modern society is the incarnation of reason, and normal behaviour is behaviour which contributes to the smooth workings of society.

Even before sociology itself was created, sociologism was dominant. It was a central core surrounded by a vast field of theories which explained modes of social behaviour in terms of the historical set to which they belonged and their position on the tradition–modernity axis. There was much talk of a global society, of the spirit of the age (*Zeitgeist*) and of modes of production. Historicism, simple or complex, was an intermediary stage between the old theories which defined behaviour in terms of membership of a culture, and the newer theories which defined it in terms of its role in society's production of itself through cultural innovations, political debates, forms of organization and forms of power. This historicism is collapsing before our very eyes. Social thought is now turning towards actors, not in order to concentrate exclusively on their subjectivity, but in order to observe every form of action, from the rational pursuit of self-interest to debates about social policies and public freedoms, to clashes between the subject and powers.

This classical sociology is now being challenged. The actors–system correspondence no longer seems 'natural', and we are no longer convinced that a universalist reason should triumph over particular interests. According to many of the best sociologists, modern society is, on the contrary, dominated by the breakdown of the correspondence between system and actors. Power is becoming concentrated, and flows of money, influence and information are controlled by restricted groups. What is known as social integration can be reinterpreted as the controls exerted by power centres over social actors who are being increasingly manipulated. At the same time, those actors are defined not so much by their roles as by their position in a market, and therefore by their own interests on the one hand and, on the other, by a subjectivity which protects the freedom of the actor against an over-organized society and defends an identity, which can mean cultural particularisms, a language, a religion, a territory or an ethnic group.

The correspondence between actor and system is being replaced by two conflicting images: that of a system without actors, and that of an actor without a system. The first image dominated the 1970s, and the second the 1980s. As utopian communism evaporated and as the new social movements rapidly collapsed in the aftermath of May 1968, social thought entered a lengthy ice age. Society was seen purely as a system of controls, repression and the reproduction of inequalities. Many reacted to the optimistic modernism of the immediate post-war period by adopting the view that any attempt at reform or to stimulate social reflexivity would merely strengthen the centre's domination over the periphery. Society was indeed a machine, but it was an infernal machine. This discourse was too far removed from reality to encourage concrete research, which therefore disappeared almost completely for a long decade in which ideological-type constructs, some of them tricked out with a few statistics, replaced sociological analysis. Their primary function was not to describe social life, but to supply an ideology consonant with the worries of the greater part of the intellectual world and the whole of society. This vision of society, which turned the critical spirit in to antimodernism, expressed the apprehensions of a socio-cultural world faced with the arrogant triumph of new technologies and consumption. Structural-Marxist discourse was the language and ideology of an intelligentsia divorced from society.

This interlude could not last for long. Whilst sociologists and philosophers were proclaiming order to be immobile, everything around them was in motion: commodity consumption, education, productive technologies and health technologies. By the beginning of the 1980s in some countries, by the middle of the decade in France and by its end in the communist countries of Central and Eastern Europe, voluntarist regimes were collapsing, and purely critical thought was giving way to the noisy triumph of the market economy, and to demands for consumption, mobility and freedom. Some wanted to be part of the triumph of liberalism. They therefore made *Homo sociologicus* part of *Homo economicus* and explained the most diverse forms of behaviour in terms of rational choices. Others took a more pessimistic view, and described social actors as stumbling through a world which was no longer illuminated by either values or norms and forms of organization, and as exchanging signals containing implicit messages, lies and traps with other actors who were stumbling through the same fog. This was a world in which everyone acted without believing in anything, except perhaps the need to save their own skins in a hostile world by learning to allay suspicion.

The insurmountable opposition between the image of a system

without actors, which was taken to extremes by Nicos Poulantzas (1974) and the Althusserean school, and that of an actor without a system, which finds its clearest expression in the work of Erving Goffman (1959), signals the decay of classical sociology. The decay can, however, become still more advanced. At one extreme, Niklas Luhmann (1984) describes the social system as a biological system which is transformed from within, mainly through a process of differentiation. This image is consonant with important aspects of our fragmented society, namely the development of art for art's sake and the respective independence of economic life, political life, the world of religion and private life. At the opposite extreme, social actors are once more seen as part of a tradition, and the analysis of action becomes a hermeneutics. There can be no possible communication between systems theory and hermeneutics. If the object constructed by classical sociology ceases to exist, it is quite understandable that major domains of social analysis should come within the remit of either philosophy or economic science. The very workings of society, its historical transformations and its concrete unity, which almost always coincides with that of a Nation-State, no longer seem to correspond to values, norms or, more generally, political projects. The objective and the subjective are separated by a social fallow land, and anyone who still believes in the existence of an organized set of institutions seems either to be deceived by a mirage or trapped by their own desires. As we have already said, the idea of post-modernity describes the decay of the classical image of society. Indeed, it could well be redefined as the idea of a post-social or post-historical era, as those terms signal an even more complete break with the experience of the last few centuries than the idea of post-modernity.

There is no necessary reason why the culture and the economy, values and interest should combine through institutional means to form a society. On the contrary, we can observe these two worlds becoming both increasingly divorced and increasingly intertwined. Whilst part of the population – the majority in the North and the minority in the South – lives in a technical and economic world, another part of it – the minority in the North and the majority in the South – is involved in a quest for a defensive identity. In European countries, East and West, some speak of open markets, whilst others want to preserve the independence and distinctiveness of the nation at all costs. Do they belong to the same society? The differences between them are greater than those between the left and the right. Even at the level of the individual, the two worlds meet and clash rather than combine; Jean Fourastié (1950), for instance, writes a hymn of praise to the 'Thirty Glorious Years' and to technological progress, but he is also a Christian thinker who is profoundly distressed by certain of modernity's effects. The Republican dream is fading: the political world is no longer solid enough to combine the defence of a cultural identity with confidence in the market. And far from overcoming them, political life is being weakened by these contradictions. The great parties which aspired to being the embodiment of societal projects are therefore going in to decline. This divorce between cultural identity and economic rationality explains the crisis of 'the social' and the almost total disappearance of a word which now seems as dated and as nostalgic as 'charity'.

The decay of the social should not, however, be seen solely as a crisis which has dangerous effects. The exhaustion of the idea of society signals above all a new stage in modernity and secularization. The Roman image of the citizen and the religion of the public good and social utility, are being replaced by the figure of a human Subject whose attempts to become free and responsible are no longer guaranteed by any law. Indeed, they are increasingly defined by a rejection of arbitrary laws. Marcuse and Foucault may well be right to denounce the new forms of social conformism and the pressures that are brought to bear in the name of hygiene or to convince us that it is in all our interests to restrain our passions, fight deviancy and promote the triumph of a scientifically-based moralism. On the other hand, these new images of social and cultural integration are being challenged by the idea of a Subject who rejects the law of social utility and variants on the logic of apparatuses, and whose demand for freedom is inseparable from desire, tradition, the Id and the We.

It is true that, as the twentieth century draws to a close, the pendulum of history is swinging from left to right, from collectivism to individualism, from revolution to rights, and from planning to the market. After having been imprisoned for so long by dictatorial apparatuses and ideologies, 'nature' does seem to be taking its revenge. Yet the idea of the Subject is no more bound up with the market economy than it is with centralized planning, which are simply contrasting variations on the logic of systems. We are, however, witnessing a conflict between an increasingly utilitarian logic of social integration and a Subject defined in terms of the individual's relationship with the self and not in terms of participation in an essence or community. As a result of the current collapse of communist or nationalist regimes, the personal subject is no longer being conflated with society as collective Subject, and the rights of man are no longer equated with the duties of the citizen.

Society was, like reason itself, a deistic expression of the old religious spirit. It was a new form of the alliance between man and the universe. That alliance can no longer exist, and the break between the human order and the order of things is ushering us in to full modernity. Ethics can no longer teach us to conform to an order; it must invite everyone to take responsibility for their own lives, and to defend a freedom that is far removed from an individualism vulnerable to every kind of social determinism. Freedom means the ability to manage the difficult relationships between the shattered fragments of rationalist modernity: sexuality, consumption, nation and company.

In an era in which there seem to be no checks on either transnational trade or the new communitarianism, many people are still drawn to the old model of society. Respectable as it may be, this nostalgia for objective reason and the *polis* cannot provide an answer to the real problems of personal and collective life. Modern man is no more a citizen of Enlightenment society than he is a creature of God. His only responsibilities are to himself.

This new development was initially associated with neo-liberalism, and with a new interest in the strategies of governments and companies as they tried to adapt to a changing environment in which there were few controls and to a world market in a constant state of disequilibrium. At almost the same time, a conception of the actor that was less militant and more suited to those who had to get by as best they could, rather than conquer the world, was beginning to gain currency. The actor began to be described as attempting to organize an environment which was no longer ruled by values, norms or even conventions. This view goes against the heritage of critical sociology, as whilst society is a system which functions only in order to promote its own power, actor and society are now divorced, and the actions of actors are inevitably both egoistical and unpredictable. At the same time, the sociology of modernization was reverting to a sociology of action which contrasted the values of freedom and responsibility with the interests of the system. The sociology of action, finally, became what it always had been, even when it was trapped in to a historicist framework, namely a sociology of the Subject. The book you have just read is part of that tendency and represents an attempt to reject both a purely critical sociology and historicism.

We must, however, be wary of constructing too strict a dichotomy between supposedly successive modes of thought. The idea of a Subject, which was once bound up with the image of the transcendental world order, became incarnated in history during the era of triumphant modernity. It then became a way of resisting the stranglehold of powers and apparatuses. The history of modernization is also, and primarily, the history of subjectivation. The views of those who interpret its history as a transition from the subjective to the objective and from conviction to responsibility not withstanding, we have to recognize that the secularization of the Subject began with what Weber calls worldly asceticism. Sociology is no longer merely the study of the rationalization and functionality of social institutions. It takes as its main object the conflict between the Subject and systems, between freedom and power. This book is a defence of modernity to the extent that it attempts to demonstrate that social life is constructed through struggles and negotiations around the implementation of the cultural orientations that go to make up what I term historicity. In today's post-industrial society, which I describe as 'programmed', these struggles no longer centre upon the social use of technology, but upon the production and mass distribution of representations, data and languages. This central assertion immediately fills the vacuum that has opened up between the economy and culture. It defines actors, who were once defined in terms of their identity, in terms of social relations, and therefore power relations; all social relations have a power dimension, or a lack of symmetry between rulers and ruled. It also replaces the idea of the market with the idea of the company – which can be economic, political or cultural – as power-centre.

The Subject opposes the logic of the system. The Subject and the system are not separate worlds, but antagonistic social movements. They are social and political actors who come in to conflict, even when the demands of the Subject are not taken up by political agents and even when the great productive systems convince many people that they are no more than agents of economic rationality, or even public servants. Society can no longer be defined as a set of institutions, or as the effect of a sovereign will. It is the creation of neither history nor the Prince. It is a field of conflicts, negotiations and mediations between rationalization and subjectivation, and they are the complementary and contradictory faces of modernity.

This assertion is an implicit critique of culturalism and economism. Their success is certainly consonant with the present decay of the idea of society, but they are both incapable of taking acount of any analysis of the other. They therefore frustrate any attempt to construct an overall theory of society or, more specifically, to understand the relationship between the economistic North and the culturalist South. Only a truly social theory, or a sociology, can offer an overall explanation rather than an interpretation of only some observable phenomena. Human beings make their own history, but they do so through social conflicts, and on the basis of cultural choices. We have not left industrial society and we have not entered post-modernity; we are building a programmed society in which the production of symbolic goods has the central role that once devolved upon the production of material goods in industrial society. It is possible that this society may see a complete divorce between the economy and culture, just as the forces of economic or scientific development created islands of rationality in a world of tradition and community at the beginning of modernity. Yet such a rupture must be seen as pathological, and it can be analysed only as a divorce between complementary domains. The political system must establish mediations between the two.

Social science must be able to see beyond the divorce between market and community, between economism and culturalism, and rediscover the unity of a system of historical action, or in other words *cultural orientations* and *social actors* which are in conflict to the extent that they are trying to give different *social forms* to those cultural orientations. Actors are no longer defined by their social situation, as they were in a class society; they must be understood to be social movements. One actor speaks of strategy and of adapting to change and the market, of operational thought and of cost–benefit calculations; the other speaks of the Subject and its freedom and of the individual's will to be an actor. These actors are in conflict, but they are united by their shared reference to a creative movement, and therefore to a hyper-modernity. And yet, as in all periods of history, these social movements can be transformed in to their opposites, or in to social anti-movements. At this point, the offensive action of the Subject is transformed in to a defensive action which is concerned with identity and community rather than freedom. At the same time, the strategies of political, economic or cultural enterprises are frustrated by the reign of money, and productive capitalism gives way to finance capitalism. At both the international level and at the level of individual industrial countries, our society is torn between conflicting tendencies. On the one hand, we are constructing a new system of historical action. On the other hand, that system is being destroyed by a dualism which divorces the economy from culture and the North from the South. North and South are no longer different continents: they are part of every country.

Since the beginning of the 1980s, there has been a sharp rise in inequality at the international level. The industrialized countries reacted to the crisis of the 1970s by making an unprecedented technological leap forward, whereas vast regions of the Third World and the intermediary countries suffered a dramatic reversal. We therefore have an acute contradiction between an economistic vision of society and a culturalist vision. In rich countries, the 'rational choice' school is reverting to the idea of *Homo economicus*; in impoverished or paralysed countries, culturalism is becoming more and more aggressive. It rejects a modernity it sees only from the outside, and looks to a mythical past to compensate for a present which has no future. Rather than taking sides or becoming involved in oratorical jousts, we must recognize that, despite their antagonisms, both these positions contain broken fragments of a new stage in modernity. It may be having difficulty in emerging, but our analysis must be able to perceive it.

It will no doubt be claimed that this image of society takes us back to the historicism that was criticized at such length in part II. A distinction must, however, be made between two very different assertions. The first and most general is that any 'modern' society must be seen as the product of its own activity, and must therefore be defined in terms of a certain mode of self-production. The second is that only industrial society, understood in the broad sense of the term, succeeds in seeing itself and constructing itself in terms of historical development and evolution. It is by no means contradictory to define our society as hyper-modern and to say that it is a product of the evolutionist thought that characterized one stage in the development of modern societies. Similarly, the classical society that produced the political philosophy of the sixteenth, seventeenth and eighteenth centuries was the modern society of the Renaissance. It created modern science and the modern State, but it thought in terms of order rather than movement, and in political rather than economic terms. The political society analysed by Machiavelli, Hobbes and Rousseau, and then the industrial society analysed by Comte, Hegel and Marx, led to the formation of a post-industrial *programmed* society in which ethical categories have the central importance that once belonged to political and then economic categories. Prior to the appearance of modernity, religious thought played the same role.

The transition from modern society to the programmed society is not a continuous process of uninterrupted progress. It takes place dramatically and slowly, just like the nineteenth-century transition from political society to economic society, or from the society of the mercantile economy and right to the society of industry and class struggle. It involves crises and turmoil. Since 1968, we have been living through the crisis and decay of industrial society, its cultural field, its social actors and its forms of political action. This crisis reached its climax at the beginning of the 1980s. It was so acute that all we could see was the conflict between the world of calculation and the world of cultural identity, and the dangers that threatened the planet if we continued to pursue a policy of uncontrolled growth. We can, however, now predict and even see the rebirth of the social. New actors are appearing. What I was the first to describe as new social movements were no more than fragile, almost monstrous, hybrid forms. These hybrids between actors of the future and the ideologies of the past looked like social centaurs. Thanks to the media and to a few intellectuals who have succeeded in escaping the discourses of the past, public opinion is, however, aware of new social problems and is outlining new debates. The main object of this book is to define the cultural field, and especially the forms of social thought, that are at stake in the social relations and conflicts, and the forms of political action that are being reorganized before our very eyes.

Nothing could be further from my intentions than to return to a deistic conception of natural law and to define modes of behaviour in terms of a harmony or disharmony with principles established by either nature or a divine creator. In my own view, my analysis is sociological because the Subject can be defined and constructed only as an actor involved in social conflicts and as the creator of historicity. It is this combination of a social conflict – and the appropriate forms of negotiation – and cultural orientations which are shared by adversaries, that defines social actors and, more directly still, social movements. This means that social life is irreducible to either the implementation of shared values or, at the opposite extreme, a class struggle which is as radical as a civil war. The Subject is therefore inconceivable in the absence of social relations and especially of the power that transforms instrumental rationality in to a system of order that seeks more and more power. Any analysis which centres on the idea of the Subject also defines the formation or destruction of the Subject in social terms.

The dichotomy between a left-wing thought which stresses the impersonality of systems – especially economic systems – and a right-wing thought which is more individualistic and liberal was bequeathed to us by the nineteenth century, and it often prevents us from seeing that a great inversion is taking place within the social sciences. One is initially tempted to say that ideological conflicts are now taking place on different fronts, that the left is defending individuals and minorities from profit and power, whilst the right remains more attached to the impersonal logic of the market. But that answer misses the real point. Whilst the nineteenth century was dominated by the economy, the twentieth has been dominated by politics and above all by resistance to totalitarianism. This should prevent us from reducing our vision of the individual to the rational pursuit of self-interest. It is resistance to absolute power that makes recognition of the ethical subject so important. So much so that the central debate is no longer one between holism and individualism, but one between the sociology of the subject and rationalist individualism, now that the systems that dominate the world appeal to the market, and not to the historical mission of the State or the mobilization of a class.

The Role of Intellectuals

Whilst it is true that certain intellectuals are trying to build the new cultural stage on which social actors quite different to those of industrial society are beginning to appear, we have an uneasy feeling that most of them are increasingly absent from public life. So much so that we have to ask ourselves if they have not in fact vanished from the centre of collective life, just as the clerics before them were swept aside when secularization triumphed and when historians replaced theologians, and scientists the interpreters of sacred texts. The intellectuals were deeply involved in secularization. They constantly spoke out against the masters of power and money in the name of the necessary progress of history, hoping that it would do away with privileges and ignorance and allow the majority to share in and manage the benefits of progress. Marx believed that the increasing socialization of production made socialism inevitable. The intellectuals therefore spoke in the name of those who had no voice, but they derived their legitimacy from their understanding of the laws of history. This made them both advisers to the modernizing Prince and defenders of the oppressed people. They were both an elite who had shaken off the influence of conventions and traditions, and revolutionaries who were convinced that science alone could destroy the *anciens régimes* and plough the ground so deeply that it would one day be possible to reap the harvest of freedom. This image of the intellectual is now an anachronism. Many intellectuals have broken with modernity, and those who have not done so have often allowed themselves to become servants of despots they believed to be enlightened, but who were merely totalitarian tyrants. This has tarnished the image of the intellectuals much more than the actions of those who took the side of fascist nationalism, as their actions were seen as marginal, if not insane. For the last hundred years, the most vigorous current in intellectual life has been the antimodernism inspired by Nietzsche and to some extent Freud. It was widely popularized by the Frankfurt School and then Michel Foucault, and the most extreme leftism eventually merged with the new liberalism to create postmodernism. The religion of the future has gradually been replaced by nostalgia for Being and for what Horkheimer called objective reason.

Many intellectuals have been fighting against the idea of the Subject for a hundred years. They have usually done so in the name of reason or history, but it was sometimes in the name of the nation. Some went back to the heritage of the clerics who once deciphered the rational order of a world which was both created by God and accessible to the human understanding. Others, who found it easier to accept that God was dead, attempted to subordinate the human conscience, not to his revelation or to the laws of the world he created, but to impersonal forces such as Progress and Evolution. The best of them became fascinated with the destruction of conventions brought about by a liberated sexuality which, because it was no longer functional, implied the presence of a death instinct as well as the life instincts. Nostalgia for Being and investigations in to sexuality combined to sustain a mode of thought which was both creative and critical of social philosophies of progress that called for a rational modern society, as opposed to the privileges and beliefs of traditional societies. They no longer dreamed of a utopian society enlightened by reason, but of escaping the stranglehold society and powers, either by taking refuge in the aesthetic experience, as the Germans have done so often since the end of the eighteenth century, or by following the example of the surrealists and Georges Bataille by breaking through the screen of consciousness in pursuit of a sexuality free from social norms. The world of the 1980s, with its appeals to economic rationalism or consumption in the North and to a threatened cultural identity in the South, was a world without intellectuals because they were so suspicious of the future.

Many, in Frankfurt and elsewhere, saw the emergence of the *consumer society* as a form of decadence. It is, however, of crucial importance because some parts of the world have seen the emergence of a 'positive' mode of thought, which can take a very mediocre form, just as the negative thought of the past could take the equally mediocre form of superstition and could sanctify human injustices. This form of thought, which appeared in the United States long before it did so in Japan and Europe, replaces guilt with desire, worries about salvation with the will to happiness, and surrender to the divine and natural order with the search for responsibility and solidarity.

The role of intellectuals is certainly not to become involved in the most commercialized forms of the consumer society. But nor is it their role to reject the consumer society as a whole or to despise demands emanating from those who have long been denied both consumption, freedom and education. They cannot ignore the fact that it can also take a higher form. Intellectuals who remain faithful to the heritage of the Enlightenment tend all too often to denounce mass society for its supposed vulgarity. They are content to denounce the poverty or the dangers of mass cultural consumption, and their talents are displayed in criticisms rather than proposals. This implies an extreme distrust of consciousness, which is in their view always a false consciousness. Their attitude is very similar to that of the Republican elite, which has always wanted to restrict power to educated or competent citizens, or even to qualified interpreters of the meaning of history. From Guizot to Lenin, many intellectuals have spoken in the name of an avant-garde. The bourgeoisie was the avant-garde of a people who could not acquire the education it needed at one fell swoop. The role of the revolutionary party was to enlighten the people and the masses who were trapped by ignorance, isolation and repression. Intellectuals have always tended to combine a desire to act in the name of the people with a distrust of government by the people.

As intellectuals become increasingly trapped in to antimodernism and adopt a purely critical stance, they exert a growing influence over the socio-cultural sector, and especially teachers and students. As their numbers increase, those in this sector are becoming discontented with their situation which is, in material terms, greatly inferior to that of their counterparts in the technico-economic sector. Yet at the same time, intellectuals are losing their influence over society as a whole. They have found it relatively easy to persuade the academic world, and even part of the press and the publishing industry, to accept their antimodernism, but they have been outflanked by the majority of people who spend more time watching television than reading books. Such people are well aware that rising standards of living have allowed them to acquire household appliances, to own a car, to have holidays and to give their children the university education that they could not afford for themselves. Do we have to view this mass culture and the influence of the media purely in terms of conformism and commodity consumption? That judgement is as crude as the claim that books written by intellectuals contain nothing but pointless obscurity and an off-putting jargon. It is in fact this mass culture, which is created and distributed mainly by television, that has provided a haven for a Subject which was persecuted and accused of every possible crime by 'high culture'. The return of the Subject can take very commercial forms, but it can also give rise to emotions, solidarity movements and discussions about the greatest problems of human life: birth, love, reproduction, sickness, death, relations between men and women, parents and children, majorities and minorities, and between the planet's rich and poor. The door was closed on social problems which are of no interest to those who reduce everything to interest or to those who talk of nothing but culture. But they are now coming back through the window of television, where the problems of education, health, immigration and many other issues are often discussed with greater competence and passion than in parliaments and universities.

Rather than turning their backs on this mass culture, intellectuals should be releasing its creativity and preventing it from being used for purely commercial purposes. They should be protecting it from demagogy and confusion. This presupposes the demolition of the barriers which all too often cut the educated off from the rest of the population. It further presupposes that students must overcome the divorce between vocational training and a general culture that is steeped in antimodernism or clings to an academicism which is domineering rather than open to lived experience. The role of the intellectuals should be to promote the emergence of the Subject by increasing individuals' will and capacity to be the actors of their own lives. The Subject comes in to conflict with the dominant logic of the system, which reduces it to being a consumer and to defending its own interests in a changing environment; the Subjet is also threatened by the flight from the social field and its diversity in to the artificial homogeneity of a communitarian tradition or in to a religious faith. The main task of the intellectuals is to build the alliance between the Subject, reason, freedom and justice. How can they not speak in the name of reason, when reason is their only defence against money, power and intolerance? How can they not defend the Subject, or the individual's autonomous thought and action, against enforced orders, inherited taboos and conformism of all kinds?

The lower intelligentsia which speaks in the name of the individual and human rights must take the place of an upper intelligentsia which speaks of nothing but the meaning of History. For too long intellectuals have allowed themselves to be seduced by powers which claimed to be the agents of reason; we must now ask those who have served tyrants to remain silent, and ask the others to do more to defend freedom against power. We must ask them to defend the authenticity of personal and collective demands against the clear conscience of the well-to-do. It will be more difficult to change the role of the intellectual in France than it is elswhere, as French intellectuals identify closely with the principles of reason and their realization in history. All the philosophies of history that display so little interest in the freedom of individuals, minorities and even majorities, have now been discredited, as have the princes they once served. Their organic intellectuals no longer inspire confidence. It is those who have been able to resist tyranny who have won the respect of the masses: the dissidents and witnesses, the victims of massacres, imprisonment and exile who are so often despised by those who repect nothing but reason, even when it becomes reason of State. Their exemplary behaviour means a great deal to those who are more familiar with deprivation than programming, who are more touched by compassion than by triumphant rides through History. Intellectual life must halt the persecution of the Subject, which has been our major concern for so long, and learn not to create a dichotomy between meaning and consciousness or individuals and society.

Full Modernity

The long century that is now coming to an end was not simply a moment of sound and fury that followed the peaceful hopes of the eighteenth and nineteenth centuries. The upheavals we have lived through have been so momentous that no one can dream of a return to the calm waters of the philosophy of the Enlightenment, even if we do have a feeling that the French Revolution is over, as François Furet puts it (Furet 1978), and even though the celebration of its bicentenary remembered only the Declaration of the Rights of Man. In doing so, it concentrated on the links between the Revolution and the long tradition, both Christian and secularized, of natural law, and ignored everything that prefigured the age of revolutions, the formation of an absolute power, the Terror and the transition from the revolutionary spirit to the spirit of the police state. We are no more making the transition from modernity to post-modernity than we are going back to the equilibrium that was destroyed by the idea of progress and development. When we try to define the 200-year period that is now drawing to a close, we have to describe it as a period of *limited modernity*. According to modernist definitions, society is the product of its own activity. The self-styled 'modern period' was therefore only partly modern. It did not completely sever the link between social life and the world order. It believed in history, just as earlier periods believed in divine creation or in communal foundation myths. At the same time, it attempted to see the social functionality or dysfunctionality of modes of behaviour as the foundations of good and evil. Whilst humanity was no longer ruled by the laws of the universe or the law of God, it was still ruled by the law of history, reason or society. The network of correspondences between man and the universe was not broken. This semi-modernity still dreamed of building a world which would be natural because it was rational.

The crisis of modernity, which some see as a break with secularization and trust in reason, can more accurately be described as a transition to a more complete modernity. This modernity is casting off all the ropes that still moor it to the quayside of a natural, divine or historical order of things. In the era of limited modernity, human beings mistook themselves for gods. Intoxicated with their own power, they imprisoned themselves in an iron cage. Its bars were not created by technology, but by an absolute power, by a despotism which aspired to modernization and which became totalitarian. From the mid nineteenth century onwards, the idea of modernity was increasingly concealed behind that of modernization, and by the mobilization of non-economic and non-modern resources in an attempt to promote development, despite the fact that development must be either spontaneous or endogenous. These tendencies combined to erase the early image of modernity, which derived all its strength from its liberating role. As the old regimes fell in to decay or were overthrown, the liberation movements became exhausted and modern society found that it was a prisoner of, on the one hand, its own might and, on the other, of the historical and cultural conditions of its realization. As we reach the end of the twentieth century modernity is vanishing, crushed by its own agents. It is no more than an accelerated avant-gardism that is turning in to a directionless postmodernity. The crisis in proto-modernity has given birth to both the games of post-modernity, the horrors of the totalitarian world and the full modernity we are now entering.

It would be more accurate to say that modern society is now faced with a choice. It can surrender completely to the logic of instrumental action and market demands. It can pursue the process of secularization to the point of suppressing every image of the Subject. It can simply try to reconcile instrumental rationality and mass consumption with the memory of inherited traditions and a sexuality freed from social norms. The alternative is to combine rationalization with subjectivation, efficiency with freedom. If we also recall that the defence of communities and the mobilization of nations is now the dominant trend in many parts of the world, it becomes clear that our second alternative is equidistant from extreme utilitarianism and the obsessive search for an identity. Reason is not reducible to self-interest or the market when it inspires the productivist spirit, and the Subject is not reducible to a community or collective Ego when it calls for a freedom which is inseparable from the critical work of reason. Liberalism and culturalism can once more be seen as decayed elements of our shattered modernity. This modernity exists only by reconciling reason and the Subject. The combination is conflict-ridden, but the conflict is one between forces which share the same reference to human creativity and which reject all essences and all principles of order.

Modernity achieved no longer uses conformity to the law of God or social utility as a criterion for evaluating modes of behaviour; its only goal is *happiness*. A happy individual is one who is aware of being a subject and of being recognized as capable of social actions designed to heighten his or her awareness of being free and creative. This personal happiness is inseparable from the desire to make others happy, from involvement in their quest for happiness and from compassion for their unhappiness. The realization of modernity requires the dissolution of the shadows of guilt and the hopes placed in a redemption which can take a political form as easily as a religious form. Purely critical modes of thought, which are inseparable from the negation of the Subject, are always hostile to modernity, and are often inspired by a combination of antimodernism and nostalgia for Being. On the other hand, whilst we must be wary of modes of thought which merely call for integration through consumption and for a consensus based upon the suppression of conflicts, perhaps the time has come to accept happiness. It is the need to reconcile reason with the Subject, which have been contrasted with one another for so long that the modern world is becoming a world of women. Men identified themselves with reason, as opposed to sentiments, interiority and tradition. As the research carried out in Italy by Simonetta Tabboni (1992) demonstrates, 'modern' women want both to control the instruments of reason and experience the joy of being Subjects, body and soul. Modernity is no longer satisfied with the spirit of conquest and its asceticism. It has no time for nostalgia for equilibrium, community and homogeneity. Modernity is freedom and labour, community and individuality, order and mobility. It is reuniting things that have long been separated and is struggling against a possible divorce between technology and identity that would now be more dangerous than ever before.

Curriculum Vitae

Are these ideas an extension of those expounded in my previous books, or do they contradict them?

I have given the name 'historicity' to the set of cultural models a society uses to produce its norms in the domains of knowledge, production and ethics. Cultural models are the issues at stake in conflicts between social movements which attempt to give them a social form consistent with the interests of various social categories. The formulation is clearly historicist. It does not take in to consideration the general problems of the social order and democracy. Unlike political philosophy, it defines a society in terms of its work, its production and its capacity to act on itself. It therefore refers to industrial society – and then post-industrial society – and not to society in general. It is obviously influenced by Marxist thought or, more simply, Marxist-influenced economic and social history. The sociology I have produced is part of modernist thought. And I now consider that it is as impossible to abandon the view that society is the product of its own cultural or economic investments as it is to abandon the idea of the Subject. The idea of a social movement is based upon a historicist approach, but it also refers to the Subject, or in other words to the freedom and creativity of a social actor who is in danger of becoming dependent upon, or alienated by, the dominant forces that are transforming him in to an agent of either their own will or a necessity which is regarded as natural. We therefore have to turn our backs on the theories of Marx and Lukács, for whom actors are important only when they are agents of historical necessity.

When I speak of historicity, I am speaking of the creation of a historical experience, and not of a position in historical evolution or in the development of spirit or the productive forces. Perhaps I was wrong to borrow a term and distort its original meaning, but my choice of terminology reflected a conscious decision to break with an evolutionist vision.

Yes, my faith in history is now exhausted and I can no longer identify the individual with the worker or the citizen. Yes, I am more afraid of the totalitarian State and of all apparatuses of power than of a capitalism which has been made more civilized by two generations of the Welfare State. Yes, I prefer democracy, even when it does not do away with injustice, to revolutions which always establish an absolute power. There are many reasons why the man I am today is not identical with the man who went to university shortly after the war. But that does not prevent me from seeing a great continuity in my own life. I am also becoming more and more clearly aware that I am part of a tradition and that my work has been influenced by St Augustine and Descartes, by the Declaration of the Rights of Man and certain militants in the labour movement, by the modernizing intellectuals of Latin America, and by Solidarity. They all resisted the established order in the name of a non-social principle of protest and action – which has to be described as spiritual, even in the case of Locke's disciples. They all accept and defend modernity, which is inseparable from rationalization, but challenge the arrogance of technological and administrative action by promoting the resistance, dissidence and freedom of the human subject.

I analysed the workers' movement as the defence of working-class autonomy against scientific management, and thus made a distinction between the workers' movement and the socialism that is influenced by a historicist faith in progress (Touraine 1965, 1966). I then defined

post-industrial society as a society in which the production of material
goods gives way to the production of cultural goods, and in which
the primary conflict is one between the defence of the Subject and the
logic of the system of production, consumption and communication
(Touraine 1969). I now define modernity in terms of subjectivation as
well as rationalization. This development was inevitable, given that I
took part in protests and demonstrations against colonial wars being
waged by my own country when I was a young adult, and then
sensed a fraternity with the intellectuals and workers who rejected
communist dictatorships in Budapest in 1956, in Prague in 1968 and
in Gdansk in 1980. My analysis of May 1968 showed that an archaic
ideology was masking the emergence of new forms of protest which
appealed to the personality and to culture rather than self-interest
(Touraine 1968). I defended those movements, and then the Latin
Americans who were fighting against injustice and dictatorships not
by launching hyper-Leninist guerrilla wars, but by calling for democracy (Touraine 1973b). The idea of a social movement, which has so
often been central to my work, is radically different to the idea of
class struggle. The latter appeals to the logic of history, whereas the
former appeals to the freedom of the Subject, even if that means
rejecting the pseudo-laws of history.

I am not unaware of the fact that a discourse which refers to ethics
or the freedom of the Subject may be short-lived. It will, however,
last longer than a discourse which appeals to history and reason. And
it is less dangerous. It now seems to me that a consumer society
which eliminates the idea of the Subject is just as unsatisfactory as the
neo-communitarian regimes which transform believers in to a political
police. If we are to avoid both Charybdis and Scylla we have to keep
our distance, or in other words defend human beings regardless of
their social roles and loyalties. We have to gamble on their capacity
for consciousness and resistance. The century that is now drawing to
a close has been too violent for us to place our trust in history or
progress. It tells us, in soft but convincing tones, that we must open
up individual and collective clearings in the forest of technologies,
rules and consumer goods, and that freedom is preferable to all of
them.

Some will say that my ideas are as fragile and as ephemeral as the
new social movements I tried to theorize at the end of the 1960s
(Touraine 1968). How, they ask, can we fail to recognize that those
movements lasted no longer than the political sects of nineteenth-
century utopian socialism, or that the appeal to the Subject simply
hides the fact that there are no real social and political actors? Some
of my critics have pointed out that whilst reliance upon God, the cult

of reason or appeals to a history are certainly fraught with danger, not least in that they may lead to a repressive theocracy in particular, they have mobilized whole nations and classes. They claim that my appeal to the Subject is no more than a faded copy of those great uprisings, or a moralistic expression of the worries of a new middle class which is more concerned with security than conflict, order than change. These criticisms are a travesty of the facts. The demise of the political programmes and apparatuses that have dominated the last hundred years is opening up an already crowded space for ethical principles and truly social movements, but those who are still looking in the opposite direction – towards the fading lights and noise of industrial society – cannot see it.

My way of thinking, like other and sometimes contradictory modes of thought, is an attempt to discover the meaning of not only new ideas, but practices of all kinds, individual and collective, which reveal the issues, actors and conflicts of a new world. Our world is dominated by strategies for making profits or gaining power, but it is also alive with liberating utopias, communitarian defences, erotic images, humanitarian campaigns, attempts to catch the eye of the other. These are the scattered fragments that will together construct a Subject which can reconcile reason and freedom, intimacy and community, commitment and non-commitment. This book has been devoted to the reconstruction of the figure of the Subject. The Subject will never be transformed in to a monument unless it disappears from history. It does not belong to the history of ideas, which is no more than part of social and cultural history, because the meaning of human behaviour is as present in day-to-day practices and organized collective actions, as in artistic and intellectual creations. There are enough discourses and new practices to convince us that we have left behind historicist thought, industrial society and the ideologies that accompanied capitalist or socialist accumulation; has not the time come to admit that we have entered our full modernity and to recognize that we live in a place and time characterized by the appearance of new social actors, a new culture and new lived experiences?

Present Position

We no longer have any faith in progress. We no longer believe that greater prosperity will lead to democratization and happiness. The liberating image of reason has given way to the disturbing theme of a rationalization which concentrates the power to take decisions at the top. We are increasingly afraid that growth will destroy basic natural equilibria, that it will lead to increased inequality on a world scale and that it will involve everyone in an exhausting process of continuous change. These worries mask the underlying fear that humanity is breaking off its alliance with nature and reverting to savagery just when it thought it had been freed from all constraints and was in control of its own destiny. Some miss traditional society, and its codes, hierarchies and rites. This is a common reaction in countries where modernization came from outside, or was imported by settlers or an enlightened despot. Others are reverting to either a secular or a religious form of the rationalist worldview which called upon human beings to cultivate reason, whose laws are the same as the laws that govern the universe. Knowledge, they say, sets us free from the passions, as well as from ignorance and poverty. Science gives man power only if he submits to the objective laws of the world. This attitude is found mainly in countries and social categories which have played a central role in a development defined primarily in terms of rationalization. Others believe mainly in the social order. They may not believe in the defence of vested interests or privileges, but they do believe in the pursuit of the common good, and they usually see society as a natural, mechanical or organic system whose laws, like those of natural phenomena, must be discovered and respected. All these arguments have something in common. They are all attempts to reconstruct a social order which is natural and to bring human beings in to harmony with the world by obeying the dictates of reason.

Sociology has always played an important role in this quest for a lost unity. Sociology came in to being in France, and was born of the constant attempts of Comte and Durkheim to reconcile modernity with social and cultural integration. Now that anticapitalist and anti-imperialist social movements have been perverted in to totalitarian regimes, many people are openly turning to the past and replacing modernity's social science with a political philosophy. Its concerns are depicted by Ambrogio Lorenzetti's fresco series in the town hall in Sienna: *Good and Bad Government*. Social categories are being subordinated to the categories of political and ethical analysis. The trajectory taken by so many thinkers of modernity from Tocqueville to Marx is now being inverted.

Yet none of these answers can eradicate the divorce between man and nature, which we experience both as a liberation and as a threat. Our collective might has become so great that we no longer know what it means to live in harmony with nature: almost everything – our food, our machines, our games – is a product of science and technology, and almost no one wants to put an end to the race for scientific discovery from which we expect new benefits. At the same time, we have the feeling that power is everywhere and that society is governed not so much by legally- and ethically-based institutions as by the demands of economic competition, the programmes of the planners, and advertising campaigns. Society, which means both technology and power, a division of labour and a concentration of resources, is becoming increasingly estranged from the values and demands of social actors. The idea of a mass or consumer society has replaced that of industrial society because it acknowledges the divorce between the worlds of production and consumption, whereas industrial society still defined human beings as workers, and in that sense defined them in the same terms as the system of production.

We no longer perceive the existence of a society organized around political institutions. We see centres of economic, political and military administration on the one hand, and the private world of needs on the other. There no longer seems to be any correspondence between actor and system. We no longer belong to a society, a social class or a nation to the extent that our lives are in part determined by the world market, and in part confined to a world of personal life, interpersonal relations and cultural traditions. Daniel Bell (1976) rightly worries about the decline of societies in which production, consumption and political management are separate worlds governed by conflicting norms. Whilst the market is replacing social norms and cultural values with competition, an obsession with identity is replacing involvement in society at the personal level and our societies are becoming increasingly unco-ordinated sets of collectivities, subcultures and individuals. Given that both collective and individual identity is fragile in a world which is exposed to market forces, there is now a no-man's-land between the market and private life. In it, we can still see the ruins of public life, but violence is on the increase as socialization declines.

What can we do to remedy a situation in which nostalgia for the One and the world order seems pointless and where the complete divorce between actor and system leads to the coexistence of a savage subjectivity and an enforced order, but not to their integration? The book you have just read attempts to provide an answer. It traces the decline of the Christian and Cartesian dualism which was repressed by the optimistic materialism of the enlightenment and then repressed even more severely by the philosophies of Progress. It then describes the antimodernist reaction against historicism that takes us from Nietzsche to the Frankfurt School and Michel Foucault. Having examined the break between a rationalist neo-liberalism which believes only in change, and a post-modernist subjectivity which cobbles together signs from past cultures, it finally puts forward the idea that the only way to avoid the fragmentation of modern society is to recognize that modernity is not based upon rationalization alone. From the very outset, it was defined by the divorce – and the complementarity – between reason and the Subject and, more specifically, between rationalization and subjectivation. Rather than taking the view that technical and economic rationality are increasingly destroying subjectivity, this book demonstrates how modernity produces the Subject, which is synonymous with neither the individual nor the role-set that is constructed by the social organization. The subject is the labour through which an individual transforms him or herself in to an actor, or in other words an actor capable of transforming a situation rather than reproducing it through his mode of behaviour.

These considerations do not originate from sociology in the strict sense of the term, but from the work of Freud. In both his theory and his practice, Freud attempts to overcome the crude distinction between the *Es* and the *Über-Ich* and to discover the foundations for an *Ich*. And for someone who so constantly denounces the illusions of the Ego and consciousness the *Ich* is inevitably an I.

The appeal to the Subject can turn against rationalism and can degenerate in to an obsession with identity or confinement in a community. It can also be a will to freedom, and can ally itself with reason to the extent that reason is a critical force. In similar fashion, reason can identify with the management apparatuses which control flows of money, decisions and information, and it can also destroy the Subject and the meaning that individuals try to give to their actions. But it can also ally itself with the social movements that are trying to defend the Subject against a concentration of resources which corresponds to a logic or power, and not the logic of reason.

The precise answer supplied by this book is that whilst reason and the subject can become estranged or mutually hostile, they can also unite, and that the agent of their union is the social movement, or in other words the transformation of the personal and collective defence of the Subject in to a collective action directed against power, which subordinates reason to its own interests. It is therefore possible to reanimate a social space which seemed to have been emptied of all content, or to have been squeezed between an internationalized economy and a privatized culture. Just as the old definition of social life as a set of correspondences between institutions and mechanisms of socialization was definitively destroyed by modernity triumphant, so the real content of modernity increasingly depends upon the ability of social movements which assert the presence of the Subject to roll back the power of ruling groups. Part III of this book is constructed around the identification of the notions of Subject and social movement.

The history of modernity is the history of *the twofold affirmation of reason and the Subject,* and it began with the split between the Renaissance and the Reformation, which not even Erasmus could overcome. Successive social movements – the revolutionary bourgeoisie, the workers' movement and then new social movements whose goals are cultural rather than economic – represent an increasingly direct call for the reconciliation of reason and the Subject. And that implies a divorce between reason and the Subject and between the subject and the individual.

These conclusions preclude any return to a philosophy of the social order or of history, even though we all feel the need for social integration, irrespective of whether we define it in religious, political or juridical terms. That is the price we have to pay for protection against all the totalitarian temptations that have swept through the world for almost a century and which have covered it with concentration camps, holy wars and political propaganda. Modernity resists all forms of totality. Modernity is a dialogue between reason and the Subject, and it can never be broken off or brought to an end because it keeps open the road to freedom.

Bibliography

Where two dates are given, the first is that of the original publication; the second that of the translation or the edition used here.

Adorno, Theodor W., Else Frankel-Brunswick, Daniel J. Levinson and R. Sanford (1950), *The Authoritarian Personality*, New York: Harper.

Albert, Michel (1991), *Capitalisme contre capitalisme*, Paris: Seuil.

Alquié, Ferdinand (1950), *La Découverte métaphysique de l'âme chez Descartes*, Paris: PUF.

Ardigo, Achille (1988), *La Sociologia oltre il post-moderno*, Bologna: Il Mulino.

Arendt, Hannah (1954), *Between Past and Future: Six Exercises in Political Thought*, London: Faber, 1961.

Ariès, Philippe (1960), *Centuries of Childhood*, London: Jonathan Cape, 1962.

Aron, Raymond (1961), *Dimensions de la conscience historique*, Paris: Plon.

Aron, Raymond (1969), *Les Désillusions du progrès. Essai sur la dialectique de la modernité*, Paris: Calmman-Lévy.

Atlan, Henri (1979), *Entre le cristal et la fumée. Essais sur l'organisation du vivant*, Paris: Seuil.

Atlan, Henri (1991), *Tout, non, peut-être*, Paris: Seuil.

Augustine St (400), *Confessions*, tr. R. S. Pine-Coffin, Harmondsworth: Penguin, 1961.

Badinter, Elisabeth (1980), *L'Amour en plus*, Paris: Flammarion.

Balandier, Georges (1985), *Le Détour: pouvoir et modernité*, Paris: Fayard.

Barel, Yves (1984), *La Société du vide*, Paris: Seuil.

Baudelaire, Charles (1863), *Le Peintre de la vie moderne*, in *Curiosités esthétiques: L'Art romantique*, Paris: Garnier, 1962.

Baudrillard, Jean (1972), *For a Critique of the Political Economy of the Sign*, tr. Charles Levin, St Louis: Telos, 1981.

Baudrillard, Jean (1977), *Forget Foucault*, tr. S. Lotringer, New York: Semiotext(e), 1987.

Baudrillard, Jean (1978), *In the Shadow of the Silent Majorities*, tr. Paul Foss, Paul Patton and John Johnson, New York: Semiotext(e), 1983.

Beck, Ulrich (1982), *Risk Society: Towards a New Modernity*, tr. Mark Ritter, London: Sage, 1992.

Bell, Daniel (1976), *The Cultural Contradictions of Capitalism*, London: Heinemann.

Bellah, Robert, et al. (1985), *Habits of the Heart: Individualism and Commitment in American Life*, Berkeley: University of California Press.

Beneton, Philippe (1987), *Introduction – la politique moderne*, Paris: Hachette.

Benichou, Paul (1948), *Morales du grand siècle*, Paris: Gallimard.

Benjamin, Walter (1982), *Paris, Capitale du XIXe siècle. Le Livre des passages, 1927–29, 1934–40*, Paris: Cerf, 1989.

Berlin, Isaiah (1969), *Four Essays on Liberty*, Oxford: Oxford University Press.

Berlin, Isaiah (1991), *The Crooked Timber of Humanity*, New York: Knopf.

Berman, Marshall (1970), *The Politics of Authenticity: Radical Individualism and the Emergence of Modern Society*, New York: Athenaum.

Berman, Marshall (1983), *All that is Solid Melts in to Air: The Experience of Modernity*, London: Verso.

Bernstein, Richard, ed. (1985), *Habermas and Modernity*, Cambridge, Mass.: MIT Press.

Besnard, Philippe (1970), *Protestantisme et capitalisme*, Paris: Colin.

Birnbaum, Pierre (1975), *La Fin du politique*, Paris: Seuil.

Birnbaum, Pierre (1982), *La Logique de l'Etat*, Paris: Fayard.

Birnbaum, Pierre and Jean Leca, eds (1982), *Sur L'Individualisme*, Paris: Presses de la Fondation Nationale des Sciences Politiques.

Bloch, Ernst (1962), *Heritage of our Time*, tr. Neville and Stephen Plaice, Cambridge: Polity.

Bloom, Allan (1987), *The Closing of the American Mind*, New York: Simon and Schuster.

Bobbio, Norberto (1984), *The Future of Democracy*, tr. Roger Griffin, Cambridge: Polity, 1987.

Bouretz, Pierre, ed. (1991), *La Force du droit: panorama des débats contemporains*, Paris: Seuil.

Bremond, Henri (1967), *Histoire littéraire du sentiment religieux en France depuis la fin des guerres de religion: l'humanisme dévot*, Paris: Armand Colin.

Brubaker, R. (1984), *The Limits of Rationality: An Essay on the Social and Moral Thought of Max Weber*, London: Allen and Unwin.

Burlamaqui, J.-J. (1751), *Eléments de droit naturel*, Paris: PUF, 1983.

Camus, Albert (1947), *The Plague*, tr. Stuart Gilbert, London: Hamish Hamilton, 1948.

Cassirer, Ernst (1932), *The Philosophy of the Enlightenment*, tr. Fritz C. A. Koelln and James P. Pettegrove, Princeton, NJ: Princeton University Press, 1951.

Castells, Manuel (1983), *The City and the Grass-Roots*, London: Edward Arnold.

Castoriadis, Cornélius (1975), *The Imaginary Institution of Society*, tr. Kathleen Blamey, Cambridge: Polity, 1987.

Castoriadis, Cornélius (1984), 'The State of the Subject Today', *Thesis Eleven* 24.

Castoriadis, Cornélius (1989), *Le Monde morcelé: Les Carrefours du labyrinthe III*, Paris: Seuil.

Cazeneuve, Jean (1980), *Sociologie de la radio-télévision*, Paris: PUF.

CFDT (1977), *Les Dégâts du progrès: Les Ouvriers face au changement technique*, Paris: Seuil.

Chartier, Roger (1990), *Les Origines culturelles de la Révolution française*, Paris: Seuil.

Claudel, Paul (1929), *Le Soulier de satin*, Paris: Gallimard.

Cohen, Jean and Andrew Arato (1992), *Civil Society and Political Theory*, Cambridge, Mass.: MIT Press.

Colin, Pierre and Olivier Mongin, eds (1988), *Un Monde désenchanté? Débat avec Marcel Gauchet*, Paris: CERF.

Colletti, Lucio (1969), *From Rousseau to Lenin: Studies in Ideology and Society*, tr. John Merrington and Judith White, London: NLB, 1972.

Collier, David, ed. (1979), *The New Authoritarianism in Latin America*, Princeton: Princeton University Press.

Comte, Auguste (1844), *Discours sur l'esprit positif*, Paris: Vrin, 1983.

Comte, Auguste (1849a), *Discours sur l'ensemble du positivisme*, Paris.

Comte, Auguste (1849b), *Catéchisme positiviste*, Paris: Garnier, 1909.

Comte, Auguste (1851–4), *Système de politique positive*, Paris: Anthropos, 1968–71.

Condorcet, Marquis de (1795), *Esquisse d'un tableau historique des progrès de l'esprit humain*, Paris: Flammarion, 1988.

Crozier, Michel (1979), *On ne change pas la société par décret*, Paris: Grasset.

Crozier, Michel (1987), *Etat moderne, état modeste. Stratégies pour un autre changement*, Paris: Fayard.

Crozier, Michel and E. Friedberg (1977), *L'Acteur et le système. Les Contraintes de l'action collective*, Paris: Seuil.

Daraki, Maria (1981), 'L'Emergence du subject singulier dans les *Confessions d'Augustin*', *Esprit* 2.

Debray, Régis (1967), *Revolution in the Revolution?*, tr. Bobbye Ortiz, Harmondsworth: Penguin, 1968.

Debray, Régis (1989), 'Etes-vous démocrate ou républicain?', *Le Nouvel Observateur*, 30 November.

Delannnoi, Gil and Pierre-André Taguieff, eds (1991), *Théories du nationalisme*, Paris: Kimé.

Deleuze, Gilles (1962), *Nietzsche et la philosophie*, Paris: PUF.

Derathe, Robert (1950), *Jean-Jacques Rousseau et la science politique de son temps*, Paris: Vrin.

Descartes, René (1637), *Discourse on the Method*, tr. Robert Stoothoff, in *The Philosophical Writings of Descartes*: volume 1, Cambridge: Cambridge University Press, 1985.

Descartes, René (1641), *Meditations on First Philosophy, with Selections from the Objections and Replies*, tr. John Collingham, Cambridge: Cambridge University Press, 1986.

Descartes, René (1649) *The Passions of the Soul*, tr. Robert Stoothoff, in *The Philosophical Writings*, Cambridge: Cambridge University Press, 1986.

Diani, Marco, ed. (1992), *The Immaterial Society. Design, Culture and Technology in the Post-Modern*, Englewood Cliffs: Prentice-Hall.

Dreyfus, Hubert and Paul Rabinow (1982), *Michel Foucault: Beyond Structuralism and Hermeneutics*, Hemel Hempstead: Harvester.

Dubet, François (1987), *La Galère. Jeunes en survie*, Paris: Seuil.

Dubet, François (1991), *Les Lycéens*, Paris: Seuil.

Dubuffet, Jean (1991), *Lettres – J. B. 1946–1985*, Paris: Hermann.

Dumont, Louis (1977), *Homo Aequalis I. Génèse et épanouissement de l'idéologie économique*, Paris: Gallimard.

Dumont, Louis (1983), *Essai sur l'individualisme. Une Perspective anthropologique sur l'idéologie moderne*, Paris: Seuil.

Dumont, Louis (1991), *Homo aequalis II. L'idéologie allemande. France–Allemagne et retour*, Paris: Gallimard.

Duras, Marguerite (1984), *The Lover*, tr. Barbara Bray, London: Bloomsbury, 1993.

Durkheim, Emile (1925), *Moral Education: A Study in the Theory and Application of the Sociology of Education*, tr. Everett K. Wilson and Herman Schnurer, New York: Free Press, 1961.

Durkheim, Emile (1928), *Montesquieu and Rousseau: Forerunners of Sociology*, tr. Ralph Mannheim, Ann Arbor: Ann Arbor Paperbacks.

Ehrard, Jean (1970), *L'Idée de la nature – l'aube des Lumières*, Paris: Flammarion.

Eisenstadt, Shmuel N. (1968), *The Protestant Ethic and Modernization: A Comparative View*, New York and London: Basic Books.

Erikson, Erik K. (1971), *Identity: Youth and Crisis*, London: Faber.

Featherstone, M., ed. (1988a), *Post-Modernism*, London: Sage.

Featherstone, M. (1988b), 'In Pursuit of the Post-Modern: An Introduction', *Theory, Culture and Society* 5.

Febvre, Lucien (1928), *Un Destin: Martin Luther*, Paris: Rieder.

Ferry, Jean-Marc (1987), *Habermas: l'éthique de la communication*, Paris: PUF.

Ferry, Jean-Marc and Alain Renault (1986), *68–86: Itinéraires de l'individu*, Paris: Gallimard.

Finkielkraut, Alain (1987), *La Défaite de la pensée*, Paris: Gallimard.

Fleishmann, Eugen (1964), *La Philosophie politique de Hegel*, Paris: Plon.

Foster, Hal, ed. (1983), *The Anti-Aesthetic: Essays on Post-Modern Culture*, Seattle: B Press.

Foster, Hal, ed. (1985), *Post-Modern Culture*, London: Pluto.

Foucault, Michel (1975), *Discipline and Punish: The Birth of the Prison*, tr. Alan Sheridan, London: Allen Lane, 1977.

Foucault, Michel (1976), *The History of Sexuality. Volume 1: An Introduction*, tr. Robert Hurley, London: Allen Lane, 1979.

Foucault, Michel (1984a), *The History of Sexuality. Volume 2: The Use of Pleasure*, tr. Robert Hurley, New York: Pantheon, 1986.

Foucault, Michel (1984b), *The History of Sexuality. Volume 3: The Care of the Self*, tr. Robert Hurley, New York: Pantheon, 1986.

Fourastié, Jean (1950), *Le Grand Espoir du XXe siècle*, Paris: PUF, second edn.

Freud, Sigmund (1913), *Totem and Taboo*, in *The Origins of Religion*, Harmondsworth: Penguin, 1985.

Freud, Sigmund (1914), 'On Narcissism: An Introduction', in *On Metapsychology: The Theory of Psychoanalysis*, Harmondsworth: Penguin, 1984.

Freud, Sigmund (1915), 'Papers on Metapsychology', in *On Metapsychology*. Harmondsworth: Penguin, 1984.

Freud, Sigmund (1920), *Beyond the Pleasure Principle*, in *On Metapsychology*, Harmondsworth: Penguin, 1984.

Freud, Sigmund (1921), 'Group Psychology and the Analysis of the Ego', in *Civilization, Society and Religion*, Harmondsworth: Penguin, 1985.

Freud, Sigmund (1923), *The Ego and the Id*, in *On Metapsychology*, Harmondsworth: Penguin, 1984.

Freud, Sigmund (1925), 'An Autobiographical Study', in *Historical and Expository Works on Psychoanalysis*, Harmondsworth: Penguin, 1986.

Freud, Sigmund (1929), *Civilization and its Discontents*, in *Civilization, Society and Religion*, Harmondsworth: Penguin, 1985.

Freud, Sigmund (1933), *New Introductory Lectures in Psychoanalysis*, Harmondsworth: Penguin, 1973.

Freud, Sigmund (1939), *Moses and Monotheism*, in *The Origins of Religion*, Harmondsworth, Penguin, 1985.

Friedmann, Georges (1936), *La Crise du progrès*, Paris: Gallimard.

Friedmann, Georges (1963), *Où va le travail humain?* , Paris: Gallimard.

Friedmann, Georges (1966), *Sept Etudes sur l'homme et la technique*, Paris: Gonthier-Médiations.

Friedmann, Georges (1970), *La Puissance et la sagesse*, Paris: Gallimard.

Friedmann, Georges (1987), *Journal de guerre 39–40*, Paris: Gallimard

Fromm, Erich (1942), *The Fear of Freedom*, London: Paul.

Fukuyama, Francis (1992), *The End of History and the Last Man*, London: Hamish Hamilton.

Furet, François (1978), *Interpreting the French Revolution*, tr. Elborg Foster, Cambridge and Paris: Cambridge University Press and Editions de la Maison des Sciences de l'Homme.

Furet, François (1988), *La Révolution 1770–1880. Histoire de la France, vol. IV*, Paris: Hachette.

Furet, François and Mona Ozouf (1988), *Dictionnaire critique de la Révolution française*, Paris: Flammarion.

Gauchet, Marcel (1983), *Le Désenchantement du monde: Une Histoire politique de la religion*, Paris: Gallimard.

Gauchet, Marcel (1988), *La Révolution des droits de l'homme*, Paris: Gallimard.

Gauchet, Marcel and Gladys Swain (1980), *La Pratique de l'esprit humain: l'institution asilaire et la pratique démocratique*, Paris: Gallimard.

Gaudemar, Jean-Paul de (1982), *L'Ordre et la production: naissance et formes de la discipline d'usine*, Paris: Dunod.

Gellner, Ernest (1983), *Nations and Nationalism*, Oxford: Blackwell.

Giacometti, Alberto (1990), *Ecrits*, Paris: Hermann.

Giddens, Anthony (1990), *The Consequences of Modernity*, Cambridge: Polity.

Giddens, Anthony (1992), *Modernity and Self-Identity: Self and Society in the Late Modern Age*, Cambridge: Polity.

Gierke, Otto (1960), *Natural Law and the Theory of Society 1500–1800*, Boston: Beacon Press.

Gilson, Etienne (1930), *Etudes sur le rôle de la pensée médiévale dans la formation du système cartésien*, Paris: Gallimard.

Goffman, Erving (1959), *The Presentation of Self in Everyday Life*, New York: Anchor.

Gorz, André (1980), *Farewell to the Working Class: An Essay on Post-Industrial Society*, tr. Michael Sonenscher, London: Pluto.

Gorz, André (1989), *Critique of Economic Reason*, tr. C Turner and G. Handyside, London: Verso.

Gouhier, Henri (1988), *La Philosophie d'Auguste Comte*, Paris: Vrin.

Goyard-Fabre, Simone (1972), *La Philosophie des Lumières en France*, Paris: Klincksieck.

Goyard-Fabre, Simone (1986), *John Locke et la raison raisonnable*, Paris: Vrin.

Groddeck, Georg (1923), *The Book of the It: Psychoanalytic Letters to a Friend*, London: C. W. Daniel, 1935.

Groethuysen, Bernard (1927), *Origines de l'esprit bourgeois en France. I: L'Eglise et la bourgeoisie*, Paris: Gallimard.

Groethuysen, Bernard (1949), *J.-J. Rousseau*, Paris: Gallimard.

Groethuysen, Bernard (1956), *Philosophie de la Révolution française*, Paris: Gallimard.

Habermas, Jürgen (1963) *Theory and Practice*, tr. John Viertel, Cambridge: Polity, 1976.

Habermas, Jürgen (1981), *Theory of Communicative Action*, tr. Thomas McCarthy, Cambridge: Polity, 1989, two vols.

Habermas, Jürgen (1983), *Moral Consciousness and Communicative Action*, tr. C. Lenhardt and S. W. Nicholsen, Cambridge: Polity, 1990.

Habermas, Jürgen (1985), *The Philosophical Discourse of Modernity: Twelve Lectures*, tr. Frederick G. Lawrence, Cambridge: Polity, 1987.

Halévy, Elie (1901–4), *La Formation du radicalisme philosophique: La Révolution et la doctrine de l'utilité 1789–1805*, Paris: Alcan.

Harré, Rom (1983), *Personal Being: A Theory for Individual Psychology*, Oxford: Blackwell.

Hazard, Paul (1935), *The European Mind 1680–1715*, tr. J. Lewis May, Harmondsworth: Pelican, 1964.

Hegel, G. W. F. (1807), *The Phenomenology of Mind*, tr. J. B. Baillie, New York: Harper Torchbooks, 1967.

Hegel, G. W. F. (1821), *Philosophy of Right*, tr. T. M. Knox, Oxford: Oxford University Press, 1967.

Heller, Agnes (1985), *The Power of Shame: A Rational Perspective*, London: Routledge.

Hobbes, Thomas (1651), *Leviathan*, Cambridge: Cambridge University Press, 1991.

Hobsbawm, Eric (1990), *Nations and Nationalism Since 1780: Programme, Myth, Reality*, Cambridge: Cambridge University Press.

Horkheimer, Max (1947), *The Eclipse of Reason*, New York: Seabury Press, 1974.

Horkheimer, Max and Theodor W. Adorno (1947), *Dialectic of Enlightenment*, London: Allen Lane, 1973.

Horkheimer, Max (1967), *Critique of Instrumental Reason*, New York: Seabury Press, 1974.

Hughes, Stuart (1958), *Consciousness and Society: The Orientation of European Social Thought*, New York: Random House.

Hyppolite, Jean (1944), *Introduction – la philosophie de l'histoire de Hegel*, Paris: Rivière.

Hyppolite, Jean (1955), *Etudes sur Marx et Hegel*, Paris: Rivière.

Jacob, Francis (1970), *The Logic of Living Systems: A History of Heredity*, tr. Betty E. Spillman, London: Allen Lane, 1983.

Jameson, Fredric (1991), *Postmodernism, or, the Cultural Logic of Late Capitalism*, London: Verso.

Jay, Martin (1973), *The Dialectical Imagination: A History of the Frankfurt School and the Institute for Social Research 1921–1950*, London: Heinemann.

Jay, Martin (1984), *Marxism and Totality. The Adventures of a Concept from Lukács to Habermas*, Berkeley: University of California Press.

Kant, Immanuel (1785), *Fundamental Principles of the Metaphysics of Morals*, tr. Thomas K. Abbott, Indianapolis and New York: Bobs-Merrill.

Kant, Immanuel (1788), *Critique of Practical Reason*, Chicago: Chicago University Press, 1949.

Kepel, Gilles (1991), *La Revanche de Dieu*, Paris: Seuil.

Khosrowkhavar, Farhad (1992), *Rupture de l'unamisme dans la révolution iranienne*, Doctorat ès lettres, unpublished.

Kohut, Heinz (1971), *The Analysis of the Self*, New York: International Universities Press.

Kohut, Heinz (1977), *The Restoration of the Self*, New York: International Universities Press.

Lacan, Jacques (1959), 'On a Question Preliminary to any Possible Treatment of Psychosis', in *Ecrits: A Selection*, tr. Alan Sheridan, London: Tavistock, 1977.

Lacan, Jacques (1960), 'The Subversion of the Subject and the Dialectic of Desire in the Freudian Unconscious', in *Ecrits: A Selection*, tr. Alan Sheridan, London: Tavistock, 1977.

Laclau, Ernesto (1979), *Politics and Ideology in Marxist Theory*, London: Verso.

Laing, Ronald D. (1960), *The Divided Self*, London: Tavistock.

Lapeyronnie, Didier (1992), *De l'Expérience – l'action*, Mémoire d'habilitation (unpublished), EHESS.

Lapeyronnie, Didier and Jean-Marie Louis (1992), *Campus Blues. Les Etudiants face – leurs études*, Paris: Seuil.

Laplanche, Jean and J.-B. Pontalis, *The Language of Psychoanalysis* (1967), tr. Donald Nicholson-Smith, London: The Hogarth Press and the Institute of Psychoanalysis, 1973.

Lasch, Christopher (1979), *The Culture of Narcissism*, New York: Norton.

Lasch, Christopher (1984), *The Minimal Self: Psychic Survival in Troubled Times*, New York: Norton.

Lash, Scott (1990), *Sociology of Post-Modernism*, London: Routledge.

Lash, Scott and Jonathan Friedman, eds (1972), *Modernity and Identity*, Oxford: Blackwell.

Lefort, Claude (1981), *L'Invention démocratique. Les Limites de la domination totalitaire*, Paris: Fayard.

Lefort, Claude (1986), *Democracy and Political Theory*, tr. David Macey, Cambridge: Polity, 1988.

Leites, Edward (1988), *The Puritan Conscience and Modern Sexuality*, New Haven: Yale University Press.

Leites, Edward (1986), *The Puritan Conscience and Modern Sexuality*, New Haven: Yale University Press.

Le Rider, Jacques (1990), *Modernité viennoise et crise de l'identité*, Paris: PUF.

Leites, Edward (1988), *The Puritan Conscience and Modern Sexuality*, New Haven: Yale University Press.

Lévi-Strauss, Claude (1971), 'Race and Culture', in *The View from Afar*, tr. Joachim Neugroschel and Phoebe Ross, Harmondsworth: Penguin, 1987.

Levinas, Emmanuel (1972), *Humanisme, de l'autre homme*, Paris: Livre de poche, 1988.

Lévy, Bernard-Henri (1991), *Les Aventures de la liberté*, Paris: Grasset.

Lewis, Geneviève (1950), *L'Individualité selon Descartes*, Paris: PUF.

Lipovetsky, Gilles (1983), *L'Ere du vide. Essais sur l'individualisme contemporain*, Paris: Gallimard.

Lipovetsky, Gilles (1987), *L'Empire de l'éphémère. La Mode et son destin dans les sociéés modernes*, Paris; Gallimard.

Lipset, Seymour Martin (1960), *Political Man: The Social Bases of Politics*, London: Heinemann.

Locke, John (1690a), *First Treatise of Government*, in *Two Treatises of Government*, Cambridge: Cambridge University Press, 1988.

Locke, John (1690b), *Second Treatise of Government*, in *Two Treatises*.

Locke, John (1690c), *Essay Concerning Human Understanding*, Oxford: Clarendon Press, 1975.

Löwenthal, Leo (1961), *Literature, Popular Culture and Society*, Englewood Cliffs: Prentice Hall.

Luhmann, Niklas (1984), *Soziale Systeme*, Frankfurt: Suhrkamp.

Lukács, Georg (1923), *History and Class Consciousness*, tr. Rodney Livingstone, London: Merlin, 1971.

Luther, Martin (1518), 'Heidelberg Disputation', tr. Harold J. Grimm, in *Luther's Works*, Philadelphia: Muhlenberg Press, vol. 31, 1960.

Luther, Martin (1525), 'The Bondage of the Will', tr. Philip S. Watson, in *Luther's Works*, vol. 33, 1972.

Luther, Martin (1536), 'The Disputation Concerning Man', tr. Lewis W. Spitz, in *Luther's Works*, vol. 33, 1972.

Lyotard, Jean-François (1979) *The Postmodern Condition*, tr. Geoff Bennington and Brian Massumi, Minneapolis: University of Minnesota Press, 1984.

Lyotard, Jean-François (1983), *The Differend: Phrases in Dispute*, tr. G. Van de Abeele, Minneapolis: University of Minnesota Press, 1988.

Lyotard, Jean-François (1986), *Le Post-moderne expliqué aux enfants*, Paris: Galilée.

MacIntyre, Alasdair (1981), *After Virtue*, London: Duckworth.

Maheu, Louis and Arnaud Sales, eds (1991), *Le Recomposition du politique*, Paris and Montréal: L'Harmattan and Presses de l'Université de Montréal.

Maffesoli, Michel (1988), *Le Temps des tribus*, Paris: Klinksieck.

Maldonaldo, Tomas (1987), *Il Futuro della modernita*, Milan: Feltrinelli.

Mallet, Serge (1963), *La Nouvelle Classe ouvrière*, Paris: Seuil.

Malraux, André (1937), *Man's Hope*, tr. Stuart Gilbert and Alastair MacDonald, New York: Grove Press, 1966.

Mandeville, Bernard de (1714), *The Fable of the Bees, or Private Vices, Public Virtues*, Harmondsworth: Pelican Classics, 1970.

Mandouze, André (1968), *Saint Augustin. L'Aventure de la raison et de la grâce*, Paris: Etudes Augustiniennes.

Manent, Pierre (1977), *Naissance de la politique moderne: Machiavel, Hobbes, Rousseau*, Paris: Payot.

Manent, Pierre (1987), *Histoire intellectuelle du libéralisme*, Paris: Calmann-Lévy.

Marcuse, Herbert (1941), *Reason and Revolution: Hegel and the Rise of Social Theory*, London: Routledge and Kegan Paul, 1955.

Marcuse, Herbert (1955), *Eros and Civilization*, London: Sphere, 1969.

Marcuse, Herbert (1964), *One Dimensional Man: The Ideology of Industrial Society*, London: Sphere, 1968.

Margolin, Jean-Claude (1965), *Erasme par lui-même*, Paris: Seuil.

Marshall, T. H. (1950), *Citizenship and Social Class*, Cambridge: Cambridge University Press.

Marx, Karl (1844), 'Economic and Philosophical Manuscripts', in *Early Writings*, tr. Rodney Livingstone and Gregor Benton, Harmondsworth: Penguin Books in association with *New Left Review*, 1975: 179–400.

Marx, Karl (1845), 'Concerning Feuerbach', in *Early Writings*: 421–3.

Marx, Karl (1845–6), *The German Ideology*, in Karl Marx and Frederick Engels, *Collected Works*, vol. 5, London: Lawrence and Wishart, 1976.

Marx, Karl (1859), *Contribution to the Critique of Political Economy*, Moscow: Progress Publishers, 1970.

Mathiez, Albert (1925–7), *La Révolution française*, Paris: Denoël, 1988.

Matter, Herbert (1988), *Alberto Giacometti*, Paris: Gallimard.

Maupeou-Abboud, Nicole de (1974), *Ouvertures du ghetto étudiante. La Gauche étudiante – la recherche d'un nouveau monde d'intervention politique 1960–1970*, Paris: Anthropos.

Mauzy, Robert (1960), *L'I'dée de bonheur dans la littérature et la poésie françaises au XVIIIe siècle*, Paris: Colin.

McLuhan, Marshall (1967), *The Medium is the Message. An Inventory of Effects*, London: Allen Lane.

Mead, George Herbert (1934), *Mind, Self and Society from the Standpoint of a Social Behaviourist*, Chicago: University of Chicago Press.

Melucci, Alberto (1982), *L'Invenzione del presente*, Bologna: Il Mulino.

Mendes, Sargo, Emmanuel (1985), *La Guerre des paysans: Thomas Müntzer et le communisme*, Unpublished thesis, Université de Paris X–Nanterre.

Merton, Robert K. (1979), *The Sociology of Science: An Episodic Memoir*, New York: Arcturus Press.

Michelet, Jules (1831), *Introduction à l'histoire universelle*, in *Oeuvres complètes* vol. 2, Paris: Flammarion, 1972.

Michelet, Jules (1843), *Des Jésuites*, in Jules Michel and Edgar Quinet, *Des Jésuites*, Paris: Pauvert, 1966.

Michelet, Jules (1846), *Le Peuple*, Paris: Flammarion, 1982.

Michelet, Jules (1852–3), *Histoire de la Révolution française*, Paris: Bibliothèque de la Pléiade, 1979.

Mongardini, Carlo (1990), *Il Futuro della politica*, Milan: Franco Angeli.

Montesquieu, Baron de (1750), *The Spirit of the Laws*, tr. Anne C. Cobler, Basia Carolyn Miller and Harold Samuel Stone, Cambridge: Cambridge University Press, 1991.

Morin, Edgar (1962) *L'Esprit du temps*, Paris: Grasset.

Morin, E. (1981), *Pour sortir du XXe siècle*, Paris: Nathan.

Mornet, Daniel (1933), *Les Origines intellectuelles de la Révolution française 1715–1787*, Paris: Colin, 1967.

Moscovici, Marie (1990), *L'Ombre de l'objet. Sur l'Inactualité de la psychanalyse*, Paris: Seuil.

Moscovici, Serge (1981), *L'Age des foules*, Paris: Fayard.

Moscovici, Serge (1988), *La Machine – faire des dieux. Sociologie et psychanalyse*, Paris: Fayard.

Mounier, Emmanuel (1949), *Le Personalisme*, in *Oeuvres III*, Paris: Seuil, 1962.

Musil, Robert (1930–3), *The Man Without Qualities*, tr. E. Wilkins and E. Kaiser, London: Secker and Warburg, 1953–60, three vols.

Nietzsche, Friedrich (1872), *The Birth of Tragedy*, tr. Francis Golffing, New York: Doubleday, 1956.

Nietzsche, Friedrich (1881), *Daybreak. Thoughts on the Prejudices of Morality*, tr. R. J. Hollingdale, Cambridge: Cambridge University Press, 1982.

Nietzsche, Friedrich (1882), *The Gay Science*, tr. Walter Kaufman, New York: Vintage, 1974.

Nietzsche, Friedrich (1885),*The Twilight of the Idols*, tr. R. J. Hollingdale, Harmondsworth: Penguin, 1968.

Nietzsche, Friedrich (1887), *The Genealogy of Morals*, tr. Francis Golffing, in *The Birth of Tragedy*, New York: Doubleday, 1956.

Nietzsche, Friedrich (1888), *Beyond Good and Evil*, tr. R. J. Hollingdale, Harmondsworth: Penguin, 1973.

Nietzsche, Friedrich (1883–92) *Thus Spoke Zarathustra*, tr. R. J. Hollingdale, Harmondsworth: Penguin, 1969.

Parsons, Talcott (1966), *Societies: Evolutionary and Comparative Perspectives*: Englewood Cliffs: Prentice-Hall.

Parsons, Talcott (1971), *The System of Modern Societies*, Englewood Cliff:s Prentice-Hall.

Pascal, Blaise (1669), *Pensées*, tr. A. J. Krailsheimer, Harmondsworth: Penguin, 1966.

Perron, Roger (1985), *Génèse de la personne*, Paris: PUF.

Polanyi, Karl (1944), *The Great Transformation*, Boston: Beacon Press.

Polin, Raymond (1953), *Politique et philosophie chez Thomas Hobbes*, Paris: PUF.

Popper, Karl (1957), *The Poverty of Historicism*, London: Routledge and Kegan Paul.

Poulantzas, Nicos (1974), *Classes in Contemporary Capitalism*, tr. David Fernbach, London: NLB.

Poulot, Denis (1869), *Le Sublime*, Paris: Maspero, 1980.

Prevost, Antoine-François (1731), *Manon Lescaut*, tr. Leonard Tancock, Harmondsworth: Penguin, 1991.

Rawls, John (1971), *A Theory of Justice*, Oxford: Clarendon Press.

Raynaud, Philippe (1987), *Max Weber et les dilemmes de la raison moderne*, Paris: PUF.

Renault, Alain (1989), *L'Ere de l'individu. Contribution – une histoire de la subjectivité*, Paris: Gallimard.

Rex, John (1991), *Ethnic Identity and Ethnic Mobilization in Britain*, London: ESRC.

Rials, Stéphane (1988), *La Déclaration des droits de l'homme et du citoyen*, Paris: Pluriel.

Ricoeur, Paul (1990), *Soi-même comme un autre*, Paris: Seuil.

Rimbaud, Arthur (1873), 'Une Saison en enfer', in *Oeuvres complètes*, Paris: Bibliothèque de la Pléiade, 1951.

Roche, Daniel (1991), *Les Français de l'ancien régime*, Paris: Armand Colin.

Rorty, Richard (1989), *Contingency, Irony and Solidarity*, Cambridge: Cambridge University Press.

Rousseau, Jean-Jacques (1750), *A Discourse on the Arts and Sciences*, in *The Social Contract and Discourses*, tr. G. D. H. Cole, London: Everyman, 1973.

Rousseau, Jean-Jacques (1754), *A Discourse on the Origins of Inequality*, in *The Social Contract and Discourses*.

Rousseau, Jean-Jacques (1762a), *The Social Contract*, in *The Social Contract and Discourses*.

Rousseau, Jean-Jacques (1762b), *Emile*, tr. Allan Bloom, Harmondsworth: Penguin, 1991.

Rousseau, Jean-Jacques (1772–6), *Dialogues de Rousseau, juge de Jean-Jacques*, Paris: Armand Colin, 1962.

Rousseau, Jean-Jacques (1778), *The Confessions*, tr. J. M. Cohen, Harmondsworth: Penguin, 1970.

Rousseau, Jean-Jacques (1782), *Reveries of the Solitary Walker*, tr. Peter France, Harmondsworth: Penguin, 1979.

Salvadori, Massimo (1981), *Dopo Marx*, Turin: Einaudi.

Sartre, Jean-Paul (1946), *L'Existentialisme est un humanisme*, Paris: Nagel.

Sartre, Jean-Paul (1948) *Situations III. Qu'est-ce que la littérature?*, Paris: Gallimard.

Sartre, Jean-Paul (1965), *Situations VII. Problèmes de marxisme II*, Paris: Gallimard.

Sartre, Jean-Paul (1960), *Critique de la raison dialectique*, Paris: Gallimard.

Scaff, Lawrence A. (1989), *Fleeing the Iron Cage: Culture, Politics and Modernity in the Thought of Max Weber*, Berkeley: University of California Press.

Schopenhauer, Artur (1818), *The World as Will and Idea*, tr. P. H. Strohl, H. Turque and C. Verdillon, London: Kegan Paul, Trench, Trubner & Co, 1891.

Schorske, Karl E. (1980), *Fin de siècle Vienna: Politics and Culture*, New York: Random House.

Schumpeter, Joseph Aloi (1912), *The Theory of Economic Development*, Cambridge, Mass.: Harvard University Press, 1951.

Sennet, Richard (1977), *The Fall of Public Man*, New York: Knopf.

Sève, Lucien, ed. (1987), *Recherche médicale et respect de la personne humaine*, Paris: Documentation française.

Sève, René (1989), *Leibniz et l'école moderne du droit naturel*, Paris: PUF.

Simon, Herbert and James March (1966), *Organisations*, New York: Carnegie Institute of Technology.

Starobinski, Jean (1957), *Jean-Jacques Rousseau. La Transparence et l'obstacle*, Paris: Gallimard, collection Tel, 1982.

Starobinski, Jean (1964), *L'Invention de la liberté 1700–1789*, Geneva: Skira.

Tabboni, Simonetta (1992), *Construire nel presente. Le Giovani donne, il tempo e il denaro*, Milan: Franco Angeli.

Taguieff, Pierre-André (1990), *La Force du préjugé: essai sur le racisme et ses doubles*, Paris: Gallimard.

Tawney, R. H. (1926), *Religion and the Rise of Capitalism*, Harmondsworth: Penguin, 1938.

Taylor, Charles (1989), *Sources of the Self. The Making of Modern Identity*, Cambridge: Cambridge University Press.

Taylor, Frederick W. (1914), *The Principles of Scientific Management*, New York and London: Harper.

Thesis Eleven (1989), 23, 'Redefining Modernity: The Challenge to Sociology'.

Thesis Eleven (1992), 31, 'Interpreting Modernity'.

Thurow, Lester (1993), *Head to Head: The Coming Economic Battle among Japan, Europe and America*, New York: Warner Books.

Tilly, Charles (1986), *The Contentious French: Four Centuries of Popular Struggle*, Cambridge, MA: Harvard University Press.

Tocqueville, Alexis de (1835–40), *Democracy in America*, tr. Henry Reeve, New York: Knopf, 1945.

Tönnies, Ferdinand (1957), *Community and Society*, Ann Arbor: University of Michigan Press.

Totaro, Francesco (1979) *Produzione del sense: forme del valore et dell'ideologia*, Milan: Università Catolica.

Toulmin, Stephen (1990), *Cosmopolis: The Hidden Agenda of Modernity*, New York: Free Press.

Touraine, Alain (1965), *Sociologie de l'action*, Paris: Seuil.

Touraine, Alain (1966), *La Conscience ouvrière*, Paris: Seuil.

Touraine, Alain (1968), *The May Movement*, tr. Leonard Fox Mayhew, New York: Random House, 1971.

Touraine, Alain (1969), *The Post-Industrial Society. Tomorrow's Social History: Class, Conflict and Culture in the Programmed Society*, tr. Leonard Fox Mayhew, New York: Random House, 1971.

Touraine, Alain (1973a), *La Production de la société*, Paris: Seuil.

Touraine, Alain (1973b), *Vie et mort du Chili populaire*, Paris: Seuil.

Touraine, Alain (1974), *Pour la sociologie*, Paris: Seuil.

Touraine, Alain (1978), *The Voice and the Eye: The Analysis of Social Movements*, tr. Alan Duff, Cambridge: Cambridge University Press.

Touraine, Alain (1984a), *Le Retour de l'acteur. Essai de sociologie*, Paris: Fayard.

Touraine, Alain, Michel Wieviorka and François Dubet (1984), *Le Mouvement ouvrier*, Paris: Fayard.

Turner, Brian S., ed. (1990), *Theories of Modernity and Post-Modernity*, London: Sage.

Turkle, Sherry (1984), *The Second Self: Computer and Human Spirit*, New York: Simon and Schuster.

Valéry, Paul (1925), 'Fragment d'un Descartes', in *Oeuvres I*, Paris: Bibliothèque de la Pléiade, 1960.

Vattimo, Gianni (1985), *La Fin de la modernité*. Paris: Seuil, 1987.

Vattimo, Gianni (1992), *The Transparent Society*, tr. David Webb, Cambridge: Polity.

Vattimo, Gianni ed. (1986), *La Secularisation de la pensee*, Paris: Seuil.

Venturi, Franco (1971), *Au Siècle des Lumières*, Paris: Mouton.

Vernant, Jean-Pierre (1989), *L'Individu, la mort, l'amour. Soi-même et l'autre en Grèce ancienne*, Paris: Gallimard.

Wahl, Jean (1929), *Le Malheur de la conscience dans la philosophie de Hegel*, Paris: Rieder.

Walzer, Michael (1965), *The Revolution of the Saints: A Study in the Origin of Radical Politics*, Cambridge, Mass.: Harvard University Press.

Weber, Eugen (1976), *Peasants in to Frenchmen: The Modernization of Rural France 1870–1914*, Palo Alto: Stanford University Press.

Weber, Max (1904–5), *The Protestant Ethic and the Spirit of Capitalism*, tr. Talcott Parsons, London: Routledge, 1992.

Weber, Max (1919), 'Science as Vocation' and 'Politics as Vocation', in H. H. Gerth and C. Wright Mills, eds, *From Max Weber: Essays in Sociology*, London: Routledge, 1970.

Weber, M. (1922), *Economy and Society*, Berkeley: University of California Press, 1979, 2 vols.

Weiner, Richard (1981), *Cultural Marxism and Political Sociology*, London: Sage.

Westbrook, Robert B. (1991), *John Dewey and American Democracy*, Ithaca: Cornell University Press.

Whyte, W. H. (1956), *The Organisation Man*, New York: Simon and Schuster.

Wieviorka, Michel (1988), *Sociétés et terrorisme*, Paris: Fayard.

Wieviorka, Michel (1991), *L'Espace du racisme*, Paris: Seuil.

Index